"Even though there is little doubt that climate change challenges the practice of democracy in multiple ways, the exact relationship between both is still insufficiently understood. Based on extensive data analysis, Frederic Hanusch demonstrates in great detail that countries that are more democratic also cope more successfully with climate change. The call for eco-authoritarianism – at times still raised in some quarters – can be soundly rejected based on Hanusch's work. *Democracy and Climate Change* is a major contribution and important reading for all who care about the future of our democracies in a warmer world."

– Frank Biermann, *Copernicus Institute of Sustainable Development, Utrecht University, The Netherlands, and Chair of the Earth System Governance Project*

"Established democracies today face a variety of troubles as the global response to climate change hangs in the balance. In this context, Frederic Hanusch has produced a timely, sophisticated and compelling empirical analysis of how democratic quality promotes effective climate policy performance, systematically bringing evidence to bear on a vital question."

– John Dryzek, *Centre for Deliberative Democracy and Global Governance, University of Canberra, Australia*

"This book represents a step-change in understanding the relationship between democratic systems and climate change mitigation. Through careful analysis of the characteristics of existing democracies, Frederic Hanusch provides compelling evidence that democratic quality has an effect on climate policy and reduction of greenhouse gases. The application of a conceptually novel account of democratic efficacy allows Hanusch to develop the politically significant argument that democratising democracy is critical in the fight against climate change."

– Graham Smith, *Centre for the Study of Democracy, University of Westminster, and Chair of the Foundation for Democracy and Sustainable Development, UK*

Democracy and Climate Change

Democracy and Climate Change explores the various ways in which democratic principles can lead governments to respond differently to climate change. The election cycle can lead to short-termism, which often appears to be at odds with the long-term nature of climate change, with its latency between cause and effect. However, it is clear that some democracies deal with climate change better than others, and this book demonstrates that overall stronger democratic qualities tend to correlate with improved climate performance.

Beginning by outlining a general concept of democratic efficacy, the book provides an empirical analysis of the influence of the quality of democracy on climate change performance across dozens of countries. The specific case study of Canada's Kyoto Protocol process is then used to explain the mechanisms of democratic influence in depth. The wide-ranging research presented in the book opens up several new and exciting avenues of enquiry and will be of considerable interest to researchers with an interest in comparative politics, democracy studies and environmental policies.

Frederic Hanusch is a postdoctoral researcher at the Institute for Advanced Sustainability Studies (IASS), Potsdam, Germany.

Routledge Global Cooperation Series

This series develops innovative approaches to understanding, explaining and answering one of the most pressing questions of our time – how can cooperation in a culturally diverse world of nine billion people succeed?

We are rapidly approaching our planet's limits, with trends such as advancing climate change and the destruction of biological diversity jeopardising our natural life support systems. Accelerated globalisation processes lead to an ever growing interconnectedness of markets, states, societies, and individuals. Many of today's problems cannot be solved by nation states alone. Intensified cooperation at the local, national, international, and global level is needed to tackle current and looming global crises.

Series Editors:

Tobias Debiel, Claus Leggewie and Dirk Messner are Co-Directors of the Käte Hamburger Kolleg / Centre for Global Cooperation Research, University of Duisburg-Essen, Germany. Their research areas are, among others, Global Governance, Climate Change, Peacebuilding and Cultural Diversity of Global Citizenship. The three Co-Directors are, at the same time, based in their home institutions, which participate in the Centre, namely the German Development Institute / Deutsches Institut für Entwicklungspolitik (DIE, Messner) in Bonn, the Institute for Development and Peace (INEF, Debiel) in Duisburg and The Institute for Advanced Study in the Humanities (KWI, Leggewie) in Essen.

Titles:

Democracy and Climate Change

Frederic Hanusch

SPONSORED BY THE

Federal Ministry
of Education
and Research

Routledge
Taylor & Francis Group
LONDON AND NEW YORK

Centre for
Global
Cooperation
Research

First published 2018 by Routledge

2 Park Square, Milton Park, Abingdon, Oxfordshire OX14 4RN
52 Vanderbilt Avenue, New York, NY 10017

Routledge is an imprint of the Taylor & Francis Group, an informa business

First issued in paperback 2019

British Library Cataloguing-in-Publication Data
A catalogue record for this book is available from the British Library

Library of Congress Cataloging-in-Publication Data
Names: Hanusch, Frederic, author.
Title: Democracy and climate change / Frederic Hanusch.
Description: Abingdon, Oxon ; New York, NY, USA : Routledge is an
    imprint of the Taylor & Francis Group, an informa business, [2017] |
    Includes bibliographical references and index.
Identifiers: LCCN 2016057929 | ISBN 9780415371162 (hbk) |
    ISBN 9780415383288 (ebook)
Subjects: LCSH: Climatic changes—Political aspects. | Climate change
    mitigation.
Classification: LCC QC903 .H3678 2017 | DDC 363.738/74561—dc23
LC record available at https://lccn.loc.gov/2016057929

ISBN: 978-0-415-37116-2 (hbk)
ISBN: 978-0-367-24804-8 (pbk)

DOI: 10.4324/9781315228983

This work and its open access publication has been supported by the Federal
Ministry of Education and Research (BMBF) in the context of its funding of
the Käte Hamburger Kolleg/Centre for Global Cooperation Research at the
University of Duisburg-Essen (grant number 01UK1810).

The original study "The Influence of Democratic Quality on Reactions to Climate Change: A Comparative Study of Climate Policies in Established Democracies" which formed the starting point for this book has been approved by the Faculty of Social Sciences of the University of Duisburg-Essen as a dissertation for the acquisition of a doctoral degree (DPhil.). The first supervisor of this dissertation was Prof. Dr. Dr. h. c. Claus Leggewie and the second supervisor was Prof. Dr. Patrizia Nanz. A viva voce took place on 5 October 2015.

The study was financially supported by the Hans Böckler Foundation.

Contents

Figures

Tables

Equations

Acknowledgements

I express my deepest gratitude to my magnificent supervisors, committee members, colleagues, friends and family. Not only have you contributed to this book, you also made the world an inspiring and better place for me during the intensive years I spent working on it. And, at the very least, you deserve the personal and handwritten dedication for which I have reserved the rest of this page.

Abbreviations

AMG	Analysis and Modelling Group
BAU	business as usual
CAN	Climate Action Network
CAPP	Canadian Association of Petroleum Producers
CCME	Canadian Council of Ministers of the Environment
CCPI	Climate Change Performance Index
CEM	Canadian Council of Energy Ministers
CESD	Commissioner of the Environment and Sustainable Development
COP	Conference of the Parties
CRA	Canadian Revenue Agency
CSD	Cross Sectional Dependence
ECan	Environment Canada
ENGO	Environmental Non-Governmental Organization
EU	European Union
FE	Fixed Effects
FMM	First Ministers Meeting
GDP	Gross Domestic Product
GHG	Greenhouse Gas
ICC	Intraclass Correlation Coefficient
IEA	International Energy Agency
IMF	International Monetary Fund
IPCC	International Panel on Climate Change
JMM	Joint Ministers Meeting
KPIA	Kyoto Protocol Implementation Act
LFE	Large Final Emitters
MP	Member of Parliament
NAFTA	North American Free Trade Agreement
NAICC-CC	National Air Issues Coordinating Committee – Climate Change
NAISC	National Air Issues Steering Committee
NCCP	National Climate Change Process
NCCS	National Climate Change Secretariat
NGO	Non-Governmental Organization
NRCan	Natural Resources Canada

NRTEE	National Round Table on the Environment and the Economy
PCO	Privy Council Office
PM	Prime Minister
PMO	Prime Minister's Office
RCESD	Report of the Commissioner of the Environment and Sustainable Development
RE	Random Effects
UNFCCC	United Nations Framework Convention on Climate Change
US	United States of America
WWF	World Wide Fund for Nature

1 Introduction

Climate change as a grievous problem combines a set of characteristics, which make it very hard to deal with, such as latency, a long time horizon, scientific complexity and free rider problems. Meanwhile, the available greenhouse gas (GHG) budget is shrinking and thus the time frame within which to protect earth system services is becoming tighter (Lenton et al., 2008; Steffen et al., 2015). In sum, this requires a broadscale transformation of contemporary societies in many fields, such as energy, land use and urbanization (WBGU, 2011). However, taking a look at established democracies separately, some appear to be more successful in dealing with climate change than others. While, for example, the United Kingdom ranks sixth in the Climate Change Performance Index (CCPI) 2015, Canada ranks fifty-eighth out of 61, with other democracies in-between (Germanwatch, 2015).

A reason for their different climate performances may be found in the ways in which democracies deal with the unintended consequences which climate change inherently produces, such as the periodicity of elections leading to short-termism, cyclical issue attention threatening enlightened understanding and dilatory as well as incremental procedures weakening their problem-solving capacities (see, e.g., Brodocz, Llanque, & Schaal, 2008; Held, 2014). Yet the characteristics of climate change and the unintended consequences of democracy might contradict each other to different degrees, e.g. some democracies perhaps find better solutions than others to overcome their short-termism, in order to be able to better deal with the long time horizon of climate change. Hence, different levels of democracy might be an explanatory factor for differences in the climate performances of established democracies.

Existing research cannot explain this observation. What is perhaps the most comprehensive and relevant study in this context merely delivers insights into trends across the spectrum of autocracy to democracy (Bättig & Bernauer, 2009). The authors study a cross section of 185 countries between 1990–2004 arguing that democratic institutions provide public goods more successfully than autocratic ones (Bättig & Bernauer, 2009). Empirical results demonstrate that the effect of democracy on climate policy commitments is positive, but that it is ambiguous in terms of GHG emissions (Bättig & Bernauer, 2009). However, the empirical data which is used is unable to distinguish between democracies. The

DOI: 10.4324/9781315228983-1

methods are incapable of providing insights into detailed mechanisms, verifying statistical trends. The theoretical literature on political institutions which is referred to might explain the different impacts of democratic and autocratic institutions, but it provides no explanation for established democracies. The Bättig/Bernauer study develops a reference point which describes where current research stands (see, e.g., Bernauer, 2013; Burnell, 2012; Cao, Milner, Prakash, & Ward, 2014; Held, 2014). So far, research has concentrated on analysing how autocracies and democracies exert influence on climate performance. Thus, how different democratic qualities influence the climate performance of established democracies is, as yet, unknown.

To close this research gap and to explain the empirical observation which has been identified, this book introduces a new perspective by asking: how does democratic quality influence climate performance of established democracies? To answer the question comprehensively, established democracies must first be distinguished between based on their democratic quality, so as to enable an evaluation of the trends which affect their influence on climate performance. Secondly, the trends need to be verified by detailed internal mechanisms and, thirdly, a generalizable concept is required which explains the results.

To achieve these objectives, this book defines democratic quality as consisting of control, equality and freedom. Climate performance is defined in terms of output (policy targets, etc.) and outcome (GHG emissions development). Moreover, a generalizable concept of democratic efficacy is provisionally outlined, which assumes that democracy's ability to produce desired and intended climate performance increases concomitantly with rising levels of democratic quality. Thereafter, empirical analysis relies on an explanatory mixed methods design. This allows richer interpretations since the main research question can be separated into two complementary analyses, which research the same phenomenon from different perspectives. First, panel regressions deliver trends for the influence of democratic quality – as measured by the Democracy Barometer – on overall climate performance – as measured by the CCPI with regard to climate policy (output) and GHG emissions development (outcome). Depending on the combinations of data, the number of countries ranges from 39–41 in the years 2004–2012, resulting in 193–326 country years. Secondly, a process tracing of Canada's Kyoto Protocol process from 1995–2012 is developed as a case study. This case study provides detailed insights into mechanisms affecting dimensions of democratic quality – evaluated by empirical translations of control, equality and freedom – and climate performance.

The study's findings demonstrate that increased democratic quality generally positively influences climate performance in established democracies. This positive influence can be observed both in terms of the output and, with certain limitations, with regard to the outcomes. The research results of both analyses are robust and synergize detailed mechanisms, verifying statistical trends. Furthermore, the mechanisms which are explored indicate that the influence upon climate performance goals might become stronger and more predictable with increasing levels of democratic quality. The concept of democratic efficacy provisionally outlined in this book can explain these findings by generalizing that democracy's ability to produce desired and intended climate performances increases concomitantly with rising levels of democratic quality.

These findings are important for academia as well as for political practice. The main implications for research are twofold: first, more research has to be carried out on the different democratic qualities of established democracies and the influence which these differences have. Secondly, this book's provisional concept of democratic efficacy has the potential to be advanced to a middle range theory, which can provide an explanatory link between democratic quality and climate performance as well as performances in other policy fields. The key practical implication has to be divided into minor recommendations, but can be summarized in a simple and yet complex manner: minimize democratic shortcomings and thus democratize democracies to make them more efficacious.

Having outlined the purpose and main results, the book proceeds in more detail. Following the introduction (Chapter 1), this book is divided into three main parts. The first part develops the bases for the analyses and starts with an evaluation of the relevance and the focus of the research (Chapter 2). Based on this, a conceptual framework can be developed, including definitions, an outline of the concept of democratic efficacy and methods (Chapter 3). The second part then comprises panel regressions as analysis I (4) and a case study of Canada's Kyoto Protocol process as analysis II (Chapters 5–10). The third and last part forges synergy beyond the two single analyses by interconnecting findings and formulating research gaps and policy recommendations (Chapter 11) as well as an overall conclusion (Chapter 12).

References

The access date of all material retrieved from the Web is 5 June 2015 unless otherwise specified.

Bättig, M. B., & Bernauer, T. (2009). National institutions and global public goods: are democracies more cooperative in climate change policy? *International Organization*, 63(2), 281–308.

Bernauer, T. (2013). Climate change politics. *Annual Review of Political Science*, 16(1), 421–448.

Brodocz, A., Llanque, M., & Schaal, G. S. (2008). Demokratie im Angesicht ihrer Bedrohungen. In A. L. Brodocz, M. Llanque, & G. S. Schaal (Eds.), *Bedrohungen der Demokratie* (pp. 11–26). Wiesbaden: VS Verlag für Sozialwissenschaften.

Burnell, P. (2012). Democracy, democratization and climate change: complex relationships. *Democratization*, 19(5), 813–842.

Cao, X., Milner, H. V., Prakash, A., & Ward, H. (2014). Research frontiers in comparative and international environmental politics: an introduction. *Comparative Political Studies*, 47(3), 291–308.

Germanwatch. (2015). *Climate Change Performance Index (CCPI)*. Retrieved from http://germanwatch.org/en/ccpi

Held, D. (2014). Climate change, global governance and democracy: some questions. In M. Di Paola, & G. Pellegrino (Eds.), *Canned Heat: Ethics and Politics of Global Climate Change* (pp. 17–28). New Delhi: Routledge.

Lenton, T. M., Held, H., Kriegler, E., Hall, J. W., Lucht, W., Rahmstorf, S., & Schell-nhuber, H. J. (2008). Tipping elements in the Earth's climate system. *Proceedings of the National Academy of Sciences of the United States of America, 105*(6), 1786–1793.

Steffen, W., Richardson, K., Rockstrom, J., Cornell, S. E., Fetzer, I., Bennett, E. M., Biggs, R., Carpenter, S. R., de Vries, W., de Wit, C. A., Folke, C., Gerten, D., Heinke, J., Mace, G. M., Persson, L. M., Ramanathan, V., Reyers, B., Sorlin, S. (2015). Planetary boundaries: guiding human development on a changing planet. *Science, 347*(6223), 736–746.

WBGU (Wissenschaftlicher Beirat Globale Umweltveränderungen/German Advisory Council on Global Change). (2011). *World in Transition – A Social Contract for Sustainability*. Berlin: WBGU.

I

The basis for the analyses

2 The unknown influence of democratic qualities on climate performance

The observation made in the introduction that different levels of democracy might be an explanatory factor for differences in the climate performances of established democracies cannot be explained by existing research. However, knowing more about this kind of democracy-climate nexus is relevant for both academia and political practice.

The following section demonstrates that academia has so far concentrated on the differences between autocracy and democracy. Hence, insights regarding the influence of democratic quality on climate performance are fragmented and provide only partial, and, unfortunately, not substantive, insights into further general patterns. Practical relevance is identified based on two of the world society's aims: a more democratic world and solutions to climate change. Combining academic and practical relevance, the focus of the book can be expressed by the main research question, which asks: how does democratic quality influence climate performance? The question demands three specific research requirements, if we are to provide a comprehensive answer taking democratic quality into account in all of its facets. More precisely, it is necessary to advance the current state of research by, first, identifying trends among democracies, secondly, detecting internal mechanisms verifying these trends and, thirdly, developing a generalizable concept that builds an explanatory link between democratic quality and climate performance.

Academic relevance: no recognition of the different influences of established democracies

Of course, climate change is neither the first, nor the only issue democracies have to deal with. And there have been numerous investigations into how democracies perform (in comparison to autocracies) in policy fields like security (see, e.g., Reiter & Stam, 2002), the economy (see, e.g., Wilensky, 2002), health (see, e.g., Mackenbach & McKee, 2013), education (see, e.g., Stasavage, 2005), social welfare (see, e.g., Kersbergen, 2003), the environment (see, e.g., Ward, 2008) and international cooperation (see, e.g., Freyburg, Lavenex, Schimmelfennig, Skripka, & Wetzel, 2011). Existing findings indicate that democracies' performances vary significantly depending on the characteristics of the issue under

DOI: 10.4324/9781315228983-3

investigation, the level of analysis and the definition and measurement of democracy. When looking for an overall trend among these studies in terms of a generalizable concept one can assume a positive influence of democracy in regard to better performance on such central issues as human rights (see, e.g., De Mesquita, Downs, Smith, & Cherif, 2005) or international peace (see, e.g., Oneal, Oneal, Maoz, & Russett, 1996; Ward, 2008), even though some studies are ambiguous in this regard (see, e.g., Runciman, 2013).

However, besides this general tendency, the introduction has, with reference to an article by Bättig/Bernauer, already exemplified the current state of research in relation to the democracy-climate nexus. The purpose of the following is therefore to evaluate more broadly where existing research stands, so as to detect useful insights and to define the research gap. Thus, existing research is organized and sorted into arguments and empirical findings which, respectively, propose both positive and negative examples of the influence of democracies upon climate performance. Two conclusions can be drawn based on that evaluation. First, the, soon to be outlined, concept of democratic efficacy suggests that it is more likely that increasing levels of democratic quality improve a state's ability to produce climate performance (see Chapter 3.2). Secondly, besides this general tendency, research is overwhelmingly focused on the differentiation of autocracy and democracy, or fragmented in terms of concentrating on single aspects of democracy which influence climate performance. Thus, the piecemeal account presented below shows us that useful insights are currently scarce and that a comprehensive book is required, which takes into account democratic quality in all of its facets.

The following section therefore proceeds by outlining the importance of concepts and operationalization. Thereafter, findings on both democracies and environmental performance in general and climate performance in particular are evaluated.

The importance of concepts and operationalization

Even though it is self-evident, it is worthwhile emphasizing that, as the evaluation of the research demonstrates, the choice of concepts and measurement tools affects the results which are achieved. As their emphasis is not on the identification of overall trends, the definitions of democracy used in case studies vary significantly, however, surprisingly, the influence of the normative definition behind existing democracy indices – which are mostly able to separate between autocracies and democracies but not between democracies themselves – has, on the whole, remained unquestioned. One of the main reasons for this might be that only a small number of democracy indices possess the required degree of validity and reliability, therefore, due to missing data, it has so far been impossible to empirically evaluate alternative normative ideas of democracy and their influence. Thus, it seems reasonable to assume that different normative conceptions of democracy might lead to variations on the results, however, there isn't currently the data or research to substantiate this assumption (Burnell, 2012, p. 823).

The second aspect influencing results is the evaluation of environmental performance (Stern, 2004). In the best case scenario, it should be comparable over time and units of analysis. Environmental performance can be divided into types of output, such as targets agreed, policies, institutions, commitments and treaty engagement (see, e.g., Boiral & Henri, 2012; Liefferink, Arts, Kamstra, & Ooijevaar, 2009; Neumayer, Gates, & Gleditsch, 2002; Recchia, 2002) and outcomes, like the concentration of pollutants (NO_x, SO_2, CO_2, etc.), emission levels and/ or emission trends (see, e.g., Jahn, 1998; Li & Reuveny, 2006; Scruggs, 2003). The separation between output and outcome remains crucial since it allows the identification of words-deeds gaps and a distinction between papers signed or institutions created and actual environmental impact. Existing studies combine or separate these elements and find that the way of measuring environmental performance influences the results with respect to the democracy-environment nexus (see, e.g., Poloni-Staudinger, 2008; Ward, 2008). It is therefore important to analyse which mechanisms lie behind the detected influences, so as to understand which elements of democratic quality influence which parts of environmental performance. Consequently, this book discusses in detail how it defines and operationalizes democratic quality and climate performance.

Democracy and environmental performance

Before undertaking a narrower investigation of democracy and climate performance, the relationship between democracy and environmental performance is evaluated, so as to see whether any additional fundamental patterns or tendencies can be detected, which would be useful for the purposes of this book. Existing arguments and empirical findings on the influence of democracy on environmental performance point in both directions, yet studies proposing a positive influence are more convincing.

Arguments which assume that democracies have a more positive relationship with environmental performance than autocracies point to the high value democracies place on quality of life, the greater long-term future orientation of democracies – compared to the focus of many autocracies on the short-term maintenance of power – the responsiveness of democratic institutions in taking care of the environmental preferences of their citizens, the opportunities for civil society to demand environmental action, the accountability mechanisms which allow voters to hold politicians to account for pollution, the electorate's ability to change governments when these fail to find adequate solutions, the way in which mistakes are publicized and informed publics are able to criticize damaging actions, the process of political learning, engagement in international cooperation and more effective governance in terms of better bureaucracies with less corruption (Burnell, 2012, p. 823; Esty & Porter, 2005; Fiorino, 2011, p. 375; Fredriksson & Wollscheid, 2007; Neumayer, 2002; Payne, 1995; Pellegrini & Gerlagh, 2006).

Fewer arguments postulate to the contrary that democracy has a negative impact on environmental performance. These arguments, when they occur, assume that democracies are wealthier and that economic growth forces environmental degradation since democratic and economic freedoms are closely related, including the freedom to pollute. Population growth is also seen as a major driver of pollution and an area which democracies do not actively control. Moreover, democracies are, due to elections, seen to be more orientated towards short-term solutions and thus only a more authoritarian state is seen as being able to deal with the transition to a steady-state society (Beeson, 2010; Gleditsch & Sverdrup, 2003; Hardin, 1968; Heilbroner, 1974; Midlarsky, 2001; Ophuls, 1977).

However, both kinds of arguments focus primarily on explanations of the different levels of influence which autocracies and democracies have on environmental performance. Thus, they provide, besides the general trend of predominantly positive arguments, only a very limited amount of useful and generalizable argumentation on the influence of different democratic qualities in established democracies.

Empirical studies also provide fragmented and mixed insights, with a weak positive tendency. First, impacts vary relative to the characteristics of democracies, e.g. parliamentary democracies appear to score better than presidential democracies, consensus democracies rate better in terms of achieving policies which are easy to accomplish and implement, but badly on substantial changes. Similarly, historic democratic capital is assumed to be more important than current democratic quality and political competition for office could be useful for environmental movements (Barrett, 2000; Binder & Neumayer, 2005; Cao, Milner, Prakash, & Ward, 2014; Fredriksson, Neumayer, Damania, & Gates, 2005; Fredriksson & Wollscheid, 2007; Poloni-Staudinger, 2008; Ward, 2008). However, "[the] literature is only just beginning to show that these processes are actually causally efficacious", which is why a closer examination of the trends and mechanisms is indispensable (Cao, et al., 2014, p. 294; Wurster, 2013). Secondly, the impact varies according to the environmental performance indicators used for output and outcome. A weak positive impact of democracy appears to exist regarding domestic environmental performance in general, international commitments, better provision of air and water quality, more stringent policies, the reduction of CO_2 and NO_x emissions, deforestation, land degradation, organics in water and long time frames in general, since democracies are assumed to be more active in monitoring and research and technology development (Barrett, 2000; Bättig & Bernauer, 2009; Bernauer & Koubi, 2009; Congleton, 1992; Desai, 1998; Farzin & Bond, 2006; Fiorino, 2011; Fredriksson & Gaston, 2000; Fredriksson et al., 2005; Fredriksson & Wollscheid, 2007; Gallagher & Thacker, 2008; Harbaugh, Levinson, & Wilson, 2002; Jancar-Webster, 1998; Li & Reuveny, 2006; Neumayer, 2002; Neumayer et al., 2002; Roberts, Parks, & Vásquez 2004; Torras & Boyce, 1998; Ward, 2008). However, some contrary and ambiguous results also exist. Studies of water quality, freshwater availability, dissolved oxygen, fecal coliform and soil erosion (Barrett, 2000; Duwel, 2010; Fisher & Freudenburg, 2004; Midlarsky, 2001), find no or ambiguous effects, while negative effects of democracy are assumed to exist in regard to deforestation and water erosion (Congleton, 1992; Midlarsky, 1998,

2001). However, empirical studies mostly remain focused on the autocracy-democracy distinctions, without distinguishing between the different types of influence which different democratic qualities might have. Even those studies researching democracies provide few relevant insights, as whether presidential or parliamentary democracies score better does not imply what influence democratic quality has on climate performance.

All in all, the findings seem to be partially contradictory and to depend on the evaluation of democracy and environmental performance (Fiorino, 2011, pp. 377–378). Almost all of the arguments and empirical findings are centred on the different ways in which democracies and autocracies influence environmental performance and thus provide almost no relevant insights into distinctions between established democracies. Thus, it is possible to identify an obvious research gap in terms of the influence of different democratic qualities and the suggestion of a positive tendency in respect to the, soon to be outlined, concept of democratic efficacy.

Democracy and climate performance

To a certain extent, the findings of the democracy-climate nexus overlap with the evaluation of the influence of democracy on environmental performance. However, the specific characteristics of climate change have to be taken into consideration to refine the focus of the book (for research overviews on climate politics beyond the democracy-climate nexus, see, e.g., Bernauer, 2013; Lachapelle & Paterson, 2013).

Arguments exist which, within the context of the comparison of democracy with autocracy and with regard to as yet unexploited democratic potential, assume that democracy has a positive influence on climate performance. These posit: first, that democracies influence climate performance more positively than autocracies as they rely on median voters as well as influential interest groups which favour the provision of public goods, like climate change mitigation, while, in autocracies, small elites seek personal wealth instead of taking care of public goods (Bättig & Bernauer, 2009, p. 286). According to this line of argument, median voters in democracies have smaller opportunity costs than their equivalents in autocracies (Bättig & Bernauer, 2009, p. 286). Democratic politicians are therefore required to provide public goods for their electorates if they want to survive, whereas autocratic leaders need to deliver private goods for their ruling elites in order to survive (Bättig & Bernauer, 2009, pp. 286–287). Moreover, it is assumed that democracies, in comparison to autocracies, provide better access to information, deliver higher levels of transparency in decision-making, encourage climate change research and establish room for pressure groups and social movements, which, together with civil society watchdogs, ensure that climate change becomes a public issue politicians have to deal with (Held & Hervey, 2009, p. 6).

Secondly, undeveloped potential opportunities have been identified in terms of facing climate change through certain democratic improvements. These include vague calls for – based on the assumption that climate change consensus is unachievable – radical democracy (Machin, 2013), global or intergenerational democracies (see, e.g., Holden, 2002) and the possibility of building democratic multi-level governance arrangements (Lidskog & Elander, 2010). Moreover, proposals for deliberative democracy to solve the climate issue have been made. This line of argument assumes that democratic leaders have to educate their constituencies, in order for free and equal democratic citizens to become "fact-regarding, future-regarding and other-regarding" (Offe & Preuß, 1991, pp. 156–157). Moreover, some authors suggest that future generations and non-humans will be able to be included in climate policy decision-making via open deliberation processes. Therefore climate science has to be better translated, so that it can be debated in public arenas and relevant networks. And policy approaches can be adjusted so as to focus on the most pressing questions, with open deliberation processes transforming private preferences into positions based on information, evidence and debate (Dryzek, n.d.; Dryzek, Norgaard, & Schlosberg, 2013; Held & Hervey, 2009, pp. 8–9; Stevenson, 2014). According to this standpoint, deliberative democracy could increase the quality and legitimacy of climate policy decision-making by dealing with climate change in all its complexity, in a fashion which is beyond the capacity of current institutions and organizations. Or, to put it simply, "representative democracy is a poor way to achieve this alone" (Held & Hervey, 2009, pp. 8–9). Besides the far-reaching approach of deliberative democracy, several more concrete elements have also been proposed to reinforce awareness of climate change: a human right to an environment which promotes human health and well-being, environmental constitutionalism and the inclusion of climate protection as a respective national objective, expanding opportunities for citizens and non-governmental organizations (NGOs) to participate in processes and to access information, environmental citizenship, climate policy mainstreaming, a transnational refocusing of democracy, so as to include elements of proxy representation for both future generations and non-human species and a more local or urban spectrum of democracy (see, e.g., Barber, n.d.; Gould, n.d.; Hayward, n.d.; Leggewie & Welzer, 2010; WBGU, 2011, p. 209). These arguments, which have been developed to face climate change democratically, are reliable and they inform the formulation of indicators for the empirical investigation of the case study, yet their importance is often diminished in deeper and more practical analyses. Moreover, no research currently exists which links all of these aspects, explaining concepts and middle range theories in the context of the question of why the different democratic qualities of established democracies might lead to better climate performance. However, it can nonetheless be concluded that ideas exist which advocate democratic improvement in the sense of a further democratization of democracy. These unexploited possibilities are assumed to have the potential to influence climate performance positively. When outlining the concept of democratic efficacy, this provides further evidence for the basic assumption that the ability to produce climate performance rises concomitantly with increasing levels of democratic quality.

Arguments which assume that democracy has a negative impact on climate performance rely heavily on consideration of the characteristics of climate change. Climate is, as one of the earth's unowned natural resources, a global common and thus not simply a straightforward environmental problem, since it also relates to questions of energy, economic development, land use, human behavior, etc. (Prins et al., 2010). Climate change is therefore characterized as a (super) wicked problem (par excellence), since it combines a set of characteristics which make it very hard to deal with, such as the shortening time horizon within which to find a solution, latency combined with a long time horizon until policy outcomes are measureable, scientific complexity ruling out an easy one-way or purely technical solution, a dynamic social context, the lack of a central global authority and free rider problems potentially leading to a tragedy of the commons and resulting in the need for a broad scale transformation (Huitema et al., 2011; Jordan, van Asselt, Berkhout, Huitema, & Rayner, 2012; Koppenjan & Klijn, 2004; Lazarus, 2009; Levin, Cashore, Bernstein, & Auld, 2007, 2012; Rae & Wong, 2012; Rittel & Webber, 1973; Sandler, 2010; Shearman & Smith, 2007; Thompson, 2006). Moreover, if policy options are identified and implemented, they have to be continuously controlled in terms of new knowledge, unpredictable developments and unforeseen tipping points, which makes a reflexive policy design necessary (Brousseau, Dedeurwaerdere, & Siebenhüner, 2012; Coenen, Huitema, & O'Toole, 1998; Dorussen & Ward, 2008; Hisschemöller, 2001; Lenton et al., 2008; Mickwitz, 2003; Pahl-Wostl, 2009; Russel, Haxeltine, Huitema, Nillsson, Rayner, & Hinkel, 2010). According to certain studies, these characteristics of climate change pose a major threat to contemporary democracies. In democracies within which the median voter happens not to prefer pro-climate policies, strong interest groups are able to lobby against active climate policies and gaps between policy announcements (output) and actual implementation (outcome) may occur, since politicians are concerned about presenting a policy, but not about its implementation (Bättig & Bernauer, 2009, pp. 287, 290–291).

Furthermore, it is assumed that democracies are not only exposed to the characteristics of climate change, but, at the same time, threatened by their democratic processes, allowing climate change contexts to undermine the democratic process itself (Brodocz, Llanque, & Schaal, 2008; Held, 2014). These arguments posit that the periodicity of elections results in short-termism and threatens sustainable policy-making. They state that the cyclical nature of issues in politics and the media complicates enlightened understanding (particularly of latent and long-term issues), that temporal and spatial incongruities mean that injustice and self-referential decision-making threaten the identities of both decision-makers and those on the receiving end of such decisions. Furthermore, they propose that the promotion of a maximization of benefits intimidates virtuous citizens and that dilatory and incremental procedures (which are important for democratic stability) threaten problem-solving capacity. Moreover, politicians might find themselves caught between the accountability required at an international level and the accountability required by their citizenry at a domestic level (Keohane, 2008).

The characteristics of climate change and the unintended consequences of democracy might also influence and even contradict each other. As a consequence of all these circumstances which complicate solution-finding for democracies, certain arguments propose (indirectly) that more "eco-authoritarian" forms of dealing with climate change, which show strong leadership and would be much more effective than democracy, are needed. This position was already popular in the 1970s and today it is often exemplified with reference to China, assuming that more autocracy leads to better policy results (see, e.g., Friedman, 2008, pp. 371–394; Hardin, 1968; Heilbroner, 1974; Lovelock, 2010; Ophuls, 1977).

When evaluating arguments which assume that democracies have a negative influence on climate change, it is important to note that these arguments primarily point to a static picture of democracy contrasted with autocracy. These provisional arguments do not take into account that different levels of democracy might be an explanatory factor for differences in the climate performances of established democracies and that, for example, some democracies perhaps find better solutions to overcome their short-termism, making them better able to deal with the long time horizon of climate change than others. Thus, arguments which set the characteristics of climate change and the consequences of democracy together are an indication that mechanisms which overlap both spheres exist. However, these arguments also quite clearly demonstrate the aforementioned research gap, since they only think in the autocracy-democracy continuum, without distinguishing between and investigating different democracies. The concept of democratic efficacy takes these considerations into account, as it assumes that democracy's ability to produce desired and intended climate performances improves concomitantly with increasing levels of democratic quality. Thus, the concept of democratic efficacy just assumes that the ability rises, but not that there is a deterministic or guaranteed positive influence.

Empirical findings which assume that democracy has a positive influence on climate performance rely overwhelmingly on research on policy outputs. This means that democracies are more likely to adopt more ambitious targets and commitments than autocracies (Bättig & Bernauer, 2009; Bernauer, 2013, p. 435; Neumayer, 2002; Stein, 2008), even though the commitments might never be intended to be met (Hovi, Sprinz, & Bang, 2012). Commitments might rely on other intentions, such as the prospect of European Union (EU) accession (McLean & Stone, 2012; Schreurs & Tiberghien, 2007), or depend on the level of governance (Dutt, 2009; Kneuer, 2012). A few studies also examine the impact of elements of deliberative democracy at the local level, assuming that deliberation builds capacity to respond to climate change and improves climate policy-making (see, e.g., Niemeyer, 2013). Studies on the influence of democracy on policy outcomes and thus actual GHG reductions are rare, often focus on the environment in general, use CO_2 as only one indicator among many, do not use panel data and apply democracy indices which are only able to separate between autocracy and democracy, rather than being able to provide useful insights into democracies themselves (see, e.g., Gleditsch & Sverdrup, 2003). The Bättig/Bernauer study we looked at earlier, based on a cross section of 185 countries between 1990–2004, finds that the effect of democracy on policy outcomes, measured in terms of emission levels and trends, is ambiguous, but assumes that democracies are likely to perform better in the long run (Bättig & Bernauer, 2009,

p. 304). Nevertheless, empirical studies only consider the autocracy-democracy continuum, instead of distinguishing between established democracies, and consequently do not research internal mechanisms beyond the local level to explain how these impact upon the influence which democracies have on climate performance.

Empirical findings which indicate that democracy has either no or a negative influence on climate performance are rare and present ambiguous results. Some studies fail to identify any effect of good governance or democracy on climate policy outcomes, which might indicate that other factors dominated outcomes (Bättig & Bernauer, 2009; Bernauer, 2013, p. 285; Bernauer & Koubi, 2009; Spilker, 2012, 2013) or that results depend upon the definition of democracy as a continuous or dichotomous indicator (Li & Reuveny, 2006). Some studies find that higher GHG per capita can be related to an effect of democracy (Congleton, 1992; Midlarsky, 1998). One study even finds that direct democracy makes the implementation of long-term effective climate change policies unlikely, since the effects of direct democracy produce rather small steps supported by a broad political elite (Stadelmann-Steffen, 2011). Thus, based on existing research it might be expected that the democracy effect on outputs is indeed stronger than on outcomes. However, besides one book on direct democracy, all research is again focused on the autocracy-democracy continuum and thus allows no insights into differences between established democracies.

The interpretation of findings on the democracy-climate nexus seems, to a certain extent, to be similar to those on democracy and environmental performance: results depend on the countries which were investigated and the democracy measurements, climate measurements and time periods which were analysed (Bättig & Bernauer, 2009, p. 292; Burnell, 2012, p. 827). Some minor indications could be identified which suggest that increasing levels of democratic quality positively influence climate performance. However, both the arguments and the empirical studies were centred on single aspects (which themselves were not empirically investigated in the majority of cases) or on the different influences which democracy and autocracy have on climate performance. None of the findings provide comprehensive insights into the differences between the influence on climate performance wielded by different established democracies. How democratic quality influences the climate performance of established democracies is thus so far unknown.

Practical relevance: a more democratic world and solutions to climate change

A more democratic world and solutions to the challenges of climate change are common aims in most parts of world society. On the one hand, the depth and breadth of knowledge about climate change and its causes and impacts has increased tremendously (IPCC, 2013, 2014a, 2014b). The effects of anthropogenic climate change, as identified by climate science, indicate some room for manoeuvre, such as a 2°C buffer zone (Randalls, 2010). To act within this room for manoeuvre GHG emissions need to be reduced to zero to avoid tremendous and partially irreversible changes in the earth system; so far tipping points have been ignored (Lenton et al., 2008). The influence such great changes in the earth system might have on human life support systems and societies could be immense. Thus, with their high percentages of GHG emissions, established democracies will also need to reduce their climate footprints.

On the other hand, some suggest that a "golden age of democracy" (Dalton, 2008, p. 251) (with respect to the number of democracies and the increase and intensification of democratic quality) is not inevitable and that democratic quality might actually decrease in many countries. The debate about a crisis of democracy is nothing new (Crozier, Huntington, & Watanuki, 1975) and arguments surrounding a so-called "post-democracy" (Andersen & Burns, 1996; Crouch, 2004) tend to somewhat rely on projections of a golden democratic age, normative simplifications and missing empirical evidence. However, contemporary democracies do nonetheless seem to be faced with several troubling developments, such as a complex and non-transparent system of representative decision-making, a marginalization of parliamentary institutions, an undermining of democratic structures through globalization, the increased importance of unelected actors, a growth in technocracy, changes in opinion-making within the public sphere and, first and foremost, internal threats from democracy itself, where the tensions caused by stresses and challenges might ultimately lead to shortcomings with regard to legitimacy and policy performance (Vorländer, 2013). All of these could weaken the influence of democratic politics on political decision-making (Papadopoulos, 2013). However, contemporary democracies founded decades and centuries ago have historically faced challenges and they seem to not only have recovered from them, but also to have renewed themselves to deal more successfully with new problems, such as climate change (Alonso, Keane, Merkel, & Fotou, 2011; Cain, Dalton, & Scarrow, 2003; Dowding, Hughes, & Margetts, 2001).

Thus, a more democratic world and solutions to the challenges of climate change are common aims in most parts of world society, albeit, the achievement of any one of these aims would be a monumental task on its own. Yet, knowing more about the democracy-climate nexus could come to be a useful factor in the development of practices which might be able to help established democracies simultaneously increase both democratic quality and climate performance.

Focus: detecting trends, exploring mechanisms and developing a concept

Taking into account both the academic and practical relevance, its focus could be narrowed down to the question of how democratic quality influences climate performance in established democracies. However, to comprehensively research how democratic quality influences climate performance in established democracies, the book needs to be adapted to meet specific research requirements.

More precisely, there are three interconnected research requirements which will frame this book. First, findings on "robust inferences about the factors that

cause variation across political units in forms and ambition levels of climate policies" are missing and there is currently no basis on which to study policy outputs
and outcomes side by side (Bättig & Bernauer, 2009, pp. 823–824; Bernauer,
2013, p. 435; Burnell, 2012). The existing body of research does not distinguish
between established democracies on the basis of their democratic quality and
there has been no evaluation of such trends and inferences in regard to their
influence on climate performance. This requirement led to panel regressions of
the Democracy Barometer and the CCPI ("analysis I").

Secondly, since spatial statistics and numeral coding will always miss nuances
which are important for dynamic policy processes, "qualitative case studies based
on 'thick description' of climate policy making remain crucial" (Bernauer, 2013,
p. 436). In particular, existing studies do not comprehensively explain what
mechanisms exist inside democracies, thus making it difficult to understand different reactions to climate change. Such mechanisms could also help verify previously detected trends. This requirement resulted in a case study on Canada's
Kyoto Protocol process between 1995 and 2012, which asked which mechanisms
link democratic quality and climate performance ("analysis II").

Thirdly, the focus of research has so far been on description rather than on
explanation and the development of an applicable theory (Cao et al., 2014,
p. 293). Thus, arguments relating to the democracy-climate nexus are fragmentary
and require a generalizable explanatory approach. Such a generalizable concept
has to function as an explanatory link between democratic quality and climate
performance. This requirement led to the development and initial outline of the
concept of democratic efficacy, which assumes that the ability to produce desired
and indented climate performance improves concomitantly with increasing levels of democratic quality. Based on the mechanisms explored in the pursuit of
the second research requirement, it was possible to advance the initially outlined
concept of democratic efficacy following empirical investigation.

In summary, these research requirements necessitate a mixed methods design,
including the possibility to explore quantitative trends, qualitatively detect
detailed mechanisms, formulate a concept of democratic efficacy and develop
synergy beyond single analyses in order to provide a comprehensive answer to the
question of how democratic quality influences climate performance. Therefore,
an adequate conceptual framework is required.

References

The access date of all material retrieved from the Web is 5 June 2015 unless otherwise
    specified.
Alonso, S., Keane, J., Merkel, W., & Fotou, M. (2011). *The Future of Representative Democ-
    racy*. Cambridge/New York: Cambridge University Press.
Andersen, S.S., & Burns, T.R. (1996). The European Union and the erosion of parlia-
    mentary democracy: a study of post-parliamentary governance. In S.S. Andersen &
    K.J. Eliassen (Eds.), *The European Union: How Democratic Is It?* (pp. 227–252).
    London: Sage.

Barber, B. (n.d.). Democracies and climate change: how cities can do what states can't. Retrieved from www.humansandnature.org/democracy—benjamin-barber-response-51.php

Barrett, S., & Graddy, K. (2000). Freedom, growth, and the environment. *Environment and Development Economics, 5*(4), 433–456.

Bättig, M. B., & Bernauer, T. (2009). National institutions and global public goods: are democracies more cooperative in climate change policy? *International Organization, 63*(2), 281–308.

Beeson, M. (2010). The coming of environmental authoritarianism. *Environmental Politics, 19*(2), 276–294.

Bernauer, T. (2013). Climate change politics. *Annual Review of Political Science, 16*(1), 421–448.

Bernauer, T., & Koubi, V. (2009). Effects of political institutions on air quality. *Ecological Economics, 68*(5), 1355–1365.

Binder, S., & Neumayer, E. (2005). Environmental pressure group strength and air pollution: an empirical analysis. *Ecological Economics, 55*(4), 527–538.

Boiral, O., & Henri, J. F. (2012). Modelling the impact of ISO 14001 on environmental performance: a comparative approach. *Journal of Environmental Management, 99*, 84–97.

Brodocz, A. L., Llanque. M., & Schaal, G. S. (2008). Demokratie im Angesicht ihrer Bedrohungen. In A. L. Brodocz, M. Llanque, & G. S. Schaal (Eds.), *Bedrohungen der Demokratie* (pp. 11–26). Wiesbaden: VS Verlag für Sozialwissenschaften.

Brousseau, E., Dedeurwaerdere, T., & Siebenhüner, B. (2012). *Reflexive Governance for Global Public Goods.* Cambridge, MA: MIT Press.

Burnell, P. (2012). Democracy, democratization and climate change: complex relationships. *Democratization, 19*(5), 813–842.

Cain, B. E., Dalton, R. J., & Scarrow, S. E. (2003). *Democracy Transformed?: Expanding Political Opportunities in Advanced Industrial Democracies.* Oxford/New York: Oxford University Press.

Cao, X., Milner, H. V., Prakash, A., & Ward, H. (2014). Research frontiers in comparative and international environmental politics: an introduction. *Comparative Political Studies, 47*(3), 291–308.

Coenen, F. H. J. M., Huitema, D., & O'Toole, L. J. (1998). *Participation and the Quality of Environmental Decision Making.* Dordrecht/Boston: Kluwer Academic Publishers.

Congleton, R. D. (1992). Political institutions and pollution control. *Review of Economics and Statistics, 74*(3), 412–421.

Crouch, C. (2004). *Post-democracy.* Malden, MA: Polity.

Crozier, M., Huntington, S. P., & Watanuki, J. (1975). *The Crisis of Democracy: Report on the Governability of Democracies to the Trilateral Commission.* New York: New York University Press.

Dalton, R. J. (2008). *Citizen Politics: Public Opinion and Political Parties in Advanced Industrial Democracies* (5th ed.). Washington, DC: CQ Press.

De Mesquita, B. B., Downs, G. W., Smith, A., & Cherif, F. M. (2005). Thinking inside the box: a closer look at democracy and human rights. *International Studies Quarterly, 49*(3), 439–457.

Desai, U. (1998). *Ecological Policy and Politics in Developing Countries: Economic Growth, Democracy, and Environment.* Albany, NY: State University of New York Press.

Dorussen, H., & Ward, H. (2008). Intergovernmental organizations and the Kantian peace. *Journal of Conflict Resolution, 52*(2), 189–212.

Dowding, K.M., Hughes, J., & Margetts, H. (2001). *Challenges to Democracy: Ideas, Involvement, and Institutions: The PSA Yearbook 2000*. Basingstoke /New York: Palgrave.

Dryzek, J.S. (n.d.). Deliberative democracy and climate change. Retrieved from www. humansandnature.org/democracy—john-dryzek-response-55.php

Dryzek, J.S., Norgaard, R.B., & Schlosberg, D. (2013). *Climate-challenged Society* (1st ed.). Oxford/New York: Oxford University Press.

Dutt, K. (2009). Governance, institutions and the environment-income relationship: a cross-country study. *Environment, Development and Sustainability, 11*(4), 705–723.

Duwel, A. (2010). Democracy and the environment: the visibility factor. *SSRN Working Paper*. Retrieved from http://papers.ssrn.com/sol3/papers.cfm?abstract_id=1582299

Esty, D.C., & Porter, M.E. (2005). National environmental performance: an empirical analysis of policy results and determinants. *Environment and Development Economics, 10*, 391–434.

Farzin, Y.H., & Bond, C.A. (2006). Democracy and environmental quality. *Journal of Development Economics, 81*(1), 213–235.

Fiorino, D.J. (2011). Explaining national environmental performance: approaches, evidence, and implications. *Policy Sciences, 44*(4), 367–389.

Fisher, D.R., & Freudenburg, W.R. (2004). Postindustrialization and environmental quality: an empirical analysis of the environmental state. *Social Forces, 83*(1), 157–188.

Fredriksson, P.G., & Gaston, N. (2000). Ratification of the 1992 Climate Change Convention: what determines legislative delay? *Public Choice, 104*(3–4), 345–368.

Fredriksson, P.G., Neumayer, E., Damania, R., & Gates, S. (2005). Environmentalism, democracy, and pollution control. *Journal of Environmental Economics and Management, 49*(2), 343–365.

Fredriksson, P.G., & Wollscheid, J.R. (2007). Democratic institutions versus autocratic regimes: the case of environmental policy. *Public Choice, 130*(3–4), 381–393.

Freyburg, T., Lavenex, S., Schimmelfennig, F., Skripka, T., & Wetzel, A. (2011). Democracy promotion through functional cooperation? The case of the European Neighbourhood Policy. *Democratization, 18*(4), 1026–1054.

Friedman, T.L. (2008). *Hot, Flat, and Crowded: Why We Need a Green Revolution, and How It Can Renew America* (1st ed.). New York: Farrar, Straus and Giroux.

Gallagher, K.P., & Thacker, S.C. (2008). Democracy, income, and environmental quality. *Working Paper 164*, Amherst: Political Economy Research Institute, University of Massachusetts.

Gleditsch, N.P., & Sverdrup, B.O. (2003). Democracy and the environment. In M.R. Redclift, & E. Page (Eds.), *Human Security and the Environment: International Comparisons* (pp. 45–70). Cheltenham: Edward Elgar.

Gould, C. (n.d.). Beyond the dual crisis: from climate change to democratic change. Retrieved from www.humansandnature.org/democracy—carol-gould-response-50.php

Harbaugh, W.T., Levinson, A., & Wilson, D.M. (2002). Reexamining the empirical evidence for an environmental Kuznets curve. *Review of Economics and Statistics, 84*(3), 541–551.

Hardin, G. (1968). Tragedy of the commons. *Science, 162*(3859), 1243–1248.

Hayward, T. (n.y.). Why taking the climate challenge seriously means taking democracy more seriously. Retrieved from www.humansandnature.org/democracy—tim-hayward-response-54.php

Heilbroner, R.L. (1974). *An Inquiry into the Human Prospect*. New York: W.W. Norton & Company.

Held, D. (2014). Climate change, global governance and democracy: some questions. In M. Di Paola, & G. Pellegrino (Eds.), *Canned Heat: Ethics and Politics of Global Climate Change* (pp. 17–28). New Delhi: Routledge.

Held, D., & Hervey, A. F. (2009). Democracy, climate change and global governance: democratic agency and the policy menu ahead. *Policy Network Paper*. Retrieved from www.policy-network.net/publications_download.aspx?ID=3426

Hisschemöller, M., & Hoppe, R. (2001). Coping with intractable controversies: the case for problem structuring in policy design and analysis. In M. Hisschemöller, R. Hoppe, W. Dunn, & J.R. Ravetz (Eds.), *Knowledge, Power and Participation in Environmental Policy Analysis* (pp. 47–72). New Brunswick, NJ: Transaction Publishers.

Holden, B. (2002). *Democracy and Global Warming*. London/New York: Continuum.

Hovi, J., Sprinz, D. F., & Bang, G. (2012). Why the United States did not become a party to the Kyoto Protocol: German, Norwegian, and US perspectives. *European Journal of International Relations*, 18(1), 129–150.

Huitema, D., Jordan, A., Massey, E., Rayner, T., van Asselt, H., Haug, C., Hildingsson, R., Stripple, J. (2011). The evaluation of climate policy: theory and emerging practice in Europe. *Policy Sciences*, 44(2), 179–198.

IPCC. (2013). The Physical Science Basis. Contribution of Working Group I to the Fifth Assessment Report of the Intergovernmental Panel on Climate Change. Full Report. Cambridge/New York: Cambridge University Press.

IPCC. (2014a). Climate Change 2014: Impacts, Adaptation and Vulnerability. Contribution of Working Group II to the Fifth Assessment Report. Cambridge/New York: Cambridge University Press.

IPCC. (2014b). Climate Change 2014: Mitigation of Climate Change. Contribution of Working Group III to the Fifth Assessment Report. Cambridge/New York: Cambridge University Press.

Jahn, D. (1998). Environmental performance and policy regimes: explaining variations in 18 OECD-countries. *Policy Sciences*, 31(2), 107–131.

Jancar-Webster, B. (1998). Environmental movement and social change in transition countries. *Environmental Politics*, 7(1), 69–90.

Jordan, A., van Asselt, H., Berkhout, F., Huitema, D., & Rayner, T. (2012). Understanding the paradoxes of multi-level governing: climate change policy in the European Union. *Global Environmental Politics*, 12(2), 43–66.

Keohane, R.O., & Raustiala, K. (2008). Toward a post-Kyoto climate change architecture: a political analysis. *UCLA School of Law, Law-Econ Research Paper*, No. 08–14. Retrieved from SSRN: https://ssrn.com/abstract=1142996 or http://dx.doi.org/10.2139/ssrn.1142996

Kersbergen, K. V. (2003). *Social Capitalism: A Study of Christian Democracy and the Welfare State* (Digital printing ed.). London: Routledge.

Kneuer, M. (2012). Who is greener? Climate action and political regimes: trade-offs for national and international actors. *Democratization*, 19(5), 865–888.

Koppenjan, J. F.M., & Klijn, E.-H. (2004). Managing Uncertainties in Networks: A Network Approach to Problem Solving and Decision Making. London/New York: Routledge.

Lachapelle, E., & Paterson, M. (2013). Drivers of national climate policy. *Climate Policy*, 13(5), 547–571.

Lazarus, R.J. (2009). Super wicked problems and climate change: restraining the present to liberate the future. *Cornell Law Review*, 94(5), 1153–1233.

Leggewie, C., & Welzer, H. (2010). Another "great transformation"? Social and cultural consequences of climate change. *Journal of Renewable and Sustainable Energy*, 2(3), 1–13.

Lenton, T.M., Held, H., Kriegler, E., Hall, J.W., Lucht, W., Rahmstorf, S., & Schell-nhuber, H.J. (2008). Tipping elements in the Earth's climate system. *Proceedings of the National Academy of Sciences of the United States of America*, 105(6), 1786–1793.

Levin, K., Cashore, B., Bernstein, S., & Auld, G. (2007). *Playing It Forward: Path Dependency, Progressive Incrementalism, and the "Super Wicked" Problem of Global Climate Change*. Paper presented at the International Studies Association 48th annual convention.

Levin, K., Cashore, B., Bernstein, S., & Auld, G. (2012). Overcoming the tragedy of super wicked problems: constraining our future selves to ameliorate global climate change. *Policy Sciences*, 45(2), 123–152.

Li, Q., & Reuveny, R. (2006). Democracy and environmental degradation. *International Studies Quarterly*, 50(4), 935–956.

Lidskog, R., & Elander, I. (2010). Addressing climate change democratically. Multi-level governance, transnational networks and governmental structures. *Sustainable Development*, 18(1), 32–41.

Liefferink, D., Arts, B., Kamstra, J., & Ooijevaar, J. (2009). Leaders and laggards in environmental policy: a quantitative analysis of domestic policy outputs. *Journal of European Public Policy*, 16(5), 677–700.

Lovelock, J. (2010) *James Lovelock on the Value of Sceptics and Why Copenhagen was Doomed/Interviewer: L. Hickman*. Retrieved from https://www.theguardian.com/environment/blog/2010/mar/29/james-lovelock (accessed 15 February 2017).

Machin, A. (2013). *Negotiating Climate Change: Radical Democracy and the Illusion of Consensus*. London: Zed Books.

Mackenbach, J.P., & McKee, M. (2013). A comparative analysis of health policy performance in 43 European countries. *European Journal of Public Health*, 23(2), 195–201.

McLean, E.V., & Stone, R.W. (2012). The Kyoto Protocol: two-level bargaining and European integration. *International Studies Quarterly*, 56(1), 99–113.

Mickwitz, P. (2003). A framework for evaluating environmental policy instruments: context and key concepts. *Evaluation*, 9(4), 415–436.

Midlarsky, M.I. (1998). Democracy and the environment: an empirical assessment. *Journal of Peace Research*, 35(3), 341–361.

Midlarsky, M.I. (2001). Democracy and the environment. In N.P.G.P.F. Diehl (Ed.), *Environmental Conflict* (pp. 155–178). Boulder, CO: Westview Press.

Neumayer, E. (2002). Do democracies exhibit stronger international environmental commitment? A cross-country analysis. *Journal of Peace Research*, 39(2), 139–164.

Neumayer, E., Gates, S., & Gleditsch, N.P. (2002). Environmental Commitment, Democracy, and Conflict. Background Report for World Development Report 2003. Washington, DC: World Bank.

Niemeyer, S. (2013). Democracy and climate change: what can deliberative democracy contribute? *Australian Journal of Politics and History*, 59(3), 429–448.

Offe, C., & Preuß, U. (1991). Democratic institutions and moral resources. In D. Held (Ed.), *Political Theory Today* (pp. 143–171). Stanford, CA: Stanford University Press.

Oneal, J.R., Oneal, F.H., Maoz, Z., & Russett, B. (1996). The liberal peace: interdependence, democracy, and international conflict, 1950–85. *Journal of Peace Research*, 33(1), 11–28.

Ophuls, W. (1977). *Ecology and the Politics of Scarcity*. San Francisco, CA: Freeman.

Pahl-Wostl, C. (2009). A conceptual framework for analysing adaptive capacity and multi-level learning processes in resource governance regimes. *Global Environmental Change-Human and Policy Dimensions*, 19(3), 354–365.

Papadopoulos, Y. (2013). *Democracy in Crisis? Politics, Governance and Policy*. Basingstoke: Palgrave Macmillan.

Payne, R. A. (1995). Freedom and the environment. *Journal of Democracy, 6*(3), 41–55.

Pellegrini, L. G., & Gerlagh, R. (2006). Corruption, democracy, and environmental policy: an empirical contribution to the debate. *The Journal of Environment & Development, 15*(3), 332–354.

Poloni-Staudinger, L. M. (2008). Are consensus democracies more environmentally effective? *Environmental Politics, 17*(3), 410–430.

Prins, G., Galiana I., Green C., Grundmann, R., Hulme, M., Korhola, A., Laird, F., Nordhaus, T., Pielke, R., Rayner, S., Sarewitz, D., Shellenberger, M., Stehr, N., & Tezuka, H. (2010). *The Hartwell Paper: A New Direction for Climate Policy after the Crash of 2009*. London: Institute for Science, Innovation & Society, University of Oxford.

Rae, A., & Wong, C. (2012). Monitoring spatial planning policies: towards an analytical, adaptive, and spatial approach to a "wicked problem". *Environment and Planning B-Planning & Design, 39*(5), 880–896.

Randalls, S. (2010). History of the 2 degrees C climate target. *Wiley Interdisciplinary Reviews–Climate Change, 1*(4), 598–605.

Recchia, S. P. (2002). International Environmental Treaty engagement in 19 democracies. *Policy Studies Journal, 30*(4), 470–494.

Reiter, D., & Stam, A. C. (2002). *Democracies at War*. Princeton, NJ: Princeton University Press.

Rittel, H. W. J., & Webber, M. M. (1973). Dilemmas in a general theory of planning. *Policy Sciences, 4*(2), 155–169.

Roberts, J. T., Parks, B. C., & Vásquez, A. A. (2004). Who ratifies environmental treaties and why? Institutionalism, structuralism and participation by 192 nations in 22 treaties. *Global Environmental Politics, 4*(3), 22–64.

Runciman, D. (2013). *The Confidence Trap: A History of Democracy in Crisis from World War I to the Present*. Princeton, NJ: Princeton University Press.

Russel, D., Haxeltine, D., Huitema, M., Nillsson, M., Rayner, T., & Hinkel, J. (2010). Climate change appraisal in the EU: current trends and future challenges. In M. Hulme, & H. Neufeldt (Eds.), *Making Climate Change Work for Us: European Perspectives on Adaptation and Mitigation Strategies* (pp. 31–52). Cambridge: Cambridge University Press.

Sandler, T. (2010). Overcoming global and regional collective action impediments. *Global Policy, 1*(1), 40–50.

Schreurs, M. A., & Tiberghien, Y. (2007). Multi-level reinforcement: explaining European Union leadership in climate change mitigation. *Global Environmental Politics, 7*(4), 19–46.

Scruggs, L. (2003). *Sustaining Abundance: Environmental Performance in Industrial Democracies*. Cambridge /New York: Cambridge University Press.

Shearman, D. J. C., & Smith, J. W. (2007). *The Climate Change Challenge and the Failure of Democracy*. Westport, CT: Praeger Publishers.

Spilker, G. (2012). Helpful organizations: membership in inter-governmental organizations and environmental quality in developing countries. *British Journal of Political Science, 42*, 345–370.

Spilker, G. (2013). *Globalization, Political Institutions and the Environment in Developing Countries*. New York: Routledge.

Stadelmann-Steffen, I. (2011). Citizens as veto players: climate change policy and the constraints of direct democracy. *Environmental Politics, 20*(4), 485–507.

Stasavage, D. (2005). Democracy and education spending in Africa. *American Journal of Political Science*, 49(2), 343–358.

Stern, D. I. (2004). The rise and fall of the environmental Kuznets curve. *World Development*, 32(8), 1419–1439.

Stevenson, H., & Dryzek, J. S. (2014). *Democratizing Global Climate Governance*. Cambridge: Cambridge University Press.

Thompson, A. (2006). Management under anarchy: the international politics of climate change. *Climatic Change*, 78(1), 7–29.

Torras, M., & Boyce, J. K. (1998). Income, inequality, and pollution: a reassessment of the environmental Kuznets Curve. *Ecological Economics*, 25(2), 147–160.

Vorländer, H. (2013). Zur Lage der Demokratie. *Zeitschrift für Politikwissenschaft*, 23(2), 267–277.

Ward, H. (2008). Liberal democracy and sustainability. *Environmental Politics*, 17(3), 386–409.

WBGU (Wissenschaftlicher Beirat Globale Umweltveränderungen/German Advisory Council on Global Change). (2011). *World in Transition – A Social Contract for Sustainability*. Berlin: WBGU.

Wilensky, H. L. (2002). *Rich Democracies: Political Economy, Public Policy, and Performance*. Berkeley: University of California Press.

Wurster, S. (2013). Comparing ecological sustainability in autocracies and democracies. *Contemporary Politics*, 19(1), 76–93.

3 The concept and the operationalization of democratic efficacy

"There is no simple answer to your question."

(Stone, 2014)

This chapter develops the conceptual framework of the book to answer the main research question of how democratic quality influences climate performance in established democracies. Therefore, it defines and operationalizes both democratic quality and general performance, setting them in relation to one another. Thereafter, the chapter differentiates the main research question and proposes the concept of democratic efficacy, assuming that democracy's ability to produce desired and intended climate performances improves concomitantly with increasing levels of democratic quality. Finally, a mixed methods approach is developed. This approach consists of a quantitative analysis which focuses on trends in the influence of democratic quality on climate performance, and a qualitative analysis which explores which mechanisms connect democratic quality and climate performance.

Defining democratic quality and general performance

To answer the question of how democratic quality influences climate performance in established democracies, two basic definitions need to be outlined: democratic quality and general performance. The following develops these two definitions in order to propose an argument about the influence of democratic quality on climate performance and to operationalize them in empirical research. Before dealing with each of the two definitions individually, both must be defined in order to avoid an overlap in the evaluation of the influence of democratic quality on climate performance.

Democratic quality indicates the level of democracy and relies on a pure understanding of democracy. Applied to Lincoln's famous distinction, a pure understanding has, on the whole, to be understood as a "government of the people" governed "by the people". Democratic quality can be divided into a substantive and a procedural part. Procedural democratic quality consists of such dimensions as liberty, participation and transparency, and is particularly relevant for policy

DOI: 10.4324/9781315228983-4

Table 3.1 General performance and democratic quality

	Substantive aspects	*Procedural aspects*
General performance	substantive general performance	procedural general performance
Democratic quality	substantive democratic quality	procedural democratic quality

Source: Based on Roller, 2005, p. 24.

processes. The realization of these dimensions helps to ensure substantive democratic quality consisting of the meta dimensions of freedom, equality and control, which are particularly relevant in terms of democratic renewal at the level of political institutions.

General performance is a "consequentialist" understanding of democracy that every state can perform regardless of whether it is democratic or autocratic. In Lincoln's words, a consequentialist understanding of whether democracy provides a "government for the people". General performance can be divided into procedural and substantive general performance. Procedural general performance consists of governmental capability, stability (of government), effectiveness and efficiency. The realization of these dimensions helps to ensure substantive general performance in certain policy subfields, like environment, security or welfare. Table 3.1 provides a basic illustration of democratic quality and general performance separated into their substantive and procedural parts.

The table indicates that general performance and democratic quality can be conceptually distinguished. Both concepts exist at substantive and procedural levels and require further clarification for empirical analysis.

Democratic quality

The understanding of democratic quality in this book is quite pragmatic and assumes that both democratic theories and empirical manifestations of democracies are overwhelmingly time-bound and that democracy is characterized by a procedural rather than a universal character. Since democracy is, on the whole, a normative concept, a few preliminary remarks are essential. Democracy "has meant different things to different people at different times and places" (Dahl, 2000, p. 3) and this is why the "history of the idea of democracy is curious" and "the history of democracies is puzzling" (Held, 2006, p. 1). In simple terms, throughout human history, people have developed many democratic theories and founded a wide range of states they described as democratic. Consequently, the term democracy has "at the same time an empirical reference and a normative, ideal connotation" (Morlino, 2012, p. 25). Hence, democracy is not a closed concept. It is possible for new dimensions of democratic quality to arise, for existing ones to develop further or to decline completely. Thus, many dimensions of democratic quality have developed both theoretically (and have probably not, or only partially, been put into practice) and empirically through the practice of democratic states and societies (and are probably not, or only partially, reflected in democratic theories) or in the interplay of both spheres. Interdependence between theories of democracy and the development of democratic practice is of crucial importance (Thompson, 2008). Hence, a definition of democratic quality has to be very open-minded about a wide range of democratic dimensions which can empirically and theoretically be combined in different ways (Bochsler & Kriesi, 2013, p. 69; Coppedge et al., 2011, pp. 255, 263; Smith, 2009, pp. 10–12). Even though such argumentation is based on certain ideals and assumes a world which will probably never be achieved, it is still a useful tool with which to judge the world we live in.

More precisely, it is assumed that (meta) dimensions of democratic quality have developed in terms of an "affirmative genealogy" (Joas, 2013). An affirmative genealogy looks to reveal the interconnections between historical reflections and arguments of justification. It assumes that scepticism about a purely rational justification of ultimate values and an analytical explanation of their development (as opposed to their construction or discovery) does not lead to relativism, postmodern arbitrariness or a destruction of values (Nietzsche, 2014), but instead to the acceptance of values. Therefore, it is important to ensure that each historical innovation of democratic quality is recognized as an innovation, while, at the same time, also preserving a recognition of the universal claim or evident nature which such an innovation can have for the people involved. The key to the development of dimensions of democratic quality has to be seen not only in contingent beliefs, world views and traditions but first and foremost in the moment in which these values gain binding empirical power, the ability to effect change and a plenary character (Joas, 2013). This occurs when theoretical and practical/ empirical spheres merge and people accept their merger.

In order to develop an open-minded approach, however, this book applies a somewhat holistic approach, evaluating both theories of democracy and democratic indices. The evaluation implies a conceptualization which has the task of identifying and organizing dimensions of democratic quality (Munck, 2009; Munck & Verkuilen, 2002). Thereby, the identification of dimensions must specify the concept by avoiding the inclusion of irrelevant dimensions and/or the exclusion of relevant dimensions. Similarly, the organization of the dimensions must avoid redundancy and conflation. Having identified (1) meta dimensions as overall guiding principles, (2) dimensions of democratic quality as conceptual criteria can be empirically translated to (3) evaluative standards stipulating what counts as high or low democratic quality (Thompson, 2008, p. 501). Lastly, evaluative standards can be differentiated to (4) indicate which conditions can be empirically evaluated to determine democratic quality (Thompson, 2008, p. 501). Based on these criteria, the definition tries to include reasonable dimensions of democratic quality which can be conceptually justified. However, "[t]here is no objective way of deriving a single framework of democratic quality, right and true for all societies" (Diamond & Morlino, 2004, p. 22). And, therefore, the definition can only be seen as a proposal for how to conceptualize democratic quality.

It is assumed, that three meta dimensions exist and these can be found, with different weightings and connotations, in almost all theories and indices of democracy. Figure 3.1 provides a basic definition of democratic quality, conceptualized in the form of meta dimensions as substantive democratic quality and related dimensions as procedural democratic quality.

Freedom, equality and control seem, as meta dimensions, to be the "boundary contested principles" of the "boundary contested concept" of democracy (Gallie, 1956; Lord, 2004 (quotation 12)). They are the basic principles which democratic movements have fought for throughout the history of democracy and are, in different connotations and weightings, the anchor points of theories of democracy, something which has lent them both empirical power and a plenary character. There are sound reasons why these three guiding meta dimensions have developed such importance and superior standing. Freedom is a basic principle since it ensures that individual rights are guaranteed while also enabling creative forces to further develop democracy. However, for all citizens to have the same ability to make use of their rights, political equality must also ensure that these citizens all have equal opportunity to influence political power. Thus, freedom and equality are interrelated. In order to decide what equality means to them and how it should be realized, citizens need the right to speak freely about it as well as equal opportunities to do so. Control, meanwhile, ensures that the will of the demos is accountably implemented under the rule of law and that their understanding of equality is actually implemented. Thus, freedom, control and equality serve much more to enable and complement than to contradict one another. Subsequently, the existence and further development of these three principles enables democratic renewal.

More precisely, control, seen as a meta dimension of democratic quality, means an accountable, independent and stable exercise of power. Clear lines of accountability ensure the control of decision-makers, as they are obliged to explain their political decisions when requested to do so by citizens, constitutional bodies, state institutions, officials, etc. (see, e.g., Bühlmann & Kriesi, 2013, pp. 53–57; Diamond & Morlino, 2004, pp. 25–26; Morlino, 2012, pp. 199–202). Accountability can be divided into vertical and horizontal parts. Vertical accountability is the kind of accountability that decision-takers or electors in representative democracies can demand from decision-makers or those elected as a result of decisions and

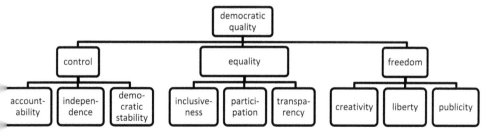

igure 3.1 Assignment of meta dimensions to the dimensions of democratic quality

policies which have already been made (see, e.g., Przeworski, Stokes, & Manin, 1999). Horizontal accountability is the accountability of decision-makers by other (state) institutions with the means to check and monitor their decisions (see, e.g., Bovens, 2007; O'Donnell, 1994). The main feature of independence as the second dimension of control is rule of law at an institutional and organizational level. A free and open access judiciary needs to be established in order to have a high quality democracy. Moreover, it is important to make authorities respect the law and establish its supremacy. This means ensuring that no unjustified connections exist between the judiciary and the legislature or the executive, as this hinders independent decisions and enables corruption. Thus, the judiciary has to be highly professionalized (see, e.g., Keith, 2002; La Porta, Lopez-de-Silanes, Pop-Eleches, & Shleifer, 2004). Stability, as the third dimension related to control, guarantees that a state is embedded within stable democratic structures, which themselves have to be secured in many different branches. Stability is characterized by governmental capability, including constraints on constitutional and executive power, the absence of destabilizing circumstances and the existence of sufficient resources for democratic institutions. A democratic government has to have the capability and autonomy to effectively govern the political process and to implement policies based on democratic procedures (see, e.g., Etzioni, 1968; Harmel & Robertson, 1986; Scharpf, 1999). Therefore, it needs different kinds of resources, such as, for example, public support (see, e.g., Chanley, Rudolph, & Rahn, 2000; Rudolph & Evans, 2005). At the same time, it is necessary to have mutual constraints on constitutional powers and executives. These can be found in veto powers in the form of, for example, an opposition with corresponding rights or the control of institutions with sufficient resources to oversee governmental policies and to inform the public about them (see, e.g., Hamilton, Madison, & Jay, 2014; Schneider, 2003; Tsebelis, 1995). Moreover, the absence of destabilizing circumstances and the presence of sufficient resources for democratic institutions is important for the stability of a democratic system. In summary, statehood has to be guaranteed and democracy so designed as to be able, depending on the government in power, to cope with a rapid turnover in personnel and wild variations within democratic institutions and their responsibilities without the basic tenets of its existence being threatened.

Equality as a meta dimension consists of inclusive, participative and transparent access to political power and thus to legislation (see, e.g., Dahl, 1956, 2000, 2006; Saward, 1998). Inclusiveness can be seen in an openness and fairness of access which guarantees the involvement of a plurality of actors. This includes the involvement of both current and future generations in the formulation and implementation of decisions. Such actors can be described as holders since they own a certain quality or resource: citizens have rights, residents occupy spatial locations, experts possess knowledge, owners share property, "beneficiaries-cum-victims" have a stake regardless of when and where they live, spokespersons represent interests and representatives have status (Schmitter, 2002, pp. 62–63). The selection of holders must be fair and unbiased, in order to guarantee that no disproportionality exists (see, e.g., Holden, 2006; Teorell, 2006; Urbinati &

Warren, 2008). Moreover, weak and marginalized actors need special consideration, including the making of appropriate arrangements and the provision of
necessary resources, so as to ensure their ability to participate. Participation as
a second dimension of equality requires not only the right to participate, but,
first and foremost, a large number of active participants, since important arguments will otherwise neither be voiced nor heard (see, e.g., Barber, 1984; Powell, 2004; Teorell, 2006). Thus, influence on decision-making through adequate
participation mechanisms (direct, intermediary, representative, etc.) is essential.
When these participation mechanisms are based on the considered judgement
of equals, then they can be described as deliberative. Something which can be
observed in the justification of policy proposals in regard to the common good
and in the ways in which other actors adjust their own positions. All this can
result in a responsiveness which reflects the results of considered judgements,
even during the implementation of policies (see, e.g., Bühlmann & Kriesi, 2013,
pp. 47–53; Fishkin, 2009; Morlino, 2012, pp. 208–211). For this purpose, public services need to be trained and made aware of these necessities (Ingram &
Schneider, 2006). The last dimension of equality, transparency, ensures access to
and traceability of all relevant information at all stages of the policy process (see,
e.g., Stiglitz, 1999). This includes ensuring that meetings with decision-making
characters are transparent and announced in advance, so that all actors are able to
participate. Moreover, the state has to provide its citizens (or the democratically
legitimized actors involved) with access to all relevant documents, so as to make
the political process publicly visible (see, e.g., Islam, 2006). Informal meetings
have to be minimized and democratically justified, since secrecy enables the dom-
ination of particular interests and corruption (see, e.g., Hollyer, Rosendorff, &
Vreeland, 2011; Lindstedt & Naurin, 2010).

Freedom as a meta dimension secures creativity, liberty and publicity. The first
of these dimensions, creativity, can be reached by competition, experimentation
and innovation, all of which enable creative potentials for more democracy (see,
e.g., Smith, 2009). Science plays an important part in creativity, since a functioning democracy needs informed citizens to develop democratic innovations.
Moreover, free thinking within science and openness to new ideas and concepts
is central for democratic renewal. Another source of creativity, competition, has
to be seen in a range of actors with different views on the issues under consideration being involved in decision-making processes and elections (see, e.g.,
Bartolini, 1999, 2000). Such a diverse setting can also result in diverse policy
options. Also, in the actors themselves competition seems to be a source of more
creative results and positions (see, e.g., Morlino, 2012). Experimentation with as
yet unestablished elements with the potential to create greater democratic quality should be allowed and supported in high quality democracies. As a second
dimension of freedom, individual, associational and organizational rights enable
autonomy and liberty. Individual liberty is a central precondition for a functioning democracy (see, e.g., Keith, 2002; O'Donnell, 2004). Civil rights of belief,
expression, physical integrity, etc. enable personal autonomy and must not only
exist, but also be actively implemented by states. Political rights, such as the

freedom of association and the right to organize empower an active public sphere and the existence of a variety of organizations (see, e.g., Linz & Stepan, 1996). If there is a free and easy way for individuals to establish organizations and if these organizations can act and express themselves autonomously free of repressing influence by third parties, then it can be assumed that freedom at an organizational level exists. Media pluralism and a free public sphere guarantee publicity as the third dimension of freedom (see, e.g., Putnam, Leonardi, & Nanetti, 1993; Sartori, 1987; Teorell, 2006; Young, 1999). It is important that different media outlets exist since they enable discourse and express opinions for public debate and judgement. The result can be an active civil society expressing its voice. It is therefore necessary that states support media pluralism and public debate through conferences, active press secretariats, publications, etc. Media also has the function of controlling political processes and raising public awareness about information and events which would otherwise be unaccessible for most individuals. Moreover, scientific results need to be translated and explained to a broader public and can be carried out by the media. Thus, public awareness of important issues under debate indicates that publicity is ensured.

To conclude, it seems obvious that there are several connections between the (meta) dimensions. It is, for example, impossible for individual liberties to exist without stable democratic structures, even though both aspects are subsumed under different dimensions. Therefore, it is more likely than unlikely that a high level of democratic quality in one dimension goes hand in hand with a high degree of quality in another closely related dimension. Moreover, some dimensions can, to a certain extent, be seen as preconditions for another dimension, such as liberty for creativity. The book is well aware of these circumstances and takes them into consideration in its empirical analysis. However, the type of organization required for the conceptualization is unable to fully account for all of these aspects, as, in order to be able to carry out the research, the level of complexity must, to some extent, be reduced.

In the next section, the aforementioned dimensions will need to be empirically translated to the situation under investigation and defined by a series of indicators. Thus clarified, the defined concept will provide guidance for comparable approaches to the evaluation of democratic quality, however, it will have to be applied to specific circumstances.

General performance

A general standard of performance as a consequentialist "government for the people" and, in terms of climate change, perhaps also "for the planet" can hypothetically be achieved by every state, regardless of whether it is democratic or autocratic. As already indicated, general performance can be divided into procedural (see, e.g., Back & Hadenius, 2008; Charron & Lapuente, 2010; Eckstein, 1971; Roller, 2005; Weaver & Rockman, 1993) and substantive general performance (see, e.g., Lane & Ersson, 2000; Pennock, 1966; Roller, 2005). This book proposes an approach wherein procedural general performance consists of the capability, stability and effectiveness and efficiency of the government. The realization of these dimensions helps to ensure substantive general performance, such as the performance in certain policy subfields like climate change. Figure 3.2 provides an overview of the detected dimensions of general performance in order of conceptualization.

The capability, stability and effectiveness and efficiency of government are the proposed qualifications in terms of procedural general performance. These three dimensions ensure that a state is able to fulfil its duties. The first dimension, governmental capability, ensures that the state has the ability to operate successfully (see, e.g., Bertelsmann-Stiftung, 2014a (Management Index); 2014b (Management Index); Weaver & Rockman, 1993). It stands for a state that is able to set and maintain strategic priorities, since – pragmatically speaking – not all duties can be fulfilled at the same time and this is why a concentration of resources is necessary. Therefore, sufficient steering capability is needed to navigate in the right direction. Moreover, a state needs to demonstrate flexibility and innovation in order to manage unexpected situations and to foster future-orientated perspectives. To do so, it needs to learn from past errors, so as to avoid future failures.

Stability forms the second dimension (see, e.g., Bertelsmann-Stiftung, 2014a (Management Index); Eckstein, 1971; Kaufmann, Kraay, & Zoido-Lobatón, 1999; Weaver & Rockman, 1993). To demonstrate stability a government needs to be able to successfully navigate conflict situations and manage any cleavages which might occur. Furthermore, destabilizing circumstances, such as too many powerful groups dictating a state's policy, must be avoided. Durability is ensured once citizens respect political institutions as a result of their performance. If this is not the case, a state might find itself unable to move forward in terms of formulating and implementing policies. A further indication of stability is the commitment to international treaties and communities. This ensures cooperation, which itself aids a state's long-term well-being, since the acceptance of international norms promotes exchange with other states and therefore makes such states more likely to be part of an international community.

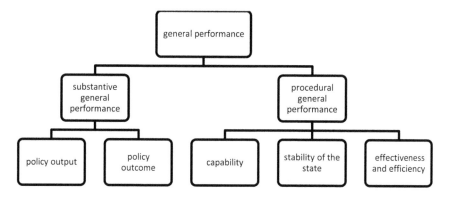

Figure 3.2 Dimensions of general performance

The third dimension of procedural general performance lies in the composition of effectiveness and efficiency (see, e.g., Back & Hadenius, 2008; Bertelsmann-Stiftung, 2014a (Management Index); Charron, 2009; Weaver & Rockman, 1993). The quality of bureaucracy seems to be of crucial importance in guaranteeing effective and efficient policy formulation and implementation, since civil servants have to ensure proceedings independent of political pressure. Thus, the state has to make proper use of its (economic, human, etc.) resources if it is to act successfully. These circumstances help to ensure that the credibility of a state's commitment to its policies is seen as being reliable.

Substantive general performance consists of two dimensions, namely the formulation and realization of policies (see, e.g., Bertelsmann-Stiftung, 2014b (Management Index); Longo, 2008; Weaver & Rockman, 1993). Hence, substantive general performance can be divided between policy output and policy outcome (Fiorino, 2011, pp. 367–371; Grumm, 1975). Output focuses on the formulation of policy plans and ratified targets, such as a Kyoto Protocol target. Outcome focuses on the results of these activities and thus the implementation of policies in terms of actual changes accomplished, as, for example, in terms of climate change, a reduction in GHG levels. It is therefore necessary to explicitly define what type of substantive general performance is applied in a study.

To conclude, it can be assumed that there are still certain links between the dimensions, but these are minimized in order to separate the dimensions as far as possible. The book is well aware of these circumstances and takes them into consideration in empirical analyses where this is deemed necessary.

Dimensions of procedural general performance are not, as in the case of democratic quality, related to specific dimensions of substantive general performance. Instead, it is assumed that all three dimensions influence policy output and policy outcome. In the next section, these dimensions will therefore have to be empirically translated to the situation under investigation. Thus, the defined concept will provide guidance for comparable approaches in the evaluation of general performance, but it will need to be applied to specific circumstances.

Conclusion

Both democratic quality and general performance can be separated into substantive and procedural (meta) dimensions. Nonetheless, procedural dimensions induce substantive dimensions, even though the relationship between them differs depending on whether they are being used to assess democratic quality or general performance. Table 3.2 illustrates the conceptualization as it has been identified and defines the fields through use of dimensions.

Table 3.2 sets a framework in terms of providing a conceptualization of the definitions of democratic quality and general performance. In order to now make use of Table 3.2's four fields to answer the question of how democratic quality influences climate performance in established democracies, an argument consisting of an hypothesis and sub-questions will be developed and translated by means of empirical analysis research methods.

Table 3.2 General performance and democratic quality with details

	Substantive (meta) dimensions	Procedural dimensions
General performance	substantive general performance (policy output, policy outcome) here: climate performance	procedural general performance (the capability, stability and effectiveness and efficiency of government)
Democratic quality	substantive democratic quality (control, equality, freedom)	procedural democratic quality (accountability, independence and stability of democratic institutions, inclusiveness, participation, transparency, creativity, liberty and publicity)

Source: Based on Roller, 2005, p. 24.

The democratic efficacy concept and argument

The book proposes an argument and related outline for the concept of democratic efficacy as the ability of a democracy to produce desired or intended climate performance. Therefore, the analytical, empirical and argumentative context is (re)considered to present the concept of democratic efficacy in the form of a drafted model, a hypothesis and a number of questions.

Analytical context

Even though the division into such classic categories as actors and structures is only an heuristic approach with many shortcomings (see, e.g., Latour, 2005), a more promising, sound and, most importantly, applicable alternative for the purposes of this book is, as yet, outstanding. With a focus on the dimensions of democratic quality, the book detaches itself from these categories, but assumes that they might be useful in order to reduce complexity and to define an analytical context for operationalization.

Although many more actors are empirically considered, this book's main actors are democracies in the form of nation states. Since their evolution, there has been "little question whether states are to be taken seriously in social scientific explanations" (Skocpol, 1985, p. 28). Even though many developments have changed the role of the state, they have not necessarily altered its importance (Compagnon, Chan, & Mert, 2012; Mol, 2007; Skocpol, 1985). The nation state still remains crucial, since its formulation and implementation of climate policy largely determines performance (Fiorino, 2011, 2014). A closer look at the nation state and the actors involved in its policy-making, allows us to see it as a policy network in the form of "sets of formal institutional and informal linkages between governmental and other actors structured around shared if endlessly negotiated beliefs and interests in public policy making and implementation" (Rhodes, 2006, p. 426). Since these types of interactions seem to have increased over the last few decades, state governments have come to resemble meta governors, often acting more strategically and reflexively than by command and control alone (Torfing & Lewis, 2011).

The structure in which the democratic nation state acts in the context of this book is a policy process. This policy process can be understood as a process in which the production of process structures by actors and the influence of these structures on those same actors are permanently interconnected.

The basic aim of the policy process heuristic is to disaggregate the complexity of a policy process into a distinct number of phases, in which the majority of actors, ideas, institutions, etc. can be integrated (Howlett & Giest, 2013; Howlett, Ramesh, & Perl, 2009).

However, since policy-making goes back and forth on a much more ad hoc and idiosyncratic basis, reality often differs from the idealized stages seen in Table 3.3 (Howlett et al., 2009). Nevertheless, to reduce complexity and to make the issue under investigation researchable, it can, in regard to climate change at the nation state level, be assumed that there has already been one (more or less) full policy process cycle. This cycle has its roots in the 1970s and 1980s, when climate change was, for the first time, recognized as a problem. Agenda setting took place in the early 1990s (1), with the proposal and choice of a solution (and thus both policy formulation and decision-making in the context of the Kyoto Protocol (2+3)). Policy implementation to put the solution into effect proceeded until 2012 (4) and when the first commitment period ended the results were able to be monitored and evaluated (5).

From a nation state's perspective, the policy process is taking place on an intermestic level. Intermesticity is characteristic of climate change policy as climate change takes place simultaneously at both international and domestic levels, which cannot be separated as they are intrinsically related (Manning, 1977; Perl, 2013; Spanier & Uslaner, 1982). Of course, the intermestic level description is closely related to and mostly interchangeable with multilevel and, probably also, foreign policy-making, as it is characterized by the complex interconnections and influences which make foreign policy in the twenty-first century very different to the foreign policy of previous centuries. In this regard one brief excuse has to be made: there are prominent voices, like Tocqueville, Locke and Lippmann, which

Table 3.3 Stages of the policy process

Stage	Applied problem-solving	Stages in policy cycle
1	problem recognition	agenda setting
2	proposal of solution	policy formulation
3	choice of solution	decision-making
4	putting solutions into effect	policy implementation
5	monitoring results	policy evaluation

Source: Adapted from Howlett, Ramesh & Perl, 2009, pp. 12–13.

assume that foreign policy issues are not compatible with democracy (Carlsnaes, 1981; Goldmann, 1986). This book will research whether this assumption is true in terms of intermestic policy-making concerning climate change. Moreover, when analysing the democracy-climate nexus no differentiation will be made between micro, meso and macro levels, since, in the context of the empirically investigated democratic nation state, dimensions of democracy are important in all three spheres.

Overall, the book tries to answer the question of how democratic quality influences climate performance in established democracies by researching democratic nation states in an intermestic level policy process from the mid-2000s to 2012 (analysis I) and the early 1990s to 2012 (analysis II). The book is aware of the shortcomings which the heuristics of the analytical context have, but assumes that they are nevertheless useful for empirical research.

Empirical and argumentative background

To develop an argument and a related concept of democratic efficacy, it is not sufficient just to know what we already know but whether existing research's assumptions are reliable. Thus, these need to be assessed and only those assumptions and findings which are convincing and can be integrated into a coherent concept will then be able to be used as the basis for this book's own arguments.

A focused reconsideration of the most reasonable arguments which assume that democratic quality has a negative impact on climate performance shows the following tendencies. First, they rely on the description of climate change as a grievous problem with characteristics such as a shrinking time horizon, scientific complexity, free rider possibilities, unforeseen tipping points, high requirements for global cooperation and the necessity for a reflexive policy design. Secondly, in the context of climate change, democracies are also threatened by the characteristics of the democratic process itself, such as the periodicity of elections with short legislative terms, the switching of issue attention undermining enlightened understanding and dilatory and incremental procedures diminishing problem-solving capacity etc. Thirdly, more general assumptions presume an inability to govern due to the complexity of societies (Crozier, Huntington, & Watanuki, 1975) consisting of citizens focused on gaining immediate, short-term advantages, an "overloaded government" which is unable to fulfil all of its functions (Birch, 1984) and politicians who are insufficiently qualified and surrounded by structures designed to focus on re-election.

These arguments are quite substantial, yet while they might describe a threat both to and of existing democracies, they do not explain how the different democratic qualities of established democracies influence climate performance. In contemporary democracies, policy-making tends not to be based on public and considered judgement by common people per se, but to be determined in reference to periodical elections and the results of opinion polls in relation to these elections, thus simply representing an aggregation of private interests. This is not to say that the democratic quality of contemporary democracies is worsening, as arguments in post-democratic research propose, but to assume that currently existing democracies are not perfect. So, yes, democracies have problems due to the specifics of climate change and their internal procedures. The characteristics of climate change and the unintended consequences of democracy might contradict each other to different degrees. However, perhaps some democracies are able to find better solutions to overcome their short-termism and to more effectively deal with the long time horizon of climate change. It is therefore necessary to distinguish between different democracies. Not all democracies have the same levels of democratic quality and this might impact upon their ability to influence climate performance.

Arguments assuming a positive influence of democratic quality on climate performance are either rare or rely on minor aspects of the democracy-climate nexus without thinking more broadly about the relationship. Thus, in terms of the focus and the relevance of the research to this book (see Chapter 2), there is a clear indication of the need for further research. Most reasonable arguments rely on an informed median voter who, as a result of post-material values and small opportunity costs, prefers the provision of public goods, with politicians being held to account and thus needing to respond to these demands. Secondly, more general arguments beyond the environment-democracy nexus are relevant when outlining the concept of democratic efficacy. These arguments assume that democracy presents the most powerful set of institutions available, guaranteeing stability and enabling political learning (Halperin, Siegle & Weinstein, 2005). Theories postulate that democracy is effective as a result of its competitiveness (Wittman, 1995), that democracy enables cooperation (Choi, 2004) and improves the quality of government (Charron & Lapuente, 2010). Thirdly, potential proposals for the potential improvement of democracy are quite vague. They assume that intergenerational democracies can be established by paying more attention to future tasks (such as climate change) and focus on what deliberative improvements could be capable of in the future. For example, how scientific and other improvements and policy evolutions, such as environmental constitutionalism, may help climate policy mainstreaming, etc. According to their advocates, these improvements might "create a democracy of public judgment rather than private opinion" (Barber, 2010, p. 168). Table 3.4 illustrates the main shortcomings and advantages identified by existing research on the democracy-climate nexus.

The shortcomings and advantages summarized in the table illustrate the context in which the concept of democratic efficacy has to fit. When focusing on the democracy-climate nexus, democracy is, however, not the only relevant factor which needs to be taken into account. Two other factors have to be taken in consideration, if we are to properly look at climate performance. In the first case, we need to consider procedural general performance, as the other type of performance a political system consists of at the procedural level. Yet, we also need to look at other factors, besides the political system, whose influence will need to be analysed when focusing on the democracy-climate nexus. Procedural general performance consists of governmental capability, stability, effectiveness and efficiency. Obviously, these dimensions have an influence on climate performance and influence or are influenced by procedural democratic

Table 3.4 Shortcomings and advantages of the democracy-climate nexus

Shortcomings	Advantages
• characteristics of democracy (issue attention cycling, etc.) • characteristics of climate change (grievous problem) • general arguments (overloaded government, etc.)	• characteristics of democracy (median voter favours climate action, etc.) • an assumed inherent potential for improvement (deliberative procedures, etc.) • general arguments (democracy enables cooperation, etc.)

quality, which then might itself influence climate performance. Other factors which have to be taken into account include, for example, political institutions, dependence on fossil fuel energy, income, population density, political culture, climate vulnerability, traditions of economic intervention and economic structures as such (Bernauer, 2013; Lachapelle & Paterson, 2013). Moreover, the book is open to all kinds of influences which might be detected by empirical analysis and include such factors as the age of the population; factors which have, as yet, not been considered in existing research. Nevertheless, while being aware of other factors, the main purpose of this book is to examine the influence democratic quality alone has on climate performance and to answer the question of how democratic quality influences climate performance in established democracies.

The concept of democratic efficacy: outline, hypothesis, questions

The concept of democratic efficacy in the form of an initial outline, hypotheses and questions has to both match and recognize the analytical, argumentative and empirical context while, at the same time, going one step further. The purpose is to provide a preliminary outline of a concept that is applicable in the general context of the democracy-climate nexus and beyond. It should be possible to enlarge it, so as to enable it to explain the relationship between democracy's ability to produce the desired and intended performance in other policy fields and levels of democratic quality in general. Thus, this book proposes a concept of democratic efficacy assuming that democracy's ability to produce desired and intended climate performance improves with increasing levels of democratic quality.

When it comes to individuals, the concept of democratic efficacy takes a different approach to those of many other empirical research concepts. Simply put, many theories assume a certain kind of individual actor and aggregate their behaviour to nation state levels (like the rational actor in collective action theories). This book, however, considers this approach oversimplified and, due to such phenomena as emergence, academically unsatisfactory (Cartwright, 2002a, 2002b; Kittel, 2006). What is instead important is that democracy as a continuous mode of operation created by humans shapes humans. This continuous mode of operation/democratic design, which is both created by and shapes humans, has the ability to produce the desired or intended climate performance. Thus, democratic efficacy assumes that democracy is capable, or, more precisely, that more democratic quality is more capable of creating those competencies required to influence climate performance, and perhaps other policy issues, positively.

This central assumption is based on the weak positive tendency detected in existing research and, more importantly, on a distinct assumption based on theories of change. That is to say that societies need high-level democratic qualities to find solutions and pathways for major transformations by design and that these are necessary in the context of climate change, in order to protect earth system services (see, e.g., Grin, Rotmans, Schot, Geels & Loorbach, 2010; Messner 2015; WBGU 2011). More democracy could imply, for example, including future generations in current decision-making, indicating that their room for manoeuvre in the coming decades and centuries should be no smaller than that of today's citizenry. This could lead to a more sustainable world, since the use of natural resources would reduce future room for manoeuvre. Resources would have to be used in a sustainable manner, supporting almost automatically a transformation to sustainability and thus better climate performance. Consequently, it is presumed that the influence of democratic quality depends on the existence of its different dimensions and the interplay between them. The more dimensions of democratic quality are present, the better they can serve their main purpose of problem solving and anticipating better futures.

Consequently, the concept of democratic efficacy expects the ability to produce climate performance to improve concomitantly with increasing levels of democratic quality. One main reason for this expectation can be seen in societies' requirement for certain democratic dimensions, such as creativity, to find solutions and pathways for major transformations, as are required in the context of climate change. Furthermore, more established democracies with more democratic quality are assumed to be better prepared to critically investigate whether they are pursuing the right policies and are in a position to respond to unforeseen challenges. Current democracies also face the challenge that they all too often rely on private opinions (which are probably more focused on present than on future advantages) or the aggregation of private opinions through polls, while the democratic ideal assumes that decision-making should rely on public judgement instead. Thus, democratic efficacy, assuming that democracy's ability to produce the desired and intended climate performance concomitantly improves with increasing levels of democratic quality, could, for political practice, be translated into the term "fixing climate change means fixing democracy" (Barber, 2010, p. 165).

The concept of democratic efficacy has to be adapted for empirical research. Therefore, an explanatory, sequential mixed methods design has been applied, using qualitative research to explain the (non-)significant results of the quantitative analysis and to advance the concept of democratic efficacy. The wording relies not on any ideological separation between a quantitative (hypothesis, independent variable, etc.) and a qualitative (guiding proposition, key explanatory variable, etc.) language, but uses both interchangeably. There is one world out there and not two in the form of a quantitative and qualitative one. While the purpose of the quantitative analysis (analysis I) is to test the basic assumption of a positive influence in terms of generalization and to detect trends, the qualitative analysis (analysis II) focuses on how and why exactly the mechanisms of influence do or don't work out. Therefore, democratic quality and general performance have to be abstractly separated, so as to evaluate the influence one has on the other, as illustrated in Table 3.5.

While the grey dotted arrow from substantive democratic quality to substantive general performance quantitatively tests the proposed influence (analysis I), the arrows leading from procedural dimensions to substantive general performance research how and why that influence takes place in the form of mechanisms (analysis II). The arrows on the right demonstrate that procedural democratic quality can take place directly (black arrow) or indirectly, in terms of an influence of procedural democratic quality on procedural general performance influencing climate performance (grey arrows) and an influence of procedural general performance on procedural democratic quality, which itself then influences climate performance (black dotted arrows). The proposed influence relies on the assumption that the dimensions of democratic quality have (in their interplay) a positive effect, e.g. the inclusion of all relevant and affected actors in combination with responsive participation structures based on considered judgement leads to a climate politics for which politicians can be held accountable by a free public sphere with the means to act as a control mechanism. Since these interactions are unknown in the context of the democracy-climate nexus, the white space in Figure 3.3 in the empty model will have to be filled in analysis II.

Thus, while analysis I researches whether trends in the proposed influence of democratic quality exist, analysis II fills the empty model with the interplay of the dimensions of procedural democratic quality with regard to their influence on climate performance and thus verifies or rejects the trends detected in analysis I.

Table 3.5 General performance and democratic quality with influences

	Substantive (meta-)dimensions	*Procedural dimensions*
General performance	substantive general performance: climate performance (policy output, policy outcome)	procedural general performance (governmental capability, stability of government, efficiency and effectiveness)
Democratic quality	substantive democratic quality (control, equality, freedom)	procedural democratic quality (accountability, independence, stability of democratic institutions, inclusiveness, participation, transparency, creativity, liberty, publicity)

Source: Based on Roller, 2005, p. 24.

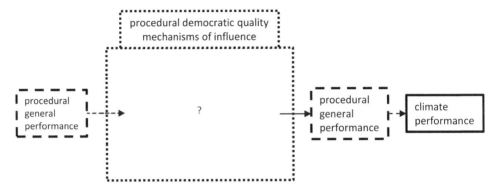

Figure 3.3 Empty model of the mechanisms of influence

To clarify the exact purposes of the overall and supplementary analyses more precisely, questions and hypothesis have to be formulated. The overall question connecting both analyses asks:

How does democratic quality influence the climate performance of established democracies?

To answer the overall question, analysis I focuses on the exploration of statistical trends and asks:

What influence does substantive democratic quality have on climate performance?

Analysis I has a primarily deductive function and looks to test the outlined concept of democratic efficacy. In this context, the following hypothesis can be formulated:

Higher levels of substantive democratic quality influence climate performance positively.

The reason for the expected positive influence is based on the concept of democratic efficacy assuming that democracy's ability to produce desired and intended climate performances improves concomitantly with increasing levels of democratic quality. Higher levels of democratic quality ensure a better level of problem solving, innovation, creativity and critical investigation; all of which are necessary if we are to solve the climate problem. Moreover, due to the worldwide spread of post-material values (including environmental aspects like the protection of the environment) (see e.g. Inglehart, 2008), it is to be expected that higher levels of democratic quality are more likely to convert these values into policy formulation and implementation. It is also to be expected that a positive influence on output (policy targets, etc.) and outcome (GHG emission development) exists, since increasing levels of democratic quality lead to more responsiveness in regard to both components of the dependent variable. However, as the evaluation of research implies, the influence might be weaker on outcome since other factors have even more influence on outcome than democratic quality.

Analysis II focuses on detailed mechanisms to explain why democratic quality and the interplay of its dimensions influence climate performance. Thus, to answer the overall question, analysis II asks:

Which mechanisms link procedural democratic quality and climate performance?

By exploring these mechanisms, analysis II operates both inductively and abductively in filling the empty model and exploring advancements of the concept of democratic efficacy. Moreover, by the identification of mechanisms, analysis II also carries out theory testing in terms of verifying or rejecting the trends explored by analysis I. Analysis II's main question is answered with the guidance of the following focusing tasks:

- an evaluation of the level of dimensions of procedural democratic quality and their (interrelated) influence on climate performance;
- a counterfactual argumentation of how more or less democratic quality would have influenced climate performance;
- a consideration of potential caveats and third factors influencing climate performance;
- a consideration of procedural general performance as an independent variable influencing procedural democratic quality and as an intervening variable influenced by procedural democratic quality;
- an exploration of whether the detected mechanisms are generalizable and how they advance the initially outlined concept of democratic efficacy.

Thus, both analyses are related to one overall research question and research the same phenomenon, the democracy-climate nexus, from different perspectives and different levels of abstraction. The drafting of an initial concept of democratic efficacy and the formulation of questions and hypotheses give guidance for empirical research. Therefore, a mixed methods design has to be developed that interconnects both analyses methodically and operationalizes the questions and hypotheses of analyses I and II.

Explanatory mixed methods research design

This book's research into how democratic quality influences the climate performance of established democracies is translated into two sub-questions, leading to two empirical analyses. Assuming that the methods follow the research question, the book applies a mixed methods design. Therefore, the mixed methods approach is explained, then the quantitative approach of analysis I, based on panel regression, is laid out and, subsequently, the qualitative empirical inquiry methods of analysis II are explicated.

Mixed methods

Mixed methods research can provide a dialogue between the two empirical analyses endorsed by the overall research question (Cao, Milner, Prakash, & Ward, 2014; Harding & Seefeldt, 2014). In this case the research approach is based on a methodology which includes philosophical assumptions that guide both the collection and analysis of data, providing advantages through the combination of quantitative and qualitative data (Brady & Collier, 2010; Creswell & Plano Clark, 2011, p. 7; Lin & Loftis, 2005; Bergmann, 2008a, p. 2; 2008b, p. 19). While quantitative analysis may be able to identify effects across units of analysis, qualitative analysis may explain how the effects work out in terms of mechanisms, etc. (George & Bennett, 2005; Gerring, 2004; Goertz & Mahoney, 2012).

This book uses mixed methods in the form of an explanatory design, which is closely related to nested analysis (Lieberman, 2005; Rohlfing, 2008). Basically, the explanatory design comes in two phases with qualitative data building upon initial quantitative results (Creswell & Plano Clark, 2011, pp. 81–86). Both analyses are thus related through the main research question they address and the case selection of analysis II, which is based on the indices values used in analysis I. Thus, the explanatory design is useful, firstly, for the assessment of trends and relationships and, secondly, for its explanation of the mechanisms leading to these trends.

Methods analysis I

Analysis I applies panel regressions to answer the question of what influence substantive democratic quality has on climate performance and to test the hypothesis that higher levels of substantive democratic quality have a positive influence on climate performance. Therefore, the next chapter of the book describes, first, how panel regressions work and what kind of panel regressions are applied and, second, how both the question and the hypotheses are operationalized.

Panel regression analysis

Regression analyses estimate the relationships between variables. They are able to identify correlations between independent and dependent variables, but not causation. Panel regression can be achieved by repeated observation of the same variable(s) using the same units of analysis.

In the context of this book, panel regressions are able to take into account changes both *within* one country – in so far as the observed variable changes over time – and *between* different countries (for the following see e.g., Allison, 2009; Firebaugh, Cody, & Massoglia, 2014; Wooldridge, 2013, pp. 466–483).

Both variations are important for an evaluation of the influence of substantive democratic quality on climate performance and they thus need to be explained in terms of their translation into empirical models.

Basically, both variations, within and between, can be combined into three models: fixed effects, random effects and a hybrid model. Fixed effects models only use variation within countries over time to calculate effects. Thus, other factors, including those omitted by the model, stay very much the same. This allows near causal interpretation, since it is very unlikely that the effect is biased. In the case of this book, fixed effects consider how climate performance in established democracies is affected when substantive democratic quality changes. Thus, fixed effects do not take into account information on differences between countries. Instead, random effects models use fixed and between effects and calculate the weighted averages of both. Thereby, all of the data is used, including information between countries. However, results cannot be causally interpreted in the same way as in the fixed effects model. In the case of this book, climate performance in between effects might not only (partially) rely on democratic quality, but also on other variables which differ between countries and are not included in the model (omitted variables bias). The usual trade-off is to estimate either fixed effects (delivering precise results but losing information) or to estimate random effects (using all available information but potentially having an omitted variables bias). However, the dominance of between variations, in particular in democratic quality data, makes it necessary to take between effects into consideration. Therefore, the third option, the hybrid model, is assumed to be the best model, since it estimates within and between effects separately. Subsequently, both fixed and – with somewhat more care – between effects can be interpreted.

This book uses a so-called hybrid model or between-within method (Allison, 2014) which combines the advantages of random and fixed effects models, allowing it to estimate both varying time and constant time variables (Allison, 2009; Schunck, 2013). As explained earlier, for the purposes of the book it might be of interest to estimate the effect over time (within) and across units (between) and this is why the hybrid model is applied in analysis I. However, the possibility of omitted variables bias in the between effects still exists and results will have to be interpreted carefully. For the hybrid model, the random effects model is used with two changes: first, the independent (varying time) variables are transformed in deviations from unit specific means and, secondly, variables are included which are the unit specific means of each independent (time-varying) variable. While the first transformation is a within transformation, the second is a between transformation. The subsequent equation of the hybrid model looks as follows:

$$y_{it} = a + b(x_{it} - \bar{x}_i) + c\bar{x}_i + dz_i + e_{it}, \ e_{it} = w_{it} \tag{3.1}$$

Equation 3.1 Basic equation for the hybrid model

In the equation, b is the estimator for the within component and identical to the fixed effects within estimation, c is the estimator for the between component and dz_i the vector of possible time constant variables (which, however, are unimportant in terms of the empirical analysis within this particular book). The hybrid model will be estimated with a calculation method which is able to evaluate robust standard errors for panel regressions with cross-sectional dependence, since it is assumed that climate policy formulation and implementation in one country might have an influence on other countries (Hoechle, 2007). Even though the Hausman test recommends random effects, its results in the context of the hybrid model mean that fixed effects – since they are always unbiased – can be interpreted. However, if, based on the Hausman test, random effects are assumed to be inadequate, the between effects will either have to be completely rejected or – due to the high amount of between variance in the data of this book – interpreted with a constant awareness of possible biases in the back of one's mind.

Of course, it might be possible to apply an even more complex panel regressions approach or to apply minimally different techniques, but, in the context of the available data, it is doubtful whether this would be advantageous for the purposes of analysis (Angrist & Pischke, 2009).

Operationalization

The operationalization of the question and the hypothesis of analysis I for the hybrid model has to consider the independent variable of interest (substantive democratic quality), the dependent variable (climate performance) and control variables. For choosing indices, measurements, etc. as variables three criteria have been considered: first, they should correspond to the aforementioned definitions of general performance and of democratic quality in established democracies; secondly, they have to provide sufficient data for the panel regressions; thirdly, this chapter considers whether they are sufficiently coherent and display satisfactory objectivity, reliability and validity. The purpose of such being to find data which can be used for empirical analysis and to exclude data which is inadequate.

The independent variable of substantive democratic quality should cover a critical mass which encompasses most democratic countries. Such indices originated in light of a democratization of democracies as the fourth or fifth wave of democratization (see, e.g., Fung & Wright, 2001; Huntington, 1997; Offe, 2003) and to distinguish between democracies in order to evaluate the different democratic quality of already established democracies (Altman & Pérez-Liñán, 2002; Berg-Schlosser, 2004; Diamond & Morlino, 2004; Plattner, 2004). So far, only the Democracy Barometer has proved to be sensitive enough to differentiate between established democracies on the basis of their democratic quality and it provides data for 70 countries in the time period from 1990–2012 (Democracy-Barometer, 2015). All other indices either do not cover enough countries over a set period of time or focus on the distinction between democracy and autocracy with little attention paid to the differences between democracies. Moreover, while the functions subordinated to each dimension differ (freedom: individual liberties, rule of law and public sphere; control: competition, mutual constraints and governmental capability; equality: transparency, participation and representation), the Democracy Barometer corresponds to this book's definition of the three principles of control, equality and freedom (Democracy-Barometer, 2015). Indicators of the functions are aggregated to an overall index by a number of procedures, resulting in an index ranging from 0–100 with higher numbers indicating a higher level of democratic quality. Thus, although the Democracy Barometer is not entirely without its critics, the decision as to which index to use as an independent variable is simple (Jäckle, Wagschal, & Bauschke, 2012, 2013; Merkel, Tanneberg, & Bühlmann, 2013). Despite its critics, the Democracy Barometer stands out both in terms of its quality and quantity when compared with other indices.

The dependent variable of climate performance should cover as many of the Democracy Barometer's country years as possible. Of course, the index should maintain coherency, objectivity, reliability and validity. Taking a closer look at existing indices and approaches measuring climate performance, it becomes clear that, while many of them (such as the World Wide Fund for Nature (WWF) Climate Score Cards (WWF & Ecofys, 2009), the (EU) Climate Action Tracker (Ecofys & Analytics, 2015), the Climate Change Cooperation Index (Bernauer & Böhmelt, 2013) and the Index of Climate Policy Activity (Schaffrin, Sewerin, & Seubert, 2015) are conceptually quite convincing, they nonetheless either lack the required data (in the form of a substantial number of countries and years) or are not transparently updated and available online. The most comprehensive and yearly updated index is the Climate Change Performance Index (CCPI), which will function as the dependent variable of this book (Burck, Hermwille, & Bals, 2014). It provides data for 58 countries from 2007–2015, whereby the climate policy component is one year older (t–1) and the emissions component three years older (t–3) than the year the index is published. It ranks countries on a scale of 0–100 with higher numbers indicating better climate performance. It is composed by indicators measuring Emission Level (30 per cent), Development of Emissions (30 per cent), Climate Policy (20 per cent), Efficiency (10 per cent) and Renewable Energies (10 per cent). Thus, the relevant output component is Climate Policy while the relevant outcome components are Emissions Level and Development of Emissions. However, the Emissions Level component "is less an indicator of the performance of climate protection than an indicator of the respective starting point of the investigated countries" (Burck et al., 2014, p. 7). Instead, the emissions development component "is comparatively responsive to effective climate policy, and therefore is an important indicator for a country's performance" (Burck et al., 2014, p. 7). Thus, the relevant outcome component used in panel regression is Development of Emissions. Moreover, Efficiency and Renewable Energies combine elements of both output and outcome and cannot be clearly categorized as either. Thus, together with the overall CCPI score and the Policy and Emission Development component, the dependent variable of the book can be thrice distinguished.

Of course, control variables also have to be taken into consideration in the context of the democracy-climate nexus (Bernauer, 2013; Lachapelle & Paterson, 2013). The purpose of these control variables is first and foremost to function as control variables in terms of minimizing omitted variables biases. All control variables are, for theoretical reasons, assumed to be important in terms of influencing climate performance. However, since the focus of this book is on the influence of democratic quality, the effects of the control variables is neither considered nor interpreted in detail. Rather, their results are assumed to perhaps deliver insights which might be of interest for further studies.

The models estimated in analysis I provide the following control variables. It is assumed that the production of oil, gas and coal influences a country's climate performance, since fossil resources and their exploitation may increase a country's dependence on them. Countries with higher production of fossil fuels may perform worse on climate performance. Also, as part of the geographical circumstances, it is expected that climate vulnerability might influence climate performance due to the higher risks of damage. Countries facing higher risks are probably more interested in successfully responding to climate change. Moreover, economic development is of crucial importance. Therefore, income, as gross domestic product (GDP) per capita, and trade openness, as imports plus exports divided by GDP, are included. It is assumed that increases in GDP per capita and economic activity lead to a decrease in climate performance. However, the degree of service industry within an economy might actually indicate better climate performance, since this means that production takes place elsewhere in the world. In this context, the book also controls Internet users, assuming that well connected societies need less transportation and thus produce less GHG. Moreover, the degree of urban population might be related to less GHG, due to increased population density and the subsequent closer proximity of residents to one another. The degree of old and young citizens within a given society might also play a role, with the assumption being that people aged 0–14 and people aged 65 and above differ in their orientation towards solving the climate challenge. While younger populations are assumed to care more about their future, older generations probably care less about the following decades and centuries.

Of course, control variables might vary in importance with regard to their influence on output and outcome. Unfortunately, general procedural performance cannot be controlled since the available indices or components either do not provide sufficient data or overlap conceptually with the Democracy Barometer. Furthermore, we lack information on some factors which might influence climate performance, such as, for example, culture. The result is a codebook including all of the variables which have been investigated or used for panel regressions.

In the empirical analysis, data is not converted to a 0–1 scale, since it is assumed that, while such a transformation might be helpful in comparing the effects of the coefficients, it is more important to be able to directly observe the original value schemes of the different variables in the coefficients (something which a transformation to another scale might hinder). The calculation of the panel regressions, the visualization of graphics and the descriptive investigations

Table 3.6 Codebook

	Variable	Specification	Source
Democratic quality (independent variable)	dembar (separate values for three principles, nine functions)	democratic quality index by Bühlmann/ Merkel/Müller/Giebler/Wessels at the Centre for Democracy Studies Aarau (ZDA); 1990–2012; 0–100 scale, higher values indicate increased democratic quality	www.democracybarometer.org/ (20.01.2015)
Climate performance (dependent variable)	CCPI (separate values for emission development, policy)	Climate Change Performance Index by Germanwatch; 2007 to 2015; 0–100 scale, higher values indicate better climate performance; values are retimed as follows: CCPI t–2, Emissions Development t–3, Climate Policy t–1	http://germanwatch.org/en/ccpi; personal contact to Germanwatch (Jan Burck) submitting detailed data
Control variables	oilgascoal	production of oil, gas, coal in mtoe; 1990–2011	www.bp.com/sectionbodycopy.do?ca (17.01.2013), Hanusch (addition of oil, gas, coal)
	income	GDP per capita, purchasing power parity (PPP) (constant 2005 international $); 1990–2011	http://data.worldbank.org/ (17.01.2013)
	tradeopenness	imports plus exports divided by GDP; 1990–2011	http://data.worldbank.org/ (22.01.2013), Hanusch (calculation)

(Continued)

Table 3.6 (Continued)

Variable	Specification	Source
internetusers	Internet users (per 100 people); 1990–2011	http://data.worldbank.org/ (16.04.2013)
vulnerability	vulnerability measures a country's exposure, sensitivity and its ability to adapt to the negative impact of climate change; ND-GAIN measures a country's overall vulnerability by considering vulnerability in six life-supporting sectors – food, water, health, ecosystem service, human habitat and infrastructure, 0–1 scale, higher values indicate higher vulnerability. 1995–2012	http://index.gain.org/ranking/vulnerability (26.01.2015)
urbans	urban population in %	http://data.worldbank.org/ (16.04.2013)
population14	population aged 0–14 (% of total)	http://data.worldbank.org/ (16.04.2013)
population65	population aged 65 and above (% of total)	http://data.worldbank.org/ (16.04.2013)
services	services etc., value added (% of GDP)	http://data.worldbank.org/ (16.04.2013)

is undertaken with STATA 12.0 software (see Appendix A for the do file, the data set is available from the author). While these quantitative investigations may detect generalizable trends, the explanatory mixed methods design requires a more qualitative case study to explain what causal connections link democratic quality and climate performance.

Methods analysis II

Analysis II asks what mechanisms link procedural democratic quality and climate performance. To answer this question analysis II investigates a case study of Canada's Kyoto Protocol process. For this purpose, this section describes how one has to understand a case study in the context of the democracy-climate nexus and which case selection criteria are applied. Thereafter, the process tracing (as the main investigation procedure based on both the content analysis of documents and expert interviews) is explained and, finally, the operationalization of analysis II is developed.

Case study and selection

A case relates to a "spatially delimited phenomenon (a unit) observed at a single point in time or even some period of time" (Gerring, 2007, p. 19). A case study is the intensive investigation of a single case with the additional aim of, at least partially, generalizing for other cases (Gerring, 2007, p. 20). Case studies enable the development of differentiated and closely focused concepts, like democratic efficacy, by extracting new ideas and they are able to see the general in the particular (Bennett & Elman, 2007, pp. 178, 180). Case studies are useful in the identification of a causal mechanism by which an independent variable influences the dependent variable, such as in the case of the assumed effect of procedural democratic quality on climate performance (Gerring, 2012, p. 215; Mahoney, 2007, p. 131).

Consequently, the main task when explaining a case study in the context of empirical research is to answer the question of what the case is a case of. The unit of analysis in this book is a democratic nation state at the intermestic level over the time period of the Kyoto Protocol policy process (beginning in 1995 and ending in 2012) with a focus on the manifestations and interrelations of dimensions of procedural democratic quality, their influence on climate performance and the causal mechanisms between these two elements. Based on the results of the case study, the concept of democratic efficacy can be evaluated and enriched in terms of hypothesis formulation and the identification of causal mechanisms. Thus, the case study is primarily so-called theory-building by identifying causal mechanisms and formulating new hypotheses as well as, to a lesser extent, theory testing by evaluating whether the general assumptions of the concept of democratic efficacy hold when researching within-case mechanisms. Hence, the case selection is important as a case is required which can help to fulfil these purposes (Gerring, 2007, p. 5).

Case selection is usually based on purposes at an intermediate level, where one knows something (at a more general level) but not everything (at a more detailed level or vice versa). However, case selection should not just be based on features of interest, importance or easily accessible data (alone). Instead, the main criterion has to be the relevance of the case to the purposes of the book, which, in analysis II, is a test or verification of the results reached in analysis I in regard to the positive influence of higher levels of democratic quality on climate performance and theory development based on identified mechanisms and their potential generalization in the context of the concept of democratic efficacy. For analysis II, a case is needed which allows for an enrichment of the concept of democratic efficacy, with insights into causal mechanisms leading to a redefinition and generation of new hypotheses, and at the same time hard proof or a thorough test of the general trend detected in analysis I.

The approach to fulfilling both purposes is the application of process tracing as a procedure which enables counterfactual analysis based on a deviant case. A deviant case is needed which allows the book to challenge the trends detected in analysis I and, through its deviancy, enables the development of new hypotheses. By counterfactual argumentation at the within-analysis level, the deviant case will also have to become a typical case in so far as this is required for the exploration of causal mechanisms (Gerring, 2007, pp. 91–93, 105–107; Mahoney, 2007, p. 125). A deviant case in the context of the democracy-climate nexus and the concept of democratic efficacy would either combine high levels of democratic quality with low levels of climate performance or low levels of democratic quality with high levels of climate performance. It seems to be more useful to research a deviant case with quite high levels of democratic quality to see democratic quality in action rather than a case where democratic quality is low or almost absent.

While there are a few cases which could be taken into consideration in this regard, the country chosen in this book is Canada. According to the concept of democratic efficacy Canada performs too well on democratic quality to perform so badly on climate performance. For example, Canada has won so many of the so-called Fossil of the Day Awards (representing the worst performance at United Nations Framework Convention on Climate Change (UNFCCC) Conferences of the Parties (COPs)) from the Climate Action Network, including five times in a row the Fossil of the Year Award, that, in 2013, it received the Lifetime Unachievement Fossil Award (CAN, 2013). Moreover, Canada is the only country to have signed and then withdrawn from the Kyoto Protocol, it scored last on the WWF Climate Score Cards and ranks very lowly in the CCPI, etc. At the same time, however, Canada reaches the highest possible scores in the Polity VI and Freedom House indices as well as being placing in roughly the ten most democratic countries in the Democracy Barometer. Thus, Canada seems to be a good choice for the exploration of the case study's main aim and should be able to shed a light on procedural democratic quality's causal mechanisms of influence on climate performance, leading to new hypotheses and a redefinition of, or challenge to, to the concept of democratic efficacy while also allowing for a challenge to the concept of democratic efficacy at a more general level.

However, as the detailed empirical analysis demonstrates, Canada turns out to be much more of a typical than a deviant case, since procedural democratic quality is much lower than the data in the Democracy Barometer implied. Thus, the results do not challenge the positive trends detected in analysis I and the concept of democratic efficacy as intensively as expected. Instead, the Canadian case verifies both the positive trends detected in analysis I and, through detected mechanisms, the concept of democratic efficacy. It also advances the concept of democratic efficacy by new and more detailed hypotheses, implying inter alia that the influence of democratic quality on climate performance becomes both more predictable and, probably, exponential with increasing levels of democratic quality.

Process tracing

The methods serve to answer the research question. In the context of analysis II, the main question asks what mechanisms link procedural democratic quality and climate performance. One procedure which enables the exploration of causal mechanisms between procedural democratic quality and climate performance is process tracing. Therefore, data collection is based on documents and expert interviews which will be analysed with content analysis. Consequently, this section explains how process tracing will be used, describes how data collection has been carried out in this study and shows the results of the content analysis.

Process tracing is not a method, but an explanatory strategy which allows researchers to chart developments, such as law-making or policy processes, over a specific time period. It can use different types of data produced by a wide range of methods, for example, expert interviews and content analysis results based on documents. Process tracing focuses on the causal mechanisms of the phenomenon under investigation and explains exactly what kinds of influence determine the interplay between an independent variable, such as democratic quality, and a dependent variable, such as climate performance, in a way which quantitative analysis cannot take into consideration (George & Bennett, 2005, pp. 206–207). More precisely, causal mechanisms describe the procedural formations of the connections between the independent and dependent variables (Beach & Pedersen, 2013, p. 25; Bennett & Elman, 2007, p. 183). Two theory-centric variants of process tracing are useful for the purposes of analysis II: theory building and, to a lesser extent, theory testing (Beach & Pedersen, 2013). Theory building process tracing focuses on what the causal mechanisms which link procedural democratic quality and climate performance are and which hypotheses are derived from these. Its procedure is based on the three steps of evidence collection, the inference of the existence of manifestations and the inference of causal mechanisms. While in analysis II the first step occurs in the form of the collection of expert interviews and documents, the second step is based on content analysis and the third step is one of genuine process tracing as it determines the relation of different manifestations in the context of the research question. The results lead to new hypotheses and, most likely, to a new concept or middle-range theory. Theory testing process tracing usually asks whether the causal mechanisms are present and function as theorized. It therefore proceeds in three steps, through a conceptualization of the causal mechanisms, an operationalization of the causal mechanisms and the collection of evidence. The focus of this book is on the detection of causal mechanisms which verify or reject the results of analysis I and/or the concept of democratic efficacy (theory testing) and thus aid a generalization which can advance the concept of democratic efficacy and subsequent hypothesis formulation (theory building). Thereby, process tracing can make use of thought experiments by varying certain criteria to receive hypothetical answers. As already outlined, counterfactual analysis asking what would happen if the independent variable, in the form of the dimensions of democratic quality, would show different manifestations is an integral part of analysis II (Levy, 2008).

As Table 3.7 demonstrates, process tracing relies on steps 1 and 2, which need further explanation. The sources of evidence for the process tracing carried out in analysis II are documents and expert interviews (Beach & Pedersen, 2013, pp. 134–140; Yin, 2009, p. 83). This sort of data triangulation from different sources ensures that the observations, which, in case studies, always exhibits a certain degree of bias, are more valid than would be the case if this book were to merely use one source (Beach & Pedersen, 2013, p. 128; Gerring, 2007, p. 185; Yin, 2009, pp. 83, 99). The documentary research carried out in analysis II is based on the principle that every document which is analysed serves the goal of answering the research question. The selection of documents was therefore not restricted but designed so as to serve this aim, thus including a wide variety of document types, such as newspaper articles, reports of the Commissioner of the Environment and Sustainable Development (CESD), memoirs of a former prime minister (PM), official UNFCCC documents, etc. Consequently, each document is analysed and weighted in the context of its background, its intention and its historical situation. Of course, these documents are not declared as objective sources of knowledge, but as pieces of evidence in need of further interpretation, since they may provide misleading information or lead to wrong conclusions, for example, by missing out important information or suggesting consensus where actual behind the scenes disagreement was extensive (Tansey, 2007, p. 486). Expert interviews therefore provide a crucial source of evidence for analysis II, as they compensate for the shortcomings of the documents and enable an analysis of those parts of the mechanisms where no evidence in the form of documents exists (Berg & Lune, 2012, pp. 112–114; Gläser & Laudel, 2010; Tansey, 2007, p. 486). Expert interviews are assumed to provide information on policy-making by first-hand testimony due

Table 3.7 Process tracing

Step 1 *data collection*	*Step 2* *data analysis and interpretation*	*Step 3* *connection of results to mechanisms*
documents expert interviews	content analysis	genuine process tracing using counterfactual thinking and detecting mechanisms for generalization

to said experts' privileged access to data which isn't publicly accessible (Tansey, 2007, p. 485). The selection of interview partners should include a group of people representative of the relevant actors and deemed to be affected by the contexts of the issue under investigation. The expert interview is a semi-structured interview conducted with a special group of experts on the issue under investigation with the aim of gaining pertinent information on Canada's climate policy-making in the context of the Kyoto Protocol process. Since the interviews are only semi-structured, not all of the questions need to be asked. The question wording is also partially flexible, allowing more inductive, deductive and abductive elements (Arksey & Knight, 1999; Gillham, 2005; Hovi, Sprinz, & Bang, 2012, p. 136). After an introductory question, the focus and concretization of the interview can be narrowed down through the experts' knowledge of the issue under investigation. All interviews used in this book were fully recorded and transcribed.

The data collection of documentary analysis and expert interviews must, in a next step, be analysed through the means of content analysis (Gläser & Laudel, 2010, pp. 199–204). Content analysis extracts information on the raw collected data from the categories highlighted in a study's theoretical basis. In the case of analysis II, this means that information is collected on procedural democratic quality, procedural general performance and climate performance. Tables are used to organize the raw data and, based on these tables, the information is then prepared according to time and content relevant aspects. Important information can be separated from unimportant information and sorted according to its relevance for the purposes of the research being undertaken. After the extraction and processing of data, content analysis interprets the processed data, taking into account contexts and historical information as well as additional concepts which relate to the research question.

The interpreted data and the dimensions of procedural democratic quality and their influences on climate performance are then analysed by process tracing along different time horizons and set in relation to one another in order to identify causal mechanisms. To do so, procedural democratic quality, procedural general performance and climate performance need to be operationalized.

Operationalization

Based on the research question of analysis II, procedural democratic quality, procedural general performance and climate performance must be operationalized. Consequently, procedural democratic quality is developed in accordance with the identified dimensions. Every dimension is empirically translated to correspond to the research purposes in the context of a democratic nation state's policy process at an intermestic level. Thereafter, indicators are identified which represent the empirically translated dimension. This table is combined with the concept of procedural general performance in order to identify any influences linking procedural democratic quality and procedural general performance. Since the dimensions of procedural general performance are already empirical translations they can function as broad indicators which need no further operationalization. The result is Table 3.8 summarizing the operationalization of analysis II, including

Table 3.8 Operationalization analysis II

Metadimension	Dimension	Empirical translation	Indicators	Direct influence of procedural democratic quality on climate performance	Findings on the (in)direct influence of procedural democratic quality on climate performance (through procedural general performance)		
					Governmental capability government sets and maintains strategic priorities government demonstrates flexibility and innovation government learns from past errors	Stability (of government) absence of destabilizing circumstances durability makes and maintains international commitments	Effectiveness and efficiency quality of the bureaucracy credibility of the government's commitment to policies government makes efficient use of available resources
control	accountability	clear lines of accountability ensure control of decision-makers	a) democratically legitimated decision-makers/government are/is in a responsible position b) results can be traced back to decision-makers (vertical accountability) c) control of decision-makers (horizontal accountability)				
	independence	independence is guaranteed through rule of law	a) no strong ties between the judiciary and the legislature and/or executive b) open and free access of judiciary c) efficient control of corruption				
	stability	policy process is embedded in stable democratic structures and democratic institutions are equipped with sufficient resources	a) democratic institutions are accepted and supported by other relevant actors and their responsibilities do not vary extremely depending on the government in power b) absence of destabilizing circumstances (like extreme threats, financial restrictions, numerous personnel changes, etc.) c) democratic institutions are sufficiently equipped to oversee the government				

equality		
inclusiveness	openness and fairness of access guarantee involvement of a plurality of relevant actors	a) involvement of those affected and relevant (holders) b) unbiased selection c) support of weak/marginalized actors
participation	participatory structures enable involved actors to influence decision-making	a) application of participation techniques as necessary (e.g. to gain consensus) b) direct/intermediary/representative, etc. influence on decision-making and thus responsive results c) room for considered judgement enables deliberation
transparency	access and traceability of all relevant information at all stages of the policy process guarantees transparency	a) phases of the process with decision-making character show a high involvement of actors since the agenda of these meetings is publicly available and participants know that they offer the opportunity to influence decision-making b) access to all relevant documents and protocols c) absence of, or democratic justification for, informal meetings

(Continued)

Table 3.8 (Continued)

Metadimension	Dimension	Empirical translation	Indicators	Direct influence of procedural democratic quality on climate performance	Findings on the (in)direct influence of procedural democratic quality on climate performance (through procedural general performance)		
					Governmental capability	Stability (of government)	Effectiveness and efficiency
					government sets and maintains strategic priorities; government demonstrates flexibility and innovation; government learns from past errors	absence of destabilizing circumstances; durability; makes and maintains international commitments	quality of the bureaucracy; credibility of the government's commitment to policies; government makes efficient use of available resources
freedom	creativity	competition, experimentation and innovation enable creative potentials for a more democratic policy process	a) equal, free and adequate competition between actors and their ideas b) during the policy process new forms are tested to enhance democratic quality c) scientists are able to undertake independent research				
	liberty	associational and organizational rights enable autonomy and guarantee liberty	a) the existence of a variety of organizations indicates organizational rights which support their free and easy establishment of organizations, including those of b) marginalized groups, are able to act and express themselves autonomously without being influenced by, or made dependent on, third parties and/or being excluded from the process				

		c) individuals can make use of their political and civil rights to state their views about the issues under consideration
publicity	media pluralism and a free public sphere guarantee publicity on the issue under debate	a) a wide range of media outlets follow the policy process
		b) a press office with responsibility for the policy process exists and this supports public debate about the issue through press conferences, publications, explanation of scientific results, etc.
		c) the issue raises public awareness and this controls the policy process

the independent and intervening variable. In the first four columns on the left-hand side of the table, procedural democratic quality is illustrated, along with its dimensions, empirical translations and indicators. In the fifth column, every direct influence of procedural democratic quality on climate performance can be inscribed, while, the sixth column on the right side of the table, leaves space for observations on the interplay between procedural general performance and procedural democratic quality in terms of its influence on climate performance. All of the raw data which is deemed to be relevant for the purposes of analysis II, be it from the documents or interviews, can be displayed in this table. Based on the completed table, a content analysis can interpret the results.

While procedural democratic quality and procedural general performance are operationalized, it is also necessary to further operationalize substantive general performance as climate performance in the context of the case under investigation in analysis II.

Substantive general performance can be separated into output (results of formulation of policies in form of targets, etc.) and outcome (results of the implementation of policies to achieve targets, etc., i.e., in the form of GHG measurements). Consequently, climate performance can also be separated into these two dimensions, while this book focuses only on mitigation and not on adaptation. The output and outcome aims can be separated into saving GHG by doing less of the same, by making a practice more efficient so that the same result can be achieved with less GHG or by stopping a practice which is producing GHG. To give an example of mobility in terms of the use of a car run by fossil fuels: one can either drive less with the same car, make it more efficient by fitting a hybrid engine in the car or stop using the car and walk instead. The fields in which output and outcome can take place are broad, since they include every action producing GHG with the potential to decrease polluting GHG. The IPCC distinguished between the five categories: (1) energy, (2) industrial processes and product use, (3) agriculture, forestry and other land use, (4) waste and (5) other (IPCC, 2006). The formulation of action in these fields can be summarized in overall reduction targets compared to a specific baseline year (Kyoto Protocol: 1990 levels) and the year or time frame within which the target should be achieved (Kyoto Protocol: 2008–2012). This target is the main point of orientation when estimating output. Moreover, the quality of output can be estimated along certain criteria, such as the objective of a specific policy formulation, its scope, integration into a holistic policy package, sufficient budget, implementation procedures and monitoring process (Schaffrin et al., 2015).

Applied to analysis II, the focus when researching whether procedural democratic quality influences climate performance is to evaluate whether the fields of action, quality of plan and aims of practice in the context of an overall Kyoto Protocol target and the "sub-targets" of policy plans are positively, negatively or not at all influenced by procedural democratic quality.

Regarding outcome, an overall numerical estimation of how much democratic quality led to how much increase or decrease in GHG is not possible within the parameters of the case study in the same way as it might be in analysis I. Instead,

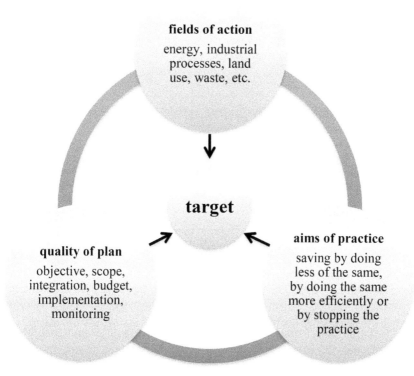

Figure 3.4 Output

analysis II evaluates whether any indications can be found which suggest that procedural democratic quality had a positive, negative or no influence on actual GHG developments and not only on targets. Thus, analysis II aims not to evaluate Canada's overall climate performance between 1995 and 2012. The focus is only on those aspects of climate performance which are influenced by procedural democratic quality. The quite holistic operationalization of climate performance is necessary to be aware of all aspects which might potentially be influenced by procedural democratic quality.

References

The access date of all material retrieved from the Web is 5 June 2015 unless otherwise specified.

Allison, P. D. (2009). *Fixed Effects Regression Models*. Los Angeles: Sage.

Allison, P. D. (2014). Problems with the hybrid method. Retrieved from www.statisti calhorizons.com/problems-with-the-hybrid-method

Altman, D., & Pérez-Liñán, A. (2002). Assessing the quality of democracy: freedom, competetiviness and participation in eighteen Latin American countries. *Democratization*, 9(2), 85–100.

Angrist, J. D., & Pischke, J. R. S. (2009). *Mostly Harmless Econometrics: An Empiricist's Companion*. Princeton, NJ: Princeton University Press.

Arksey, H., & Knight, P. (1999). *Interviewing for Social Scientists: An Introductory Resource with Examples*. London/Thousand Oaks, CA: Sage Publications.

Back, H., & Hadenius, A. (2008). Democracy and state capacity: exploring a J-shaped relationship. *Governance – an International Journal of Policy Administration and Institutions*, 21(1), 1–24.

Barber, B. (1984). *Strong Democracy: Participatory Politics for a New Age*. Berkeley: University of California Press.

Barber, B. (2010). Fixing climate change means fixing democracy. In C. Bieber, B. Drechsel, & A.-K. Lang (Eds.), *Kultur im Konflikt* (pp. 165–168). Bielefeld: Transcript.

Bartolini, S. (1999). Collusion, competition and democracy – Part I. *Journal of Theoretical Politics*, 11(4), 435–470.

Bartolini, S. (2000). Collusion, competition and democracy – Part II. *Journal of Theoretical Politics*, 12(1), 33–65.

Beach, D., & Pedersen, R. B. (2013). *Process-tracing Methods: Foundations and Guidelines*. Ann Arbor: University of Michigan Press.

Bennett, A., & Elman, C. (2007). Case study methods in the international relations subfield. *Comparative Political Studies*, 40(2), 170–195.

Berg-Schlosser, D. (2004). The quality of democracy in Europe as measured by current indicators of democratization and good governance. *Journal of Communist Studies and Transition Politics*, 20(1), 28–55.

Berg, B. L., & Lune, H. (2012). *Qualitative Research Methods for the Social Sciences* (8th ed.) Boston: Pearson.

Bergmann, M. M. (2008a). Introduction: whither mixed methods? In M. M. Bergmann (Ed.), *Mixed Methods Research. Theories and Applications* (pp. 1–7). Los Angeles/London/New Delhi/Singapore: Sage.

Bergmann, M. M. (2008b). The straw men of the quantitative-qualitative divide and their influence on mixed methods research. In M. M. Bergmann (Ed.), *Advances in Mixed Methods Research. Theories and Applications* (pp. 11–22). Los Angeles/London/New Delhi/Singapore: Sage.

Bernauer, T. (2013). Climate change politics. *Annual Review of Political Science*, 16(1), 421–448.

Bernauer, T., & Böhmelt, T. (2013). National climate policies in international comparison: the Climate Change Cooperation Index. *Environmental Science & Policy*, 25, 196–206.

Bertelsmann-Stiftung. (2014a). *Bertelsmann Transformation Index*. Retrieved from www.bti-project.org/materialien/bti-2014

Bertelsmann-Stiftung. (2014b). *Sustainable Governance Indicators*. Retrieved from www.sgi-network.org/2014/Downloads

Birch, A. H. (1984). Overload, ungovernability and delegitimation – the theories and the British case. *British Journal of Political Science*, 14(April), 135–160.

Bochsler, D., & Kriesi, H. (2013). Varieties of democracy. In H. Kriesi, S. Lavenex, F. Esser, J. Matthes, M. Bühlmann, & D. Bochsler (Eds.), *Democracy in the Age of Globalization and Mediatization* (pp. 69–102). Basingstoke: Palgrave Macmillan.

Bovens, M. (2007). Analysing and assessing accountability: a conceptual framework. *European Law Journal*, 13(4), 447–468.

Brady, H. E., & Collier, D. (2010). *Rethinking Social Inquiry: Diverse Tools, Shared Standards* (2nd ed.). Lanham, MD: Rowman & Littlefield Publishers.

Bühlmann, M., & Kriesi, H. (2013). Models for democracy. In H. Kriesi, S. Lavenex, F. Esser, J. Matthes, M. Bühlmann, & D. Bochsler (Eds.), *Democracy in the Age of Globalization and Mediatization* (pp. 44–68). Basingstoke: Palgrave Macmillan.

Burck, J., Hermwille, L., & Bals, C. (2014). *The Climate Change Performance Index. Background and Methodology.* Retrieved from http://germanwatch.org/en/download/8579.pdf

Burnell, P. (2012). Democracy, democratization and climate change: Complex relationships. *Democratization, 19*(5), 813–842.

CAN (2013). Canada wins "Lifetime Unachievement" Fossil Award at Warsaw climate talks. Retrieved from http://climateactionnetwork.ca/2013/11/22/canada-wins-lifetime-unachievement-fossil-award-at-warsaw-climate-talks/#sthash.YzajiVyi.dpuf

Cao, X., Milner, H. V., Prakash, A., & Ward, H. (2014). Research frontiers in comparative and international environmental politics: an introduction. *Comparative Political Studies, 47*(3), 291–308.

Carlsnaes, W. (1981). Foreign policy and the democratic process. *Scandinavian Political Studies, 4*(2), 81–108.

Cartwright, N. (2002a). In favor of laws that are not ceteris paribus after all. *Erkenntnis, 57*(3), 425–439.

Cartwright, N. (2002b). The limits of causal order, from economics to physics. In U. Maäki (Ed.), *Fact and Fiction in Economics: Models, Realism, and Social Construction* (pp. 137–151). Cambridge: Cambridge University Press.

Chanley, V. A., Rudolph, T. J., & Rahn, W. M. (2000). The origins and consequences of public trust in government – a time series analysis. *Public Opinion Quarterly, 64*(3), 239–256.

Charron, N. (2009). Government quality and vertical power-sharing in fractionalized states. *Publius – the Journal of Federalism, 39*(4), 585–605.

Charron, N., & Lapuente, V. (2010). Does democracy produce quality of government? *European Journal of Political Research, 49*(4), 443–470.

Choi, A. (2004). Democratic synergy and victory in war, 1816–1992. *International Studies Quarterly, 48*(3), 663–682.

Compagnon, D., Chan, S., & Mert, A. (2012). The changing role of the state. In F. Biermann & P. Pattberg (Eds.), *Global Environmental Governance Reconsidered* (pp. 237–263). Cambridge, MA: MIT Press.

Coppedge, M., Gerring, J., Altman, D., Bernhard, M., Fish, S., Hicken, A., Kroenig, M., Lindberg, S. I., McMann, K., Paxton, P., Semetko, H. A., Skaaning, S.-E., Staton, J., Teorell, J. (2011). Conceptualizing and measuring democracy: a new approach. *Perspectives on Politics, 9*(2), 247–267.

Creswell, J. W., & Plano Clark, V. L. (2011). *Designing and Conducting Mixed Methods Research* (2nd ed.). Los Angeles: Sage Publications.

Crozier, M., Huntington, S. P., & Watanuki, J. (1975). *The Crisis of Democracy: Report on the Governability of Democracies to the Trilateral Commission.* New York: New York University Press.

Dahl, R. A. (1956). *A Preface to Democratic Theory.* Chicago: University of Chicago Press.

Dahl, R. A. (2000). *On Democracy.* New Haven, CT/London: Yale University Press.

Dahl, R. A. (2006). *On Political Equality.* New Haven, CT: Yale University Press.

Democracy-Barometer. (2015). *Democracy Barometer.* Retrieved from www.democracybarometer.org/dataset_en.html

Diamond, L., & Morlino, L. (2004). The quality of democracy – an overview. *Journal of Democracy, 15*(4), 20–31.

Eckstein, H. (1971). *The Evaluation of Political Performance: Problems and Dimensions*. Beverly Hills, CA: Sage Publications.

Ecofys, & Climate Analytics (2015). *Climate Action Tracker*. Retrieved from http://cli mateactiontracker.org

Etzioni, A. (1968). *The Active Society: A Theory of Societal and Political Processes*. London/ New York: Collier-Macmillan Free Press.

Fiorino, D. J. (2011). Explaining national environmental performance: approaches, evidence, and implications. *Policy Sciences*, *44*(4), 367–389.

Fiorino, D. J. (2014). Too many levels or just about right? Multilevel governance and environmental performance. In I. M. Weibust, & James Meadowcroft (Eds.), *Multilevel Environmental Governance: Managing Water and Climate Change in Europe and North America* (pp. 15–35). Cheltenham: Edward Elgar Publishing.

Firebaugh, G., Cody, W., & Massoglia, M. (2014). Fixed effects, random effects, and hybrid models for causal analysis. In S. L. Morgan (Ed.), *Handbook of Causal Analysis for Social Research* (pp. 113–132). New York: Springer.

Fishkin, J. S. (2009). *When the People Speak: Deliberative Democracy and Public Consultation*. Oxford/New York: Oxford University Press.

Freedom House (2013). *Freedom in the World 2013*. Retrieved from www.freedomhouse. org/report-types/freedom-world

Fung, A., & Wright, E. O. (2001). Deepening democracy: innovations in empowered participatory governance. *Politics & Society*, *29*(1), 5–41.

Gallie, W. B. (1956). Essentially contested concepts. *Proceedings of the Aristotelian Society*, *56*, 167–198.

George, A. L., & Bennett, A. (2005). *Case Studies and Theory Development in the Social Sciences*. Cambridge, MA: MIT Press.

Germanwatch. (2015). *Climate Change Performance Index (CCPI)*. Retrieved from http:// germanwatch.org/en/ccpi

Gerring, J. (2004). What is a case study and what is it good for? *American Political Science Review*, *98*(2), 341–354.

Gerring, J. (2007). *Case Study Research: Principles and Practices*. New York: Cambridge University Press.

Gerring, J. (2012). *Social Science Methodology: A Unified Framework* (2nd ed.). Cambridge/ New York: Cambridge University Press.

Gillham, B. (2005). *Research Interviewing: The Range of Techniques*. Maidenhead/New York: Open University Press.

Gläser, J., & Laudel, G. (2010). *Experteninterviews und qualitative Inhaltsanalyse als Instrumente rekonstruierender Untersuchungen* (4th ed.). Wiesbaden: VS-Verlag.

Goertz, G., & Mahoney, J. (2012). *A Tale of Two Cultures: Qualitative and Quantitative Research in the Social Sciences*. Princeton, NJ: Princeton University Press.

Goldmann, K. (1986). Democracy is incompatible with international politics: reconsideration of a hypothesis. In K. Goldmann, S. Berglund, & G. Sjöstedt (Eds.), *Democracy and Foreign Policy* (pp. 1–44). Aldershot: Gower.

Grin, J., Rotmans, J., Schot, J., Geels, F. W., & Loorbach, D. (2010). *Transitions to Sustainable Development: New Directions in the Study of Long Term Transformative Change*. New York: Routledge.

Grumm, J. G. (1975). The analysis of policy impact. In F. Greenstein, & N. Polsby (Eds.), *Policies and Policy-making Handbook of Political Science* (Vol. 6). Reading, MA: Addison-Wesley Publishing Company.

Halperin, M., Siegle, J., & Weinstein, M. (2005). *The Democratic Advantage: How Democracies Promote Prosperity and Peace.* New York/London: Routledge.

Hamilton, A., Madison, J., & Jay, J. (2014). *The Federalist Papers.* Mineola, NY: Dover Publications, Inc.

Harding, D., & Seefeldt, K. (2014). Mixed methods and causal analysis. In S. L. Morgan (Ed.), *Handbook of Causal Analysis for Social Research* (pp. 91–110). New York: Springer.

Harmel, R., & Robertson, J. D. (1986). Government stability and regime support – a cross-national analysis. *Journal of Politics, 48*(4), 1029–1040.

Held, D. (2006). *Models of Democracy* (3rd ed.). Cambridge /Malden, MA: Polity.

Hoechle, D. (2007). Robust standard errors for panel regressions with cross-sectional dependence. *Stata Journal, 7*(3), 281–312.

Holden, M. (2006). Exclusion, inclusion and political institutions. In R. A. W. Rhodes, S. A. Binder, & B. A. Rockman (Eds.), *Political Institutions* (pp. 163–190). Oxford: Oxford University Press.

Hollyer, J. R., Rosendorff, B. P., & Vreeland, J. R. (2011). Democracy and transparency. *Journal of Politics, 73*(4), 1191–1205.

Hovi, J., Sprinz, D. F., & Bang, G. (2012). Why the United States did not become a party to the Kyoto Protocol?: German, Norwegian, and US perspectives. *European Journal of International Relations, 18*(1), 129–150.

Howlett, M., & Giest, S. (2013). The policy-making process. In E. Araral, S. Fritzen, M. Howlett, M. Ramesh, & X. Wu (Eds.), *Routledge Handbook of Public Policy* (pp. 17–28) New York/Abingdon: Routledge.

Howlett, M., Ramesh, M., & Perl, A. (2009). *Studying Public Policy: Policy Cycles & Policy Subsystems* (3rd ed.). New York: Oxford University Press.

Huntington, S. P. (1997). After twenty years: the future of the third wave. *Journal of Democracy, 8*(4), 3–12.

Inglehart, R. F. (2008). Changing values among western publics from 1970 to 2006. *West European Politics, 31*(1–2), 130–146.

Ingram, H., & Schneider, A. L. (2006). Policy analysis for democracy. In R. E. Goodin, M. Moran, & M. Rein (Eds.), *The Oxford Handbook of Public Policy* (pp. 169–189). Oxford: Oxford University Press.

IPCC. (2006). *IPCC Guidelines for National Greenhouse Gas Inventories.* Retrieved from www.ipcc-nggip.iges.or.jp/public/2006gl/pdf/0_Overview/V0_1_Overview.pdf

Islam, R. (2006). Does more transparency go along with better governance? *Economics and Politics, 18*(2), 121–167.

Jäckle, S., Wagschal, U., & Bauschke, R. (2012). Das Demokratiebarometer: "basically theory driven"? *Zeitschrift für Vergleichende Politikwissenschaft, 6*(1), 99–125.

Jäckle, S., Wagschal, U., & Bauschke, R. (2013). Allein die Masse macht's nicht – Antwort auf die Replik von Merkel et al. zu unserer Kritik am Demokratiebarometer. *Zeitschrift für Vergleichende Politikwissenschaft, 7*(2), 143–153.

Joas, H. (2013). *The Sacredness of the Person: A New Genealogy of Human Rights.* Washington, DC: Georgetown University Press.

Kaufmann, D., Kraay, A., & Zoido-Lobatón, P. (1999). *Governance Matters.* Washington, DC (1818 H St., NW, Washington 20433): World Bank, Development Research Group World Bank Institute, Governance, Regulation, and Finance.

Keith, L. C. (2002). Constitutional provisions for individual human rights (1977–1996): are they more than mere "window dressing"? *Political Research Quarterly, 55*(1), 111–143.

Kittel, B. (2006). A crazy methodology? On the limits of macro-quantitative social science research. *International Sociology, 21*(5), 647–677.

La Porta, R., Lopez-de-Silanes, F., Pop-Eleches, C., & Shleifer, A. (2004). Judicial checks and balances. *Journal of Political Economy, 112*(2), 445–470.

Lachapelle, E., & Paterson, M. (2013). Drivers of national climate policy. *Climate Policy, 13*(5), 547–571.

Lane, J.-E., & Ersson, S. O. (2000). *The New Institutional Politics: Performance and Outcomes.* London/New York: Routledge.

Latour, B. (2005). *Reassembling the Social: An Introduction to Actor-Network-Theory.* Oxford/New York: Oxford University Press.

Levy, J. S. (2008). Counterfactuals and case studies. In J. M. Box-Steffensmeier, H. E. Brady, & D. Collier (Eds.), *The Oxford Handbook of Political Methodology* (pp. 627–644). Oxford: Oxford University Press.

Lieberman, E. S. (2005). Nested analysis as a mixed-method strategy for comparative research. *American Political Science Review, 99*(3), 435–452.

Lin, A. C., & Loftis, K. (2005). Mixing qualitative and quantitative methods in political science: a primer. APSA Annual Conference, Washington, DC, 1 September.

Lindstedt, C., & Naurin, D. (2010). Transparency is not enough: making transparency effective in reducing corruption. *International Political Science Review, 31*(3), 301–322.

Linz, J. J., & Stepan, A. C. (1996). *Problems of Democratic Transition and Consolidation: Southern Europe, South America, and Post-communist Europe.* Baltimore, MD: Johns Hopkins University Press.

Longo, F. (2008). Quality of governance: impartiality is not enough. *Governance: An International Journal of Policy Administration and Institutions, 21*(2), 191–196.

Lord, C. (2004). *A Democratic Audit of the European Union.* Basingstoke/ New York: Palgrave Macmillan.

Mahoney, J. (2007). Qualitative methodology and comparative politics. *Comparative Political Studies, 40*(2), 122–144.

Manning, B. (1977). Congress, executive and intermestic affairs – proposals. *Foreign Affairs, 55*(2), 306–324.

Merkel, W., Tanneberg, D., & Bühlmann, M. (2013). "Den Daumen senken": Hochmut und Kritik. *Zeitschrift für Vergleichende Politikwissenschaft, 7*(1), 75–84.

Messner, D. (2015). A social contract for low carbon and sustainable development: reflections on non-linear dynamics of social realignments and technological innovations in transformation processes. *Technological Forecasting and Social Change, 98*, 260–270.

Mol, A. P. J. (2007). Bringing the environmental state back in: partnerships in perspective. In P. Glasbergen, F. Biermann, & A. P. J. Mol (Eds.), *Partnerships, Governance and Sustainable Development: Reflections on Theory and Practice* (pp. 214–238). Cheltenham/ Northampton, MA: Edward Elgar Publishing.

Morlino, L. (2012). *Changes for Democracy: Actors, Structures, Processes.* Oxford: Oxford University Press.

Munck, G. L. (2009). *Measuring Democracy: A Bridge between Scholarship and Politics.* Baltimore, MD: Johns Hopkins University Press.

Munck, G. L., & Verkuilen, J. (2002). Conceptualizing and measuring democracy – evaluating alternative indices. *Comparative Political Studies, 35*(1), 5–34.

Nietzsche, F. (2014). *On the Genealogy of Morals* (2nd ed.). Arlington, VA: Richer Resources Publications.

O'Donnell, G. (1994). Delegative democracy. *Journal of Democracy, 5*(1), 55–70.

O'Donnell, G. (2004). Why the rule of law matters. *Journal of Democracy, 15*(4), 32–46.

Offe, C. (2003). *Demokratisierung der Demokratie: Diagnosen und Reformvorschläge*. Frankfurt/ New York: Campus.

Pennock, J. R. (1966). Political development, political systems, and political goods. *World Politics, 18*(3), 415–434.

Perl, A. (2013). International dimensions and dynamics of policy-making. In E. Araral, S. Fritzen, M. Howlett, M. Ramesh, & X. Wu (Eds.), *Routledge Handbook on Public Policy* (pp. 44–56). New York/Abingdon: Routledge.

Plattner, M. F. (2004). The quality of democracy. A skeptical afterword. *Journal of Democracy, 15*(4), 106–110.

Powell, G. B. (2004). Political representation in comparative politics. *Annual Review of Political Science, 7,* 273–296.

Przeworski, A., Stokes, S. C., & Manin, B. (1999). *Democracy, Accountability, and Representation*. Cambridge/New York: Cambridge University Press.

Putnam, R. D., Leonardi, R., & Nanetti, R. (1993). *Making Democracy Work: Civic Traditions in Modern Italy*. Princeton, NJ: Princeton University Press.

Rhodes, R. A. W. (2006). Policy network analysis. In R. E. Goodin, M. Moran, & M. Rein (Eds.), *The Oxford Handbook of Public Policy* (pp. 425–447). Oxford: Oxford University Press.

Rohlfing, I. (2008). What you see and what you get: pitfalls and principles of nested analysis in comparative research. *Comparative Political Studies, 41*(11), 1492–1514.

Roller, E. (2005). *The Performance of Democracies: Political Institutions and Public Policy*. Oxford: Oxford University Press.

Rudolph, T. J., & Evans, J. (2005). Political trust, ideology, and public support for government spending. *American Journal of Political Science, 49*(3), 660–671.

Sartori, G. (1987). *The Theory of Democracy Revisited*. Chatham, NJ: Chatham House Publishers.

Saward, M. (1998). *The Terms of Democracy*. Cambridge: Polity Press Blackwell.

Schaffrin, A., Sewerin, S., & Seubert, S. (2015). Toward a comparative measure of climate policy output. *Policy Studies Journal, 43*(2), 257–282.

Scharpf, F. W. (1999). The choice for Europe: social purpose and state power from Messina to Maastricht. *Journal of European Public Policy, 6*(1), 164–168.

Schmitter, P. C. (2002). Participation in governance arrangements: is there any reason to expect it will achieve "sustainable and innovative policies in a multi-level-context"? In H. Hubert, P. Getimis, G. Kafkalas, & R. Smith (Eds.), *Participatory Governance in Multi-level Context* (pp. 51–69). Opladen: Leske+Budrich.

Schneider, A. (2003). Decentralization: conceptualization and measurement. *Studies in Comparative International Development, 38*(3), 32–56.

Schunck, R. (2013). Within and between estimates in random-effects models: advantages and drawbacks of correlated random effects and hybrid models. *Stata Journal, 13*(1), 65–76.

Skocpol, T. (1985). Bringing the state back in. In P. B. Evans, D. Rueschemeyer, & T. Skocpol (Eds.), *Bringing the State Back In* (pp. 3–37). Cambridge: Cambridge University Press.

Smith, G. (2009). *Democratic Innovations: Designing Institutions for Citizen Participation*. Cambridge: Cambridge University Press.

Spanier, J. W., & Uslaner, E. M. (1982). *Foreign Policy and the Democratic Dilemmas* (3rd ed.). New York: Holt, Rinehart, and Winston.

Stiglitz, J. E. (1999). *On Liberty, the Right to Know, and Public Discourse: The Role of Transparency in Public Life*. Paper presented at the Oxford Amnesty Lecture, 27 January 1999.

Retrieved from http://citeseerx.ist.psu.edu/viewdoc/download?doi=10.1.1.594.93& rep=rep1&type=pdf (accessed 15 January 2017).

Stone, J. (2014) Interview on Canada's Kyoto Protocol Process/Interviewer: F. Hanusch.

Tansey, O. (2007). Process tracing and elite interviewing: a case for non-probability sampling. *Ps-Political Science & Politics*, 40(4), 765–772.

Teorell, J. (2006). Political participation and three theories of democracy: a research inventory and agenda. *European Journal of Political Research*, 45(5), 787–810.

Thompson, D. (2008). Deliberative democratic theory and empirical political science. *Annual Review of Political Science*, 11, 497–520.

Torfing, J., & Lewis, J. M. (2011). *Interactive Policy Making, Metagovernance, and Democracy*. Colchester: ECPR Press.

Tsebelis, G. (1995). Decision-making in political-systems – veto players in presidentialism, parliamentarism, multicameralism and multipartyism. *British Journal of Political Science*, 25, 289–325.

Urbinati, N., & Warren, M. E. (2008). The concept of representation in contemporary democratic theory. *Annual Review of Political Science*, 11, 387–412.

WBGU (Wissenschaftlicher Beirat Globale Umweltveränderungen/German Advisory Council on Global Change). (2011). *World in Transition – A Social Contract for Sustainability*. Berlin: WBGU.

Weaver, R. K., & Rockman, B. A. (1993). *Do Institutions Matter?: Government Capabilities in the United States and Abroad*. Washington, DC: The Brookings Institution.

Wittman, D. A. (1995). *The Myth of Democratic Failure: Why Political Institutions are Efficient*. Chicago: University of Chicago Press.

Wooldridge, J. M. (2013). *Introductory Econometrics: A Modern Approach* (5th ed.). Mason, OH: South-Western Cengage Learning.

WWF, & Ecofys. (2009). G8 *Climate Scorecards*. Retrieved from www.wwf.se/source. php/1253675/G8%20Climate%20Scorecards%202009.pdf

Yin, R. K. (2009). *Case Study Research: Design and Methods* (4th ed.). Los Angeles, CA: Sage Publications.

Young, I. M. (1999). State, civil society, and social justice. In I. Shapiro & C. Hacker-Cordón (Eds.): *Democracy's Value* (pp. 141–162). Cambridge: Cambridge University Press.

II

An empirical analysis of the democracy-climate nexus

4 Analysis I

More leads to more – positive statistical trends

Analysis I asks what influence substantive democratic quality has on climate performance. The corresponding hypothesis assumes that higher levels of democratic quality positively influence climate performance.

Results indicate that more substantive democratic quality has a positive influence on overall climate performance and climate policy performance (output) and, with certain limitations, on GHG emissions development (outcome). Thus, results overwhelmingly verify the hypotheses and deliver findings supporting the concept of democratic efficacy. Panel regressions are estimated based on data from the Democracy Barometer and the CCPI. Depending on the combination of data used, the number of countries ranges from 39–41 from 2004–2012, resulting in 193–326 country years.

To reach these findings (for Stata commands see Appendix A), the analysis graphically and statistically explores available data ("Exploring the data of the Democracy Barometer, the Climate Change Performance Index and the control variables") and thereafter runs panel regressions on the influence of substantive democratic quality on climate performance ("A mostly positive relationship"). The findings are put into context and discussed in the concluding section ("Discussion").

Exploring the data of the Democracy Barometer, the Climate Change Performance Index and the control variables

The purpose of data exploration is to clarify the data structure of applied indices and control variables, in order to ensure a reasonable interpretation of the results. The data used in this book, of course, depends on real world characteristics of the countries under investigation. A critical investigation in the form of a graphical and statistical exploration is therefore necessary to evaluate what kind of data is used in panel regression analyses. The following section therefore proceeds by exploring data for the independent variable (substantive democratic quality) in the Democracy Barometer, for the dependent variable (climate performance) in the CCPI and for the control variables. Thereafter, the cumulative data is compared.

A first exploration of the Democracy Barometer provides insights into why the Democracy Barometer is useful for the purpose of analysis.

DOI: 10.4324/9781315228983-6

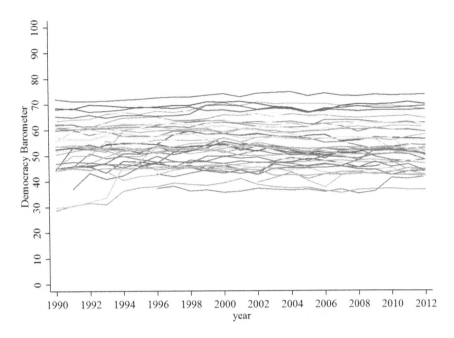

Figure 4.1 Democracy Barometer over time

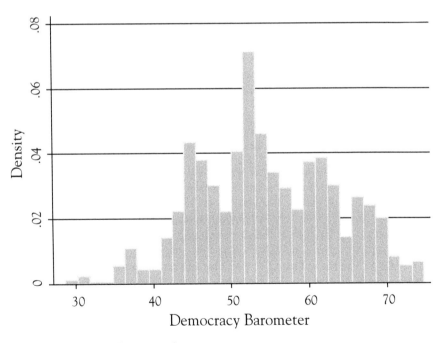

Figure 4.2 Democracy Barometer density

Table 4.1 Key numbers from the Democracy Barometer

Variable	Observations	Mean	Standard deviation	Minimum	Maximum	ICC
dembar	1068	54.6490	8.7946	28.7883	74.7380	.9404

The grey lines showing the countries' substantive democratic quality values indicate that in the case of the Democracy Barometer there don't seem to be many changes over time. The intraclass correlation coefficient (ICC) underlines that graphical impression with numbers: 94 per cent of the variation within the Democracy Barometer is the result of so-called between variation between countries and thus only 6 per cent of the variation is the result of so-called within variation, which covers variation within countries over time. Therefore, it can be assumed that democracies are, due to their institutions, typically quite stable countries and that changes within their structures take a lot of time since compromises have to be found, laws have to be made and implemented, etc. This is a reasonable assumption, as democracies do not change that much from one year to another, but stay quite stable over time, only witnessing procedural changes. A closer look at the histogram also shows that the Democracy Barometer features a nearby normal distribution.

The climate performance index used for panel regressions is the CCPI. It consists of a policy component and two emission components as well as components focusing on renewable energy and energy efficiency. As dependent variables in the panel regressions countries' overall scores in the CCPI are used to provide an overall estimation of all five components. Moreover, the policy component is used to evaluate output. Lastly, the emissions level component "is less an indicator of the performance of climate protection than an indicator of the respective starting point of the investigated countries", while the emissions development component "is comparatively responsive to effective climate policy, and therefore is an important indicator for a country's performance" (Burck, Hermwille, & Bals, 2014, p. 7). Thus, the emissions development component is used for outcome.

The CCPI varies substantially over time and seems to be close to a normal distribution. While the overall between variation of the CCPI of 68 per cent demonstrates that variations take place more often between than within countries, the emissions development and policy components show that the within and between variance is almost the same in both cases. However, the CCPI seems to be capable of substantial distinctions, also in terms of its components. The CCPI and the Democracy Barometer overlap between the mid-2000s and 2012.

Lastly, a brief exploration of the control variables provides an overview of aspects such as their distribution, which can be useful when interpreting the findings of the panel regressions.

The exploration of control variables might be of interest in regard to the ICC: with Internet users only one control variable has an ICC indicating more within

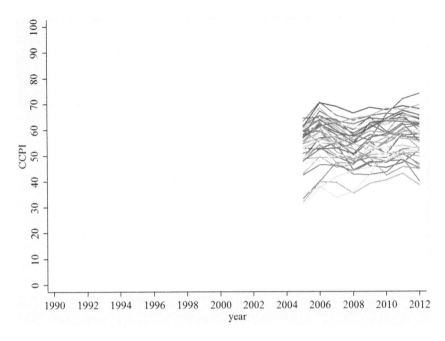

Figure 4.3 CCPI over time

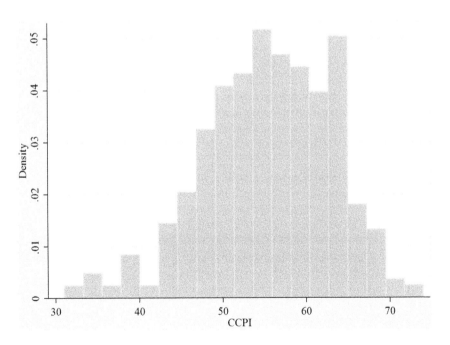

Figure 4.4 CCPI density

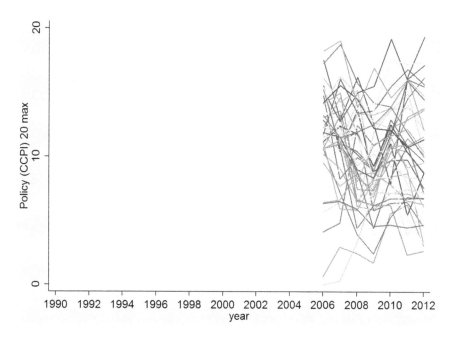

Figure 4.5 CCPI policy component over time

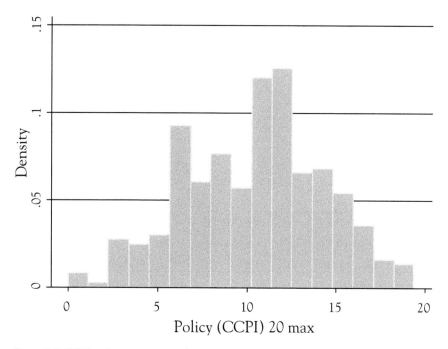

Figure 4.6 CCPI policy component density

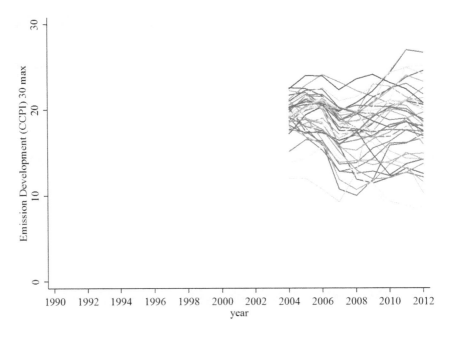

Figure 4.7 CCPI emission development over time

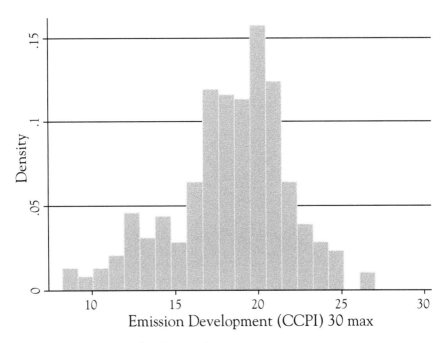

Figure 4.8 CCPI emission development density

Table 4.2 Key numbers from climate performance indices

Variable	Observations	Mean	Standard deviation	Minimum	Maximum	ICC
CCPI	368	55.4660	7.6826	31.0024	74.0037	.68335
emissions developmentCCPI	412	18.3713	3.4723	8.2262	27.0484	.46492
policyCCPI	322	10.4555	3.8560	0	19.3846	.53467

Table 4.3 Key numbers from the control variables

Variable	Observations	Mean	Standard deviation	Minimum	Maximum	ICC
oilgascoal	1540	53.5082	178.3891	0	1501.449	.9937
income	1475	16747.88	12276.37	1197.76	74021.46	.9380
trade openness	1439	.8440	.5089	.1230	3.7104	.8303
vulnerability	1206	.3174	.0685725	.1836	.4562	.9834
urbans	1496	68.0600	15.4607	25.547	97.4854	.9733
internet users	1318	24.5433	27.0768	.0001	96.6184	.2221
population14	1497	24.0029	8.2177	13.2818	45.8640	.9177
population65	1497	10.9362	4.7220	3.0494	23.3868	.9354
services	1338	61.2533	9.9647	15.8984	86.7317	.6494

than between variation, followed by services and trade openness. Thus, most variation of the control variables relies on between variations, which is why the between effect in panel regressions has to be taken into consideration, with the relevant amount of caution.

In terms of case selection, Figure 4.9 explores the Democracy Barometer-CCPI relationship in more detail to show, besides the characteristics which have already been mentioned, that Canada is the deviant case previously considered to be useful for the purposes of analysis.

Focusing on the means of both the Democracy Barometer (mdembar) and the CCPI (mCCPI), Australia, Canada, Luxembourg and the United States (US) can be identified as cases which fulfil the criteria of deviant cases, with quite high levels of democratic quality but low levels of climate performance. Due to the aforementioned selection criteria and the outstanding role Canada has played in regard to the Kyoto Protocol process, it is the case which will be researched in depth, since it seems to provide the most useful example for the purposes of analysis.

Based on the data exploration, panel regressions can be calculated with the Democracy Barometer and the CCPI. It seems the data from the indices and the

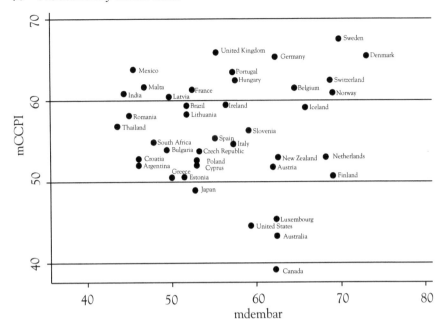

Figure 4.9 Democracy Barometer and the CCPI

control variables includes enough variation, is almost normally distributed and that significant effects may therefore be found.

A mostly positive relationship

The analysis proceeds by applying a Hausman test and a test on cross sectional dependence (CSD) followed by panel regressions, themselves including a description and comparison of the results before a conclusion (4.3) which discusses the findings in the context of the research question and hypothesis.

In the context of this book, a test on CSD examines whether different countries influence each other, so that one can check the influence which one country might have on another. The test implements two semi-parametric tests (Frees, 1995, 2004; Friedman, 1937) and one parametric procedure (Pesaran, 2004). The null hypothesis assumes that the residuals are not correlated. The null hypothesis has to be rejected if $p < 0.05$. The CSD is calculated in minimized fixed effect (FE) and random effects (RE) models, only including the main independent variable of interest in terms of the Democracy Barometer values and the different CCPI components.

The results of the test on CSD indicate in every combination that the null hypothesis has to be rejected and thus that CSD exists. Moreover, the assumption that substantive democratic quality in one country influences substantive democratic quality in other, e.g. neighbouring countries, is also theoretically plausible due to diffusion effects, etc. Similar theoretical assumptions might also be true for other independent variables, such as economic indicators, etc. Consequently, the panel regressions are calculated with CSD consistent standard errors (Hoechle, 2007).

The Hausman test helps to decide whether a fixed effects or a random effects model is more appropriate. The null hypothesis assumes that the preferred model is random vs. fixed effects (Greene, 2008, pp. 180–251). More precisely, the null hypothesis assumes that the unique errors are not correlated with the regressors and thus the random effects estimators are the same as the fixed effects estimators. The test calculates whether the unique errors are correlated with the regressors. If $p < 0.05$ the null hypothesis has to be rejected, then one can assume that fixed effects are more appropriate. If $p > 0.05$, then one can assume that random effects are more appropriate.

The Hausman test delivers mixed results. In the case of the emissions development component, the null hypothesis has to be rejected and thus fixed effects would be more appropriate. In both other cases, random effects might be more appropriate. Since a hybrid model exists which is able to calculate both within (fixed effects) and between estimations, a final decision is not necessary. Due to its mixed results, the Hausman test even endorses the hybrid model. Moreover, in the context of the research question, it is theoretically plausible to research what influence different levels of substantive democratic quality across countries have on climate performance and what influence changing levels of substantive democratic quality within one country have on climate performance. However, in the case of the emissions development component, the result means that the between effects have to be rejected or – due to the high dominance of between variance in the data of this book – interpreted with a high level of awareness of the possibility of biases due to omitted variable biases. However, due to the

Table 4.4 Test on cross-sectional dependence

Independent variable	Dependent variable	CSD based on fixed effects estimations	CSD based on random effects estimations
dembar	CCPI	.0000	.0000
dembar	emissiondevelopment CCPI	.0000	.0000
dembar	policyCCPI	.0000	.0000

Note: p is significant if < 0.05.

Table 4.5 Hausman test

Independent variable	Dependent variable	Hausman test result
dembar	CCPI	.8075
dembar	emissiondevelopmentCCPI	.0165
dembar	policyCCPI	.4942

Table 4.6 Panel regression results

CCPI	Model 1		Model 2	
	Within	Between	Within	Between
dembar	.2447* (.0875)	.3757*** (.0278)	−.1751 (.1327)	.2197* (.0751)
oilgascoal	−.0888*** (.0125543)	−.0066* (.0022)	−.1086*** (.0121)	−.0094*** (.0008)
income	−.0011** (.0003)	−.0001 (.0001)	−.0022*** (.0003)	.0001 (.0002)
vulnerability	−112.6676** (35.6423)	35.3240*** (4.6934)	−95.6701*** (7.3242)	10.3365 (8.1622)
trade openness			7.3575* (2.4409)	1.8825 (1.7167)
urbans			.1518 (.1425)	−.10928*** (.0124)
internet users			.0507 (.0617)	.1864* (.0634)
population14			−1.9658** (.4221)	2.3508** (.4633)
population65			−2.0574** (.4248)	3.0150** (.7607)
services			.2606** (.0700)	−.2750*** (.0296)
countries		41		39
country-years		287		232
r²		0.2694		.5240

Policy CCPI (output)	Model 1		Model 2	
	Within	Between	Within	Between
dembar	.3209* (.1231)	.0403 (.0221)	.2829+ (.1307)	−.0307 (.0652)
oilgascoal	−.0147 (.0204)	−.0039⁺ (.0019)	−.0314 (.0283)	−.0066* (.0018)
income	−.0002⁺ (.0001)	.0001⁺ (.0000)	−.0006* (.0002)	−.0314 (.0282)
vulnerability	−152.2479** (30.7744)	1.6815 (1.9860)	−132.0815* (48.1273)	−10.7792⁺ (4.9211)
trade openness			4.7132** (1.0830)	.3751 (.5260)
urbans			.3180* (.1014)	−.0520*** (.0062)

Policy CCPI (output)	Model 1 Within	Model 1 Between	Model 2 Within	Model 2 Between
internet users			−.0826[+] (.0380)	.1442** (.0230)
population14			−.8880 (.6304)	.7247*** (.1123)
population65			−1.1864** (.2212)	.9777** (.1642)
services			−.0465 (.0390)	−.0128 (.0320)
countries		41		39
country-years		246		193
r²		.1346		.3653

Emission development CCPI (outcome)	Model 1 Within	Model 1 Between	Model 2 Within	Model 2 Between
dembar	.02406 (.1019)	.1113* (.0382)	.1175 (.0938)	.1718* (.0695)
oilgascoal	−.0264* (.0082)	.0016** (.0003)	−.0392** (.0096)	.0017** (.0004)
income	−.0007*** (.0001)	.0001 (.0001)	−.0009*** (.0001)	.0001 (.0001)
vulnerability	80.7564** (18.5517)	−8.3471*** (1.5860)	109.0386** (22.5255)	−14.9530*** (2.2151)
trade openness			1.3343 (1.9186)	.6630*** (.1202)
urbans			.0322 (.0905)	.0376*** (.0052)
internet users			−.0268 (.0219)	−.0347 (.0211)
population14			.4026 (.3239)	.2010 (.1947)
population65			−.1181 (.1688)	.0888 (.3038)
services			.1677** (.0411)	−.0757* (.0237)
countries		41		39
country-years		326		268
r²		2.4199		2.5388

Note: Driscoll/Kraay standard errors in parentheses. ***≤0.001, **≤ 0.01, *≤ 0.05, *+≤ 0.1.

high dominance of between variance, it seems reasonable to reject results not directly but instead to consider whether these are reasonably interpretable. In other words, although between as well as within effects of CCPI and policy CCPI can be interpreted, since within effects are never biased and the Hausman test allows the interpretation of the between component as part of random effects, the between effect of the emissions development CCPI has nonetheless to be treated with extreme caution.

Two models are calculated for each climate performance component. The small model (model 1) includes only four key variables, however, these variables are believed to have a significant impact on climate performance. The variables in question are substantive democratic quality, income as GDP per capita, climate vulnerability and oil, gas and coal production. The broad model (model 2) additionally includes variables for trade openness, the percentage of the population which lives in urban areas, the percentage of people under the age of 14, of people over the age of 65 years and of services as percentage of GDP. There are good reasons why these factors also influence climate performance. Their inclusion may reduce omitted variable biases and provide additional insights, leading to the identification of further research gaps.

The CCPI delivers reliable results. r^2 is, with values ranging from 0.1346 to 0.4199 in model 1 and 0.3653 to 0.5388 in model 2, very high. To interpret the strength of the effects correctly, it is important to recognize that the Democracy Barometer and the overall CCPI range from 0–100, with higher scores indicating better democratic quality and climate performance respectively. Elsewhere the range differs and the policy component of the CCPI ranges from 0–20 and its emissions development component from 0–30. In both cases, higher scores once more indicate better climate performance.

The influence of democratic quality on the overall CCPI, including all components (policy, emissions development, emissions level, renewable energies and efficiency), shows a significant positive within effect in model 1 of .2447. This means that when democracies increase their score in the Democracy Barometer by 1, this causes an increase of 0.2447 in the CCPI. Additionally, both between effects are positive and significant. The effects of 0.3757 and 0.2197 mean that the different levels between democracies also influence the CCPI positively: a difference of 1 in the Democracy Barometer is therefore related to higher values of 0.3757 or 0.2197 respectively in the CCPI.

The influence of democratic quality on climate policy output is also markedly positive. In models 1 and 2, we can also see significant within effects of 0.3209 and 0.2829 respectively. Since within effects are totally reliable, the effect is quite considerable, particularly when you take into account that the climate policy component only ranges from 0–20, which means that an increase of 1 in the Democracy Barometer leads to an increase of 0.3209 or 0.2829 respectively in the CCPI.

Also, in terms of emissions development as the component which measures outcome, significant positive between effects of 0.1113 and 0.1718 can be detected. However, the between effects of the emissions development component have to be interpreted very cautiously: the Hausman test indicated that random effects, and thus perhaps between effects, would basically not be appropriate for the emissions development component. Thus, even though a significant positive effect exists, the effect might be the result of other factors not included in the model. The results of the models have to be interpreted with certain limitations and cannot be taken for granted in the same way as the overall CCPI and the policy component.

Overall, even though certain limitations regarding outcome must be recognized, there is strong evidence that increasing and higher levels of democratic quality have a significant positive effect on climate performance. Out of 12 effects based on the Democracy Barometer not one turned out to be significantly negative. On the contrary, all of the significant effects recorded turned out to be positive. Thus, there is no evidence indicating a negative influence of increasing democratic quality on climate performance in established democracies. These results now need to be theorized and discussed in the context of both the research question and the hypothesis of analysis I in order to conclude what general assumptions can be drawn for the democracy-climate nexus.

Discussion Analysis I

Analysis I asks what influence substantive democratic quality has on climate performance. The corresponding hypothesis assumes that higher levels of democratic quality influence climate performance positively. Results of the panel regressions allow, with one limitation, a straightforward answer and confirmation of the hypothesis. As previously theorized, substantive democratic quality mainly has a positive influence on climate performance in established democracies.

More precisely, findings regarding the influence of democratic quality on overall climate performance as measured by the CCPI confirm the hypothesis. One within and both between effects are significantly positive. Recognizing that the models using the CCPI as a dependent variable also include all of its components (policy, emissions development, emissions level, renewable energies and efficiency), it is reasonable to assume that the whole package of democratic quality and climate performance actually fit together and do not contradict each other. Almost the same can be said in regard to output as measured by the climate policy component of the CCPI, which also confirms the hypothesis. Both within effects are significantly positive, which can almost be seen as causal proof, since these effects cannot be biased by other factors. Taking into account the dominance of between variance (of 94 per cent) in the Democracy Barometer, these effects are even more remarkable.

However, findings on the outcome variable measured by the emissions development component of the CCPI are not that clear. Between effects in both models are significantly positive, indicating that higher levels of democratic quality can be related to better scores in the emission development component. However, these findings must either be cautiously interpreted or entirely rejected, since the Hausman test informed us that the between effects might be biased. Nevertheless, recognizing the high between variance in the data, a cautious interpretation of the results is outlined. The following interpretation is only possible since effects are estimated with a hybrid model, allowing for the differentiation of changes *within* one country as well as heterogeneity *between* countries. The argumentation, which is related to the results of the climate policy component, is as follows: countries which become more democratic also increase their climate policy performance. However, there is no significant representation of this in the between models. An explanation might be seen in the fact that the application of new modes or improvements of democratic quality are often related to specific policy subfields. When such formulations take place, people, politicians and other actors are motivated to use these new democratic tools and are ambitious in producing substantial policies. However, this effect seems to become irrelevant once the increase of substantive democratic quality has taken place, since the enthusiasm from the starting phase has faded. If one compares the findings from the emissions development component with those of the climate policy component, the significant positive effect moved from within to between models, which might make sense. While the process of establishing new democratic procedures is often related to the formulation of policies, the implementation and thus the influence of emission development takes place in existing democratic institutions. These do not change that easily and that is why the between component is more important. This supposed pattern is tentative, in need of further empirical checks and formulates a research gap. However, existing research on the different influence of democracy and autocracy on climate performance has already detected ambiguous results regarding outcome (see, e.g., Bättig & Bernauer, 2009). Therefore, the significant positive between effects on outcome can only be assumed with certain restraints.

Moreover, analysis I formulates a distinct set of research gaps. In order to distinguish between democracies and the climate performance of different democracies, better and more data is required. Future research should also pay attention to the distinction of between and within models, especially the relationship that might exist regarding the influence of substantive democratic quality on climate policy and emission development. Lastly, and even though the panel regressions focus on the influence of substantive democratic quality, certain control variables show significant and noticeable influences that indicate the requirement for further investigation. This can be demonstrated by the results of the variable indicating the vulnerability of a country to the consequences of climate change. In most models, vulnerability delivers significant results, but the influence can be seen in different directions, e.g. it seems as if states which become more vulnerable over time make weak policies. These ambiguous results are in need of more research. Ambitious small island states are probably too often identified as the most vulnerable countries, with the statistical results seeming to indicate that other vulnerable countries do not care that much about their future.

Thus, the findings of analysis I mostly verify the proposed hypothesis, while results regarding outcome have to be treated with a certain amount of caution. Analysis I endorses the previously outlined concept of democratic efficacy, assuming that the ability to produce desired or intended climate performance rises concomitantly with increasing levels of democratic quality. Of course, one general limitation of panel regressions is their limited probabilistic character, which doesn't allow for possibilistic interpretations with the inclusion of counterfactuals, alternative developments, etc. The findings rely on historical information on climate performance and thus provide no opportunity for explaining why a qualitative analysis follows this quantitative analysis. Thus, analysis II has not only to verify or reject the results of analysis I through the exploration of mechanisms which research whether the observed correlation follow hints on causality, it has also to evaluate what alternative developments other than empirical observations might be possible.

References

The access date of all material retrieved from the Web is 5 June 2015 unless otherwise specified.

Bättig, M. B., & Bernauer, T. (2009). National institutions and global public goods: are democracies more cooperative in climate change policy? *International Organization*, 63(2), 281–308.

Burck, J., Hermwille, L., & Bals, C. (2014). *The Climate Change Performance Index. Background and Methodology*. Retrieved from http://germanwatch.org/en/download/8579.pdf

Frees, E. W. (1995). Assessing cross-sectional correlations in panel data. *Journal of Econometrics*, 69(2), 393–414.

Frees, E. W. (2004). *Longitudinal and Panel Data: Analysis and Applications in the Social Sciences*. Cambridge /New York: Cambridge University Press.

Friedman, M. (1937). The use of ranks to avoid the assumption of normality implicit in the analysis of variance. *Journal of the American Statistical Association*, 32(200), 675–701.

Greene, W. H. (2008). *Econometric Analysis* (6th ed.). Upper Saddle River, NJ: Prentice Hall.

Hoechle, D. (2007). Robust standard errors for panel regressions with cross-sectional dependence. *Stata Journal*, 7(3), 281–312.

Pesaran, M. H. (2004). General diagnostics tests for cross section dependence in panels (August 2004). *CESifo Working Paper Series No. 1229; IZA Discussion Paper No. 1240*. Retrieved from https://ssrn.com/abstract=572504 (accessed 16 February 2016).

5 Analysis II

Canada's Kyoto Protocol process, 1995–2012 – a case study perspective

"We were not taking full advantage of our democratic opportunities, which is sad when you think about it."

(Stone, 2014)

Analysis II asks which mechanisms link procedural democratic quality and climate performance. The empirical case which is investigated is Canada's Kyoto Protocol process between 1995 and 2012. A period which turns out to be not quite as deviant as was previously assumed, since democratic quality in the specific policy process is lower than the Democracy Barometer scores assumed. Thus, results in the form of explored mechanisms indicate that decreasing levels of democratic quality influence climate performance negatively. Hence, the findings point in the opposite, but logically same, direction as analysis I and verify the positive trends detected there. The mechanisms which have been identified as linking procedural democratic quality and climate performance even indicate that, with increasing levels of democratic quality, the positive influence on climate performance becomes more predictable and stronger. This assumption is based on the observation that dimensions of procedural democratic quality form mechanisms through which they influence each other, and thereby climate performance, positively. Cases of this can be seen in, for example, transparency ensuring accountability by requiring higher levels of inclusiveness and participation, which results in more responsiveness and a reduction of particular interests. etc. Thus, there is a positive kind of self-enhancement of the existing dimensions of procedural democratic quality, which, in turn, increase the ability of democratic quality to produce the desired and intended climate performance as theorized in the concept of democratic efficacy. Minor caveats only seem to exist very occasionally and at an intermediate stage. For example, when one democratic dimension is in need of another, but the partnering dimension does not exist (e.g. in the absence of participatory structures, well-organized inclusiveness might immobilize decision-making rather than facilitate it).

To reach these findings, the analysis first clarifies the Canadian conditions influencing climate performance, including the internal and external contexts, the political system and the sources of GHG. Secondly, Canada's climate policy-making is explained by an outline of climate policy development, an overview of

DOI: 10.4324/9781315228983-7

the competencies of relevant actors in the climate policy-making processes and an examination of common explanatory models. Thirdly, the empirical analysis of democratic quality and its influence on climate performance in the context of the Kyoto Protocol process is prepared by outlining the background before COP 1.

Canadian circumstances

A famous Canadian civil servant once described Canada quite substantially in just one sentence:

> Separated from the British Isles by a three-thousand-mile ocean, situated next to the United States, living in a country which covers half of the North American continent, with our heterogeneous population, our two cultures and our two languages, we have developed a parliamentary practice of our own based on British principles and yet clearly Canadian.
>
> (Beauchesne, 1958 [1922], p. 8)

Even though Beauchesne precisely situates Canada in the world of nations, this chapter has to go one step deeper inside Canadian circumstances since a wide array of them affects Canada's climate policy performance. Democratic quality might be one of them. The goal of this chapter is twofold: first, to familiarize ourselves the wide array of circumstances that may affect climate performance in order to focus entirely on mechanisms regarding the influence of democratic quality on climate performance in the case study and, secondly, to identify the first indications of a democracy-climate nexus in Canada. Through an analysis of all three circumstances (internal and external contexts, the political system and GHG sources), a better picture emerges of the context in which climate policy-making takes place and, most importantly, of the magnitude of the influences involved. First, it is shown that Canada's geography and political culture build a framework within which Canadians produce and deal with GHG emissions. Secondly, federal government has two tasks or roles: (1) to develop and implement federal law and (2) to coordinate the provinces, so that they implement these laws. This case study focuses on these two roles without taking a closer look inside provinces and territories. Thirdly, emissions profiles indicate an overall increase in GHGs, with, inter alia, a considerable contribution to the energy sector.

Canada's internal and external contexts

Distinguishing between internal and external contexts for the purposes of analysis, two aspects seem to be of special importance in understanding Canada and Canada's way of climate policy-making as well as its GHG development: Canada's geography and its economy which is very much the result of its geographic circumstances and political culture.

First, regarding the internal context, it is almost impossible to overlook the fact that Canada is the second largest country in the world. The direct effects of the country's size on its climate policy are obvious (Dion, 2011): travelling takes a lot of time and resources and the population is mostly based near to the border to the US and is faced with very cold winters and hot summers, with corresponding cooling and heating necessities. Energy resources and interests in exploiting them range from oil sands in Alberta or Saskatchewan to hydro energy in Quebec, which is why large differences in the reduction costs of GHGs exist between provinces. In its early years, the Canadian economy could be described by the so-called staple thesis. Developed by W. A. Mackintosh and Harold Innis, this thesis focused on the economic development of Canada through an export based economy centred around resource extraction and primary industries (farming, fishery, fur trade, forestry, mining, etc.) (Howlett, Netherton, & Ramesh, 1999, pp. 81–100). Today, Canada's growing economy is still very energy intensive and relies heavily on the extraction of natural resources – especially of oil sands – however, it has nonetheless become much more diverse and cannot be explained by the staple thesis alone (Howlett et al., 1999, pp. 319–325). Moreover, Canada is experiencing immigration driven population growth, with an increase rate of over 25 per cent from 27.632 million inhabitants in 1990 to 34.702 million in 2012 (IMF, 2014). Obviously, all these people travel, heat, etc. and are thus important factors in Canada's GHG emissions development.

Secondly, the physical characteristics of Canada's geography do not alone determine the internal context, the country is also shaped by its political culture. As already explained, Canada has a high rate of immigration and is, in comparison to other countries, often mentioned as an example of a quite well functioning multicultural society (Banting & Kymlicka, 2010). A similar situation already existed when Canada was founded in 1867, with the competing (and unequal) influences of aboriginal people, the French, the British and many more groups. Thus, it would be incorrect to identify one unifying threat in terms of its political culture (Wiseman, 2007, p. 264). Changes and continuity are simultaneously present as countervailing tendencies (Wiseman, 2007, pp. 271–272): Immigrants and modern Canadians are very alike, they are flexible and relocate for employment, they marry each other, use the same media, travel around the country on a regular basis, etc. At the same time, old ideologies have taken hold. Atlantic Canada seems to rely on more traditional (political) practices than the steadily transforming West. An ideological polarization still exists in British Columbia and Ontario remains the moderate English hegemon, while the persistence of the French Canadians, with failed sovereignty referendums in 1980 and 1995, continues to be a major political theme in Quebec. Quebec, like some other provinces, has even left the national climate policy process on several occasions and accepted the Kyoto Protocol acting as a nation upon itself. However, if one tries to define "the" Canadian identity, it is probably the debates about Canadian identity itself which have contributed most to its development. These include the rejection of (parts of) the US-American way of life and the self-identification as a kinder and gentler US, more precisely Canada and the US "differ in their fundamental organizing principles: Canada has been, and is, a more class-aware, elitist, law-abiding, statist, collectivity-orientated and particularistic (group-orientated) society than the United States" (James & Kasoff, 2008, pp. 278–279; Lipset, 1990 (quotation 8)). Thus, Canada has developed a political culture where public consultations within a federal system play a considerable role and diverse influences are able to be articulated. As Chapters 6–9 will demonstrate, this diverse identity, with its consequent public consultations, also (partially) exists within Canada's climate politics.

The external context can also be divided into two categories: geography and political culture. The proximity to the US as the only border to another state is clearly the dominating geographic factor and, briefly explained, the US is Canada's best friend whether it likes it or not. The two economies are largely integrated due to the Free Trade Agreement of 1989 and the North American Free Trade Agreement (NAFTA) of 1994. The US is also Canada's most important export and import partner. For example, at the UNFCCC level, Canada pleaded for a fairer approach which would take account of emissions in the country where Canada's resources are consumed (Dion, 2011, p. 27a). Due to the countries' interconnectedness, Canada's policy often mirrors that of the US and this can also, in part, be seen in its climate policy, for example, with the Kyoto targets (Dion, 2011; Harrison, 2012).

Canada's political culture in the international sphere is to some extent equivalent to its consultative tradition at the domestic level. Often characterized as a middle power, Canada is generally in favour of multilateral solutions (James & Kasoff, 2008, pp. 3–6; Tomlin, Hillmer, & Hampson, 2008). Due to their attempts to present balanced views and to find truly multilateral solutions, Canada and its diplomats are very well received by other states. Although that general approach has changed somewhat over the past few years, a survey has recently still ranked Canada as the most admired and esteemed nation out of a selection of 50 countries (Reputation-Institute, 2014). Even though Canada's climate policy has developed in a multilateral tradition within the UNFCCC, the influence of the regime, the final results of the climate policies and Canada's reputation at the international level have to be seen through a different lens, as Chapters 6–9 will demonstrate.

Canada's political system and its policy-making

The main features of Canada's political system can be found in a combination of a slightly modified British Westminster parliamentary system with a first past the post electoral system and a highly decentralized federalism, resulting in, strong executives at federal, provincial and territorial levels (Marleau & Montpetit, 2005). To explain the system and to indicate what effects it has on the democracy-climate nexus, this chapter: outlines its basic structures; explains the parliamentary system; analyses the decentralized federalism; and examines how the government works, especially in terms of its intermestic policy-making.

The political system has its origins in the British North America Act of 1867, a statute of the British Parliament, and has, over time, been expanded upon, mainly by means of written and unwritten conventions, most prominently, by the Charter on Rights and Freedoms in 1982. Law-making is shared amongst federal, provincial and territorial governments. The supreme authority is the law. The head of state is the British monarch, represented by the governor general, who is

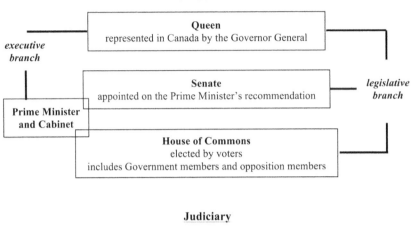

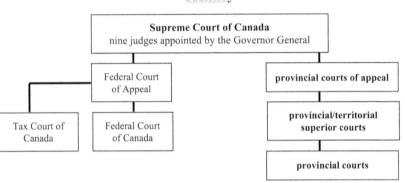

Figure 5.1 Canada's system of governance
Source: Based on Forsey (2016).

appointed by the monarch on the recommendation of the PM. In political practice, the monarch and the governor general mainly act on the advice of the PM
without having much power. The Parliament consists of a lower house, the House
of Commons, which is directly elected by voters, and an upper house, the Senate,
which members are appointed to on a regional basis by the governor general on
the PM's recommendation. In the first past the post electoral system for the lower
house, only candidates who receive the highest number of votes in their district
gain a seat. The PM is appointed by the governor general and is, by convention, the leader of the strongest party following a general election. After having
accepted the appointment of the governor general as the leader of the strongest
party, the PM then appoints his or her Cabinet. Moreover, the governor general
formally appoints judges to the Supreme Court, prorogues and dissolves Parliament and holds the position of, amongst others, commander-in-chief. However,
as already explained, the powers of the governor general are in practice very weak
and, when faced with a strong PM, the holder of the position rarely invokes his

or her prerogative, particularly as the PM recommends who becomes governor general. Courts or the judiciary oversee the work of government and governing processes, but play almost no part in judging substantive policies. Their position was also weakened in a constitutional reform in 1992 and this is why intergovernmental negotiations in the federal system have very much replaced courts in their influence in affecting changes in the political system (Inwood, O'Reilly, & Johns, 2011). This same system is reproduced in all provinces and, with slight variations, in the territories, whereby the federal government is connected to the provinces and territories through a number of institutions. Therefore, the Canadian political system can be divided into three different levels: federal, national (comprised of federal-provincial-territorial collaborations) and provincial.

The parliamentary system was founded by section 17 of the Constitution Act 1867. It established "one parliament for Canada consisting of the Queen, the Upper House styled Senate and the House of Commons". The legislature of the Parliament is bicameral and legislation has to be adopted by both houses. However, even though the Senate formally possesses almost the same powers as the House of Commons, it has no right to initiate financial legislation such as tax issues. Since senators are not appointed by the provinces and have little influence on federal decision-making processes, the Senate is not a forum to negotiate regional differences. Instead, the House of Commons is the elected chamber of the Canadian Parliament. In the first past the post electoral system, also known as the simple plurality system, a seat in the House belongs to candidates who won their districts through a majority of the votes cast. This electoral system means it is hard for smaller parties to be represented in the House and the majority government usually receives less than 50 per cent of the votes cast. Subsequently, Canada has mainly been characterized, at least at the federal level, by a two-party system (Liberals and Conservatives plus the small Quebecois), which seems to have now transformed into a three-party system with a strong New Democratic Party. One important parliamentary institution is the caucus. It unites members of the same party from both houses and meets regularly in camera to internally debate political issues and differences. The legislative process itself is organized in three main stages.

In the first stage, the Cabinet stage, the government decides for which of its policies it wants to start a legislation process. After consultations, a memorandum to the Cabinet is prepared, which is considered by the Cabinet. A Cabinet Committee debates the memorandum and writes a report, ratifies it and sends it to the specific department to prepare a draft bill. After being reviewed by the relevant minister and by the leader of the House, the latter of these introduces the bill in Parliament. The House then has a first and a second reading, a committee and a report stage for detailed study, followed by a third reading and vote. The same procedure is repeated in the Senate. After the third reading, the bill awaits royal assent, which, in practice, means that the bill becomes an act. Finally, the act comes into force, either immediately or at a later point, depending on the specific procedure decided upon.

Federalism is an essential characteristic of Canada's political system. Canada's federalism has its roots in the regional differentiation of provinces and territories

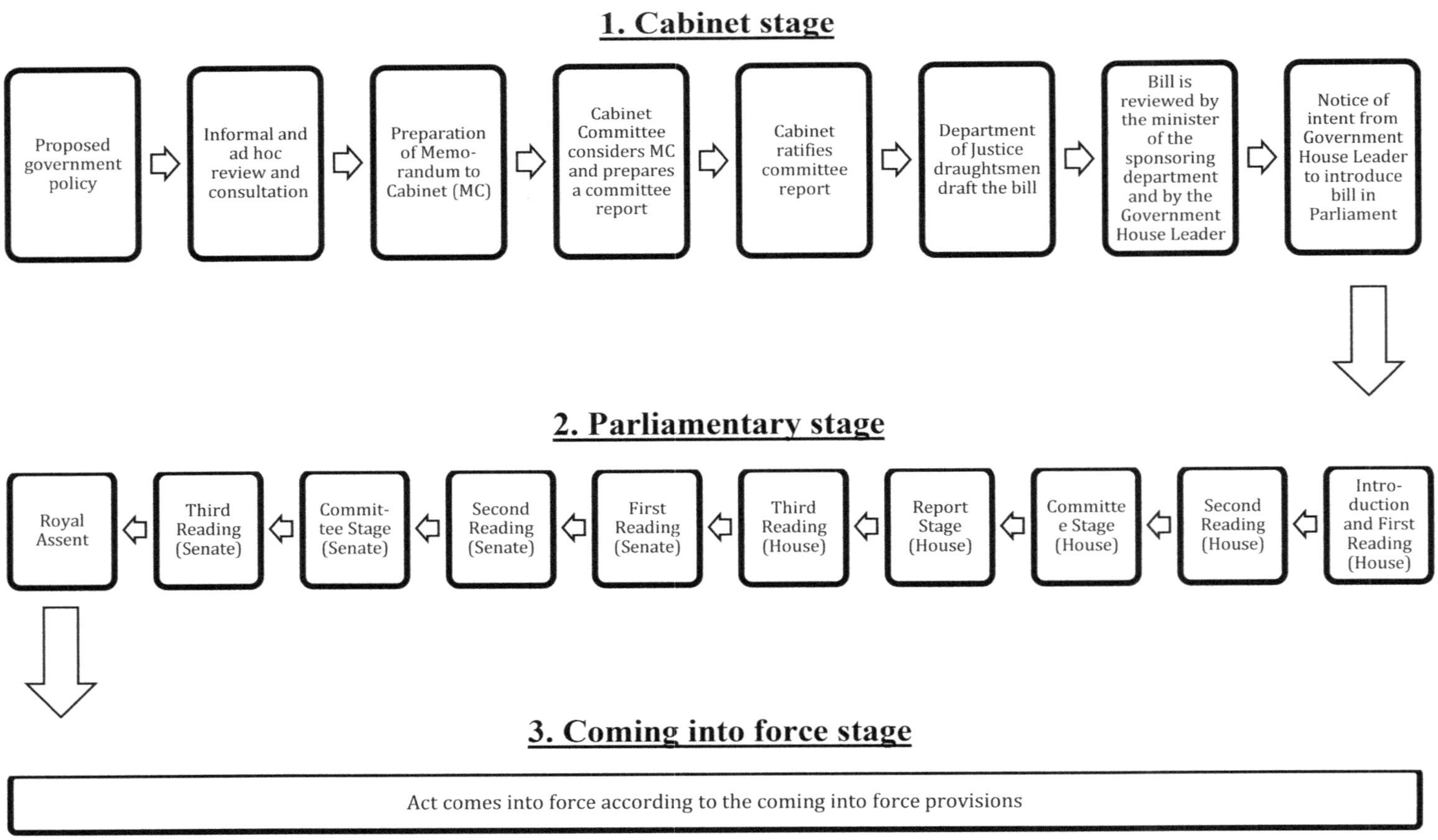

1. Cabinet stage

| Proposed government policy | → | Informal and ad hoc review and consultation | → | Preparation of Memo-randum to Cabinet (MC) | → | Cabinet Committee considers MC and prepares a committee report | → | Cabinet ratifies committee report | → | Department of Justice draughtsmen draft the bill | → | Bill is reviewed by the minister of the sponsoring department and by the Government House Leader | → | Notice of intent from Government House Leader to introduce bill in Parliament |

⟹

2. Parliamentary stage

| Introduction and First Reading (House) | → | Second Reading (House) | → | Committee Stage (House) | → | Report Stage (House) | → | Third Reading (House) | → | First Reading (Senate) | → | Second Reading (Senate) | → | Committee Stage (Senate) | → | Third Reading (Senate) | → | Royal Assent |

⟹

3. Coming into force stage

Act comes into force according to the coming into force provisions

Figure 5.2 Legislative process
Source: Based on Barnes (2012).

and stems from its cultural and colonial background. From time to time Quebec still attempts to become a sovereign state and the country's aboriginal people often call for more autonomy (Bakvis & Skogstad, 2008, p. 18). Moreover, provinces and territories are far from having an equal economic background. Over the years, the federal state has had to transfer more and more competencies to the provinces and territories in order to prevent a national collapse. At the same time, especially in the twentieth century with the foundation of the welfare state, more coordination has become necessary (Watts, 2002). The party system is also very regionally orientated; this is why regional and national groups of the same party can display huge differences and a certain level of incongruence in their programmes, and regional branches of parties usually claim more provincial autonomy. The federal state lacks a system of effective representation of provincial interests and concentrates much authority in the hands of the PM (Bakvis & Skogstad, 2008, p. 8). Taking all of these features into account, one can conclude that the Canadian federalized state has, in practice, often been characterized by conflict, instability and a lack of ability to enforce its authority when pursuing fundamental policies. Since, by constitution, no institutionalized intergovernmental mechanisms exist, the federal state is an autonomous law-maker. At the same time though, the provinces can also act quite autonomously (Watts, 1999, p. 77). And, due to a lack of institutionalized procedure, at least three forums are used to coordinate federal-provincial diplomacy (Bakvis & Skogstad, 2008, p. 9; Macdonald et al., 2013, p. 44; Simeon, 1972): First Ministers Meetings (FMMs), as meetings of the PM and the provincial and territorial premiers, meetings of provincial and territorial premiers without the PM (partially institutionalized since 2003 as the Council of the Federation) and meetings of federal and provincial ministers in a specific policy field. Having no binding decision-making procedures, these forums have no further institutional basis and only a small amount of political influence (Brühl-Moser, 2012). According to Canadian courts, the agreements of the forum do not have the character of legally binding contracts; they "do not trump the fundamental parliamentary principle that each government should be responsible to its own legislature" (Simeon & Nugent, 2008, p. 96). Not surprisingly, Canada is often categorized as the most decentralized state worldwide and intergovernmental policy-making is usually organized informally and on specific topics (Bakvis & Skogstad, 2008, p. 9). Since there is no need to cooperate by law, the consultations do not always lead to decisions where the federal state, the provinces and territories are in line, but in many cases bilateral solutions between the federal state and the specific provinces are negotiated and provinces are often allowed to opt out if they disagree with the resolutions (Painter, 1991). This lack of institutionalization exists in almost every circumstance: there is no statutory foundation, nor are there any fixed schedules, voting and/or decision-making procedures, etc. (Brown, 2006, p. 68; Papillon & Simeon, 2004, p. 128; Simeon, 2006, p. 68; Simeon & Nugent, 2008). However, Canadian federalism has survived by generating the necessary flexibility when interpreting and adapting to the problems at hand, with mixed results in terms of policy performance.

Federalism and democracy are two separate principles of political systems. Federalism is primarily designed to organize different regional interests. It is often assumed that federalism has the potential to positively influence democratic quality due to more efficient policy performance on a regional level, the possibility to be innovative, etc. (Benz, 2003, pp. 1, 10). Nevertheless, those arguments are very general in nature and we want to take a closer look at different types of federalism and their influence on different types of democracy (Benz, 2003, p. 10). In the Canadian case, federalism allows decisions between the federal and provincial level, but this comes at a high price since Canadian federalism seems to reduce democratic quality (Benz, 2003, pp. 19–21; Simeon & Cameron, 2002): informal coordination in the absence of institutionalization is usually not very transparent, the forums within which meetings take place are purely accountable to other institutions or voters, executives at the federal, provincial and territorial level dominate negotiations and parliaments and parties are often not involved in the negotiations, etc. Thus, federal, provincial and territorial governments work together in a so-called executive federalism with certain shortcomings in democratic quality (Inwood et al., 2011, pp. 3–4, 7–8, 445).

In general, the way federalism influences policy performance depends on the specific type of federalism (competitive, collaborative, etc.) and the policy field (Bakvis & Skogstad, 2008, p. 12; Biela, Kaiser, & Hennl, 2013, p. 6). Moreover, one has to distinguish between the right to decide (formulation and decision-making) and the right to act (implementation) (Braun, 2000; Keman, 2000). As one can imagine looking back at the issues discussed above, Canadian provinces and territories can play a huge role in this regard. Therefore, it depends very much upon whether both levels already have their own views and programmes in a given policy field or whether one or both of those levels comes into the discussion free of any preliminary specifications (Harrison, 1996, pp. 8–9). Regarding climate change, the constitution states that the ownership of natural resources belongs to the provinces and territories and this is why they hold many jurisdictional cards when it comes to determining climate change policy.

To sum up Canadian federalism in the context of the purpose of the case study, one can expect democratic quality and climate performance to have limitations due to the characteristics of Canadian executive federalism. This negative influence is to be taken into account when trying to analyse the influence of democratic quality on climate performance.

Having explained the parliamentary system and federalism, the way the government functions remains as an important characteristic of Canada's political system. The executive authority is formally the remit of the governor general in consultation with the Privy Council, however, in practice, it is the governor general acting on the advice of the PM (Marleau & Montpetit, 2005; PCO, 1998). By constitution, the governor general chooses the members of the Privy Council, but, in practice, the PM nominates the members as personal and confidential advisors. Most of the nominees are ministers. Moreover, PMs decide upon their ministers and their competencies.

Since decision-making within the Cabinet is not very formalized, PMs can heavily influence the working structure of the Cabinet as an instrument through which to achieve their goals (Schacter & Haid, 1999, pp. 2–4). Thus, decision-making is very much rooted in its time and dependent on the PM. After the Cabinet has decided on specific policies, more detailed work is then carried out within Cabinet Committees. Nevertheless, neither the PM, nor the ministers, nor the Privy Council have much to do with the implementation of policies. Once they have been decided upon and the first steps taken, for example, public communication or legislative action have been initiated, there is – apart from, in some cases, the auditor general – no structural monitoring by the Privy Council or any other institution. On the whole, the Cabinet trusts the sponsoring department of a policy to ensure that it will be implemented (Schacter & Haid, 1999, p. 21). However, the clerk of the Privy Council (the head of public services) undertakes weekly discussion with deputy ministers on the progress of broader political commitments made by the Cabinet. Thus, decision-making is more or less overseen by the Privy Council, but not monitored in any real detail (Schacter & Haid, 1999, pp. 29–33).

The Prime Minister's Office (PMO) and the Privy Council support the PM. The PMO is politically orientated and works primarily to coordinate with ministers and the party, handles parliamentary issues and briefs the PM on general developments at the national and international levels. The Privy Council is, however, operationally orientated and the key institution in developing government policy and direction. As the public service department of the PM, it focuses on a wide range of topics and responsibilities, including the work of the Cabinet, relations with the provinces, the appointment of key positions within the government and the functioning of decision-making processes as advised by the PM. Two other institutions which are worth mentioning in regard to the financial and personal aspects of decision-making are the Treasury Board, as the employer and manager of public services, and the Department of Finance, as the ministry controlling the budget.

Regarding the democracy-policy-performance nexus it has to be noted that the way governmental decision-making takes place obviously influences policy results. However, the democratic component and its influence on the results are less clear. The government, once elected, has, in its decision-making, no further legally binding democratic components. Therefore, it is hard to estimate the concrete interplay between democratic quality and general performance in the exclusive circle of executive decision-making at this stage besides noting that there is not much democratic influence required when the government makes its decisions.

Since climate policy-making in the context of Kyoto takes place at the intermestic level, it is important to explain how policy at this level is made in Canada's political system. The treaty-making process for international treaties like the Kyoto Protocol can be split into the following phases (Morrissette, 2011): first, an explanatory phase is overseen by the Privy Council, where general interests and important sections of any intended treaty are identified and discussed; secondly,

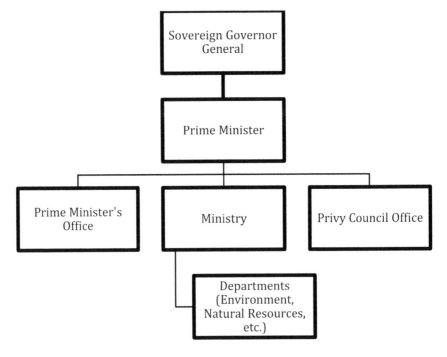

Figure 5.3 Executive institutions
Source: Based on PCO (n.d.).

a negotiation mandate is granted by the Cabinet; thirdly, the negotiation process itself takes place; and, fourthly, the treaty is finalized in a phase which includes the authorization of the negotiation results by the Cabinet and the signing of the treaty by the governor general. At no point in this process does the Parliament have any substantial influence, since its non-binding consultative role lacks the authority to alter the contents of the treaty.

In many countries, federal governments sign, ratify and implement international treaties. However, in the Canadian political system, this is not the case, since in many policy fields implementation falls within the authority and jurisdiction of the provinces and territories, which often results in conflict, due to different preferences amongst provinces, territories and the federal state. In the case of environmental treaties, the federal government, the provinces and the territories all share responsibility. Canada created the Council of Ministers of the Environment (CCME) as an institution to coordinate environmental issues between provincial, territorial and federal ministers. In practice, the consultation of the provinces and territories before signing a treaty with shared jurisdiction is either negotiated by the CCME or informally, which is why powerful provinces can usually play a strong role in such agreements. However, there is no legally binding guarantee that the federal government will respect agreements negotiated with the provinces and territories when signing a treaty. In practice, bilateral agreements are often made between specific provinces and the federal state, in which the federal government offers, for example, subsidies in order to persuade regional governments to sign up to a treaty (Rabe, 2007, p. 434).

The democratic quality of policy-making in intermestic policy fields seems to be low on average: Most researchers state that the PM determines the proceedings and their results (Gecelovsky, 2011, p. 226). Moreover, consultants are often involved in the policy process, which raises questions as to the legitimation of this "invisible public service" (Howlett, 2013, p. 165). Canada seems in many regards to be the Western state where foreign policy-making is furthest removed from parliamentary business and at its closest to the executive. Indeed, it appears that the trend is towards even more executive control of policy-making (Thunert, 2003). The only very brief lively dialogue on foreign policy with an impetus towards opening foreign policy to the broader public seems to have been without any real influence (Ayres, 2006). The combination of the dominance of the federal executive in producing foreign policy and signing international treaties and the dominance of the federal, provincial and territorial executives in implementing policies appears to negatively impact upon democratic quality and its possible influence on policy results. However, the informality of this process would also allow the executive to include the public in the policy-making process. Due to the functioning of the government as explained above, policy performance very much depends on the PM, the Cabinet's views and political will, while democratic quality only seems to have marginal influence.

To sum up, a look at analysis from 1971 seems to be insightful. Doern and Aucoin write in their book on *The Structures of Policy-making in Canada* that the "extent to which there is public involvement in the inter-election political process in Canada has been limited and sporadic" and they see a "need for newer instruments of citizen participation" (Doern & Aucoin, 1971, p. 279). After analysing Canada's policy-making structures, it seems that not very much has changed since 1971. The executive and, especially, the PM seem to be very dominant in the political process, while representatives in the House have almost no say in the making of public policy and there seems to be a distinct lack of accountability (Atkinson, Marchildon, Phillips, Rasmussen, Béland, & McNutt, 2013; Howlett, 2013, p. 65; Inwood et al., 2011, p. 58; Simpson, 2001).

However, when it comes to the Kyoto Protocol process, the federal government has two tasks or roles: (1) to develop and implement federal law; and (2) to coordinate the provinces so that these laws are implemented. The following case study will explicitly focus on these two roles without taking a closer look at the provinces and what they themselves do in regard to climate change. In both roles, the executive seem to be the most important players, while other actors don't appear to be essential in the policy process. Thus, in contrast to the results of the Democracy Barometer, which describes Canada as a high-profile democracy, several weaknesses within the Canadian political system seem to combine when looking at the characteristics of climate change and the Kyoto Protocol. Therefore, it is also important to look at what the main sources of GHG development are. Analysing which level of government takes the decisions in policy-making and which actors take what positions helps us to understand which are the dominant forces behind Canada's GHG emissions.

The sources and the development of GHG emissions

The impacts of climate change in Canada are diverse due to the similarly diverse geography of the country. Since climate change occurs most significantly with temperature increases in higher latitudes, Canada will likely face the biggest issues in the north of the country. This could lead to both positive and negative implications, such as the possibility that the exploitation of resources will become easier because of the reduction in sea ice and/or the necessary adaptation (parts of) Canada's Aboriginal people might come to be faced with as their native environments change (White, 2010, p. 3). Thus, climate change will, inter alia, have an impact on Canada as a fossil fuel exporting country, but it will also raise questions about the way Canadians live in an energy intensive economy. When taking a look at the democracy-climate nexus in Canada, it is therefore crucial to know where the country's GHGs originate and how they are developed.

When compared with their state in the Kyoto Protocol base year of 1990 with 591 Mt CO_2 eq., Canada's overall emissions rose steadily in the 2000s with a peak of 749 Mt CO_2 eq. in 2007, before experiencing a downward tendency to 702 Mt CO_2 eq. in 2011, which was closely related to the international financial crisis from 2007 onwards (ECan, 2013, p. 19). Also, Canada's per capita emissions grew steadily in the 1990s starting with 21.3t CO_2 eq./capita, stabilizing in the 2000s with a peak in 2000 reaching 23.4t CO_2 eq./capita and then falling following the financial crisis of 2007/2008 to 20.4t CO_2 eq./capita in 2011 (ECan, 2013, p. 20). However, with no year showing per capita emissions below 20t CO_2 eq., Canada has one of the highest per capita emissions levels worldwide. As in many industrialized Western countries, the GHG intensity per GDP declined in Canada (ECan, 2013, p. 19). However, compared to total emissions, the GHG intensity did not decline fast enough to capture the steadily growing overall emissions. Having a look at the GHGs themselves, between 1990 and 2011, CO_2 remains the most relevant gas, accounting for more than three-quarters of total emissions (ECan, 2013, p. 46).

When trying to explain the increase in GHG emissions the two most important sectors are energy and transport, which together produced 81 per cent of Canada's emissions in 2011 (ECan, 2013, p. 21). To give just two examples: in the energy sector, oil sands increased by 453 per cent from 1990 to 2011, while, in the same time frame, the number of motor vehicles increased by 50 per cent (ECan, 2013, pp. 50, 55). In absolute terms, the whole energy sector increased by 103 Mt CO_2 eq. and there was significant increase in land use, rising from −62 Mt CO_2 eq. in 1990 to 87 Mt CO_2 eq. in 2011 (ECan, 2013, p. 22). Since certain sources of GHG emissions, like oil sands, are not equally distributed among the provinces, very different emission profiles emerge regionally, e.g. in the middle of the investigated time frame, in 2002, Alberta had per capita emissions of around 72 Mt CO_2 eq. while Quebec's emissions only reached 12 Mt CO_2 eq. (Bjorn et al., 2002, p. 21).

Of course, so far, this data has told us very little about the influence which democratic quality might have on Canada's climate performance. However, it has become clear which main sources, drivers and sectors Canadian policy processes would have had to address to achieve the Kyoto target of an average annual emissions reduction of 6 per cent from 1990 levels during the commitment period of 2008–2012. The data also shows that many factors, such as an increasing exploitation of oil sands and an increasing population, clearly led to higher emissions rates (Schwanen, 2006, pp. 292–293).

Climate policy-making

While the previous chapter explained circumstances which might have influenced climate performance and in which climate policy-making was embedded, this chapter seeks to take a more precise look at how climate policy-making developed, who its most relevant actors were and what explanatory models currently exist. It is demonstrated that, even though at the federal and national levels, a couple of climate change plans were developed, they were neither strong enough, nor well enough implemented to reach the Kyoto Protocol target. The climate policy-making actors and procedures which were identified seem to have been very strongly influenced by federalism, a strong executive, shared jurisdiction and mixed authorities in regard to international treaty formulation and implementation. Existing research literature generally tries to explain the development and performance of Canada's climate policy on the basis of five factors: intergovernmental policy-making with the characteristics of federalism, Canada's economy, proximity to and integration with the US, Canada's geography and the lack of political will or leadership.

Canada's climate policy development

Canada first announced a concrete stabilization target at the Toronto conference on The Changing Atmosphere: Implications for Global Security in 1988 under the government of PM Mulroney (Progressive Conservative Party). The target set was to reach levels 20 per cent below those of 1988 by 2005. As a result of a task force established after the conference in 1988, at the 1990 UN conference in Bergen, the goal changed to a stabilization of GHGs at 1990 levels by 2000. This target became part of the federal government's Canada's Green Plan for a Healthy Environment in 1990. In the same year, federal, provincial and territorial governments released a National Strategy on Global Warming with the same target.

In 1992, Canada became the first industrialized country to sign and ratify the UNFCCC. In the same year, a first Joint Ministers Meeting (JMM) took place as a collaboration between the CCME and the Council of Energy Ministers (CEM) to elaborate the further planning of Canada's climate policy. In 1993, Jean Chrétien (Liberal Party) came into office as the new PM and, in 1995, Canada's National Action Programme on Climate Change was released as the first overall programme on climate policy by federal, provincial and territorial governments.

At the COP in Kyoto in 1997, Canada agreed to a reduction target of 6 per cent below 1990 levels between 2008–2012, even though the JMM had previously agreed on a target of stabilization. After Canada signed the Kyoto Protocol in 1998, the first ministers (PMs at federal, provincial and territorial levels) established an intensive National Climate Change Process (NCCP) to develop an implementation strategy which would look at whether and how to achieve the 6 per cent target. The National Climate Change Secretariat (NCCS) was also founded at this point, and, in close collaboration with the JMM, it helped to organize the process. Besides regular JMMs, a consultative process with 16 issue tables between 1998–2000 was initiated as a main constituent part of the NCCP. The issue tables included c. 450 governmental, non-governmental and business experts, whose job it was to evaluate the impacts, costs and benefits related to climate change in specific climate relevant policy fields. After the issue tables finalized their reports in 2000, national stakeholder sessions took place country-wide to discuss results and seek input on how to implement policies. The process resulted in Canada's National Implementation Strategy on Climate Change and Canada's First National Climate Change Business Plan. Additionally, the federal government released its *Government of Canada Action Plan 2000 on Climate Change* (Government of Canada, 2000).

In 2002, further stakeholder sessions took place and there was public involvement in the debate surrounding the federal government's *Discussion Paper on Canada's Contribution to Addressing Climate Change* (Government of Canada, 2002b). Due to disagreements between the federal government and some provinces (particularly Alberta), the NCCP came to an end in 2002, even though the NCCS continued to exist until 2004. In 2002, the NCCP also released the *National Climate Change Business Plan* (NCCP, 2002) and the federal government published its *Climate Change Plan for Canada* (Government of Canada, 2002a), based on its earlier discussion paper. In the same year, Canada ratified the Kyoto Protocol. Still governed by the Liberal Party, Paul Martin became the country's new PM in 2003. After the process between the federal, provincial and territorial levels ended, the federal government set up some bilateral agreements with the provinces between 2003 and 2005. In 2005, the federal government hosted the COP and released a plan called *Project Green: Moving Forward on Climate Change. A Plan for Honouring our Kyoto Commitment* (Government of Canada, 2005).

In 2006, the governing parties changed and, in 2007, the new Conservative Party government under PM Stephen Harper released *Turning the Corner: An Action Plan to Reduce Green House Gas Emissions and Air Pollution* (ECan, 2007b). This plan ignored the Kyoto target and had the goal of reducing 2006 levels

Table 5.1 Climate change plans and reduction targets

Year	International	Federal plan	Federal-provincial plan	Target	Base year emissions (Mt CO_2 eq.)	Projected emissions target (Mt CO_2 eq.)
1988	PM Mulroney sets target at the The Changing Atmosphere: Implications for Global Security conference			20% below 1988 levels by 2005	588	470 in 2005
1990	UN conference in Bergen	Canada's Green Plan for a Healthy Environment	National Strategy on Global Warming	to have stabilized at 1990 levels by 2000	590	590 in 2000
1993		Announcement by PM Chrétien		20% below 1988 levels by 2005	588	470 in 2005
1995			Canada's National Action Programme on Climate Change	66Mt below 1995 levels by 2010	640	574 in 2010
1997	COP 3 in Kyoto			6% below 1990 levels by 2012	590	555 in 2012
2000		Action Plan 2000		65Mt per year during the commitment period to reach the Kyoto COP target	590	555 in 2012
2000			Canada's National Implementation Strategy on Climate Change	no target, but part of Kyoto implementation		

(Continued)

Table 5.1 (Continued)

Year	International	Federal plan	Federal-provincial plan	Target	Base year emissions (Mt CO_2 eq.)	Projected emissions target (Mt CO_2 eq.)
2000			Canada's First National Climate Change Business Plan	no target, but part of Kyoto implementation		
2002		A Discussion Paper on Canada's Contribution to Addressing Climate Change		no target, but part of Kyoto implementation		
2002		Climate Change Plan for Canada		6% below 1990 levels by 2012	590	555 in 2012
2002			National Climate Change Business Plan 2002	"Canada's National Climate Change Business Plan 2002 is not a summary of the plan that may be required to achieve the Kyoto targets." (p. 2)		
2005		Project Green: Moving Forward on Climate Change		6% below 1990 levels by 2012	590	555 in 2012
2007		Turning the Corner		20% below 2006 levels by 2020	719	575 in 2020

2007	A climate change plan for the purposes of the Kyoto Protocol Implementation Act	6% below 1990 levels by 2012	590	555 in 2012
2008	A Climate Change Plan for the Purpose of the Kyoto Protocol Implementation Act	6% below 1990 levels by 2012	590	555 in 2012
2010	COP 15 in Copenhagen	17% below 2005 levels by 2020	731	607 in 2020
2010	A Climate Change Plan for the Purposes of the Kyoto Protocol Implementation Act	17% below 2005 levels by 2020 mentioned (even though the KPIA forced the government to meet the Kyoto target)	731	607 in 2020
2011	A Climate Change Plan for the Purposes of the Kyoto Protocol Implementation Act	17% below 2005 levels by 2020 (even though the KPIA forced the government to meet the Kyoto target)	731	607 in 2020
2012	A Climate Change Plan for the Purposes of the Kyoto Protocol Implementation Act	17% below 2005 levels by 2020 (even though the KPIA forced the government to meet the Kyoto target)	731	607 in 2020

Source: Based on climate change plans (CCME, 1990; ECan, 2007a, 2008, 2009, 2010, 2011, 2012; Government of Canada, 2000, 2002a, 2002b, 2003, 2005, 2006a, 2007a, 2007b, 2008; NCCP, 2000b, 2001, 2002) and NRTEE (2012, p. 29). Mt CO_2 eq. can vary slightly since calculations of the base year change.

of emissions by 20 per cent by 2020. In response, the opposition parties in the Canadian Parliament adopted the Kyoto Protocol Implementation Act (KPIA) in 2007, voting through the act against the votes of the governing minority party. This forced the Minister of the Environment to prepare yearly plans stating how to achieve the Kyoto target. As a result of the KPIA, the government released six climate change plans between 2007–2012. In 2011, Canada announced that it would withdraw from the Kyoto Protocol in 2012, indicating that it did not cover the largest global emitters (China and the US). As Canada's climate change plans had never included enough mitigation policies to meet the target, nor had these plans ever been fully implemented, Canada would have fallen far short of the 6 per cent target anyway.

Table 5.1 summarizes these developments by providing an overview of reduction targets and climate plans announced at international conferences or on the federal or federal-provincial level.

Competencies of actors in climate policy-making processes

Climate change affects a wide range of actors. However, the actors and the policy-making structures differ considerably. In Canada, competencies in the policy field of climate change are neither conclusively, nor clearly arranged; the constitution includes no reference to environmental matters. In 1997, the Supreme Court ruled that the environment was "as such, a subject matter of legislation under the Constitution Act, 1867". As it was put there, "the Constitution Act, 1867 has not assigned the matter of 'environment' sui generis to either the provinces or Parliament. . . . Rather, it is a diffuse subject that cuts across many different areas of constitutional responsibility, some federal, some provincial" (Glenn & Otero, 2012, p. 492; Hogg, 2009; Supreme Court, 1992, pp. 63–65; Valiante, 2009). Thus, the constitutionality of climate change is also a very complex subject of unclear definition. A final court decision on climate change does not exist. It is expected that it would assume that jurisdiction over climate change is shared (Chalifour, 2010). And, whether the federal level can act alone or if the provinces and territories have to be involved seems to depend on the concrete policy instruments used (Lucas & Yearsley, 2011). The reason for this lies in the shared jurisdictional authority: the federal government has the right to formulate and sign international treaties like the Kyoto Protocol, but provinces and territories own, for example, the natural resources within their realms. Shared authority and the need to coordinate intergovernmental politics without fixed procedures thus characterize the formulation and implementation of policies (Macdonald et al., 2013, p. 45). Since this case study concentrates on the Kyoto Protocol, the federal government and its two main climate policy responsibilities will form the focus of this investigation: to develop more or less democratic federal climate policy and, where necessary, to coordinate the national process with provinces and territories to develop national climate policy and to ensure its implementation.

The actor with the final say at the federal level is, of course, the PM, backed up by the PMO and the Privy Council. However, the PM was only partially able to influence critical and important situations in climate policy-making during the Kyoto Protocol negotiations in 1997 or the ratification in 2002. This behaviour changed significantly when Stephen Harper became PM in 2006 and showed leadership on the climate agenda (Macdonald, 2008). Although the broader influence of climate policies led to many departments becoming involved in climate policy-making during our time period (e.g. from finance, Indian and northern affairs through to industry), Environment Canada (ECan) and Natural Resources Canada (NRCan) had the lead on the issue, with different foci based on their responsibilities (Macdonald et al., 2013, pp. 46–47). Parliament seems to be weak when it comes to climate policy-making based on international treaty ratification. Due to its non-binding consultative role it is unable to change the treaty's content. Nevertheless, it has its role in the legislative process, where federal climate policies are made. Parliament can also be a player during minority governments, when it is occasionally able to pass acts in opposition to the governing party. Since the PM and the ruling Cabinet belong to the same party, parties themselves do appear to be indirectly involved in the climate policy process, yet, as actors per se, parties are not very influential (Inwood et al., 2011, p. 211). However, even though it seems that party difference is not that important (H. A. Smith, 2008, p. 47), the role of party membership cannot be ignored. Besides state institutions, there are also non-governmental actors (which will not be explained in detail here) from civil society based environmental non-governmental organizations (ENGOs) and, most importantly, from business organizations, especially in the oil and gas sector. At the provincial level, the structure of state institutions and other actors is very similar to that at the federal level, albeit with differences regarding the actors' levels of influence and whether they focus on more active or passive climate policy approaches (Macdonald et al., 2013, p. 47).

The procedures and structures which have evolved in Canadian climate policy-making are a combination of the specificity of the climate change problem and the aforementioned characteristics of Canada's political system: the authority to make international treaties lies in the hands of the federal government, while implementation cannot be carried out without the support of the provinces, especially as they own many of the resources required. Canadian federalism is also one of the most decentralized federal systems worldwide, either lacking or with very weak fixed rules and institutional arrangements for coordinating federal-provincial policy-making. Consultation mechanisms implemented to find answers in these structural circumstances often vary in quality and intensity, have no binding character and frustrate both federal and provincial governments (Morrissette, 2011, p. 593). As the following case study will show in more depth, Canada's involvement in the Kyoto Protocol seems to mirror at least some of these circumstances. Perhaps to some extent this is also a result of federal policy instruments, such as fiscal, regulatory or voluntary instruments, being limited, but provincial governments are aware of short-term costs related to climate policy, greatly differing reduction costs among the provinces and the possibility for both the federal and the provincial sides to pass the buck, etc. (see, e.g., Harrison, 1996; Macdonald, 2009; Macdonald et al., 2013; Samson, 2001).

Based on these characteristics of Canadian federalism and their implications for international treaty formulation and implementation, the most important structures in Canadian climate policy-making are the FMMs, the JMMs and their temporarily initiated bodies, such as the NCCS created for the NCCP, as well as diverse ad hoc and other informal meeting structures.

FMMs are composed of the PM and his counterparts at the provincial level. Even though climate change would probably have been an issue which required debating at a FFM, FMMs only very rarely talked about climate policy in this study's time period. More precisely, the FMMs only explicitly discussed climate policies once: in their meeting after the Kyoto Conference in 1997, arranged to discuss the 6 per cent target agreed upon in Kyoto. A second request was made in 2002 by the provincial and territorial PMs to discuss ratification, but this was rejected by then PM Jean Chrétien. Instead, from 1993 onwards, the JMMs formed an important part of national climate change related negotiations. JMMs are a collaboration of the CEM and the CCME, both composed of federal, provincial and territorial ministers. JMMs played an especially important role until 2002, but nonetheless have no binding character and it is possible for a government to opt out of adopting their conclusions (Bakvis, Brown, & Baier, 2009).

The system behind JMMs is quite elaborate: a National Air Issues Coordinating Committee – Climate Change (NAICC–CC) by assistant-deputy-ministers reported to the National Air Issues Steering Committee (NAISC) by deputy ministers report to the JMM (Macdonald et al., 2013, p. 48). The NCCP initiated in 1998 was organized around the JMM. The federal-provincial NCCP was bureaucratically backed up by the NCCS, which was co-directed by an official from the federal government and one official from a provincial government. Public hearings, consultations, etc. have a strong tradition in Canadian environmental policy-making. The first public hearings took place in 1984, then in 1986 the National Task Force on Environment and Economy (NTFEE) was established and conducted multi-stakeholder forums (Samson, 2001, p. 211). This tradition was reinvaded during climate policy-making, especially during the existence of the NCCP. However, the NCCP only existed between 1998–2002 in a very intense phase of climate policy-making in Canada and no equivalent body existed in the aftermath.

To sum up, Canada's climate policy-making actors and procedures seem to be very much influenced by federalism, strong executives, shared jurisdiction and mixed authority regarding international treaty formulation and implementation. Regarding the democracy-climate nexus it appears as if it is highly dependent on partially institutionalized (ad hoc) consultation and decision-making procedures.

Common explanatory models

Existing literature overwhelmingly characterizes Canada's environmental policy as possessed of a high level of vertical fragmentation in a decentralized policy field (Inwood et al., 2011, p. 178; Toner, 2002). Since where GHGs are emitted is irrelevant on a global scale, climate change seems to pose a major threat to such a fragmented system. More precisely, common explanatory models seem to focus on five factors when looking at the development and performance of Canada's climate policy: intergovernmental policy-making in federal systems, Canada's economy, the proximity to the US, Canada's geography and the lack of political will or leadership. Even though existing research assesses some aspects of democratic quality in the context of climate policy-making, this never takes the form of a comprehensive evaluation, nor does it attempt to analyse the influence of democratic quality on climate performance.

Most researchers identify intergovernmentalism in Canadian federalism as the dominant factor in climate policy-making (Macdonald et al., 2013, pp. 37–60). According to these explanations, Canadian federalism, with its constitutional restrictions in regard to climate performance, limits the possibility of it fulfilling its international commitments like the Kyoto Protocol, especially at the implementation stage (Harrison, 2010, p. 193; Weiburst, 2003, p. 288). Intergovernmentalism hinders the process of ensuring that the burden of reducing emissions is fairly shared among Canada's provinces (Dion, 2011, p. 23a). To function, it needs the broad participation of governments and stakeholders without being able to give them any guarantees of success (Samson, 2001). Not surprisingly, this system only worked with a number of informal elements until 2002 and subsequently, after 2003, it ceased to produce any climate policy results (Macdonald et al., 2013, pp. v–vi). The implementation of international treaties, like the Kyoto Protocol, is complicated in Canada, since their ratification has no direct legal effect and the authority to implement changes lies in the hands of the provincial administrations (Glenn & Otero, 2012, pp. 491–492) and is in need of strong federal leadership and coordination (Drexhage & Murphy, 2010, pp. 20–22).

The fact that the national economy is energy intensive and closely related to its counterpart in the US provides a second explanatory factor. According to this line of argumentation, the influence of the economy on climate performance can be explained by a historical dependence on low-cost fossil fuels to offset high energy costs and thus high rates of GHG emissions when producing and exporting raw materials (Halucha, 1998, p. 298). The primacy of economic development over climate protection is seen as an obvious consequence of the National Energy Programme 1980 (Glenn & Otero, 2012, pp. 493–494). The gas and, in particular, oil (sands) extraction industries are both very strong and growing, since they are supported by both the federal and many provincial governments as main drivers of economic growth (Eberlein & Doern, 2009, pp. 30–31; Huot, Fischer, & Lemphers, 2011; Levi, 2009). And, according to some authors, industry campaigning – for example, shortly before the ratification of the Kyoto Protocol – clearly indicated that the industry preferred a responsible approach in terms of not slowing down (short-term) economic growth (Macdonald, 2001; Toner, 2002).

A third aspect which helps to explain Canada's climate performance is the close connection between the US and Canada, especially in trade relations.

According to researchers, the closeness between these two states in regard to climate politics can be exemplified by their behaviour during the negotiations of the Kyoto Protocol, when Canada simply tried to stay within a 1 per cent range of the US regardless of what had been nationally agreed before the conference (H. Smith, 2008, p. 210). The reason for wanting to stay so close to the US can be seen in Canada's trade dependency, with the US being Canada's most important import and export partner and every change in terms of energy costs, etc. thus being a disadvantage to Canada's economy (Halucha, 1998, p. 298).

The fourth factor described by current literature is usually only very briefly mentioned at the beginning of books or articles – probably because it is such a constant factor – and is the combination of Canada's geography. Compared to other parts of the world with more densely concentrated populations, Canada's population is quite spread out, so meeting with someone in person involves travelling longer distances. Similarly, most of the country lives with cold winters, hot summers and a growing population. Moreover, the concentration of emissions varies considerably within the country, which is why reduction costs also vary and, so far, no solution has been found to resolve this problem. According to researchers who stress that geography plays a major role, geography as a factor does help to explain Canada's climate performance, but does not excuse or justify it (Dion, 2011, p. 42a).

The fifth factor in the list of explanations is a bit vague in its contours, but is mentioned frequently in research. According to the literature, there was a lack of political will and leadership in Canada. Inside the country's federal executive, provinces and territories no individual, nor government, took a strong leadership role or supported the climate agenda with the necessary (financial) resources and political will, especially when it came to implementation and the fight over whether commitments and investments would be honoured following subsequent elections (Macdonald, 2009; Stilborn, 2003, p. 12).

Common explanatory models often combine certain factors to describe Canada's climate policy. Whether democratic quality has an effect on climate performance or the characteristics of climate change affect democratic quality is unclear. When it comes to climate policy-making in Canada various articles can be found, yet these are often not formulated in relation to democratic quality and very few tendencies emerge on the interplay between climate performance and democratic quality. The first tendency which can be found is the view that Canadian international treaty-making in relation to the Kyoto Protocol (both the formulation of the target in 1997 and its ratification in 2002) was characterized by a lack of democratic quality, since neither the provinces, nor Parliament were able to influence federal executive decision-making (Harrington, 2005, pp. 468–469). Another aspect seems to be that the reporting of information to the public and Parliament was often incomplete and, overall, very much piecemeal (Bjorn et al., 2002, pp. 54–55). Moreover, while climate change plans were often designed to engage with citizens, in the end, polls on support of climate policies returned mixed results (Stilborn, 2003, pp. 14–15).

Existing analysis is far from providing a clear picture of the democracy-climate nexus and related mechanisms. It seems as if there are a couple of problematic democratic areas in regard to climate policy-making, but these are only tendencies and require further research.

Climate policy before COP 1: a brief background of Canada as a first mover

The time frame before negotiations leading to Kyoto, and thus the time frame before the period investigated in regard to the democracy-climate nexus started, is the phase in which the very first climate policies were made.

As already explained Canada acted as a first mover during this initial phase, hosting climate change conferences in 1984, 1988 and 1990. Most prominently, it hosted the 1988 conference The Changing Atmosphere: Implications for Global Security, with more than 300 scientists and policy-makers from 46 countries and organizations (Bramley, 2000). At the conference, PM Mulroney (Progressive Conservative Party) agreed to a target which foresaw a 20 per cent reduction below 1988 levels by 2000. However, the goal changed at a UN conference in Bergen in 1990, where a task force was established, which suggested stabilizing GHG emissions at 1990 levels by 2000. This target later became the goal of the federal government's Green Plan for a Healthy Environment, which focused primarily on information provision, voluntary action and, in 1990, a National Strategy on Global Warming at the federal-provincial level. Consequently, PM Mulroney and Canadian experts were acknowledged as early leaders on the issue (H. A. Smith, 2008, p. 48). As a result of the conference in 1988 and its recognition as a leader in climate change policy, Canada had a broad basis from which to deal with the issue. In some of their meetings, different stakeholders were involved in the formulation of policies and negotiations, like Members of Parliament (MPs) who attended the second World Climate Conference in 1990.

A further formalization of climate policy-making took place after 1990. A JMM between the CCME and the CEM took place in light of the signing and ratification of the UNFCCC in 1992 and looked to design further steps within Canada's climate policy-making, aimed at achieving a stabilization of GHG emissions at 1990 levels by 2000. As a result of these meetings, the deputy ministers of Natural Resources and ECan established a NAISC and National Air Issues Coordinating Committee (NAICC).

Evidence of involvement in these early years are however rare. In a strategic overview, the CCME announced that in addition to the JMM it had formed, a multi-stakeholder group to help facilitate the preparation of Canada's negotiating position (CCME, 1992, p. 8). However, no other information can be found on this multi-stakeholder group, neither about its meetings nor its composition, which probably means that its influence was limited and/or very informal. Nevertheless, PM Mulroney stood for very active environmental policy-making and, in 2006, he was proclaimed the "greenest prime minister in Canadian history" (*Corporate Knights Magazine*, 2005, p. 28).

In 1993, Jean Chrétien (Liberal Party) became Canada's new PM and he committed himself to a reduction target of 20 per cent of 1988 emissions levels by 2005 during the election campaign. However, a meeting of federal and provincial energy and environment ministers on 17 November 1993 only looked to develop options for stabilizing emissions by 2000 and for further reductions by 2005 (Bramley, 2000; Macdonald, 2010). In early 1994, a JMM again charged a multi-stakeholder group, this time the Measures Group for the Climate Change Task Group of the NAICC, with the development of a national climate programme (Bramley, 2000). This group put forward 88 measures in their final report, *Measures for Canada's National Action Program on Climate Change*, but the selection procedure for determining the chosen stakeholders does not appear to have been documented, nor indeed does there appear to be any other information on the group's make-up. The 88 measures were used for an assessment made by the Climate Change Task Group in 1995, which concluded that it was unlikely that the proposed initiatives would be strong enough to reduce emissions in a substantive way (Bramley, 2000). In the aftermath, there was conflict between Environment Minister Copps, who was in favour of regulations, and Natural Resources Minister McLellan, who was in favour of voluntary action (Macdonald, 2010). McLellan overwhelmingly won the battle with the *Voluntary Challenge and Registry* document forming a central part of the subsequent programme. A programme which, at the end of the day, only marginally reduced Canada's GHG emissions (Simpson, Jaccard, & Rivers, 2008, p. 59). As a result of these developments, federal, provincial and territorial governments released Canada's *National Action Programme on Climate Change* (NAPCC) in 1995 (Government of Canada, 2004). However, the whole process between 1993–1995 can be characterized as a relatively informal consultation process (Bjorn et al., 2002, p. 111). According to a report by the Commissioner of the Environment and Sustainable Development (CESD), the NAPCC was implemented inadequately in the following years since "there is no clear assignment of roles and responsibilities, no national communication programme, no implementation plan, limited provision for regular, results-based monitoring of progress and no consolidated summary-level reporting to Parliament" (CESD, 1998). Since the report also concludes that "the strategic direction of the NAPCC needs to be substantially rethought", the policy process of the Kyoto Protocol built an almost completely new policy process, which had to be adopted due to the ineffectiveness of the old one (CESD, 1998).

So, where did Canada stand at the beginning of the formulation of the Kyoto Protocol in 1995? Canada behaved as a first mover and leader on the climate file, hosted conferences and gained an international reputation. However, the programmes designed to reduce emissions seemed, as the CESD states, to be inadequate. Moreover, the role of democratic quality is not foreseeable since information on aspects such as the composition of the multi-stakeholder groups involved is very cursory, which could also be seen as an indication of their influence, which, as already stated, was either informal or unimportant. Nevertheless, climate scientist John Stone characterized the early years of climate policy-making in Canada as a committed and open period, indeed, as "a golden age" compared to more recent developments (Stone, 2014).

References

The access date of all material retrieved from the Web is 5 June 2015 unless otherwise specified.

Atkinson, M. M., Marchildon, G. P., Phillips, P. W. B., Rasmussen, K. A., Béland, D., & McNutt, K. (2013). *Governance and Public Policy in Canada: A View from the Provinces.* North York, Ontario: University of Toronto Press.

Ayres, J. (2006). Civil society participation in Canadian foreign policy: expanded consultation in the Chrétien years. In P. James & M. O'Reilly (Eds.), *Handbook on Canadian Foreign Policy* (pp. 491–512). Lanham, MD: Lexington Books.

Bakvis, H., Brown, D. M., & Baier, G. (2009). *Contested Federalism: Certainty and Ambiguity in the Canadian Federation.* Don Mills, Ontario: Oxford University Press.

Bakvis, H., & Skogstad, G. (2008). Introduction: Canadian federalism. In H. Bakvis & G. Skogstad (Eds.), *Canadian Federalism: Performance, Effectiveness, and Legitimacy* (pp. 2–20). Toronto: Oxford University Press.

Banting, K., & Kymlicka, W. (2010). Canadian multiculturalism: global anxieties and local debates. *British Journal of Canadian Studies, 23*(1), 43–72.

Barnes, A. (2012). The legislative process: from policy to proclamation. Retrieved from www.parl.gc.ca/Content/LOP/ResearchPublications/prb0864-e.htm (accessed 17 February 2017).

Beauchesne, A. (1958 [1922]). *Rules and Forms of the House of Commons of Canada, with Annotations, Comments and Precedents; A Compendium of Canadian Parliamentary Practice, Prepared for the Use of Members of Parliament* (4th ed.). Toronto: Carswell.

Benz, A. (2003). Föderalismus und Demokratie. Eine Untersuchung zum Zusammenwirken zweier Verfassungsprinzipien. *Polis* (57), 1–33.

Biela, J., Kaiser, A., & Hennl, A. (2013). *Policy Making in Multilevel Systems: Federalism, Decentralisation, and Performance.* Colchester: ECPR Press.

Bjorn, A., Duminuco, S., Etcheverry, J., Gore, C., Harvey, D., Lee, I., MacDonald, D., MacIntyre, K., Riddle, R., Scott, D., Soltay, T., Stewart, K., Zupancic, T. (2002). *Ratification of the Kyoto Protocol: A Citizen's Guide to the Canadian Climate Change Policy Process.* Toronto: Sustainable Toronto.

Bramley, M. (2000). *A Climate Change Resource Book for Journalists.* Retrieved from www.pembina.org/reports/CCRB-e.pdf (accessed 17 February 2017).

Braun, D. (2000). Territorial division of power and public policy-making: an assessment. In D. Braun (Ed.), *Public Policy and Federalism* (pp. 27–56). Aldershot: Ashgate.

Brown, D. (2006). Still in the game: efforts to tame economic development competition in Canada. In K. Harrison (Ed.), *Racing to the Bottom? Interjurisdictional Competition in Canada* (pp. 49–72). Vancouver: UBC Press.

Brühl-Moser, D. (2012). Der Föderalismus Kanadas: interstaatlich, exekutiv und asymmetrisch. In I. Härtel (Ed.), *Handbuch Föderalismus–Föderalismus als demokratische Rechtsordnung und Rechtskultur in Deutschland, Europa und der Welt.* (pp. 627–669). Berlin/Heidelberg: Springer.

CCME. (1990). *National Action Strategy on Global Warming.* Winnipeg, Manitoba: CCME.

CCME. (1992). *Strategic Overview.* Winnipeg, Manitoba: CCME.

CESD. (1998). *Report of the Commissioner of the Environment and Sustainable Development. Chapter 3*. Retrieved from www.oag-bvg.gc.ca/internet/English/parl_cesd_199805_03_e_9343.html

Chalifour, N. (2010). The constitutional authority to levy carbon taxes. In T. Courchene & J. R. Allan (Eds.), *The State of the Federation 2009. Carbon Pricing and Environmental Federalism* (pp. 177–195). Montreal/Kingston: McGill-Queen's University Press.

Corporate Knights Magazine (2005). Greenest PM in Canadian history. *Corporate Knights Magazine*, 4(1): 28.

Dion, S. (2011). The fight against climate change: why is Canada doing so little? *The Tocqueville Review/La Revue Tocqueville*, XXXII(2), 21a–46a.

Doern, G. B., & Aucoin, P. (1971). Conclusions and observations. In G. P. Doern & P. Aucoin (Eds.), *The Structures of Policy-making in Canada* (pp. 267–279). Toronto: Macmillan of Canada.

Drexhage, J., & Murphy, D. (2010). *Climate Change and Foreign Policy in Canada: Intersection and Influence*. Canadian International Council. Retrieved from http://indiaenvironmentportal.org.in/files/IISD_ClimateChangeForeignPolicy_Drexhage_Murphy.pdf (accessed 17 February 2017).

Eberlein, B., & Doern, G. B. (2009). German and Canadian multi-level energy regulatory governance: introduction, context, and analytical framework. In B. Eberlein & G. B. Doern (Eds.), *Governing the Energy Challenge* (pp. 3–37). Toronto: Toronto University Press.

ECan. (2007a). A climate change plan for the purposes of the Kyoto Protocol Implementation Act 2007. Retrieved from www.parl.gc.ca/Content/HOC/Committee/391/ENVI/WebDoc/WD3067248/391_ENVI_Rel%20Doc_PDF/A%20Climate%20Change%20Plan-e.pdf (accessed 17 February 2017).

ECan. (2007b). *Turning the Corner. An Action Plan to Reduce Greenhouse Gas Emissions and Air Pollution*. Ottawa: Environment Canada.

ECan. (2008). A climate change plan for the purposes of the Kyoto Protocol Implementation Act 2008. Retrieved from www.ec.gc.ca/doc/ed-es/p_124/CC-Plan-2008_eng.pdf (accessed 17 February 2017).

ECan. (2009). A climate change plan for the purposes of the Kyoto Protocol Implementation Act 2009. Retrieved from http://publications.gc.ca/collections/collection_2010/ec/En56-183-2009-eng.pdf (accessed 17 February 2017).

ECan. (2010). A climate change plan for the purposes of the Kyoto Protocol Implementation Act 2010. Retrieved from http://publications.gc.ca/collections/collection_2010/ec/En56-183-2010-eng.pdf (accessed 17 February 2017).

ECan. (2011). A climate change plan for the purposes of the Kyoto Protocol Implementation Act 2011. Retrieved from http://publications.gc.ca/collections/collection_2011/ec/En11-11-2011-eng.pdf (accessed 17 February 2017).

ECan. (2012). A climate change plan for the purposes of the Kyoto Protocol Implementation Act 2012. Retrieved from www.ec.gc.ca/Publications/98673EA5-AD03-4D6A-93B4-1CDF2088BF43/KPIA-Plan-2012—April-25-_E_02.pdf (accessed 17 Februry 2017).

ECan. (2013). *National Inventory Report 1990–2011: Greenhouse Gas Sources and Sinks in Canada. Part 1*. Retrieved from http://unfccc.int/national_reports/annex_i_ghg_inventories/national_inventories_submissions/items/7383.php

Forsey, E. A. (2016). *How Canadians Govern Themselves*. Retrieved from www.lop.parl.gc.ca/About/Parliament/senatoreugeneforsey/book/assets/pdf/How_Canadians_Govern_Themselves9.pdf (accessed 17 February 2017).

Gecelovsky, P. (2011). Of lightning bolts and legacies revisited: another look at the prime minister and Canadian foreign policy. In C. Kukucha & D. Bratt (Eds.), *Readings in*

Canadian Foreign Policy: Classic Debates and New Ideas (pp. 217–227). Toronto: Oxford University Press.

Glenn, J.M., & Otero, J. (2012). Canada and the Kyoto Protocol: an Aesop fable. In E.J. Hollo, K. Kulovesi, & M. Mehling (Eds.), *Climate Change and the Law* (pp. 489–507). Dordrecht: Springer.

Government of Canada. (2000). *Government of Canada Action Plan 2000 on Climate Change*. Retrieved from http://publications.gc.ca/collections/Collection/M22-135-2000E.pdf (accessed 17 February 2017).

Government of Canada. (2002a). *Climate Change Plan for Canada*. Retrieved from http://manitobawildlands.org/pdfs/CCPlanforCAN27Nov02.pdf (accessed 17 February 2017).

Government of Canada. (2002b). *A Discussion Paper on Canada's Contribution to Addressing Climate Change*. Retrieved from http://publications.gc.ca/collections/Collection/En4-4-2002E.pdf (accessed 17 February 2017).

Government of Canada. (2003). *Climate Change: The Federal Investment 1997–2002. Comprehensive Report*. Retrieved from http://publications.gc.ca/collections/Collection/M174-3-2002E.pdf (accessed 17 February 2017).

Government of Canada. (2004). *Historical Information*. Retrieved from http://web.archive.org/web/20050412021402/http://www.climatechange.gc.ca/english/canada/goc_historical.asp.

Government of Canada. (2005). *Project Green. Moving Forward on Climate Change. A Plan for Honouring Our Kyoto Commitment*. Retrieved from http://publications.gc.ca/collections/Collection/En84-15-2005E.pdf (accessed 17 February 2017).

Government of Canada. (2006a). *Canada's Clean Air Act*. Retrieved from http://publications.gc.ca/collections/Collection/En84-46-2006E.pdf (accessed 17 February 2017).

Government of Canada. (2007a). *Ecoaction. Action on Climate Change and Air Pollution*. Retrieved from www.ec.gc.ca/doc/media/m_124/brochure/brochure_eng.pdf (accessed 17 February 2017).

Government of Canada. (2007b). *Regulatory Framework for Air Emissions*. Retrieved from https://www.ec.gc.ca/doc/media/m_124/report_eng.pdf (accessed 17 February 2017).

Halucha, P. (1998). Climate change politics and the pursuit of national interests. In F.O. Hampson, & M.A. Molot (Eds.), *Canada among Nations 1998. Leadership and Dialogue* (pp. 285–304). Toronto/Oxford/New York: Oxford University Press.

Harrington, J. (2005). Redressing the democratic deficit in treaty law making: (re-)establishing a role for parliament. *McGill LJ, 50*, 465–509.

Harrison, K. (1996). *Passing the Buck: Federalism and Canadian Environmental Policy*. Vancouver, BC: UBC Press.

Harrison, K. (2010). The struggle of ideas and self-interest in Canadian climate policy. In K. Harrison, & L.M. Sundstrom (Eds.), *Global Commons, Domestic Decisions: The Comparative Politics of Climate Change* (pp. 169–200). Cambridge, MA/London: MIT Press.

Harrison, K. (2012). Multilevel governance and American influence on Canadian climate policy: the California effect vs. the Washington effect. *Zeitschrift für Kanada-Studien, 32*(2), 45–64.

Hogg, P.W. (2009). Constitutional authority over greenhouse gas emissions. *Alberta Law Review, 46*(2), 507–520.

Howlett, M. (2013). *Canadian Public Policy: Selected Studies in Process and Style*. Toronto/Buffalo, NY/London: University of Toronto Press.

Howlett, M., Netherton, A., & Ramesh, M. (1999). *The Political Economy of Canada: An Introduction* (2nd. ed.). Don Mills, Ontario: Oxford University Press.

Huot, M., Fischer, L., & Lemphers, N. (2011). *Oilsands and Climate Change. How Canada's Oilsands are Standing in the Way of Effective Climate Action.* Retrieved from https://www.pembina.org/reports/us-oilsands-and-climate-briefing-note-201109b.pdf

IMF. (2014). *World Economic Outlook Database.* Retrieved from www.imf.org/external/pubs/ft/weo/2014/01/weodata/index.aspx

Inwood, G. J., O'Reilly, P. L., & Johns, C. M. (2011). *Intergovernmental Policy Capacity in Canada: Inside the Worlds of Finance, Environment, Trade, and Health.* Montreal: McGill-Queen's University Press.

James, P., & Kasoff, M. J. (2008). *Canadian Studies in the New Millennium.* Toronto/Buffalo, NY: University of Toronto Press.

Keman, H. (2000). Federalism and policy performance: a conceptual and empirical inquiry. In U. Wachendorfer-Schmidt (Ed.), *Federalism and Political Performance* (pp. 196–227). London: Routledge.

Levi, M. A. (2009). *The Canadian Oil Sands. Energy Security vs. Climate Change.* Retrieved from www.cfr.org/content/ . . . /Oil_Sands_CSR47.pdf

Lipset, S. M. (1990). *Continental Divide: The Values and Institutions of the United States and Canada.* New York: Routledge.

Lucas, A., & Yearsley, J. (2011). The constitutionality of federal climate change legislation. *SPP Research Paper, 4*(15), 1–38.

Macdonald, D. (2001). The business campaign to prevent Kyoto ratification. Paper presented at the Annual Meeting of the Canadian Political Science Association. Retrieved from ftp://host-209-183-10-27.static.dsl.primus.ca/cpsa-acsp/paper-2003/macdonald.pdf

Macdonald, D. (2008). Climate-change policy making by the Stephen Harper Government: a case study of the relationship between public opinion and environmental policy. Paper presented at the Annual Meeting of the Canadian Political Science Association, Vancouver.

Macdonald, D. (2009). The failure of Canadian climate change policy: veto power, absent leadership and institutional weakness. In D. L. Vannijnatten, & R. Boardman (Eds.), *Canadian Environmental Policy: Prospects for Leadership and Innovation* (pp. 152–166). Toronto: Oxford University Press.

Macdonald, D. (2010). Federal CC action consolidated chronology, May 2010. Unpublished paper.

Macdonald, D., Gordon, D., Bidordinova, A., Monstadt, J., Scheiner, S., Kern, K., Pristupa, A., Hayden, A. (2013). Allocating Canadian greenhouse gas emission reductions amongst sources and provinces: learning from Germany and the EU. Retrieved from www.environment.utoronto.ca/AllocatingGHGReductions2013/docs/AllocatingGHGReductions2013.pdf

Marleau, R., & Montpetit, C. (2005). *House of Commons Procedures and Practice. 1. Parliamentary Institutions.* Retrieved from www.parl.gc.ca/marleaumontpetit/DocumentViewer.aspx?DocId=1001&Sec=Ch01&Seq=3&Language=E (accessed 17 February 2017).

Measures Working Group for the Climate Change Task Group of the National Air Issues Coordinating Committee (1994). *Measures for Canada's National Action Program on Climate Change, Final Report,* June.

Morrissette, F. (2011). Provincial involvement in international treaty making: the European Union as a possible model. *Queen's LJ, 37*(2), 577–616.

Natural Resources Canada. Efficiency and Alternative Energy Branch (1996). *Canada's Climate Change: Voluntary Challenge and Registry (VCR),* November, 1995 Progress Report.

NCCP. (2000b). *Canada's National Implementation Strategy on Climate Change*. Retrieved from https://web.archive.org/web/20030610062703/http://nccp.ca/NCCP/pdf/media/JMM-fed-en.pdf (accessed 1 March 2017).

NCCP. (2001). *Progress Report*. Retrieved from https://web.archive.org/web/20051026104315/http://www.nccp.ca/NCCP/pdf/11574_ClimateReportV2.pdf (accessed 1 March 2017).

NCCP. (2002). *Canada's National Climate Change Business Plan 2002*. Retrieved from www.ibrarian.net/navon/paper/Canada_s_National_Climate_Change.pdf?paperid=410984. (accessed 17 February 2017).

Painter, M. (1991). Intergovernmental relations in Canada – an institutional analysis. *Canadian Journal of Political Science – Revue Canadienne de Science Politique*, 24(2), 269–288.

Papillon, M., & Simeon, R. (2004). The weakest link? First minister conferences in Canadian intergovernmental relations. In J. P. Meekison (Ed.), *The State of the Federation 2002* (pp. 113–140). Montreal/Kingston: McGill-Queen's University Press.

PCO. (1998). Decision-making processes and central agencies in Canada: federal, provincial and territorial practices – Canada. Retrieved from www.pco-bcp.gc.ca/index.asp?lang=eng&page=information&sub=publications&doc=aarchives/decision/canada-eng.htm

PCO. (n.d.). The structure of the federal government. Retrieved from www.pco-bcp.gc.ca/docs/images/pub_decision_9-e.gif

Rabe, B. G. (2007). Beyond Kyoto: climate change policy in multilevel governance systems. *Governance – An International Journal of Policy Administration and Institutions*, 20(3), 423–444.

Reputation-Institute. (2014). *Country RepTrak Report*. Retrieved from www.reputationinstitute.com/thought-leadership/country-reptrak

Samson, P. R. (2001). Canadian circumstances: the evolution of Canada's climate change policy. *Energy & Environment*, 12(2), 199–215.

Schacter, M., & Haid, P. (1999). *Cabinet Decision-making in Canada: Lessons and Practices*. Retrieved from http://iog.ca/wp-content/uploads/2012/12/1999_April_cabinet2.pdf

Schwanen, D. (2006). Canada and the Kyoto Protocol: when reality sets in. In A. F. Cooper & D. Rowlands (Eds.), *Canada Among Nations 2006* (pp. 292–318). Montreal/Kingston: McGill-Queen's University Press.

Simeon, R. (1972). *Federal-provincial Diplomacy; The Making of Recent Policy in Canada*. Toronto/ Buffalo, NY: University of Toronto Press.

Simeon, R. (2006). *Federal-provincial Diplomacy: The Making of Recent Policy in Canada* (with a new preface and postscript). Toronto: University of Toronto Press.

Simeon, R., & Cameron, D. (2002). Intergovernmental relations and democracy: an oxymoron if there ever was one. In H. Bakvis & G. Skogstad (Eds.), *Canadian Federalism: Performance, Effectiveness, and Legitimacy* (pp. 278–295). Toronto: Oxford University Press.

Simeon, R., & Nugent, A. (2008). Parliamentary Canada and intergovernmental Canada: exploring the tensions. In H. Bakvis & G. Skogstad (Eds.), *Canadian Federalism: Performance, Effectiveness, and Legitimacy* (pp. 89–111). Toronto: Oxford University Press.

Simpson, J. (2001). *The Friendly Dictatorship*. Toronto: McClelland & Stewart.

Simpson, J., Jaccard, M. K., & Rivers, N. (2008). *Hot Air: Meeting Canada's Climate Change Challenge*. Toronto: Emblem/McClelland & Stewart.

Smith, H. (2008). Canada and Kyoto: independence or indifference. In B. Bow & P. Lennox (Eds.), *An Independent Foreign Policy for Canada* (pp. 207–221). Toronto: University of Toronto Press.

Smith, H. A. (2008). Political parties and Canadian climate change policy. *International Journal, 64*(1), 47–66.

Smith, J., & Mount Allison University. Centre for Canadian Studies. (2004). *Federalism.* Vancouver: UBC Press.

Stilborn, J. (2003). Canadian intergovernmental relations and the Kyoto Protocol: what happened, what didn't. Canadian Political Science Association Conference. Retrieved from www.cpsa-acsp.ca/paper-2003/stilborn.pdf

Stone, J. (2014) Interview on Canada's Kyoto Protocol Process/Interviewer: F. Hanusch.

Supreme Court (1992). *Friends of the Oldman River Society v. Canada (Minister of Transport)*, [1992] 1 S.C.R. 3. Retrieved from https://scc-csc.lexum.com/scc-csc/scc-csc/en/829/1/document.do (accessed 2 February 2017).

Thunert, M. (2003). Akteure, Kräfteverhältnisse und Einflussgrößen im außenpolitischen Entscheidungsprozess Kanadas. In W. V. Bredow (Ed.), *Die Außenpolitik Kanadas* (pp. 53–81). Wiesbaden: Westdeutscher Verlag.

Tomlin, B. W., Hillmer, N., & Hampson, F. O. (2008). *Canada's International Policies: Agendas, Alternatives, and Politics.* Don Mills, Ontario/New York: Oxford University Press.

Toner, G. (2002). Contesting the green: Canadian environmental policy at the turn of the century. In U. Desai (Ed.), *Environmental Politics and Policy in Industrialized Countries* (pp. 71–120). Cambridge, MA: MIT Press.

Valiante, M. (2009). The courts and environmental policy leadership. In D. L. VanNijnatten & R. Boardman (Eds.), *Canadian Environmental Policy and Politics: Prospects for Leadership and Innovation* (pp. 30–45). Don Mills, Ontario: Oxford University Press.

Watts, R. (1999). *Comparing Federal Systems* (2nd ed.). Montreal/Ithaca, NY: McGill-Queen's University Press.

Watts, R. (2002). The distribution of powers, responsibilities and resources in federations. In A. L. Griffiths (Ed.), *The Handbook of Federal Countries, 2002* (pp. 448–471). Montreal/Kingston: McGill-Queen's University Press.

Weiburst, I. (2003). Implementing the Kyoto Protocol: will Canada make it? In D. Carment, F. O. Hampson, & N. Hilmer (Eds.), *Canada Among Nations* (pp. 287–311). Don Mills, Ontario: Oxford University Press.

White, R. R. (2010). *Climate Change in Canada.* Toronto/New York: Oxford University Press.

Wiseman, N. (2007). *In Search of Canadian Political Culture.* Vancouver: UBC Press.

6 1995–1997

Chrétien makes use of the prerogative

The mistake that perhaps was made that this wasn't an issue of general public knowledge or general public discourse. And that, of course, is what we should have started engaging much earlier than what happened.

(*Confidential1, 2014*)

Canada found itself in a good position when negotiations leading to the Kyoto Protocol started with COP 1 in 1995. In the 1980s, Canada had positioned itself as a first mover and developed the first national climate change policies. Yet, national negotiations between the federal government and the provinces and territories became much more intense when a decision on a potential target for COP 3 had to be found. The governments agreed upon a target, but during negotiations at Kyoto the federal government decided to change its position to a much more ambitious target than previously negotiated at the national level, leading to domestic controversy in the aftermath.

Between 1995–1997, developments were not focused on making substantial and far-reaching policies, but on very few events, especially the Kyoto Protocol target. They took place at national and international levels and were, originally, somewhat cursory, resulting in the first trends on the democracy-climate nexus as opposed to the more substantial findings which can be found in the subsequent time frames. However, these trends are necessary first observations for more fundamental insights into later developments.

In light of this, what mechanisms link democratic quality and climate performance? The results indicate that non-existent and/or poorly developed democratic quality and a lack of interplay have either a negative or no influence upon climate performance, with the consequence that climate performance depends on other circumstances which stem from democratic embeddedness. Of special importance in this regard were accountability, the indirect influence of inclusiveness and participation on effectiveness, efficiency and a transmission belt between the national and international spheres.

DOI: 10.4324/9781315228983-8

Accountability: basic vertical but almost no horizontal accountability (national)

Clear lines of accountability are essential to ensure the control of decision-makers. Basic accountability structures can be found in a hierarchy which was established at the beginning of the 1990s to deal with climate change (CESD, 1998). It had the structure shown in Figure 6.1, dominated by federal and provincial executives.

Between 1995–1997, the whole process was centred on the JMMs making the most important decisions and, consequently, provincial and federal governments had an influential role. JMMs took place periodically, usually once or twice a year. The NAICC-CC, as the other important committee established in June 1997, should have served as the main institution of federal coordination, but had no documented terms of reference (CESD, 1998). The NAICC-CC was a body that engaged and consulted with stakeholders, but was primarily a federal-provincial committee (Confidential1, 2014). In principle, lines of accountability existed and it is clear that the final decision-making took place in the FMMs, while the JMMs were most important for climate policy development. Thus, vertical accountability, in terms of the possibility of tracing back the results of decision-making, existed in principle, yet there doesn't appear to have been any horizontal accountability and control over decision-makers other than in the course of elections. At least no evidence can be found which shows any other equivalent forms of horizontal accountability, as neither transparent terms of reference existed, nor did actors outside the government have the possibility of obtaining institutionalized views from within the decision-making process. Which brings us to the question of which actors were informally involved.

Inclusiveness: incomplete and biased by enlightened officials (national)

Inclusiveness is democratically guaranteed by openness and fairness of access so that a plurality of relevant and affected actors is involved. However, there was

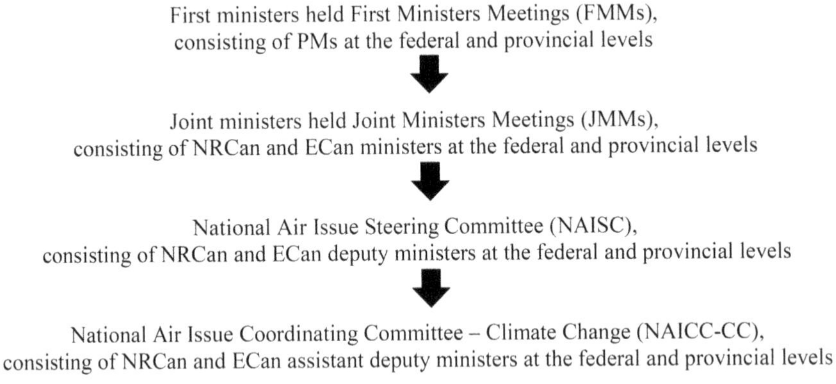

First ministers held First Ministers Meetings (FMMs),
consisting of PMs at the federal and provincial levels

Joint ministers held Joint Ministers Meetings (JMMs),
consisting of NRCan and ECan ministers at the federal and provincial levels

National Air Issue Steering Committee (NAISC),
consisting of NRCan and ECan deputy ministers at the federal and provincial levels

National Air Issue Coordinating Committee – Climate Change (NAICC-CC),
consisting of NRCan and ECan assistant deputy ministers at the federal and provincial levels

Figure 6.1 Accountability structures

only very limited consideration of including actors from outside the executive. Even though the federal government included the provinces and territories in the decision-making process, the involvement of other groups was "much more informal", without "any formal process or structure for determining what those were" (Cleland, 2014) and limited to an "informed climate policy public" (Confidential1, 2014). Moreover, these processes either did not reach out to or failed to attract the attention of high-ranking decision-makers (Cleland, 2014). Thus, "the mistake that perhaps was made was that this wasn't an issue of general public knowledge or general public discourse" since implementation relies on the "Canadian citizenry as a whole" (Confidential1, 2014). During this early phase of the Kyoto Protocol process the approach "was in need of having a more formal and systematic way of engaging stakeholders" (Confidential3, 2014).

However, it seems that the government believed it was pretty well informed and knew where everybody stood, what groups had to be involved and that the really relevant groups were actually involved. Even though its setup was never formalized, the government organized a working group shortly before COP 3 which included industry, business and environmental organizations (Heinbecker, 2014). Paul Heinbecker, head of the Canadian delegation at COP 3 and consequently involved in domestic preparations, felt that the government "had a pretty good picture of where everybody stood", even though he did not "meet with anybody actually" as he was represented by members of his staff at meetings (Heinbecker, 2014).

These circumstances seem to show an understanding of officials as *enlightened officials* who seemed to believe that they knew what people would have said had they been asked and who subsequently only invited the participation of those actors whom they thought were the most important ones. Whether or not officials actually informally selected the most relevant groups without any systematic approach, the level of inclusiveness can nonetheless be characterized as incomplete and problematic. Access to the decision-making process was neither open nor fair and it did not guarantee the involvement, and thus the possible influence, of a broader public or a plurality of actors, especially not those from weak or marginalized sectors of society. The lack of accountability and the influence of inclusiveness on climate performance cannot be estimated, however, it seems to have been overwhelmingly dependent on the executive and its preferences. So, participation was limited, but, in what ways did those who could participate influence the process?

Participation: rule of the executive (national)

Participatory structures should enable democratically involved actors to influence decision-making by leaving room for considered judgement and responsive results. In the case of the formulation of the Canadian Kyoto target, it seems that where clear rules for inclusiveness were missing, domestic participatory structures were unlikely to exist. An aspect that can be evaluated in such an informal setting is the influence of different actors through informal participation. When looking at the different actors involved, industry, especially the oil industry, and the provinces were clearly very influential. In some cases, we can also speak of a merger of these actors, since "provinces like Alberta saw it [the Kyoto Protocol target] as a threat to the oil and gas industry" (Confidential1, 2014; Stone, 2014 (quotation)).

"[T]he principle mechanism was the federal-provincial one", which dominated, especially in the form of the JMM as an executive-based sort of participatory structure (Slater, 2014). The federal government tried to play a more active role "in pushing action", while "[t]here was no provincial interest in doing anything" (Slater, 2014). Such informal participation seems to have encouraged ENGOs to become effective, yet they themselves "were more interested in making sure that they were right than [that] they were being effective" (Confidential1, 2014). The Parliament, as another relevant actor in terms of democratic quality, didn't have that much influence in general, but the Committee on Environment and Sustainable Development served as "a good forum for exchanging views on different aspects" (Confidential1, 2014). The Parliament "was part of this gigantic synthesis that would take place, but they didn't and don't have the authority to say no" (Heinbecker, 2014). Thus, even though the Canadian Parliament probably did not play a very influential role, it seems to have been the place where information and arguments were debated and transmitted into party politics. The question could be raised as to whether the Parliament was adequately informed and equipped to influence the process and if it held decision-makers accountable:

> "The reality is: unless you are heavily involved within the bureaucracy, in that process, even parliamentarians are kind of shut out. . . . And so, as a parliamentarian, if you ever get a contact at the management level or at the analyst level or someone who is actually working on the files, you hang on to them for your life because they can give you the straight goods. And, the other part of that process is having really good relationships with well-connected outsiders. So, I always worked to develop relationships with scientists and environmental experts who actually had more access to the bureaucratic process than I did, because of the nature of the way we managed as politicians. And, the other problem is that in a lot of parliamentary offices there were only, out of 306 MPs, four or five of us had people in our offices that were actually environmental experts."
>
> (Kraft Sloan, 2014)

Thus, as will be shown in the following time frames, the CESD, which in the time leading up to the Kyoto Protocol did not produce a report, became a central democratic institution. In other respects, the Parliament was hardly able to influence climate policy-making and it can be assumed that more profound knowledge about climate change would probably have resulted in more active climate policies, yet, at that time, scientists only possessed peripheral functions (Stone, 2014). Representative participation relies heavily on an adequate information basis and, when such a basis exists, it can be expected that it will have a positive influence on climate performance.

This information indicates that overwhelmingly informal participatory structures enabled an executive dominated climate policy-making environment. Canada's climate policy field is still in its conceptualization phase and has not been completely democratically institutionalized. This might be the reason why the role of the government and its preferences are so important, and the influence of such a democratically non-institutionalized participatory setting on climate performance is almost entirely unpredictable.

Indirect mechanisms: no effectiveness and efficiency without inclusiveness and participation (international)

After the process came to be very much dominated by federal-provincial executives at the national level, the dynamic of the process seemed to change as the date of COP 3 in Kyoto approached. The process gradually began to take place much more at the international level as decisions in the form of concrete reduction targets had to be made. Throughout the course of these developments, indirect mechanisms of involvement and participation on effectiveness and efficiency as procedural general performance were established.

It was at this time that the process stepped up to the ministerial level. This occurred on a very ad hoc basis and shortly before Kyoto (Cleland, 2014). The most important JMM, presided over by NRCan Minister Goodale (Simpson, Jaccard, & Rivers, 2008, p. 35), took place on 12 November 1997, just one month before Kyoto. The meeting was a "politicians only" discussion about a consensual national target for negotiations at COP 3. This consensual national target emerged as a stabilization of GHGs at 1990 levels (Confidential3, 2014), a target which the federal government and every province and territory were able to agree on. More precisely, it was "agreed that it would be reasonable to seek to reduce aggregate greenhouse gas emissions in Canada to their 1990 levels by approximately 2010". According to Robert Slater, the standstill this represented can be seen, politically speaking, as a "sort of nice positioning" (ECan, 1997; Slater, 2014).

However, this consensus did not last very long. It changed significantly when the federal government announced just a few days before COP 3 started that it wanted to reduce GHG emissions to a rate 3 per cent below 1990 levels by 2010 and by a further 5 per cent below this level by 2015 (Bramley, 2000, p. 3). Even more surprisingly for many of those previously involved, the target was later changed again, with the decision this time being made at the international level. During the negotiations at COP 3, the Canadian government decided "out of the blue" to "come in with [a proposal of] minus 6%" below 1990 levels between 2008–2012 (Slater, 2014). Thus, the government did not see the standstill consensus as binding in the context of international negotiations where "this zero target was going to leave us embarrassed" (Heinbecker, 2014). Consequently, according to Heinbecker, "there was a disagreement in a context in which everybody knew that the initial agreement wasn't tenable" (Heinbecker, 2014).

These different views on the binding character of a previously reached consensus can be seen as a result of the way preparations were organized.

The consensus on a standstill was reached at a FMM while the preparations took place at a different level between the two leading departments, ECan and NRCan. So, there were no big overlaps between these two platforms by executive dominated organizational structures, while, at the same time, "[t]here were tensions and growing tensions because the deed on this issue was with the Environment Department and the Natural Resources Department" (Heinbecker, 2014). Indeed, this was why Heinbecker from Foreign Affairs ultimately led the delegation.

Overall, it seems as if there was some confusion about the delegation's room for manoeuvre and whether they had the authority to change the standstill consensus. From a democratic point of view, these developments could be counterfactually interpreted as being as complex as they were simple. Without having involved all relevant and affected actors beforehand and without having established a clear participatory structure (which would have made the previously made agreement more legitimate and binding for both the delegation to Kyoto and the PM at home), a very poorly defined negotiation mandate existed. This had an indirect influence upon procedural general performance and more precisely upon effectiveness and efficiency, since it diminished the credibility of the government's commitment to policies and undermined their ability to translate conflicting objectives into a coherent policy. Thus, for a task as complex as dealing with climate change, the democratic preconditions for effectiveness and efficiency would seem to have existed. Furthermore, it can be expected that the implementation of a target negotiated via the method described above would be even more complicated since the international target lacked responsivity in regard to the target reached by national executives. So, what precisely happened in Kyoto to lead to a target of minus 6 per cent and how do these developments relate to the democracy-climate nexus?

Participation: briefed NGOs (international)

Being involved in an international delegation is one step, but, as empirical evidence shows, having influence on decision-making through participatory structures is another step. During COP 3, the importance of the different groups in attendance can be illustrated by the typical daily procedure, which ensured that representatives of NGOs formed the last group to speak:

> "We would start at six with the core of the delegation. It would be me and the Natural Resources and the Environment leaders who were there. . . . Then we would bring in the subject matter negotiators. . . . And, we would, in the course of this, prepare to brief the ministers, which would happen at about 7.30. . . . And then, we would bring in the NGO part of the delegation at about 8.30. . . . And then, as the last thing, at about 9.30, we'd brief the NGOs who were not part of the delegation."
>
> (Heinbecker, 2014)

Thus, NGOs could not participate in every stage of the decision-making procedure, but were briefed before official negotiations started. The closer the negotiations came to the final decision-making, the less officials, who indicated that they knew where all affected and relevant actors stood, knew in what way to negotiate and what the Canadian target would be since "this was always a very closely developed and guarded policy within the liberal government ranks" and even officials "within the government weren't even knowledgeable about what our target would be" (Confidential1, 2014). Therefore, it seems that participation was seen, in a functional way, as a "mixed blessing":

> "It helps to get the support and it helps afterwards in selling the idea whatever it is. But at the very moment of negotiations, that's where secrecy has to prevail in my judgement."
>
> (Heinbecker, 2014)

The relationship between participation and climate performance at the international level was complex. NGOs were neither left aside, nor could they participate in decision-making or in the preparation of the decision-making process, instead, they were briefed every morning and had access to information. Considered judgement was only possible within the government.

The question as to whether the NGOs meant more to the government than a way of gaining acceptance for their policies probably has to be left open. Even though such debates regularly occur, e.g. in regard to a democratic European foreign policy (Sjursen, 2011), the question of to what extent elements of a democratic foreign policy can be implemented at an international level and at what point secrecy has to prevail has yet to be decided, be it in practical policy-making or in science, and thus remains a research gap. Perhaps it is necessary to develop other democratic mechanisms which connect the national and international levels as opposed to merely allowing NGOs to be part of a delegation and to be briefed. Whether and how that would influence climate performance is unclear. However, if actors outside the government were unable to have much influence on decision-making, which actors inside the government were involved in final decision-making?

Accountability: missing accountability leads to unpredictability (international)

Democratic policy-making at the international level also requires clear lines of accountability which ensure a degree of control over decision-makers. However, the influence of meetings which took place before the negotiations in Kyoto started was marginal and they only seem to have contributed to an overall synthesis without possessing any binding character (Heinbecker, 2014). In the end, decision-making remained in the hands of political representatives, with "politicians weighing the circumstances and the situation and the politics and making decisions" (Heinbecker, 2014).

In regard to the 6 per cent target agreed upon at COP 3, the PM was clearly the decision-maker and he himself stated that he had a "personal preoccupation" with protecting the environment and thus reacted impatiently when the actions of opponents, such as businesses, the provinces, the Cabinet or bureaucrats, made agreement on targets unlikely (Chrétien, 2007, pp. 383, 385). According to Edward Goldenberg, a senior policy advisor to PM Chrétien 1993–2003, the PM was also in favour of more active climate change policies:

EG: He, the prime minister, was very strong/very much personally an environ-
        mentalist. And, I remember one time he was on the telephone on this –
        I believe on this issue with President Clinton – and I only heard – we were
        actually in Moscow when he phoned – and I don't remember what exactly
        about it was but he said to him "You know, when we get into these jobs, we
        have to do things, we have to be able to look at ourselves in the mirror and
        say we have done things that are right. For the long run. And, this is one of
        those."
FH: The climate issue?
EG: Yeah. Yeah. So he believed very strongly.

(Goldenberg, 2014)

In the end, the whole decision-making process was very informal and not embedded in a previously developed scheme or economic models. Instead, more and
more concentric circles developed around ministers Steward from ECan and
Goodale from NRCan (Confidential1, 2014; Heinbecker, 2014):

> "But a decision was made in the end by the prime minister after consulta-
> tions on the phone from Kyoto with two ministers and me and the prime
> minister at the other end. And, the prime minister decided that we would
> do, instead of doing a little bit more than the Americans, we would do a little
> bit less. . . . We didn't go back and, you know, run economic models. . . . In
> the Canadian system, there is so much power concentrated in the prime
> minister that it's, you know, he really is kind of elected to autocracy."

(Heinbecker, 2014)

Even though Canada's close relationship with the US made it negotiate within
a 1 per cent range of the US target and the actors who were personally involved
might overestimate their roles and influence upon the process, the influence of
the PM on the 6 per cent target nonetheless becomes quite obvious when reading
through the accounts.

According to John Godfrey, Liberal MP and Minister of Infrastructure and
Communities, the PM could make such decisions without thinking "through
very clearly what the implications of making this commitment would be" and
understanding "what kind of an effort it would take to reach these targets"
(Godfrey, 2014). The power of the prerogative allows him to act, according to
Goldenberg, as an "elected autocrat" (Heinbecker, 2014). The way Chrétien

used the power of the prerogative in individual decisions allowed him to make decisions independent of any horizontal control and with only very limited vertical control.

Thus, the lack of suitable accountability mechanisms ensured that the PM, as the elected head of government, made the final decision. However, it was a decision that did not rely on any previously negotiated mandate, which would have made his acting from a perspective of democratic quality more legitimate, and this makes it hard and almost impossible to hold him accountable. The PM probably did not have much interest in acting in a more formalized fashion, since this could have been highly problematic domestically, where a non-binding consensus existed and actors who were interested in a less ambitious target could turn out to be strong opponents during ongoing negotiations. Thus, at this point there was almost no horizontal accountability in the form of efficient control of the decision-maker. Moreover, the decisions which were made are, without specific information from inside the closer governmental circle, almost impossible to trace and this is why there was also a lack of democratic quality in respect to vertical accountability. In this case, the lack of accountability had no impact on climate performance, however, a non-environmental PM could have used their prerogative to achieve a much less ambitious target at Kyoto. Thus, responsiveness also becomes an important element for intermestic policies which develop between the national and international spheres.

Participation: the long shadow of insufficient responsiveness (national-international exchange)

In terms of democratic quality, responsiveness is a fundamental value which ensures that previously agreed preferences become policies and are implemented. Even though stakeholders in previous consultations at the national level might have had an influence on the overall synthesis and partially led to the support Canada developed for Kyoto mechanisms, they had no influence on the agreed target (Confidential1, 2014), which is clearly the dominant element since it determined how many GHG emissions the country was allowed to create. Taking into account the difference of 6 per cent between the standstill consensus reached prior to COP 3 and the final target, the target the federal government agreed upon with the provinces and territories was neither reached in a democratic manner, nor was the target used as a binding mandate at international negotiations. According to Heinbecker, the provinces, of course, "tried to make the argument that a deal was a deal", but he argues that they did not seriously believe that the government could stay at the 0 per cent target; the agreement was in his view "not a deal that was considered unbreakable" (Heinbecker, 2014). Even though the analysis provided by Heinbecker might be seen as a traditional and usual way of governmental policy-making, in terms of responsiveness, it is highly problematic, since he declares the transmission belt to be more or less completely negotiable.

Consequently, from their perspective, the "provinces treated that as being completely overturned" and the actions of the government as not being in line with the previously agreed target (Confidential3, 2014; Oulton, 2014). According to a high-ranking official from the Government of Alberta, they "were told very firmly and clearly that to negotiate a protocol was a very different step from ratifying the protocol" (Confidential3, 2014). The argument made by the government does not seem to have been very sound, but was nonetheless the "preamble that led to the post-Kyoto process" (Confidential3, 2014).

After the target was agreed upon, there was a clear domestic lack of a calculation of what such a target meant (although such a calculation and discussion could have been included in a preliminary participatory process, enabling the government to act responsively). Consequently, at a FMM on 11–12 December shortly after COP 3, the first ministers agreed inter alia that no region should bear an unreasonable burden and that a detailed understanding of different implementation options and their costs and benefits would have to be evaluated. Moreover, and of great significance for the influence of democratic quality on climate performance, the meeting concluded that

> "a process must be established, in advance of Canada's ratification of the Protocol, that will examine the consequences of Kyoto and provide for full participation of the provincial and territorial governments with the federal government in any implementation and management of the Protocol; and federal, provincial and territorial ministers of the environment and energy work together to consider jointly the appropriate courses of action."
>
> (CESD, 1998)

Missing responsiveness can easily be identified after COP 3 ended and the process came back to a domestic level. Not surprisingly, the provinces and territories swiftly forced a national process which clearly analysed how implementation could be worked out. Consequently, a lack of binding agreements led to a situation where a national process started right from the beginning with its conclusion completely open.

From the point of view of the democracy-climate nexus, the transmission belt between the domestic and the international level would appear to be of considerable relevance. If there is no such belt, then every democratic quality could be as high as possible domestically – which it, however, was not in the Canadian process leading up to COP 3 – without having to be translated into an international negotiation framework. Therefore, any form of participation focused on something that has to be negotiated internationally has to take into account that its procedures do not stop at the domestic border but reach further. Otherwise, responsive results matching previously agreed consensus will not be possible and the implementation will become even harder since people will be unable to identify themselves with the target. As a result, the federal government agreed to a sort of *ex post facto responsiveness* by declaring that signing a treaty and ratifying it are two different steps and the provinces would have the opportunity to participate in the process when developing an implementation plan. The Canadian case seems to be a good example for a misguided exchange between the domestic and international levels, demonstrating that even though a government might agree upon a very ambitious target, its implementation can become complicated when localized actors, such as the provinces, show no interest in accepting such a target. Thus, responsiveness as an element of democratic quality can be seen to be of considerable importance for climate performance.

Results: first insights into the negative influence of low democratic quality

What results can be distilled from the aforementioned developments in regard to the influence of manifestations of dimensions of democratic quality on climate performance?

The first finding is a mechanism which links a lack of inclusiveness with informal participatory structures and makes it almost impossible to hold decision-makers accountable for their decisions. Domestically, between 1995–1997, no broader public was involved in the decision-making process, the selection procedure remains unknown and environmental and industry groups were not brought together systematically. In such a setting, it is almost impossible to trace back results to decision-makers (vertical accountability) or to control decision-makers (horizontal accountability). Due to these circumstances, the executive dominates policy-making and the PM, in particular, can act upon his or her own preferences. A second finding is the detected indirect mechanism of inclusiveness and participation on the procedural general performance dimension of effectiveness and efficiency, especially on the credibility of the government's commitment to an agreed consensus and the role of the government in translating conflicting issues into a coherent policy. Since several relevant and affected actors were not involved before or during COP 3 and no clear participatory structure existed which would have made any consensus more legitimate and binding, the negotiation mandate was, from the point of view of the provinces, very clear (stabilization), while the federal government interpreted this prior agreement as being non-binding. Thus, inclusiveness and participation seem to be a precondition for functioning effectiveness, efficiency and better climate performance. The third finding also deals with accountability. Where no accountability for a PM exists and he or she can at the same time make use of a strong prerogative, he or she can act upon his or her own preferences and without any restrictions. The influence of a lack of accountability on climate performance is thus, in this case, completely non-existent. The fourth finding is the lack of a transmission belt which produced a feedback-loop of *ex post facto responsiveness*: in a FMM right after COP 3 the federal government had to agree to establish a broad process before ratification in order to evaluate possible options for implementation. Possibly the whole process of implementation was already useless at that point as the actors felt completely shut out and yet had to implement a target they had never agreed on beforehand. It is therefore to be expected that a lack of responsiveness has a negative influence on climate performance.

To sum up, the first time frame shows the very first evidence that low dimensions of democratic quality and their interplay lead either to a negative impact or a lack influence, with the consequence that climate performance depends on other circumstances beyond democratic processes. Meanwhile, there has so far been no evidence to show that more democratic quality would necessarily lead to better climate performance. Moreover, it seems that this book could partially reframe the debate about Canada's climate policy. Since Canada is a highly fragmented country and climate change is such a complex issue, a promising solution would appear to be to design a fully democratic policy process which takes these circumstances into account. All other factors are either almost unchangeable (Canada's geography, interdependence with the US and the structure of the economy) or unable to solve the problem alone (the PMs can show as much leadership as they want, but if the provinces do not follow them to implement their decisions, then nothing is going to happen). Democratic quality could function as an important factor in regard to an active climate policy and the other three time frames will try to shed more light on this possibility (see Chapters 7–9).

References

The access date of all material retrieved from the Web is 5 June 2015 unless otherwise specified.

Bramley, M. (2000). *A Climate Change Resource Book for Journalists*. Retrieved from https://www.pembina.org/reports/CCRB-e.pdf (accessed 17 February 2017).

CESD. (1998). *Report of the Commissioner of the Environment and Sustainable Development*. Chapter 3. Retrieved from www.oag-bvg.gc.ca/internet/English/parl_cesd_199805_03_e_9343.html

Chrétien, J. (2007). *My Years as Prime Minister* (1st ed.). Toronto: A.A. Knopf Canada.

Cleland, F.M. (2014). Interview on Canada's Kyoto Protocol process/Interviewer: F. Hanusch.

Confidential1. (2014). Interview on Canada's Kyoto Protocol process/Interviewer: F. Hanusch.

Confidential3. (2014). Interview on Canada's Kyoto Protocol process/Interviewer: F. Hanusch.

ECan. (1997). Canada's Energy and Environment Ministers agree to work together to reduce greenhouse gas emissions (Press release, 12 November).

Godfrey, J. (2014). Interview on Canada's Kyoto Protocol process/Interviewer: F. Hanusch.

Goldenberg, E. (2014). Interview on Canada's Kyoto Protocol process/Interviewer: F. Hanusch.

Heinbecker, E. (2014). Interview on Canada's Kyoto Protocol process/Interviewer: F. Hanusch.

Kraft Sloan, K. (2014). Interview on Canada's Kyoto Protocol process/Interviewer: F. Hanusch.

Oulton, D. (2014). Interview on Canada's Kyoto Protocol Process/Interviewer: F. Hanusch.

Simpson, J., Jaccard, M. K., & Rivers, N. (2008). *Hot Air: Meeting Canada's Climate Change Challenge*. Toronto: Emblem/McClelland & Stewart.

Sjursen, H. (2011). Not so intergovernmental after all? On democracy and integration in European foreign and security policy. *Journal of European Public Policy, 18*(8), 1078–1095.

Slater, R. (2014). Interview on Canada's Kyoto Protocol process/Interviewer: F. Hanusch.

Stone, J. (2014). Interview on Canada's Kyoto Protocol process/Interviewer: F. Hanusch.

7   1998–2002

Futile consultations

"So, I mean the process isn't very rational. I mean why should you expect that? It is a democracy."

(Cleland, 2014)

"Just, in the end, this was simply a process that would end up immobilizing decision-making rather than facilitating decision-making."

(Oulton, 2014)

Canada agreed at COP 3 to a minus 6 per cent target. As a result of that decision, contrasting the previous national consensus on standstill reached with provinces and territories, a FMM immediately after COP 3 decided to establish a process before ratification which would provide for "full participation of the provincial and territorial governments with the federal government in any implementation of the Protocol" (FMM, 1997). Therefore, the second time frame would seem to be insightful in regard to the Canadian attempt to establish a (democratic) climate policy process.

This time frame is characterized by two developments: first, the emergence of the NCCP, with its most intense phase from 1998–2000 – called the "table process" – and a less intense phase from 2000–2002; secondly, federal developments beside the NCCP, including national stakeholder sessions and ratification in 2002.

As in the previous time frame, 1995–1997, this chapter asks what mechanisms link democratic quality and climate performance. The results indicate that interrelations between different dimensions of democratic quality are highly important. When interrelations between dimensions with high democratic quality work out, their influence on climate performance seems to be exponentially positive, however just one dimension can have a negative impact on climate performance. Thus, the results suggest an exponential influence of interrelated dimensions of democratic quality on climate performance.

DOI: 10.4324/9781315228983-9

National activities in the form of a National Climate Change Process

In order to research the (lack of) influence of democratic quality on climate performance, some basic information about the NCCP between 1998–2000 is necessary. Following the FMM's statement at their meeting of 11–12 December 1997, a JMM on 24 April 1998 decided on a process to develop a National Implementation Strategy on Climate Change and the foundation of a NCCS that would run it. As part of the NCCP, 15 issue tables for seven key sectors, eight cross-cutting themes (transportation, electricity, Kyoto Protocol mechanisms, technology, carbon sinks, credit for early action, public education and outreach, agriculture and agri-food, the forestry sector, buildings, industry, enhanced voluntary action, municipalities, science and adaptation, tradeable permits) and an Analysis and Modelling Group (AMG), which integrated results and usually also counted as a table, were established to find options for implementation (NCCP, 2003). The tables were comprised of over 450 experts from academia, industry, NGOs and the government and analysed, with funding from the Climate Change Action Fund, the status quo in their foundation papers, identifying opportunities and challenges in the reduction of GHG emissions and the adaptations which would be required in their fields. The results were summarized in the final report of the AMG to be taken into consideration when devising a national implementation strategy (CESD, 2001, pp. 17–18).

Even though the NCCP continued after 2000 when the tables process ended, its method of proceeding changed and became less structured. The results of the tables were used when devising a discussion document, published in June 2000 for consultations in national stakeholder sessions taking place that summer in major cities to discuss options for the first phase of the National Implementation Strategy on Climate Change in the form of a first National Climate Change Business Plan (CESD, 2001, pp. 17–18). In 2001, there were two federal-provincial stakeholder working groups: the Emissions Allocation and Burden Sharing Working Group and the Domestic Emissions Trading Working Group, which continued work on the tables' themes, but without many further proceedings on the main issues (Bramley, 2014). Even though the NCCS continued to exist until 2004, the final product it published in the context of the NCCP was a second National Climate Change Business Plan in 2002, which, like the first National Climate Change Business Plan, is mainly a collection of federal and provincial climate change initiatives.

Insufficient responsiveness: the reason why the NCCP was initiated

In terms of democratic quality, the first question which has to be asked is: why was such an expansive NCCP – with the potential to be highly democratic – initiated? No reference to the establishment of such a process can be found in the period before Canada agreed to the minus 6 per cent target at Kyoto. Even though counterfactual arguing has the constraint that it never became reality, it seems conceivable to argue that, if only Canada had agreed to the previous consensus of stabilization, the FMM would not have forced such a comprehensive process. In this counter argumentation, the process would not have been established – or at least not with the same intensity – had the government acted responsively at COP 3; i.e., in all likelihood, the NCCP was probably only initiated as a result of insufficient responsiveness and the high degree of dissatisfaction following the COP 3. However, in regard to responsiveness as an indicator of participation, it has to be recognized that the stabilization decision was not very inclusive since only the provinces and territories were involved while other actors were missing. Thus, it is a lack of responsiveness as part of Canadian executive federalism which seems not to go hand in hand with high democratic quality.

Governmental capability, effectiveness and efficiency: preconditions for a democratic policy process

As empirical evidence demonstrates, governmental capability, effectiveness and efficiency as dimensions of procedural general performance seem to be preconditions for a functioning (democratic) policy process. A secretariat, e.g. which adequately manages the NCCP by showing a high level of bureaucratic quality, would seem to provide the basis for a successful policy process. Yet, were these preconditions fulfilled in the Canadian case?

The NCCS comprised of federal, provincial and territorial officials and was created "to manage the NCCP, including the sixteen issue tables/working groups . . ., which examined and analysed the impacts, costs and benefits of options to address climate change", while the JMMs were created to "develop direction" (Government of Canada, 2006, p. 63; NCCP, 2003). According to David Oulton, Chair of the NCCS throughout its existence from 1998–2004, the NCCS lacked any clear legal authority, but had four tasks, namely: (1) "to coordinate the development of domestic policy for implementation of Kyoto"; (2) "to work on what the implications are for Canada of ratifying the protocol before any ratification decision is taken . . . [and] start getting the Provinces ready to start to do those things that we're going to have to do to actually implement the protocol"; (3) "to bring in the other stakeholders"; and (4) "to monitor international consultation and negotiations about climate change since our domestic policies are necessarily linked to international policies" (Committee, 1998; Oulton, 2014). So, stakeholders had to be brought in to find out "what programs and policies Canada will have to put in place in order to successfully implement [the Kyoto Protocol targets]" (Oulton, 2014), which sounds very much like an expert function. However, a high-ranking official from Alberta who was involved in the NCCP saw the role of the secretariat as being "to have as neutral as possible [a] secretariat that was providing fair information to the whole process and was not biased to one or other jurisdiction" (Confidential3, 2014) and which could indicate that those involved at least put different emphases on the several tasks. It seems that the elected federal and provincial governments established the secretariat together to manage a national process, but the role was thin on specifics and authority, while policy direction remained with the JMMs. Thus, it seems as if there were "no clear and transparent agreements or arrangements between the federal government and the provinces and territories that specifically defined their respective roles and responsibilities for achieving Canada's climate change commitments" (CESD, 2001).

Elements of a democratic task can be suggested in the management of the 16 tables/working groups, but a clear statement of the direction in which said management should have been leading, including time lines or final products, is missing. Based on the sources looked at so far, a continuum with two extremes of democratic quality – and of course their combination – can be envisaged: (1) a policy process which simply used the knowledge of the 450 experts, while decisions remained the remit of the JMMs, as a means of acquiring consultancy, since the ministries were simply not equipped with sufficient knowledge to develop options for addressing climate change or (2) a policy process which was truly democratic in many respects and enabled the actors involved to influence decision-making. Option 1 would, of course, lead to lower democratic quality than option 2.

In terms of the NCCS, both democratic quality and its possible influence on climate performance rely on an indirect mechanism. A clear definition of the management of the NCCP by the NCCS would portray a government which showed high procedural general performance in several dimensions: in setting and maintaining strategic priorities; in learning from past errors/previous climate policy processes (especially the formulation of the Kyoto target); and in the coordination of conflicting issues and the efficient use of resources. Without a clear description of how the NCCS should manage the NCCP, the democratic nature of the process was open to question. Had the definition of the management style included the clear purpose of achieving high levels of democratic participation, then democratic quality and – as part of that indirect mechanism – the influence of democratic quality on climate performance might have been more likely. In the circumstances, it is, to some extent, up to the NCCS and other more powerful actors like the JMMs or FMMs to determine whether and how democratic the process will be. Nevertheless, the involvement of so many experts can be seen as an indicator of democratic purpose, however, the democratic extent of the gesture depends on whether they were only consulted or were actually involved in and able to participate in the process.

One element which was closely related to the composition and role of the NCCS was the purpose of the NCCP, which was to have been managed by the NCCS. More precisely, if the purpose of the NCCP was to have been democratic and to achieve climate performance, then several interesting insights can be expected. According to the NCCP itself, its purpose was to "examine the impact, costs and benefits of implementing the Kyoto Protocol and the various implementation options open to Canada" and by doing so to "engage governments and stakeholders in examining the impacts, costs and benefits of addressing climate change" (NCCP, 2003). Again, the purpose sounds like a very general task without any specifics. According to John Dillon, who represented the Canadian

Council of Chief Executives in the NCCP, the main question the NCCP was meant to answer was "Can we meet the Kyoto target?" in order to "inform a decision about whether Canada should ratify the Kyoto Protocol" (Dillon, 2014).

Thus, the official purpose of the NCCP was to examine various implementation options for the Kyoto Protocol and at the same time to engage governments and stakeholders. For other participants, it was a more fundamental question, namely, not only to develop policy options, but to examine whether the Kyoto target stood any chance of being met and thus to inform political decision-makers about whether to ratify the Kyoto Protocol. Having said this, it is also claimed that what the process was not about was making decisions (or at least suggestions which were in some way binding) on preferred policies or developing (intergovernmental) agreements, etc. It was about developing options with various stakeholders and governments which had different views on the scope of the NCCP.

Overall, the process seems to have been more an expert's policy process, which was dedicated to developing knowledge on climate change policies. It was not a fully democratic process since the participants' mandates were too limited in terms of influence, responsiveness, etc. However, there were at least some elements of engagement and thus also the possibility of an influence upon climate performance. The preconditions of effectiveness, efficiency and governmental capability are thus fulfilled, but only to a certain general extent, similarly, it can be said that there was a partially democratic purpose for the policy process, but not that this was its main intention. For a more precise understanding, it is necessary to have a closer look at the democracy-climate nexus, starting with existing accountability structures.

Inclusiveness: somewhere between expert workshops and democratic involvement

Inclusiveness in a democratic sense is characterized by open and fair access, which ensures that a plurality of relevant and affected actors is involved while the selection of said actors remains unbiased and weak and marginalized actors are included. And, as the 450 participants on the NCP's 15 issue tables and one working group were members of federal, provincial, territorial and municipal governments, representatives of industry, business and academia and employees of environmental groups, it would, at first glance, appear as if this was a broad and inclusive process (CESD, 2001, p. 9).

However insightful they are in terms of democratic quality and their mandate, both the tables and the process as a whole had to develop options for implementation; this was their original purpose and the reason for their composition. Initially, small expert tables were intended, which would have been composed of a neutral chair, a co-chair from the government and five or six experts (Dillon, 2014). The tables should have received knowledge and ideas from the most knowledgeable and important actors as a form of consulting, yet this proposal raised concern amongst environmental groups and businesses in terms of who would and who would not be involved (Dillon, 2014). The result was "a lot of pushing and pulling on some of those tables to get more people involved" and, even though it was ultimately up to the government to decide on the participants, "if you wanted to be involved and could make a reasonable case for having expertise relevant to the table's work and/or represented a stakeholder whose interests would be affected, then you could become involved", which resulted in many more participants than had previously been intended (Confidential2, 2014; Dillon, 2014). As more and more actors wanted to be involved in the process, the way ECan and NRCan sorted out who was allowed to take part was through a self-selection mechanism. Basically, the NCCS contacted associations or networks in relevant fields and asked them to select those people whose expertise suited the purposes under negotiation and who would therefore be able to participate in an informed way (Bennett, 2014; Oulton, 2014). However, self-selection could perhaps have been too unspecific, since it partially led to a selection of people who only negotiated in favour of their organizations instead of attempting to find the best options for all concerned. For instance, certain companies chose to send public relations experts instead of engineers, which reduced the level at which they could really contribute to proceedings (Bennett, 2014). Such examples probably form one of the reasons why, for example, the prominent David Suzuki Foundation ENGO felt that the process was useless and refused to take part in it (Bramley, 2014). So, as we can see, not all (relevant) actors accepted the process.

Moreover, no members of the broader public were involved, which supports the suggestion that the process was still very much based on the original idea of having small expert tables to provide knowledge in a field where the ministries were insufficiently informed. Nevertheless, involving a certain amount of relevant and affected actors on the basis of valid criteria is an important first step in the process of becoming democratically inclusive, the next one is to have an unbiased selection process, which also ensures that marginalized groups are represented. Since the meetings themselves took place across Canada, it is clear that actors from one region were not preferred over those from another (Confidential3, 2014).

Resources were also provided for ENGOs with limited budgets, e.g. they were asked to carry out studies required for the process and were paid for their work or had their transportation costs covered. However, in some cases, these kinds of support was not sufficient, since certain organizations simply lacked qualified and knowledgeable people who would have been capable of participating in such an intensive process (Oulton, 2014). Moreover, the participation rate of aboriginal people was very low, probably because there was no mechanism in place which was designed to ensure the involvement of marginalized groups (Bramley, 2014; Oulton, 2014). Almost the same circumstances can be identified for people from low-income and impoverished backgrounds, who were not involved at all (Oulton, 2014). Neither of these groups were even involved enough to have been able to have recommended the provision of more resources to help them participate, "they couldn't get close enough to be able to make themselves heard or to know about it even necessarily" (Oulton, 2014). Thus, there might be a connection between inclusiveness and liberty, since only the actors who were involved were able to express themselves in terms relevant to the process. When an actor is not involved, he or she is unable to create a voice about the issue under consideration. Furthermore, labour groups and trade unions were inadequately represented (Bramley, 2014). Political parties were also not represented, although they might have used the information produced by the tables to help them to develop parallel policies. A possibility which was brought up by John Bennett, who has worked for several ENGOs, such as the Climate Action Network, and has, since 2009, been the executive director of the Sierra Club. He describes the reaction of public servants to his proposal as follows: "they just looked at me like I was crazy" (Bennett, 2014). Finally, (and this might demonstrate that the tables were still expert workshops and not representative of Canadian society) no members of the broader public were involved at any stage in the process – no ordinary citizens, whether they were willing and informed or not, were able to participate.

The question of whether inclusiveness was present at the NCCP between 1998–2000 provides at least three insights. First, the NCCP was planned as a series of small experts' workshops from the very start. These experts needed to be independent and to be able to figure out the best solutions in various climate relevant fields based on their own knowledge. Thus, the process was not designed to be inclusive in a democratic manner. Its purpose was of a different kind and should have been a consultation of experts on issues which the government felt were underrepresented in its departments. The inclusion of experts would have been exclusive and knowledge-based, yet it could have fulfilled the government's initial purpose and intent.

Secondly, in 1998 when preparing the NCCP the ministries, due to pressure from a number of sources, changed the way they included people. The expert groups were suddenly no longer small, nor only filled with genuine experts. In the end, each table had an average of over 28 participants, with many of those in attendance as much interested in negotiating the best possible resolution for their own organizations as in finding the best solution for all concerned. When the process was opened to more participants and actors became involved who were not merely working as independent experts to reach a common resolution, the rules of the game, or more precisely the design of the process, should have been changed. A second process should have been established alongside the expert tables, with a close connection to these but a different mandate. For example, this second process could have focused on reaching a consensus as to whether any, and if so which, of the knowledge-based options developed by the small expert tables would work in societal practice or if other solutions were required. Instead, a mixed process emerged with some sound democratic elements. The sound democratic elements were various and can be summarized with the following examples: neither actors from industry nor actors with ENGO backgrounds reported any bias in the composition of the tables; the associations and umbrella organizations involved were allowed on a subsidiarity principle to decide which people would be best suited for the purposes of the process; a culture of participation at ECan existed which was able to function as a resource during the course of the table work; both money and resources were provided, so as to help involve organizations with restricted budgets; and circulating meetings across Canada ensured that no regions or local actors were left out.

Thirdly, a certain group of actors (aboriginal, low income, etc.) and the broader public were only partially involved or totally missing. Thus, some groups and members of the broader public had no chance to be heard. Even though it is unclear in what direction the involvement of those people would have changed the results of the process, it seems as if without their involvement the results can hardly be deemed to be responsive to those people. Moreover, inclusiveness and liberty are related to each other, to gain liberty you need to be involved: only those groups who are involved in and knowledgeable about the issue under consideration are able to express themselves and to raise their voices autonomously. Furthermore, this can only happen when they are aware that said policy process is taking place, which, with the NCCP, obviously was not the case.

In terms of the democracy-climate nexus, it has to be asked whether and how inclusiveness as a dimension of democratic quality influenced climate performance. A twofold answer can be given in regard to the form of inclusiveness existing in the NCCP between 1998–2000: overall inclusiveness was not intended, but developed partially and was subsequently in many regards in existence but incomplete. Therefore, the facility to build knowledge across many organizations and people, especially in the climate community was provided, however, the broader public was not represented and that is why the result could not be fully responsive. The overall influence of that partial involvement on climate performance might be considered to be slightly positive, yet it seems that it is also dependent on certain other dimensions. The intermediate impact of the way inclusiveness was organized in terms of climate performance is just as important as its direct impact, since, without open and fair access to the process, the participatory structures were only able to work with the incomplete set of actors involved. Thus, the question that now becomes important is: did clear participation structures exist which were able to deal with all the actors involved and did, for example, mechanisms exist which also tried to absorb the voices of those actors who were not directly involved in the process?

Participation: discontinued

Participatory structures should enable the actors involved to influence decision-making, providing circumstances in which, for example, considered judgement and responsive results are possible. However, it seems an impossible task to find any of these in the structure of the NCCP. A closer look at the participatory structures of the NCCP makes it increasingly obvious that the process lacked a design which would have guided the process through from its beginning to its end, either covering all the steps in-between or providing some sort of moderation, which would have ensured a direction throughout the process, developing structures towards an outcome. In many regards, it seems as if the only clear participatory structure the tables had was that those involved met on a regular basis and talked about their topic or shared information and the like. However, there seems to have been little in the way of planning or conception when it came to questions such as: how exactly the people involved (should have) acted as representatives; whether other representative actors, like parliamentarians, should have been involved; how citizens' views should have been included in the process; and how exactly all of the results should then have influenced climate policy-making, etc.

Some of those involved describe the NCCP as a "delaying tactic" implemented by the government with the aim of letting "two years go by without doing anything" (Bramley, 2014). Others see it as a sham process, which enabled the government to have various experts "appearing in public that they were consulting" without actually doing anything as a result of this consultation (Confidential2, 2014). Former Minister of the Environment, David Anderson, described the process – even though, in his view, the process was pretty well organized – as an endless back and forth, in which "you never thought to get to the end of the debate", since it was almost impossible to reach a consensus on specific numbers with all the different actors involved (Anderson, 2014). This indicates that the characteristics of climate change probably make precise decisions impossible – even though such precision may not always be necessary and can be used by some actors as an excuse or a delaying tactic – and that the process lacked a participatory structure designed to achieve results and reach consensus. Anderson identifies two main issues in the structure of the process which led to the non-delivery of a consensus on final results: first, the process' focus on industrial organizations led to a misrepresentation of Canadian industry, as such organizations are not representative of the full spectrum of industry in Canada. Secondly, the excessively detailed JMMs ensured that discussions often got bogged down in minor details (Anderson, 2014).

In almost the same vein, Robert Slater, Senior Assistant Deputy Minister during the NCCP at ECan, describes the reason why the process did not work out as a "bloody mystery" (Slater, 2014). According to his analysis, the politicians involved never had any real interest in the (results of the) process and, ultimately, they were so strongly influenced by the diverse interests participating in the process that rational policy-making and a way out of the process became impossible (Slater, 2014).

An issue which arose in relation to reaching a consensus and finding a way out of the process, and which was probably related to the endless debates, was that there were different interpretations of the purpose of the whole process. Even though an official purpose, as described above, existed, those involved had different perspectives. Whereas the initial purpose of the creators of the process was to identify and integrate concrete ideas on how to implement the Kyoto Protocol, the process developed into more of an educational exercise, producing material which was also used in the aftermath (Cleland, 2014; Dillon, 2014; Slater, 2014). While these differences were to some extent marginal and could probably have been included in a standard policy process, the different interpretations of the main purpose of the process and a lack of common understanding in this regard led to an endless debate.

An official document from the NCCS demonstrates that it was unclear whether the tables should educate, provide an expert knowledge base, develop consensus policy options or indeed do something else entirely different or all the above (which would ideally have had an impact on the participatory structures). The document describes how the tables "were asked to analyse all possible options and to not strive for consensus" (NCCS, 2000a, p. 1). Thus, even though the NCCS and the NCCP were consistently consequent in terms of promoting the initial goal – the expert tables should analyse all options – the participants and other officials appear to have taken a somewhat different view of the proceedings. However, in the end "[m]ost of the tables actually came up with sort of a consensus position" (Bennett, 2014). This clearly demonstrates that the official purpose and the purposes of those involved were not the same.

Analysis of the aftermath of the process also demonstrates that participants on the tables were under the impression that a consensus should be reached. At a conference of the Canadian Political Science Association in 2003, a paper presented by Jack Stilborn, who worked for the Research Branch at the Library of Parliament, argued that the goal of the NCCP was "to contribute discernibly to the emergence of consensus among the stakeholders involved in the Issue Tables and subsequent consultations" (Stilborn, 2003, p. 14). That the tables were nonetheless not officially intended to reach a consensus is, in terms of the participatory structures, quite insightful, since such an understanding of bringing people together is clearly more directed towards expert tables, which leaves the decision completely in the hands of the politicians involved. This would mean that, other than influencing the various options which were developed, the NCCP was not intended to have an impact upon decision-making. It seems obvious that the goals of the NCCP and the participatory structures were either unclearly defined, miscommunicated or misinterpreted and that this made it difficult for the process to reach a consensus conclusion. The option papers themselves support this view: while, for example, the central aim of the municipalities table was, according to its final paper, to provide concrete policy recommendations (not options), the transportation table was very much focused on reviewing all possible options and providing only brief recommendations at the end (NCCP, 1999a, 1999b). Thus, "part of the problem was the lack of absolutely clarity of its [NCCP] intent" (Confidential3, 2014).

It can be expected that without a clear intention of what the tables (thought they) should do, a considered judgement was always going to be unlikely. However, the tables interpreted the main purpose of their establishment, the way they organized their work provides insights into whether they provided room for deliberation. Yet, information on how the tables proceeded is hard to come by and can only be found in the papers of the tables themselves. For example, the Agriculture and Agri-Food Climate Change Table only mentions very briefly that it had 15 meetings at various places in Canada and that the recommendations were a result of research and deliberation (NCCP, 2000c). The papers from the other tables are similarly vague.

As an important basis for the proceeding of the tables, the government decided not to debate whether climate change was real or not, ensuring that the focus was on solutions to climate change right from the start (Bennett, 2014). Nevertheless, some tables "were having fairly aggressive discussions, which is a bureaucratic term for meaning that there were differences of view" (Oulton, 2014), but, at the same time, there were also tables which focused much more on problem solving by "actually talking about policies that might work" (Dillon, 2014). Thus, the debates at the tables often began with heated conversations, moving on to dynamic and civilized discussions. A lot of information was produced and conflicts would presumably have resulted from the interpretation of such information (Confidential3, 2014). These characterizations indicate that the tables' participants were able to share and produce information as experts within their specific themes, but were unable, or had no modes of deliberation or consensus finding mechanisms at hand which would have helped them, to pass judgements on the information they were producing.

Thus, it seems that one of the main problems with the way the discussions at the tables were organized was that they were unable to reach a consensus within set time limits, since the table work was restricted to a specific time frame and a decision on a ratification vote would have to be taken within a few years of the establishment of the NCCP. In such an ill-defined setting, one aspect becomes important which might be underestimated in democratic research, namely that the participants felt that their work was useless and that they sensed a lack of self-efficacy. During the process, they neither knew whether nor how their work and the information they were producing would influence any forthcoming policies and/or GHG developments and this can be considered to be an important factor in regard to their individual and collective performances (Bandura, 1995, 1997; Bandura & Locke, 2003):

> "So many of them [participants of the tables] felt that they were not very influential in the process. Yes, they got in the door to be part of the process but, no, I don't think they viewed their roles to be those of significant players."
>
> (Confidential2, 2014)

To sum up, the participatory structures were clearly at the very least poorly defined and were thus not entirely successful. Some of the participants and officials involved could not see why the process achieved so little traction, whereas others characterized the whole process as window dressing and some made structures outside the process, like the ways the associations involved worked, which accounts for the endless debates. The main purpose of the tables also remained at least partially unclear, with interpretations ranging from education and officially analysing all options through to achieving a consensus and reaching a decision as to whether to ratify Kyoto. However, some of the tables actually worked quite well in terms of evaluating and producing information about their topics, as their final options papers overwhelmingly demonstrate. The tables' output remained productive as long as their purpose was assumed to lie in the production of information. That the process was not based on sound deliberation and the establishment of room for considered judgement can be seen in the fact that discussions became aggressive and heated when it came to the interpretation of the information and the endless debates this resulted in. According to F. Michael Cleland, the process was dominated by a short-term perspective in terms of meeting the Kyoto target instead of looking for pathways to a long-term low carbon future. This is the reason why, for example, long-term future-orientated technology projects received no attention, since they were not related to the Kyoto Protocol (Cleland, 2014). As "all group thinking processes tend to become dominated by conventional thinking", the NCCP was also faced with certain shortcomings, such as proposing that "it's all gonna be renewables" without taking the role of energy efficiency into consideration adequately, nor the necessary changes this would imply in the configuration of the energy system (Cleland, 2014). Consequently, participants felt that they had no influence in the long run, although this would have been one of the process's main tasks in terms of democratic quality, i.e. enabling those involved to influence decision-making. Instead, the tables were discontinued without having formulated a roadmap on how their results would be (in)directly integrated into the policy-making process.

What does all this mean for the influence of participation on climate performance? *Discontinued participation* only occurred to generate information, it produced no consensus on action and had no clear roadmap on how results would influence policy-making, thus rendering it, to a certain extent, worthless. Nevertheless, a good information base is the right starting point for participation and the education of participants as a result of the production of information can be welcomed, as it would have increased the pool of people who know more about climate change and have enabled new policy options. Yet, the influence that the information produced in the process and the newly educated participants were able to have would have been limited and mostly indirectly effective, since the table process ended with the production of option papers. Of course, these would have been used in further stakeholder consultations, but this nonetheless only forms the first step of a truly participative process.

Despite the direct shortcomings which can be identified in the lack of/ imperfect participatory structures, no interview partner suggested that the failure of the table process could be related to the lack of involvement of members of the broader public in the process. Yet, the involvement of all affected and relevant actors might have been a necessary precondition for the process gaining traction and creating broader political interest, since the broader public demanded it.

However, explaining how the tables worked and what information they produced, leads us to two other important dimensions. Transparency and publicity are also relevant factors in a democratic policy process, ensuring that all relevant information is accessible and actively shared.

Transparency and publicity: no explanation to the broader public

Informal meetings also took place alongside the official participatory structures of the table process. Such meetings raise the question of transparency, since transparency stands for access and traceability of all relevant information at all stages of the policy process. In terms of the JMMs, David Anderson describes the decision-makers' informal meetings as a necessary step in finding out how the other side intended to behave in official negotiations, a sort of *functional informality*, so to speak:

> "There were a substantial number of informal sessions, phone calls, lunches, whatever. Largely these were in preparation for the formal meetings. You know, so you get a discussion as to where or how far can the other side go. How far can the other person go? What will they do? What is the make or break issue for them?"
>
> (Anderson, 2014)

According to David Oulton, informality was also helpful in the table process. Oulton describes his open door policy as a necessity when dealing with conflicting views and requiring a neutral stance which was able to decide in a way which was acceptable to the conflicting parties (Oulton, 2014). The question is whether trust and information about the actors' positions really justified a certain degree of informality in the process. Such informality led to lobbying and circumstances in which "clearly economic interests" had a better chance of being heard than did marginalized voices, since representatives of economic interests had the argument of generating employment on their side (Confidential3, 2014).

While, in the right circumstances, informality can help to build trust and resolve conflicts before they take on a public dimension, it can also open the door to controversial lobbying. In terms of effectiveness and efficiency, the government has to coordinate conflicting objectives in a coherent policy. Such coordination could come in the form of informal arrangement, but perhaps a better process design could make such informal conflict solving redundant. The question is what effect does informality have on democratic quality achieving climate performance? So far, it can only be concluded that such informality existed and that there might have been a tendency for informality to have been used more intensively by stronger and more resource rich actors. Whether a process free of informality would have produced better results can in any case be doubted.

The most important point of reference in this regard is probably the way in which the business as usual (BAU) projection concept was transparently created. All measures were evaluated on the basis of the BAU concept, however, the BAU concept was not always made public in Canada, "[s]o you often had a situation where the government was saying: 'We are going to reduce emissions by X megatons relative to the business as usual', but we did not actually know what the business as usual projection was" (Bramley, 2014).

Besides such in-process transparency, the other aspect of transparency combined with publicity is the way in which information about the process was disseminated to the broader public. For this purpose, a website was launched which provided information about the NCCP and, for example, contained reports from the issue tables, but not agendas of the meetings, since "nobody asked for those sorts of things" (Confidential3, 2014; Oulton, 2014 (quotation)). The purpose of providing transparency through a website and presentations in the Senate and parliamentary committees, in the Cabinet, the provinces, etc. was to have a concrete influence on the policy process results (Oulton, 2014). The effect of such transparency efforts and information provision should be to ensure that it becomes uncomfortable for industry to oppose active climate policies and that every actor is either convinced of the merits of the policy and thus supports it or at least does not hinder the federal government in ratifying the treaty (Oulton, 2014). However, "in the end, that didn't happen", and one main reason for this was that the communication of the costs of the policy instruments to the broader public did not work out as intended (Oulton, 2014). Thus, information to an informed climate policy community was quite transparently provided, but "in engaging the broader Canadian citizenry in this discussion, a much more effective job could have been done" (Confidential1, 2014).

One main aspect of transparency can be found in the way in which the issues were explained to the broader public. Maybe the broader public needed to be better sensitized and the issues to be better arranged in terms of lending them a proactive or *explanatory transparency*. Transparency seems to not only be provided through the accessibility and traceability of relevant information, but also through the explanation of this information to those who themselves would otherwise not visit the websites provided, nor read or necessarily understand the option papers resulting from the tables. Thus, transparency is, in this regard, closely connected to the public sphere and media plays a key role as a transmitter of information and a source of public education. Therefore, it becomes important to find out whether the media succeeded in reaching the broader public. However, the way the media reported on the NCCP seems not to have had an impact on policy-making. The focus was more on other policy fields, while reporting about climate issues was concentrated on announcements and on the question of whether climate change was real. In comparison to other policy fields, such as economics and federal-provincial relations, climate policy received little coverage and does not appear to have been considered to be as important (Goldenberg, 2014; Oulton, 2014).

Obviously, without media reporting on the NCCP, little influence could be had over either it or later climate performance. What might be missing here is something that again could be called a transmission belt in the form of the aforementioned *explanatory transparency*. There should have been explanatory transparency in the form of a press secretariat, which not only launched a website with option reports but also translated the option papers into everyday language, explained what these would mean in practical terms for the lives of Canadians and tried to get in contact with the media to ensure that these issues were covered. However, since the broader public was not involved and could not participate in the process, they probably did not recognize what had happened and did not demand *explanatory transparency*. Without such elements, the influence of transparency and publicity on climate performance was marginal, however, if the two dimensions had been further developed for the broader public, then a positive influence could have been expected.

Follow-up to the tables

Even though the NCCP continued after 2000 when the table process ended, its proceedings changed in a way which made the whole process become almost irrelevant in terms of the democracy-climate nexus. However, in order to evaluate all the possible influences which democratic quality, or a lack thereof, could have had on climate performance, a brief follow-up on what happened after the tables were concluded is necessary.

The results of the table process can be found in a discussion document published in June 2000, which was used at national stakeholder sessions that took place in the summer of 2000 in major cities, outlining the first phase of a *National Implementation Strategy on Climate Change* in the form of a *First National Climate Change Business Plan* (CESD, 2001, pp. 17–18). Officially, the purpose of these 14 one-day sessions, which took place in each province and territory (with the exception of two in Ontario), was to tie up the options produced by the tables with invited experts and other actors and the stakeholder input being reported to the JMMs (Delphi Group, 2000; NCCS, 2000b).

The stakeholder sessions proceeded as follows: (1) presentations by officials about the NCCP; (2) a question and answer session; (3) discussions on sector-based and broad themes in the form of input about the global situation from the participants and closing remarks by officials. Since the stakeholder sessions were one-day workshops, only a small amount of time could be devoted to procedures which enabled the participants to influence decision-making. Thus, it was overwhelmingly the case that these sessions only produced different opinions regarding what options to prioritize, without any further participative structure which would have enabled consensus and decision-making or greater involvement of the broader public. Not surprisingly, one of the main messages of the stakeholder sessions was as follows:

> "Participants noted that to act effectively on climate change, Canadians need to have a greater understanding about the issue, be engaged in changing their own behaviours that result in GHG emissions and be supportive of various actions on climate change. To this end, participants suggested that a broader public consultation on climate change should focus on education and awareness to ensure that Canadians are part of the solution."
>
> (Delphi Group, 2000, p. 7)

After the stakeholder sessions in 2000, the roles of the NCCS and the NCCP became increasingly unimportant in terms of managing a national climate policy process. In order to be comprehensive, it is noteworthy to mention that in 2001 at least two federal-provincial stakeholder working groups existed. The Emissions Allocation and Burden Sharing Working Group and the Domestic Emissions Trading Working Group both continued to work on themes of the tables but without much in the way of impact upon substantial policies (Bramley, 2014). However, their influence and importance seems to have been very limited since only one interview partner mentioned these two groups and no remarks about them could be found in any documents.

Notably, during the NCCP of 2000–2002, environmental and industry groups remained influential. Consultants appointed by the NCCS influenced the NCCP indirectly, without generally achieving much recognition, as they (helped to) set up the process, constructed models or carried out analyses (Oulton, 2014). Such consultants are, of course, not democratically legitimated actors. It is therefore necessary that the participants agree with the work of the consultants, however this cannot be ascertained with the information available. The concrete work carried out by consultants thus represents somewhat of a black hole. However – even though the Kyoto Protocol was ratified in the end – industry representatives probably had the most impact on proceedings between 2000 and 2002, since, according to David Oulton, they were very effective in terms of hindering the implementation of a major economic instrument which would have been neces- sary in terms of active climate policies (Oulton, 2014).

Overall, the role of the NCCP itself became obvious when "the wheels fell off the national process" in 2002, since it played almost no role any more when decisions on the process of ratification had to be made, informality increased and decisions were moved up to a higher level (Oulton, 2014). The NCCS existed until 2004 and undertook stakeholder sessions again in 2002 in the context of a federal discussion paper (analysed below in "Federal Activities") as well as providing little acknowledged evaluations of some policies. A final product of the NCCS, which was published in the context of the NCCP, was the 2002 *National Climate Change Business Plan*, which is more or less a list of activities which the provinces and the federal government were undertaking. In light of the 2002 federal *Climate Change Plan for Canada* (Government of Canada, 2002a), it would seem that the *Business Plan* had no great impact upon policy-making. However, the influence of consultants and industry seems to have been noteworthy as well as the increasing informality as decision-mak- ing came closer. The stakeholder sessions in 2000 as in the case of the tables included a range of invited actors, but they were never truly participative in terms of allowing the actors to influence proceedings – rather the sessions were based on the acquisition of information – nor were any mechanisms applied to deliberate with those involved to reach a consensus. Responsiveness cannot be developed in such a setting. Thus, after the table process ended, the NCCP failed to be of any further significance for insights into the democracy-climate nexus. It might be the case that we can only counterfactually assume that a bet- ter process design, including an idea of how consensus could be reached via the table process and translated into concrete policies, would have had a positive influence on climate performance.

Creativity: incompletely designed experiments can fail

Nevertheless, the fact that such a broad process as the NCCP was established at all could be praised in terms of democratic quality and described as a democratic experiment which should have influenced climate performance.

It was not only the FMMs' main purpose to ensure that the process would be public but also the wish of the PM, who "was very insistent that it has to be, there had to be exhaustive discussion". And, it is for this reason that the federal government did not use their "political force to advance things very far" (Anderson, 2014). The process was "really an experiment", since the government had not run a process with that much public engagement before (Oulton, 2014). However, at the end "this was simply a process . . . that would end up immobilizing decision-making rather than facilitating decision-making" by creating diverse views which were "more articulate and more forceful" than at the beginning of the process, whereby it would have been necessary to become "more consensus-based in the sense that people have to feel warm and comfortable before moving forward" (Oulton, 2014).

Thus, even though undertaking such a complicated and experimental process has to be ranked highly in terms of democratic quality, the experiment's overall influence on climate policy-making probably was nonetheless more negative than its absence would have been. In terms of creativity it is not only important to perform an experiment, but also to plan the experiment well and to ensure during the experiment that new forms of democratic engagement continue to be tested and innovations are enabled. This doesn't seem to have been the case with the NCCP. The experiment demonstrates that even a process which should have led to increased democratic quality can lead to even worse climate performance results. The reason seems to be that an incomplete democratic policy process, if not performed in an almost holistic way, can result in less climate performance, since only partially or deficiently applied democratic elements can make decision-making even harder. It seems that the characteristics of climate change and democratic quality require the different dimensions of democratic quality in a policy process to perform together at a very high level, so that interrelations can work to maximum effect. This is the only way that the climate problem can and will be solved completely. Top-down policy-making cannot be as holistic as required to solve the climate problem with all its subsidiary problems (involving lifestyle changes, etc.) and partially applied democratic elements can even make the situation worse.

Results of the NCCP and their influence: no warm feelings

What are the overall results of the NCCP that was in effect 1998–2002 in terms of the influence of democratic quality on climate performance?

First, there is a more direct impact in the form of the plans which were developed, including programmes which could be implemented based on the NCCP. The aforementioned option papers formed the first step. And, these were bundled together in the AMG's final report, which played an important role in bringing together the different views and option papers emerging from the table process. The AMG was entirely comprised of officials from federal and provincial departments and they were responsible for the final form of the report and, ultimately, for determining what was deemed to be important and how it was to be interpreted. The AMG stated that its final report was "not be viewed as a plan of action" but rather as an "order of magnitude", since its findings were "too coarse and many of its major assumptions too speculative" (NCCP, 2000a, pp. vii–viii). Again, it is unclear whether the results of the process were moved up to a higher level of political decision-making in order to aid concrete policy-making. Similarly, there was once more a lack of a deliberately informed decision-making process which, for example, pulled all the threads together. However, the options developed at the tables did nonetheless to some extent form the bases for the actions listed in the *National Implementation Strategy* and the *National Business Plan*, which were adopted at the JMM meeting on 16–17 October 2000. These papers provided an overview of actual programmes and of a strategy proposed by the NCCS (NCCP, 2000b, pp. 1, 12).

At the same time as the *National Implementation Strategy* and the *National Business Plan*, the federal government launched a new *Action Plan 2000* and reported in a national report to the UNFCCC that the *Action Plan 2000* drew on many of the options developed by the tables. Therefore, even though we can't trace it, it would appear that the tables and the work in the ministries did have an influence on the formulation of the *Action Plan 2000* (Government of Canada, 2006, p. 64). However, even though the NCCP was mentioned as a source of options in a federal discussion paper which led to a federal climate change plan in 2002 (Government of Canada, 2002b, p. 6), neither the *National Implementation Strategy* nor the *National Business Plan* were mentioned as options sources or as guidelines in the federal climate change plan of 2002 or in the subsequent plans. The government seems to have only partially used options developed by the tables for their climate policies, which, according to an official from ECan, was "surprising for many of us that participated in the issues/issues table process", because "many of the most promising policy options and technologies that were identified were not captured in the subsequent climate change plans, critically the *Action Plan 2000* and the *2002 Climate Change Plan*" (Confidential5, 2014). Moreover, the *Action Plan 2000* was developed within the federal ministry without any further transparent participation of other actors, which is why the influence of democratic quality on the plan can be deemed to have been even more marginal.

Furthermore, in 2001, the NCCS published a progress report on the *National Business Plan*, in which it listed – without mentioning the GHG reductions the programmes had probably made – the policies, their progress (in qualitative terms) and the next steps (NCCP, 2001). The impact the progress report might have had on some of the numerous programmes which it evaluated, inter alia many programmes which were initiated as part of the federal *Action Plan 2000*, is almost impossible to estimate. It might be the case that "some programmes were enriched, other programmes . . . they [the government] simply let run out" (Oulton, 2014). Regarding the 2002 plan, some of the options in the plan and the AMG report were partially developed, but the process "did not come up with what you might describe as a coherent plan in every aspect" (Anderson, 2014). In the end "it really was a series of objectives rather than a detailed plan" and even though there was a "plan", there were many issues which "led the plan to get sidelined and not to be implemented" (Anderson, 2014).

However, it is impossible to trace the impact of individual options from the democratically incomplete tables through to their influence on climate change plans and policy programmes ending up in GHG reductions, since the documentation and data on these paths is missing and interviews do not provide adequate information on which to base an analysis of their impacts. Based on the information available, their concrete influence seems to have been marginal.

Secondly, besides the more or less direct influence of incomplete democratic quality formed by the options developed at the tables and carried through into programmes on emissions, a more indirect influence can be found. Even though the NCCP was unable to create a common decision or plan, it may have had a long-term impact (Cleland, 2014) through the educational impact of its 450 plus experts. Those experts who attended the tables and exchanged views with other specialists were able to use their knowledge afterwards and thus the process "created a large diverse body of people who had a really good understanding of energy and what could be done to address climate change" (Confidential3, 2014). The involvement of so many participants at least led to an educated understanding of climate change. This knowledge base and the options, modelling and ideas developed during the NCCP, and in particular during the table process, indirectly influenced Canada's climate policy over the following years. However, the same difficulties encountered in the first time frame, with the lack of both a transmission belt and sufficient attempts to determine a democratic foreign policy, seem to persist in the second time frame from 1998–2002. The results of the NCCP had almost no influence on the international sphere. In fact, governmental proceedings at the international level "were seldom a reflection of the information that they got in connection with these consultation processes [NCCP]" (Confidential2, 2014).

To sum up, even though approximately 450 participants were involved in the NCCP, there were no clear participatory structures which would have enabled the participants to influence decision-making with their findings. The information provided in interviews, in which people speak of "fairly aggressive" debates, also lead to the conclusion that there was frequently an absence of room for considered judgement and attempts at deliberation. Indeed, at the end of the process, contrary views which had existed at the start of the process seem to have become more engrained rather than to have modified as a result of discussion and exposure to different perspectives. Since the tables only occasionally produced options and the way in which the AMG used these options for their final report remains lost in the non-transparent ministerial machine which developed climate change plans, responsiveness cannot really be expected. However, the NCCP did at least have an indirect influence on climate performance through its knowledge production.

In the absence of a participatory design which clearly defines how the results of a well-arranged and inclusive process are traced into the political decision-making process and determine policies, it can be concluded that the NCCP probably had no/not satisfactorily demonstrable influence upon climate performance. Even though the participants who were involved left the process knowing more about climate change, inclusiveness without participation can be more damaging than non-inclusion in terms of its influence on climate performance, since it leads to a situation within which no consensus exists which can be channelled into policies and their implementation.

Federal activities

In the context of the Kyoto Protocol process, an investigation of the federal level between 1998–2002 is also of importance for the democracy-climate nexus. And, in order to understand the following analysis, some basic information about federal developments in Canada is required.

As already mentioned, climate policy-making's main stages at the federal level between 1998–2002 were the climate change plans of 2000 and 2002, which themselves resulted from a discussion paper and several stakeholder sessions. The *Action Plan 2000* only intended to meet one third of the necessary GHG reductions to reach Canada's Kyoto target. The *2002 Climate Change Plan* focused on reductions which had to be made by large corporations and the so-called large final emitters (LFE) in a drive to reduce GHG emissions by 91 Mt CO_2 eq., leaving 60 Mt CO_2 eq. of reductions required to reach the Kyoto target. In terms of ratification, the federal government had already announced at COP 6 in 2001 that the acceptance of credit for reductions opened the way to ratification. In September 2002, the PM announced that Canada would vote on ratification by the end of the year, which gave rise to arguments with the provinces, since some of them (especially Alberta) were, as a JMM in October 2002 indicated, not in favour of ratification. Their objection included a list of 12 principles which had to be fulfilled in the views of the provinces before ratification could take place (Parliament, 2002). However, the House of Commons nonetheless voted for ratification in December 2002 with the PM completing the process soon thereafter.

Before having a closer look at two distinct process phases in 2002, namely national stakeholder consultations and the way to ratification, a more general analysis investigates the federal level between 1998–2002, asking: what influence did democratic quality at the federal level have on climate performance?

Effectiveness, efficiency and capability: a precondition for a (democratic) process

Once more, governmental capability, effectiveness and efficiency seem to be basic preconditions for a (democratic) policy process which is able to influence decision-making and policy outcomes. In this respect, two ministries are of particular importance at the federal level between 1998–2002. At the time, they held completely different views on policy. This difference of views hindered the development of strategic priorities and, both ministries seemed to be unable to accept the decisions of the democratic policy process, whose results were dependent on the participants and the process itself. Subsequently, we can assume that the impact of democratic quality will be diminished, as the ability to compromise and take on board different views is a perquisite to democratic quality being able to have much influence on the policy-making process.

In regard to climate policy-making, ECan and NRCan were a "very unmatched pair" (Anderson, 2014) and had a "dysfunctional relationship" (Slater, 2014), since their foci were quite different. While NRCan was meant to ensure that natural resources could be exploited and to secure the necessary infrastructure for said exploitation, ECan was meant to protect the environment (Cleland, 2014). Thus, the relationship varied from "a bit formal to occasionally quite toxic and occasionally quite strongly cooperative", often depending on the style and personalities of the senior leaders and their ability to work together (Cleland, 2014). Due to these characteristics, the Canadian delegation was called a "three headed monster" (Confidential5, 2014). ECan and NRCan didn't always work together with the Foreign Affairs Ministry with the same impetus and this is why their relationship also tended to be "somewhere between conflictual and full on warfare" at the international level (Confidential5, 2014).

A policy process can only really start and fully function when the government in power and all of its different departments allow the process, and the results which this engenders, to take place and come about unhindered. Hardly any process can occur without this simple sounding precondition and its absence makes the chances of democratic quality impacting on climate performance much slimmer.

Transparency, participation, accountability: "It's a bit of a gestalt"

From a democratic perspective, participatory structures should enable the actors involved to influence decision-making. According to the CESD, the "co-operation of other levels of government and other stakeholders is generally required to fully implement the measures" (CESD, 2001, p. 20). However, cooperation needs the kind of structure which enables decision-making. According to John Godfrey, the PM has to "show leadership, to mobilize, to recruit all those people to the cause and to, for example, enlist" and thus to organize "all of these resources or assets, whether it's public opinion, whether it's MPs, whether it's media, whether its environmental organizations, whether it business", otherwise debates occur that lead to neither results nor tangible influence (Godfrey, 2014).

In terms of democratic quality, it is, of course, not just a case of one person, the PM, having to show leadership, it is much more about the democratic design of the process. Nevertheless, without the PM setting strategic priorities and leading the process, climate policy-making in Canada seems to be almost impossible. And, this means that the aforementioned preconditions of governmental capability, effectiveness and efficiency are of particular relevance in terms of participation. One important player in the overall design of democratic participation could be the Parliament. So far, many of the participatory structures which adopt indirect mechanisms comprised of societal actors in the form of NGO industry representatives, etc. have been analysed, particularly in regard to the table process, since those same groups were involved. While direct forms of participation as a procedure of direct democracy were non-existent during the whole period of investigation, representative participation structures existed and have to be evaluated at the federal level to assess the amount of influence Parliament and its elected members were able to have and whether and how such representative participation may have influenced climate performance.

One of the preconditions of participatory structures enabling parliamentarians to influence decision-making was not fulfilled, since it was said that "[r]eporting to Parliament remains fragmented and piecemeal and summary-level information is still incomplete" and that is why "Parliament's ability to provide effective oversight is hampered by the continued lack of consolidated summary-level reporting" (CESD, 2001, pp. 1, 23). The evaluation of the CESD shows that neither did the government ensure transparency nor could Parliament control the government since there was insufficient information available. Where parliamentarians are not well informed, departments can, to a certain extent, do what they like and this might explain why they do not have a great deal of interest in performing an informative function (Kraft Sloan, 2014). Consequentially, the department "gets anxious when parliamentarian start to learn things, because then it makes their job harder" (Kraft Sloan, 2014). Consolidated summaries of policy-making, especially in a field as diverse and multifaceted as climate change, seem to be a precondition to influencing decision-making. Indeed, transparency is a precondition to any parliamentary activities.

Moreover, the Standing Committee on the Environment and Sustainability tried to influence the negotiating position of the Canadian government at international negotiations by writing an official letter to the government. The letter had to be answered by the department and it had to explain what Canada's position was and how climate active policies would be ensured (Kraft Sloan, 2014). Furthermore, said committee and some of its members, such as Clifford Lincoln and Charles Caccia, were able to put pressure on the government by stating in public that it was not progressive enough in terms of climate change policy (Godfrey, 2014). Of course, one scenario in which Parliament's influence can be limited is "when Parliament starts pushing, then other forces start pushing back" (Kraft Sloan, 2014).

Thus, campaigns like an official letter or arguing in public based on the legitimacy a committee has amongst elected parliamentarians could influence climate policy-making. Sufficient information from the departments would, however, form a prerequisite condition for such a strategy. Nevertheless, estimating the influence of such campaigns seems only to be possible in a broad sense. Consequently, Karen Kraft Sloan characterizes all such influences which merge together as formulating a gestalt:

"At events or things like that where family members were present and I introduced them to my kids or my husband then he [PM Chrétien] would always
say "Karen, she always bugs me about the environment. Don't worry, we are
going to ratify Kyoto. We are going to do better." You know. So, I think that
he always felt that where he had done a lot of work on certain policy fields,
he hadn't done it on the environment. I think they knew that they had to
move forward on Kyoto. So, it's a bit of a gestalt, . . . you have this information from different sources and you have this one thing that comes finally
into your mind."

(Kraft Sloan, 2014)

What can be concluded from these insights regarding the role of Parliament as a
representative form of democratic influence on climate performance? It is pretty
clear that transparency is a precondition for any possible influence of Parliament
on decision-making, since only adequate information can enable parliamentarians to follow policy issues in detail and to hold their ministers accountable for
their decisions. When a sufficient degree of transparency is available, parliamentarians and parliamentary committees are able to influence climate performance
to a certain extent through public pressure or campaigns. Again, the finding that
dimensions of democratic quality only work and are able to influence climate
performance when simultaneously present is of central significance. For example,
it is almost impossible for Parliament to create public support or to control its
executives when a process is non-transparent and information, as recommended
by the CESD, is either unavailable or inaccessible due to a lack of prior processing. Nevertheless, representative influence seems to constitute a kind of influence which can be created in public and, at the same time, is able to access
and sway decision-makers when making decisions such as going for ratification.
However, when certain groups within Parliament start to push the process in one
direction, other forces will inevitably start to push back and this can result in a
certain degree of neutralization.

Another area in which a lack of transparency affects participation is in the
existence of informal channels of influence upon decision-making. This includes
calls to the PMO, as Karen Kraft Sloan, who was a parliamentary secretary to the
environment minister, recalls:

FH: Would you say that there were actors that were able to influence the process
very strongly? And, which actors were these and how did they do that?
KS: They probably just called the PMO.
FH: So, easy?
KS: Ya. Well, you call the Prime Minister's Office, and you call PCO, and
you say 'What the fuck are they doing?' You know. 'Are they out of their
minds?' Pardon my language, but you know.

(Kraft Sloan, 2014)

As already explained, in the first time frame, the question is whether total transparency is the most democratic option, since aspects like trust probably do not

occur in the same way in such circumstances. Yet, while informality could, in certain circumstances, be trust building, conflict solving, etc., it does open the door to controversial lobbying, probably especially so in processes in which some voices are not adequately captured by the participatory structures provided.

While some of the (informal) discussions were civil and argumentative, other meetings, especially when the oil and gas industry and Alberta's provincial interests came together, were unabashedly confrontational (Anderson, 2014). Not surprisingly, as the PM remembers, "most of the hand-wringing came from the anti-government, pro-U.S. ideologues on the right, including the Canadian Alliance, Ralph Klein of Alberta, Mike Harris of Ontario, the Canadian Council of Chief Executives and the *National Post*" (Chrétien, 2007, pp. 386–387). The influence of these informal campaigns through the actors mentioned by Anderson and Chrétien is clearly demonstrated by the gains achieved by the Canadian Association of Petroleum Producers (CAPP). The CAPP represents the oil and gas sector and was very influential through informal participation, gaining a special price from NRCan Minister Dhaliwal for emitting a ton of CO_2 despite ratification of the Kyoto Protocol and the release of the *Climate Change Plan for Canada* of 2002. More precisely, on 18 December 2002, one day after Canada ratified the Kyoto Protocol, Dhaliwal sent a letter to the CAPP stating that the costs for reductions for Canadian companies would not be higher than $15 per ton of CO_2 nor would Canada force reductions greater than 15 per cent below projected business-as-usual emissions for 2010, which were numbers which had not been published in any previous plans. Two days later, the Canadian media reported that in fact the $15 rate had not even been previously debated in Cabinet (Macdonald, 2010). As Jason Myers, Policy Chief at Canadian Manufacturers and Exporters, said in January 2003, the $15 rate was a result of industry pressure negotiated by CCME, circumstances which were confirmed by Paul Fauteux, an official from ECan (Macdonald, 2010). Thus, in 2002, informal influence could be utilized as a significant policy instrument, impacting upon the price of carbon (Bramley, 2014). Since the $15 rate was not the result of considered judgement, it can be concluded that a lack of democratic quality in this case led to worse climate performance.

Besides the oil and gas industries and the respective provinces in which they are located, David Anderson argues that senators, academics and consultants played an influential role in terms of both formal and informal support for an active climate policy at the federal level. He states that, although their contribution is often not recognized and that of environmental groups overestimated, these groups were able to make themselves heard while churches and trade unions remained relatively unimportant (Anderson, 2014). More precisely, Anderson argued that environmental groups' lack of influence resulted from their arguing for "dramatic measures" in a way which would not have been accepted by the broader public, as people did not want to be faced with the consequences of such hard measures (Anderson, 2014).

The role of such actors as consultants and academics seems to have been quite clear. Even though academics might be quite neutral and can be seen as a source of evidence-based advice with which to inform policy decisions, most consultants tend – based on the fact that they are or belong to companies – to have at least some financial interest in proceedings and only limited legitimation. Therefore, it is important to look at what part of political decision-making process academics and consultants take part in, since, as David Anderson argues, their contributions can have a major influence on public opinion through the media. Their role is important, but has to be clearly defined in terms of democratic quality. While academia could play a role at the beginning of the process in terms of ensuring that other actors are well informed, they should also function as a form of consultative control mechanism during the later phases of the process, commenting on and publicly critiquing the results of the policy process. Consultants might instead be necessary for their neutrality, as it can be expected that they would be more neutral than most other participants and would therefore be able to play a constructive role in regard to organizing the policy process and wrapping up reports. However, insofar as such is likely to be possible, an alternative would be moderators who have neither financial nor content-based interests in the problems the policy process deals with and thus are able to work voluntarily, such as, for example, retired officials. Whether the role of these actors is best defined and applied in the way described here or could perhaps be applied differently, the most important objective is to define their role in the first place, since it could otherwise result in them having an unclear and perhaps informal influence upon proceedings.

Furthermore, participation can be researched by looking at the way the federal government included actors in the delegation to COPs and enabled them to influence negotiations. As Matthew Bramley, who participated at COPs for the Pembina Institute, explains, members of the delegations received more information, but were not allowed to speak to the public and could also not participate in all meetings. He preferred not to be part of the delegation since COPs were the most important event of the year for getting media coverage (Bramley, 2014). Additionally, delegations to the COPs were used by ENGOs as a means of training new staff members. By attending the COPs younger staff members were able to get used to international climate negotiations and these thus formed an important part of knowledge building for those attending as members of delegations (Bennett, 2014). So, involvement and participation could result in an educational effect, which itself could ultimately also have an influence on climate performance, since the accumulation of knowledge ensures that more participants are able to contribute considered judgements. Otherwise, one could decide not to be part of the delegation and receive media coverage and thus influence proceedings through public opinion. As already explained above, weak and marginalized groups were rarely included in the NCCP, yet they were to some extent represented in the delegations at COPs.

However, was the transmission belt strong enough to ensure some form of responsiveness? At least in regard to the inclusion of carbon sinks in the negotiations, the transportation of ideas seemed to work out (Stilborn, 2003, p. 14). Albeit, even though the same actors were to some extent involved, there doesn't appear to have been a clear structure which determined how policy options from the national or federal level were translated into a cohesive frame for negotiations. Thus, the influence of the involvement in delegations at COPs seems to be restricted to serving as a source of information and education, without having substantive influence on the negotiations themselves, since the government controlled which meetings other actors could participate in.

Overall, at the federal level, participation and its interrelations with transparency, accountability and any form of transmission belt do not appear to have been as structured or as traceable as in the NCCP. Yet, importantly, Parliament does seem to have played a role and to have been able, through a representative form of participation, to influence decision-making. However, at the same time, informal ways of involvement also existed which were quite influential, e.g. as we have seen with the $15 rate. Moreover, the first time frame lacks a clear transmission belt. Even though the forms of influence were complex, likely quite weak and hardly traceable, tendencies indicate that more participation and its interrelations with other dimensions of democratic quality did have a positive impact on climate performance. However, only those actors whose associational and organizational rights enabled autonomy were able to participate and articulate their opinions.

Publicity: uncoordinated public education and counter-education in a free public sphere

Media pluralism and a free public sphere guarantee publicity of the issue under debate and raise public awareness, e.g. through the translation of scientific results. Even though public education programmes were quite numerous (Public Education and Outreach Table, awareness and understanding programmes of the *National Climate Change Business Plan*, activities under the Climate Change Action Fund as well as NGO and industry activities, etc.), they were focused on specific actions and did not raise public awareness in general, thus they failed to constitute a proper substitute for a national programme, which did not exist (CESD, 2001, p. 18). However, some of the individual programmes did begin to work and, while some confusion still existed about the causes, effects and solutions, 87 per cent of Canadians believed the scientific premises of climate change (Government of Canada, 2001, p. 143; Olivastri, 2014). Nevertheless, there still wasn't a national programme, even though recommendations to this end had already been made by the CESD in previous years. Education seems to be a source of potential influence on citizens, especially in regard to a problem like climate change, which it is impossible to resolve without the cooperation and actions of citizens.

In more general terms, the assumption of publicity would be that media pluralism and a free public sphere guarantee publicity due to the presence of a press secretariat or similar body, which explains climate change to the broader public, raising public awareness, so that the policy process can be controlled and decision-makers be held accountable. However, David Anderson asks why actors opposing

Kyoto implementation were so effective and complains that, although "[I] can't document this, but I think there was a major influence on our media through public relations firms in Canada, putting over negative information about climate change and Kyoto", with support from climate change deniers related to US oil and gas interests (Anderson, 2014). For example, the Government of Alberta commissioned a full page spread opposing Kyoto in a monthly newspaper (Bramley, 2014). While it is, of course, part and parcel of the freedom of the press that actors are able to publish any opinion they want to, there does seem to be a bias in the possibilities different actors and groups have in terms of articulating their opinions and views through the media, with those that are able to afford big campaigns consequently receiving more attention. In the same vein as the campaign mentioned by David Anderson, PM Stephen Harper later, as part of a campaign of the Alliance against Kyoto, wrote a fundraising letter to supporters, claiming that the Kyoto Protocol was based on "tentative and contradictory scientific evidence" (Simpson, Jaccard, & Rivers, 2008, p. 95). He further wrote that the Kyoto Protocol "focuses on carbon dioxide, which is essential to life, rather than upon pollution" and that "Kyoto is essentially a socialist scheme to suck money out of wealth-producing nations" (Simpson et al., 2008, p. 95).

Thus, media outlets were used to argue against all scientific evidence opposing active climate policies. As many studies have already found (Crow & Boykoff, 2014), the way the media is structured in North America with a pro and a contra-discussant can lead to a lack of clarity in an issue like climate change. Therefore, the media seemed to have, to some extent, actually had a negative impact on the public debate around climate change in terms of climate performance. In other words, a free public sphere also allows *counter-education* in terms of climate change deniers publishing articles which contradict climate science evidence. However, it is also doubtful whether the mere presentation of two opinions stands for a qualified democratic understanding of a public sphere. However, the very fact that the Canadian media was to some extent able to make climate change a publicly debated issue made it clear that it was a serious issue that had to be considered. Some ministers, such as those from NRCan and the Finance Ministry, were under strong pressure from industry, especially those industries located in Alberta, and media reporting about climate change and why it had to be addressed seriously helped to balance some of the pressure being felt (Confidential1, 2014).

The media can help to spread facts instead of opinions. The way publicity and the media influenced climate performance is however ambiguous and probably dependent on the position of the specific newspaper, TV channel, etc. Media outlets with more left wing inclinations tend to promote a more climate active policy, while media outlets with right wing inclinations tend to promote more inactive climate policies. Moreover, the more resources an actor has, the better they are able to strongly influence campaigns through opinions published by media outlets. Thus, publicity can have a positive impact on climate performance by educating citizens and balancing debates based on facts. However, a North-American understanding of balancing opinions can lead to skewed media influence, as scientifically disproven theories are able to feature on an equal foot-ing with commonly accepted findings based on thorough research.

National stakeholder sessions

In 2002, to foster the climate policy-making process, the federal government pub-lished a discussion paper for national consultations with provinces and stakehold-ers, aimed at identifying a way forward to meet the Kyoto commitments – this resulted in a federal climate change plan and the ratification of the Kyoto Proto-col. The NCCP itself ended since some provinces, principally Alberta, did not follow or failed to reach a consensus with the federal government. Even though the discussion paper was a federal paper, the NCCP undertook the stakeholder sessions, since the federal paper was intended to be a basis for ratification, based on consensus with the provinces and therefore federal, provincial and territorial ministers requested a national discussion. The overall process in 2002 was organ-ized as follows: first, the discussion paper was considered at a JMM on 21 May 2002, secondly, one-day consultations with 900 stakeholders followed in every jurisdiction and, thirdly, a preferred approach was meant to be identified and a plan developed for which consultation would be sought that autumn (Govern-ment of Canada, 2002b, pp. 1, 37).

Participation: weak indirect responsiveness

Based on the table process, elements of responsiveness can be identified through very indirect influence in terms of the results of the AMG. Two out of four options, (1) and (3), became part of the discussion paper, for which it "provided use-ful information" and, moreover, "guidance for the design for proposals included in Option 4" (Government of Canada, 2002b, p. 16). The four options were: (1) as "broad as practical" domestic emissions trading; (2) all targeted measures; (3) a mixed approach, including domestic emissions trading, targeted measures and international permits; and (4) an adjusted mixed approach. Since the options developed by the tables ran through many stages, such as the selection of AMG members and further development in the ministries, and the members of the AMG were public servants, those involved only had a very indirect democratic influence. Right from the beginning, the government favoured option 4, devel-oped by the government, describing it in the discussion paper "as an option that could be modelled over summer months if the input and advice from consulta-tions confirm that" (Government of Canada, 2002b, p. 23). Such a recommenda-tion was not made for any other of the four options and this is why it is doubtful whether the consultations were open in terms of their results.

Even though the influence of the tables was not intended as part of a straight process when the AMG began its work in 1998, in further development by the AMG and the ministries, they and their options influenced the discussion paper by options (1) and (3) as well as indirectly in the form of option (4). Since the table process itself was already democratically incomplete and its results only indirectly became part of the discussion paper through the AMG, the influence

of that democratic incompleteness on climate performance is too cursory to identify any positive or negative effects. Nevertheless, possibly the stakeholder sessions can shed more light on the democracy-climate nexus.

Inclusiveness: almost completely inclusive

To envision the purpose of inclusiveness in terms of democratic quality, it might
be helpful to characterize it. Inclusiveness is described in the context of openness
and fairness of access, which should guarantee the involvement of a plurality of
relevant and affected actors. According to the discussion paper, 900 stakeholders
were identified and invited to be involved in the 14 sessions, with 433 of those
invited finally attending (Marbek Resource Consultants & Stratos, 2002, p. 3).

   The selection procedure itself seems to have been quite inclusive and transparent. According to the NCCS, the number of participants "needed to be
manageable and reasonably balanced between stakeholder groups" (Marbek
Resource Consultants & Stratos, 2002, p. 3). Therefore, the NCCS developed a
list for civil society groups (environmental, health, financial, labour, aboriginal,
consumer, municipal and academia) and industry representatives (business and
industry associations as well as energy, transportation, manufacturing, resource
processing, agriculture and forestry). The stakeholder names were collected
through the National Air Issues Coordinating Committee (NAICC), via a list
of participants from consultations held in 2000, through membership lists of the
15 issue tables, working group and federal departments' contacts. To fill gaps, an
Internet search was also undertaken (Marbek Resource Consultants & Stratos,
2002, p. 3). This exercise resulted in the identification of 900 stakeholder representatives, who received two invitations by email or fax with advice on online
background material (Marbek Resource Consultants & Stratos, 2002, p. 3). To
balance between civil society and industry participants, a "one organization,
one representative" guideline was applied, however this was relaxed when the
response rate fell below 50 per cent, which could be critical in terms of democratic quality, since the representative effect of the balanced approach could
thus be limited (Marbek Resource Consultants & Stratos, 2002, p. 3). Finally,
433 stakeholders plus 186 officials from federal, provincial and territorial governments attended.

   In terms of inclusiveness, the sessions were probably even better compiled than
the table process. It seems affected and relevant actors were involved, that the
selection procedure was not particularly biased in either direction and that weak
and marginalized groups, like aboriginals, were also included. Thus, a system of
open and fair access guaranteed the involvement of a plurality of actors (Confi-
dential5, 2014).

   However, there might be one limitation: out of the 433 participants (without
government representatives) only 35.1 per cent were civil society actors while
53.6 per cent came from industry (and 11.3 per cent were experts). Thus, in the
end, there was an imbalance regarding these two groups, perhaps because of the
relaxation of the "one organization, one representative" guideline. Nevertheless,

Table 7.1 Summary of workshop attendance in 2002

Workshop city	Total # invited	Civil Society						Industry				Total All Stake-holders	Total Government Participants	Total Stakeholder and Government Participants
		Expert	ENGOs	Consumers	Munici-palities	Other	Sub-total Civil Society (ex. experts)	Industry/ business associations	Resource sector firms	Manufacture, transport firms	Sub-total Industry			
Vancouver	122	6	9	2	1	2	14	5	19	5	29	49	12	61
Calgary	107	7	8	1	4	6	19	13	15	5	33	59	18	77
Regina	60	2	8	2	3	0	13	6	7	0	13	28	24	52
Winnipeg	87	2	17	2	2	3	24	4	9	0	13	39	20	59
Montréal	78	7	5	0	2	4	11	8	8	2	18	36	19	55
Toronto	176	9	9	0	2	4	15	25	9	8	42	66	11	77
Ottawa	98	5	7	1	1	5	14	24	4	0	28	47	20	67
Fredericton	80	6	5	1	1	2	9	3	8	2	13	28	13	41
Charlottetown	14	0	4	0	1	0	5	0	2	0	2	7	6	13
Halifax	44	2	3	0	1	1	4	6	6	1	13	19	13	32
St. John's	32	1	2	1	2	1	6	6	3	3	12	19	9	28
Yellowknife	36	0	7	0	1	1	9	3	5	0	8	17	5	22
Whitehorse	46	0	5	1	0	2	8	2	4	0	6	14	10	24
Iqaluit	29	2	0	0	0	1	1	2	0	0	2	5	6	11
TOTALS	1009	49	89	11	20	32	152	107	99	26	232	433	186	619

Source: Marbek Resource Consultants & Stratos (2002, p. 81).

in terms of inclusiveness, a plurality of relevant actors was involved in the stakeholder sessions. However, as the first time frame showed, inclusiveness alone does not necessarily lead to a predictable influence on climate performance and can immobilize decision-making by producing views which are even more restrictive than those held before consultations, thus having a negative effect on climate performance. Nevertheless, the involvement of affected and relevant actors is an important precondition for responsive participation and can be ranked highly in terms of democratic quality, yet it does not automatically lead to an influence on climate performance which can be clearly estimated. Participatory structures, or the lack thereof, determine what influence involved parties can have on climate performance and these are required if the participating actors are to influence the development of policy.

Participation: show, tell and collect views, but with no influence on direction

To estimate what influence the public consultations should have, it is necessary to take a look at their purpose. According to a briefing on the public consultations, the goal was to "increase awareness and understanding . . . and to provide an opportunity for Canadians to send the Government of Canada their views" (NCCS, n.d.). What precisely should be done with these Canadian views and how they should influence the discussion paper remains unclear. However, another reason why the process was initiated was that members of the government felt that they "were getting captured, if you will, by the loudest voices in industry and the loudest voices would be those that were worried about the implications and would not be in favour of ratification" (Oulton, 2014). Again, the question remains as to whether the process was really open to new results and to allowing people to influence the decision-making processes or whether the government merely tried to use it to sell its preferred policies.

The stakeholder sessions probably were more of a "show" to build public awareness and to influence dominating voices in the public climate debate rather than a real attempt to invite external influence on a federal climate plan. To get a more precise picture of the participatory structure, it is necessary to have a closer look at the organization of the sessions themselves. Consultants (Marbek Resource Consultants and Stratos Inc.) under contract at the NCCS organized the sessions (Marbek Resource Consultants & Stratos, 2002, p. 4) and a generic agenda and focus questions were applied at all sessions.

In terms of the transparency of the participatory structures and participation itself, the clear outline of the day and the focus questions are positive since they provide a framework and help to orientate participants. The focus questions are well organized to enable the participants to understand the discussion paper, since questions on clarification are possible. The next step, the collection of views, could indicate that this is to be used as a basis for further discussion at the end of the session, enabling other arguments. Question 3.a. appears to be a summing up in terms of receiving a final picture, which would suggest whether the stakeholders would accept the mixed approach, which, according to the discussion paper,

Table 7.2 Generic agenda

7:30–8:30	Registration and Continental Breakfast
8:30–8:45	Welcome and Agenda Review
8:45–9:00	NAICC Overview Presentation
9:00–9:30	AMG Presentation on Analysis
9:30–10:45	Q&A and Focused Discussion on AMG Presentation
10:45–11:00	Break
11:00–11:30	Presentation of Federal Discussion Paper
11:30–12:30	Initial Discussion of Federal Discussion Paper
12:30–1:30	Lunch
1:30–3:45	Dialogue on Federal Discussion Paper (based on focus questions)
3:45–4:00	Break
4:00–4:25	Summing Up What was Heard
4:25–4:30	Next Steps/ Closing Remarks

Source: Marbek Resource Consultants & Stratos (2002, p. 4).

the government preferred (option 4). Nevertheless, involving a wide range of stakeholders and letting them express their views are two preconditions for participation. Whether enough room for considered judgement was available remains doubtful. Moreover, there has to be a clear procedure which describes the process and allows the views received to influence the development of a climate change plan and ensure that its implementation is based on the sessions taking place.

The summary report of the stakeholder sessions concludes "[t]here was a very strong consensus from virtually all participants that climate change was a real problem, requiring action by all elements of society", but there were "widely divergent views with respect to ratification of the Kyoto Protocol", with industry against ratification and ENGOs and other participants, such as municipalities, representatives of renewable energy industries and some aboriginal organizations, in favour (Marbek Resource Consultants & Stratos, 2002, pp. ii, 11–12). Industry preferred another approach, which foresaw longer time frames, less restrictive targets and harmonization with the US approach (Marbek Resource Consultants & Stratos, 2002, p. ii). Regarding the four options on the discussion paper, "[p]articipants were generally unable or unwilling to indicate a preference among the options proposed", while industry to some extent favoured option 4 and ENGOs option 1 (Marbek Resource Consultants & Stratos, 2002, p. iv). The results of the consultations were intended to "inform the development of the next iteration of a draft implementation plan for meeting Canada's Kyoto commitments" and to be presented at a JMM in October 2002 (Marbek Resource Consultants & Stratos, 2002, p. v).

Table 7.3 Focus questions

Focus Questions on the Analysis

---

1. *Do you have any questions of clarification on the Analytical Work?*

   - Assumptions used
   - Definition of the case studies

2. *What comments do you have on the findings/learnings of the Analytical Work in terms of:*

   - Cost – effectiveness/impact on GDP
   - Competitiveness – overall and by sector
   - Distribution of costs and benefits across the country

Focus Questions on the federal Discussion Paper

---

1. Recognizing that federal, provincial and territorial ministers of Energy and Environment agreed that the federal Discussion Paper will serve as the main focus of the workshops, the intent is to focus on workable options that would enable Canada to meet its commitments of the Kyoto Protocol.

   What are your views on the overall approach to respond to climate change?

2. Instruments and Design Features

a. *What are your views on possible designs of a Domestic Emissions Trading (DET) system (e.g. with respect to allocation, coverage, offsets)?*

   - Option 1 – Broad as practical
   - Option 2 – No DET
   - Option 3 – Mixed Approach (Large final emitter)
   - Option 4 – Adjusted Mixed Approach

b. *Which Targeted Measures (TM) and/or type of policy instruments are most relevant to your province/territory and sectors?*

c. *For purchase of International Emission Permits, what is the appropriate balance between:*

   - Domestic action and international purchases
   - Government and private purchases

3. Preferred Option or Mix of Policy Instruments

a. *What are your views on the mix of policy instruments to be used in designing a workable plan to meet Canada's Kyoto target? Why? (e.g. competitiveness, distribution of costs and burden, co-benefits, contribution to Kyoto commitments, etc.)*

b. *What are the risks involved in meeting Canada's Kyoto target and how should they be managed? What are the risks of not ratifying the Protocol?*

Source: Marbek Resource Consultants & Stratos (2002, p. 5).

Thus, what also seems to be the case after the stakeholder sessions is that only different stakeholder voices were collected, with no attempt to bring these voices, which seem to be as conflicting as after the table process, together to form a consensus. While industry favoured some elements of option 4, ENGOs were more in favour of option 1. Similar differences remained in regard to the remaining decision on ratification of the Kyoto Protocol. However, the results, which, of course, were mainly comprised of different views, were meant to influence the next round of the formulation of an implementation plan. Such a second round was planned for autumn 2002, with broader consultations, which were again intended to provide the opportunity to express views on Canada's response to climate change via a website (www.talkclimatechange.ca) or via email, combined with extended focus groups for in-depth feedback from randomly selected members of the general public in urban, rural and remote places across Canada and resulting in a report (NCCS, n.d.). However, these activities, which, in regard to democratic quality, sound so promising, never took place, probably because the PM announced in September that Canada would ratify the Kyoto Protocol in 2002 and that more or less ended the whole national climate policy process. Thus, the first round of stakeholder sessions were not followed by a second round, even though it might have been a good element in the participative structure, since it could have led to decisions or helped to develop the public debate in a direction other than that which it ultimately took. Once again, only a first step was made in terms of collecting views. Nevertheless, it seems as if the federal government achieved its objective by getting a better impression of "what the state of play" was. This first step concluded that climate change was viewed as being real and that there was not such a big debate about this anymore, yet that there also wasn't much awareness about what everyone could do individually to help avert or slow climate change (Oulton, 2014).

It seems that at least some of the efforts undertaken and presented above in terms of public education and the like had a certain influence. However, people were nonetheless unable to translate the climate change task of cutting GHG emissions into their own lives and behaviour. There appears to be a very indirect influence of inclusiveness and participation on climate performance in that it informs the government how well-educated the public is and which steps could have a positive impact on climate performance moving forward, allowing the government to focus its policies much better.

At the end of 2002, the federal government published a *Climate Change Plan for Canada*, which briefly mentioned that certain options relied on the work of issue tables (Government of Canada, 2002a, p. 19). The plan also acknowledges that stakeholder sessions took place. However, very little information about them can be found, with only a short section stating that the stakeholder sessions in 2002 favoured option 4 of the discussion paper:

"In the May 2002 Discussion Paper, the Government of Canada suggested that option 4, the Adjusted Mixed Approach, could form the basis for a workable approach to meeting Canada's Kyoto target. The consultations supported further examination of this option. Over the summer, federal officials developed a more articulated version of option 4, which also responded to some of the issues raised by the previous AMG modelling and to the views expressed during the stakeholder consultations."

(Government of Canada, 2002a, p. 61)

This statement is almost a contradiction of the consultants' summary report, which identified no preferences among the participants. Industrial representatives did tend to favour some elements of option 4, but the ENGOs present were generally in favour of option 1. Such a reinterpretation by the government clearly indicates that the stakeholder sessions were not influential and that the game was ultimately played at a different level, namely between the provincial, territorial and federal governments. However, the plan indicates that further consultations were required and would be undertaken to move forward on ratification (Government of Canada, 2002a, p. 19).

The federal government developed its climate policy plan based on a discussion paper which already favoured one specific option. Basically, claiming the stakeholder sessions favoured option 4 of the discussion paper, although the sessions themselves did not reach any consensus in this respect, strongly indicated the amount of influence the stakeholder sessions had. So, in the end, the influence of the national stakeholder sessions remained marginal, also in light of the way in which executive federalism could end policy processes in Canada. One reason for this might be that the participatory structures did not include the provinces in a way which might possibly have helped lead to a consensus. To some extent the findings are similar to those of the table process: there was a high level of inclusiveness, yet there was a lack of participatory structures which could have used mechanisms of considered judgement and consensus finding to enable democratically qualified influence. The way results are included in any further climate change plan or implementation remains non-transparent in the departments and, on the whole, appears to have been of marginal impact regarding the direction developed. As only the precondition of inclusiveness is fulfilled, and the interrelation with participation cannot be established due to a lack of participatory structures, it would appear that the stakeholder sessions had almost no influence besides informing the government, so that it could better focus on achieving its intended policies.

Ratification

The year 2002 was the year in which the Canadian government wanted to move forward with its decision on ratifying the Kyoto Protocol. Since developments around ratification are of importance for the democracy-climate nexus they are analysed separately.

Participation: lobbying by Parliament and potential veto power

Parliament is a representative organized way of participation. As part of the process of ratification Parliament, or, to be more precise, the Liberal parliamentarians began to intervene by lobbying in favour of ratification. One initiative with relevance to democratic quality in regard to ratification is a letter which was used by Liberal parliamentarians to promote ratification of the Kyoto Protocol and to show support for the position of the PM. According to John Godfrey, who initiated the campaign, he got in touch with MPs and the PMO, telling Chrétien that "[w]e are going to lobby, we're encouraging you by writing you a letter to sign the Kyoto Protocol" (Godfrey, 2014). Sixty-two MPs and 15 senators signed the letter stating:

> We are writing to bring to your attention the fact that there is widespread support for ratification of the Kyoto Protocol within the Liberal Caucus. . . . For these reasons, we, the undersigned members of the National Liberal Caucus, reaffirm our government's commitment to ratify the Kyoto Protocol in 2002.

The letter made it clear to the PM that there was support within the National Liberal Caucus (Anderson, 2014; Kraft Sloan, 2014). According to Kraft Sloan, those signing the letter could "either say that this is a reflection of their constituency or that they know that this is the right thing to do", which relates the letter directly to aspects of legitimation, since it takes into account that the MPs and senators reflected the will of their constituencies and acted responsively (Kraft Sloan, 2014). The letter was, in the end, a sign of support and part of the representative participative influence parliamentarians created. Notably, parliamentarians like Karen Kraft Sloan connected the letter with the wishes of the electorate as a way of legitimation. In her case this meant showing that she felt she had the backing of her voters in supporting ratification and that it was therefore the right thing to do. Even though the influence of the vote in favour of ratification by Parliament cannot be estimated exactly, the short time frame of 10 days between the letter and the announcement by the PM make it reasonable to assume a certain level of influence as part of the overall synthesis. When Parliament finally voted on ratification – the vote (Liberals, New Democrats, Bloc Québécois in favour; Canadian Alliance, Progressive Conservatives against) was not binding for the government – the additional support gained by the positive result was, according to David Anderson, not very high, but a vote against ratification might nonetheless have acted as a veto which could have stopped the ratification process entirely (Anderson, 2014).

Based on the legitimacy of their constituencies, MPs had at least two ways of using representative influence to intervene in the climate policy process leading to ratification: first, by lobbying public support for a specific position through, for example, the signing of a letter to the PM; secondly, it seems that, although a confirmation of the government's position through a positive vote in Parliament did not lead to additional support, a vote against the government's position might – even though it was a non-binding vote – have led to significant changes in terms of Parliament exercising a veto over ratification.

Accountability: on hold for the time being

Even though ratification is not the same as a new policy plan with substantial instruments which lead directly to GHG reductions, it is a landmark in terms of confirming the target agreed to in 1997 and is binding at the international level. Thus, it is necessary to analyse whether the final decision on ratification occurred democratically in terms of a sufficiently transparent and accountable manner and whether these dimensions of democratic quality had any influence on climate performance.

As the most important person in the decision-making process, Chrétien decided that in 2002 the time was ripe for making a final decision on ratification (Chrétien, 2007, pp. 388–389). Ratification was in his view a statement of Canadian values and a pledge for the reduction of GHGs (Chrétien, 2007, pp. 388–389). Even though there was still no concrete implementation plan, he "thought it was important first to establish an obtainable target and then to figure out how to meet it step by step, year by year", since, he claimed, without having a "set destination in mind, you'll never get anywhere" (Chrétien, 2007, pp. 388–389). Anderson describes this way of acting in the context of the struggle to build a national consensus, where the PM "couldn't force it, he knew that, but he did want it" and yet wanted to build momentum and hoped that ratification could be one step in that direction (Anderson, 2014). While Chrétien mentions the democratic importance of the debates taking place in Parliament, civil society receives no further recognition (Chrétien, 2007, pp. 388–389). He held the view that ratification would be the act which would set the goalposts while concrete steps to meet the target would follow, even though the NCCP had already taken place and developed a number of options. According to Edward Goldenberg, senior policy advisor to the PM, Chrétien wanted to change the rules of the game since he saw this as the only way to drive policy development forward towards ratification and he assumed that Canada's bureaucracy would follow suit thereafter (Anderson, 2014).

Nevertheless, the decision to ratify first and worry about implementation later did not reflect overall consensus inside the government. It appears a long shadow of insufficient consensus, which could and should have been reached through the NCCP, was cast over the government in the months preceding ratification and that this was exemplified when NRCan Minister Dhaliwal confirmed in September that, even though Canada will ratify the Kyoto Protocol, it "has no intention of meeting the conditions" (The Canadian Press, 2002). Officials were not satisfied with the decision to ratify, since there was no consensus on meeting the target, rather the government tried to "work within it [Kyoto Protocol] to see how much of it could be made flexible" (Confidential1, 2014). Also, in Heinbecker's opinion, it became evident that the "government was not serious about implementation" due to endless consultations and discussions about a ratification, in which they were "setting ourselves up for failure" (Heinbecker, 2014).

A lack of consensus allowed partially accountable decision-making in terms of vertical accountability; the decision can easily be traced back since it was clear who made the decision and the way in which it was made was similarly transparent, with all sources and interviews pointing in the same direction. However, horizontal control is almost impossible in regard to the PM's decisions. Perhaps counterfactually Parliament might have been in a position to influence public opinion with a veto vote on ratification, however, this did not occur. Thus, the step-by-step approach favoured by the PM was also a way of delaying accountability in terms of shifting implementation to a future date. Accountability was only partial in the form of vertical accountability, but much of this accountability as a whole was passed on to future decision-makers and this is why the overall influence of such incomplete accountability would appear to have been negative. Postponing accountability indicates a lack of accountability which has a negative influence on climate performance.

Result: climate relevant actors promote even more diverse directions

The federal government decided to ratify without striving for consensus any further, since it was convinced that it was unable to reach such a consensus. Consequently, it suspended a request by the provinces for a JMM in October 2002. In the end, Canada's executive federalism might have been an important source of influence on the destruction of national cooperation, with a negative impact on the possible influences of democratic quality in climate policy-making (Goldenberg, 2014). Alberta abandoned national climate policy-making since it was not satisfied with the announcement made by the PM that Canada would ratify Kyoto, while their "analysis showed that we [Canada] could not actually achieve those reductions in the time that was indicated with the kind of costs that everyone talked about being supportable" (Confidential3, 2014). According to an official from Alberta, the decision to ratify was not based on sound analysis and remained a major hiccup in the climate policy process (Confidential3, 2014). This is, however, brought into question by the information produced by, for example, the tables and the fact that the characteristics of climate policy ensure that a 100 per cent guarantee of specific numbers is unrealistic.

However, the plan to ratify Kyoto first and worry about details later did not work out, as Chrétien himself realized in the aftermath (Chrétien, 2007, pp. 388–389). He recognized that implementation failed to go as far as necessary to reach substantial reductions and to meet the Kyoto target. Thus, democratic quality during ratification might have had a positive influence in terms of participation in the form of lobbying through Parliament, while shifting accountability to future generations would seem to have negatively influenced climate performance. After ratification, many positions became even more inflexible, probably because the NCCP had no participatory structures which provided room for considered judgement and consensual decision-making and would have allowed different views to come together and find a common position.

Conclusion of national and federal activities

This conclusion focuses on the dimensions of democratic quality which are relevant for climate performance and on detecting the mechanisms of influence which determine the relationships such dimensions have with both factors. The quite varied findings are then collated in the conclusion and set in context, so as to be able to make more fundamental assumptions about the democracy-climate nexus.

Interview partner: a negative impact of democratic quality?

It might be helpful to first get an impression of what those who were directly involved in Canada's Kyoto Protocol policy process think of the nexus. David Anderson argues that the Kyoto Protocol process was "highly democratic", which allowed climate change deniers to raise their voices, took too much time and did not result in consensus, which is why he identifies a "negative impact upon results" (Anderson, 2014). The question in terms of the suggestions made by David Anderson is whether an open process which involves many voices and allows them to articulate themselves is the same as a democratically qualified process. It probably is not. A high ratio of democratic quality would stand for much more than only involving loud voices. Such a process would, for example, foresee the involvement of silent voices and/or those who require further assistance to make themselves heard. It would involve ensuring that all of the different voices involved were brought together in a participative setting which allowed those involved to argue based on considered judgement. And, it would also mean that the conclusions of such a process would ultimately be responsive and would be able to have an influence on decision-making and much more. It would, therefore, appear that Canada's Kyoto Protocol policy process only made a very first step in the direction of a truly democratic process and that David Anderson's view might, in many respects, be correct in regard to, say, the NCCP, where many voices were ultimately more opposed to each other than before the process.

In the end, when he speaks of how democracy "allowed differences and disagreements to come out to be focused on" (Oulton, 2014), David Oulton argues, to some extent, quite similarly to David Anderson, stating that an excess of democracy allowed too many voices into the system. Oulton suggests that a powerful government "might have been able to make the decisions that we needed and put up with the tough decisions on moving money around and making, you know, all that sort of thing" (Oulton, 2014). On the one hand, this shows the same interpretation of democracy in terms of the democratic merit of letting all voices speak and, on the other hand, the importance of participative mechanisms which are able to draw voices together. Consequently, Oulton draws the conclusion that only a powerful central government could have solved the problem, since democratic elements were unable to deal with the issue. Such misunderstandings lead to discussions about whether an eco-dictatorship or something similar might be the only solution for dealing with climate change.

The view that democracy allowed too many actors to raise their voices and made policy-making and strong leadership more difficult is almost unanimous amongst those involved. An official who interpreted democracy first and foremost as inclusiveness also came to this conclusion, stating that analysing

> "democracy in a sense that it's going to be reflecting the full range of stakeholders and the difference of counterbalancing and influences can make it more difficult to take the kind of leadership and strong decisions and policies that might be necessary in order to implement climate change."
> (Confidential1, 2014)

Moreover, another relationship exists, but its elements need to be separated in order to evaluate the influence of democratic quality on climate performance. This relationship is the one between democracy and federalism. Obviously, they are very much interrelated, e.g. in terms of the question of how provinces should be integrated into a democratic policy process, but at the same time they have to be separated in a way which allows for a distinction between Canada's executive federalism and the democratic quality of the climate change process per se. Executive federalism seems to be able to destroy a democratic policy process, especially when the provinces feel that they are not represented. Nevertheless, these circumstances seem to represent another argument for a sound participative process in which the provinces are adequately integrated and less power rests in institutions such as the JMMs. An official from Alberta also noted how, in terms of democratic quality, the provinces and their elected governments were accountable to their constituencies in the provinces and thus had to represent their will, which did not always concur with that of the constituencies of the federal government (Confidential3, 2014). Thus, the way the provinces, as democratically elected representative governments, are included in participative structures throughout the process is once more of special importance, if the impression of inconsistent decision-making is to be avoided. Nevertheless, the official from Alberta also identified some benefits of democracy in terms of shared information, a common understanding and the beginnings of a dialogue (Confidential3, 2014).

Asked what he would do differently in terms of designing the process based on the knowledge received in the course of the process, David Anderson mentioned four issues, three of them related to democratic quality: (1) "I would not have made the change to our target that Mr Chrétien made"; (2) [he] would work for "greater discipline within the industrial organizations"; (3) "[w]e should have had a schedule with timelines for the provinces which were tighter than we had"; (4) "there should have been better coordination between . . . the Federal Department of Natural Resources and the Federal Department of Environment" (Anderson, 2014). The target change at Kyoto, which was already identified at the end of the first and the beginning of the second time frame as lacking responsiveness and an action which could lead to disaffection amongst actors involved with concluding the previous target, is mentioned by Anderson and clearly related to democratic quality. The third issue Anderson mentions is a schedule with timelines, especially in regard to the federal government's work with the provinces.

Such a deadline-based policy process structure could have been part of a participative setting which worked through previously agreed upon steps. Fourthly, Anderson mentions the fight between NRCan and ECan, which was already identified as part of a procedural general performance precondition for a democratic policy process to happen. While others argue that climate change would need strong leadership, Anderson brings up another factor which could bring democracy to a decision point in terms of crucial decisions such as those required in regard to climate politics: namely, a dramatic event (Anderson, 2014). However, even though such a dramatic event could be defined as a precondition, it is, in regard to the closing time frame, perhaps not something which can be seen as an alternative.

To sum up the insights of those who were in central roles during the 1998–2002 time frame, it is obvious that one of the central findings can be seen in the fact that a democratic policy process was, in their minds, the same as an inclusive policy process, which, however, is exemplary of a restricted understanding of democracy. However, they also mentioned that the failure to bring voices together was a key problem and one which a participative setting may have resolved. Even though inclusiveness led to shared information and the like, the overall effect of democratic quality was categorized as negative, due to a restricted understanding of democratic quality which failed to consider that, for example, inclusiveness without participation is not highly democratic but rather democratically incomplete, since the different actors left the process with more opposing views than at the beginning and interrelations, like those between inclusiveness and participation, could not be established.

Findings: further evidence on a complex relationship

The interpretation of the findings is divided between the two modes of operation: the national and the federal developments.

The national investigation of the NCCP from 1998–2002 illustrates three findings. The first finding is a pre-process issue. First, it deals with governmental capability in the form of a government which learns from past errors as well as being able to set up and maintain strategic priorities in regard to defining a clear purpose for the NCCP. Secondly, it deals with effectiveness and efficiency in terms of coordinating conflicting objectives into a coherent policy as well as making efficient use of available resources. Both are preconditions for a functioning democratic policy process and, if applied, would have been able to influence climate performance by defining a management role for the NCCS. This means that the management role and the purpose of the NCCP, as defined by the (federal and provincial) governments, should have been expressed with a democratic purpose, since the lack of any intention to have a feasible influence upon decision-making simply diminishes the likelihood of the participants feeling any form of self-efficacy, etc. Thus, when the initial purpose of the process is not defined in a democratic way, it seems unlikely that the process and its participants will be able to change much to make the process more democratic and thus influence climate performance. In other words, democratic quality and its potential influence on climate performance can only develop insofar as governments allow (conventional) democratic quality to happen within a policy process. The second finding is quite substantial in regard to the democracy-climate nexus. While inclusiveness, in terms of involving almost all relevant – probably not all affected – actors in the process, was catered for, participatory structures remained almost non-existent. The table process was initially planned as small expert workshops and would have needed – following its expansion to 450 participants – a structural redesign. A critical mass of actors was involved, however, these were more or less used as consultants who worked on climate change issues on which the government needed expertise and developed substantial options and modelling. Furthermore, there was a (potentially intentional) lack of participatory structures with a clear sense of purpose, which would have allowed participant actors to influence policy-making and thus ensure responsive results. There was also no room for considered judgement, which would have allowed for some form of consensus and helped to bring the many disparate voices together. Once more, this does not appear to have been intended by either the JMMs or the government. One could therefore speak of *discontinued participation*: the actors were there but participation was not really applied. Thus, in the end, the views of those involved were even more opposed than before, the process gained no traction and only very indirectly (through knowledge production, modelling of the AMG, etc.) influenced any policies. In terms of the influence of democratic quality on climate performance, all of the above means that inclusiveness without suitable participatory structures can have a negative impact on climate performance. Albeit, it seems counterfactually conceivable to argue that inclusiveness with suitable participatory structures could have had a significant positive impact on climate performance. A third finding exists in terms of creativity. As far as Canada is concerned the whole NCCP can, of course, be described as an experiment, even though it is debatable to what extent the process was meant to be democratic. While new forms of engagement were tested (the extent and durations of which were quite substantial) and a new bureaucratic body (the NCCS) was established with the purpose of managing the NCCP, it all lacked a holistic (democratic) design and consequently, in many instances, failed to lead to any truly democratic influence. Neither the purpose of the process initially nor the participatory structure applied was democratic. Indeed, the process was not intended to increase democratic quality but to allow for government consultation with experts, consequently competition between actors was only given lukewarm encouragement. Ultimately, creative attempts in the form of an incompletely designed experiment can, when for example providing inclusiveness without participation, end up having either no or negative influence upon climate performance.

Overall, the process influenced climate performance in at least two (indirect) ways: through the options prepared and the modelling of the AMG, which was used in the ministries to develop climate change plans, as well as through the formation of a knowledge base of educated experts, who used the knowledge they acquired subsequently. One interesting insight is that most activities during a policy process seem to take place in the meta-dimension equality. This seems the most important dimension in the course of the policy process and a good reason why process design should pay special attention to equality during the planning of democratic policy processes. However, the influence of the NCCP was overwhelmingly negative, since it immobilized decision-making rather than facilitating it. The overall influence of democratic quality cannot only be measured in terms of whether more or less democratic quality has a positive or negative influence on climate performance during the NCCP. The situation is in many ways characterized by interdependencies and interrelated mechanisms. Most importantly, inclusiveness alone can have a negative impact on climate performance, while, in combination with a high level of participation, it seems to be very promising and likely to result in a positive influence. Other dimensions follow this model: while their influence alone seems to be marginal, their interrelations (e.g. *explaining transparency* and *publicity*) are more promising and more likely to influence climate performance in a positive way. Thus, it would seem reasonable to conclude that the more interrelations can be successfully developed (due to high levels of democratic quality in several dimensions), the higher the likelihood of positive influence upon climate performance will be. Thus, the suggestion made in the first time frame that democratic quality might be an important factor can be put more precisely: it is not a question of yes or no, but dependent on the existence of interrelated dimensions. The further suggestion therefore would be: democracy has to be a holistic venture in almost every instance, otherwise it cannot make use of all its positive potentials in terms of a positive influence of democratic quality on policy performance.

Moreover, based on investigations at the federal level from 1998–2002, three findings can be identified.

The first empirical finding is almost the same as that already identified for the NCCP between 1998–2002. Namely, that effectiveness, efficiency and governmental capability are all preconditions for the successful occurrence and functioning of a policy process. In the specific case of Canada's federal climate policy development between 1998–2002, huge differences existed between the two most important departments, NRCan and ECan. Since neither wanted to lose control over the process and its results, a truly democratic process could not occur. Thus, governmental forces must at least agree on a process design which allows for influential results, if there is to be a successful democratic policy process.

Secondly, participatory structures were of importance, especially in representative terms and in regard to Parliament as well as to the delegations to the COPs. Parliament could – based on the precondition that it had enough information about the issues being discussed – influence climate policy decision-making in three instances: first, through official letters from a committee to the government, in which said committee asked what concrete plans existed for (international) negotiations. Secondly, parliamentarians were able to build public support and to lobby for certain political decisions, such as ratification, by writing an official letter of support to the PM. Thirdly, it seems as if the Parliament might counterfactually have been able to veto the policy proposals, even though decisions like the ratification of the Kyoto Protocol do not require a vote in Parliament for authorization. Moreover, another way in which participatory structures were able to influence climate performance was through the composition of the delegations to the COPs. Either societal actors could be part of the official delegation and educate themselves through participation in governmental meetings or they could use the media to make their positions public. While these more formal ways of participation seemed to positively influence climate performance, informal lobbying and a lack of transparency – as already observed during the first time frame – did the opposite, as the $15 rate guarantee demonstrates.

A third main finding also deals with participation, which demonstrates the importance of that dimension for the democracy-climate nexus. The findings from the stakeholder sessions in 2002 resemble those from the table process: every voice was able to express its position, but no attempt was made to bring disparate voices together. Instead, the government reinterpreted the results of the sessions so as to suggest that the participants favoured the same position as the government (option 4 of the discussion paper), which was simply not the case. Thus, even though involvement was again pretty well organized, there was a lack of suitable participatory structures. Similarly, there is a lack of any kind of concrete summary or documentation of whether, or indeed how, the views expressed in the stakeholder sessions influenced the climate change plans. It therefore seems very likely that the government overwhelmingly developed the option it favoured right from the beginning.

Overall, besides the observation that dimensions of procedural general performance are preconditions for a democratic policy process, important findings regarding the democracy-climate nexus can be made by assessing the federal level between 1998–2002. First, an active parliament, which is equipped with sufficient resources through the existence of other dimensions of democratic quality, such as transparency and information about the policy issue, can, on the one hand, build public pressure to influence and control decision-making and, on the other hand, could – counterfactually – act as a veto power. Secondly, during the stakeholder sessions in 2002, inclusiveness was, as was the case during the table process, fairly well arranged, yet participatory structures were once more almost completely absent. This time the influence was neither positive nor negative, since the government had already decided which option it preferred and would develop into a climate change plan. As at the national level, equality is the most active meta-dimension at the federal level and many activities around the democracy-climate nexus operate within or as a result of equality.

Further interpretation of findings: exponential increase?

Bringing all the empirical evidence, analysis and observation together, it appears that a democratic process needs to be intended and designed to be democratic by the government initiating the process. It seems unlikely that the process can develop democratic forces on its own initiative in the absence of certain circumstances. In this regard, the officials who design and supervise the process must also be trained to ensure that they understand what a truly democratic policy process design means; just because someone works at a certain ministry or is a minister does not necessarily mean that this person knows what high democratic quality stands for. Officials have to be educated in terms of democratic quality.

Probably the most important overarching finding of the second time frame is that it is becoming increasingly obvious that the dimensions of democratic quality are very much interrelated. If these interrelations can be successfully established, then their influence on climate performance is higher; concurrently, incomplete or only partially applied dimensions of democratic quality can lead to even worse climate performance. Thus, when interrelations between dimensions of democratic quality can be established – insofar as all the different dimensions are of a high level – they seem to have an exponential influence on climate performance. This means that it is not the additive sum of the influences of the dimensions of democratic quality which characterize its overall influence. Instead, the interrelations are more than just the sum of the different dimensions in terms of their exponential function. At the same time, when only low or intermediate levels of democratic quality exist, positive and negative deflections are possible. The existence of some dimensions can, in the absence of an interrelation with other dimensions (e.g. inclusiveness without participation), even have a negative impact upon climate performance, as is seen in the fact that participants' views become more inflexible after the process than they were before.

One can call this whole phenomenon or the hypothesis formulated based on the findings of the Canadian case so far *the exponential influence of interrelated dimensions of democratic quality on climate performance*. Thus, the main suggestion made in the first time frame – that democratic quality functions as an important factor for an active climate policy – seems to match findings in the second time frame and can be formulated more precisely in terms of the exponential influence explained above. However, it seems as if fully applied democratic quality can be an important influence or catalyst in this regard.

References

The access date of all material retrieved from the Web is 5 June 2015 unless otherwise specified.

Anderson, D. (2014). Interview on Canada's Kyoto Protocol process/Interviewer: F. Hanusch.

Bandura, A. (1995). *Self-efficacy in Changing Societies*. Cambridge/New York: Cambridge University Press.

Bandura, A. (1997). *Self-efficacy: The Exercise of Control*. New York: W.H. Freeman.

Bandura, A., & Locke, E. A. (2003). Negative self-efficacy and goal effects revisited. *Journal of Applied Psychology*, 88(1), 87–99.

Bennett, J. (2014). Interview on Canada's Kyoto Protocol process/Interviewer: F. Hanusch.

Bramley, M. (2014). Interview on Canada's Kyoto Protocol process/Interviewer: F. Hanusch.

CESD. (2001). *October Report of the Commissioner of the Environment and Sustainable Development*. Chapter 6—Climate Change and Energy Efficiency—A Progress Report. Retrieved from www.oag-bvg.gc.ca/internet/docs/c106ce.pdf (accessed 22 February 2017).

Chrétien, J. (2007). *My Years as Prime Minister* (1st ed.). Toronto: A.A. Knopf Canada.

Cleland, F.M. (2014). Interview on Canada's Kyoto Protocol process/Interviewer: F. Hanusch.

Confidential1. (2014). Interview on Canada's Kyoto Protocol process/Interviewer: F. Hanusch.

Confidential2. (2014). Interview on Canada's Kyoto Protocol process/Interviewer: F. Hanusch.

Confidential3. (2014). Interview on Canada's Kyoto Protocol process/Interviewer: F. Hanusch.

Confidential5. (2014). Interview on Canada's Kyoto Protocol process/Interviewer: F. Hanusch.

Crow, D. A., & Boykoff, M. T. (2014). *Culture, Politics and Climate Change: How Information Shapes Our Common Future*. Abingdon/New York: Routledge.

Delphi Group. (2000). National Climate Change Stakeholder Sessions. Paper presented to National Air Issues Coordinating Committee – Climate Change (NAICC-CC). August 2000.

Dillon, J. (2014). Interview on Canada's Kyoto Protocol process/Interviewer: F. Hanusch.

FMM. (1997). News Release – Joint Communiqué December 12, 1997. Retrieved from www.scics.ca/en/product-produit/news-release-joint-communique-first-ministers-meeting-ottawa-december-12-1997/ (accessed 05 June 2024).

Godfrey, J. (2014). Interview on Canada's Kyoto Protocol process/Interviewer: F. Hanusch.

Goldenberg, E. (2014). Interview on Canada's Kyoto Protocol process/Interviewer: F. Hanusch.

Government of Canada. (2001). *Canada's Third National Report on Climate Change*. Actions to Meet the Commitments under the United Nations Framework Convention on Climate Change. Retrieved from http://unfccc.int/resource/docs/natc/cannce3.pdf (accessed 3 March 2017).

Government of Canada. (2002a). *Climate Change Plan for Canada*. Retrieved from http://manitobawildlands.org/pdfs/CCPlanforCAN27Nov02.pdf (accessed 17 February 2017).

Government of Canada. (2002b). *A Discussion Paper on Canada's Contribution to Addressing Climate Change*. Retrieved from http://publications.gc.ca/collections/Collection/En4-4-2002E.pdf (accessed 17 February 2017).

Government of Canada. (2006). *Canada's Fourth National Report on Climate Change*. Actions to meet commitments under the United Nations Framework Convention on Climate Change. Retrieved from http://unfccc.int/resource/docs/natc/cannc4.pdf (accessed 22 February 2017).

Heinbecker, E. (2014). Interview on Canada's Kyoto Protocol process/Interviewer: F. Hanusch.

Kraft Sloan, K. (2014). Interview on Canada's Kyoto Protocol process/Interviewer: F. Hanusch.

Macdonald, D. (2010). Federal CC Action Consolidated Chronology May 2010. Unpublished paper.

Marbek Resource Consultants, & Stratos (2002). National stakeholder workshops on climate change – summary report. August 2002. Retrieved from https://web.archive.org/web/20041214110215/http://www.nccp.ca/NCCP/national_stakeholders/pdf/final_report/finalStakeholdersAug8_e.pdf (accessed 22 February 2017).

NCCP. (1999a). *Municipalities Table Options Paper*. Retrieved from http://publications.gc.ca/collections/Collection/M22-132-10-1999E.pdf (accessed 2 March 2017).

NCCP. (1999b). *Transportation and Climate Change: Options for Action*. Retrieved from http://publications.gc.ca/collections/Collection/M22-132-16-1999E.pdf (accessed 2 March 2017).

NCCP. (2000a). *An Assessment of the Economic and Environmental Implications for Canada of the Kyoto Protocol.* Retrieved from https://web.archive.org/web/20051215185942/ http://www.nccp.ca/NCCP/pdf/AMG_finalreport_eng.pdf (accessed 22 February 2017).

NCCP. (2000b). *Canada's National Implementation Strategy on Climate Change.* Retrieved from https://web.archive.org/web/20060906095903/http://www.nccp.ca/NCCP/pdf/ media/JMM-fed-en.pdf (accessed 22 February 2017).

NCCP. (2000c). *Options Report. Reducing Greenhouse Gas Emissions from Canadian Agriculture.* Retrieved from http://agrienvarchive.ca/fed/download/optionsfinal2.pdf (accesssed 22 February 2017).

NCCP. (2001). *Progress Report.* Retrieved from https://web.archive.org/web/20 051026104315/http://www.nccp.ca/NCCP/pdf/11574_ClimateReportV2.pdf (accessed 1 March 2017).

NCCP. (2002). *Canada's National Climate Change Business Plan 2002.* Retrieved from www.scics.ca/wp-content/uploads/CMFiles/conferences/830749020_e.pdf (accessed 22 February 2017).

NCCP. (2003). *National Process.* Retrieved from http://web.archive.org/web/2005110 1194706/http://www.nccp.ca/NCCP/national_process/history/index_e.html

NCCS. (2000a). *Distillation of Phase One Proposals from Issue Tables.* Retrieved from https://web.archive.org/web/20040310214521/http://www.nccp.ca/NCCP/pdf/phase_ one_proposals-05-200_en.pdf (accessed 2 March 2017).

NCCS. (2000b). Media advisory. Federal, provincial and territorial officials invite stakeholders to provide input to first climate change business plan (Press release 25 May 2000). Retrieved from https://web.archive.org/web/20040428062803/http://nccp.ca/ NCCP/pdf/media/Stakeholders-Media-Advisory.pdf (accessed 22 February 2017).

NCCS. (n.d.). *Public Consultations on Climate Change* [backgrounder]. Retrieved from https://web.archive.org/web/20040428053423/http://nccp.ca/NCCP/national_stake holders/pdf/public_consultations_e.pdf (accessed 22 February 2017).

Olivastri, B. (2014). Interview on Canada's Kyoto Protocol process/Interviewer: F. Hanusch.

Oulton, D. (2014). Interview on Canada's Kyoto Protocol process/Interviewer: F. Hanusch.

Simpson, J., Jaccard, M. K., & Rivers, N. (2008). *Hot Air: Meeting Canada's Climate Change Challenge.* Toronto: Emblem/McClelland & Stewart.

Slater, R. (2014). Interview on Canada's Kyoto Protocol process/Interviewer: F. Hanusch.

Standing Committee on Natural Resources and Government Operations (1998): Meeting protocol 4 June 1998. Retrieved from www.parl.gc.ca/HousePublications/Publica tion.aspx?Mode=1&Parl=36&Ses=1&Language=E&DocId=1038831&File=0 (accessed 22 February 2017).

Stilborn, J. (2002). Library of the Parliament. *The Kyoto Protocol: Intergovernmental Issues.* (PRB 02–21E). Retrieved from http://publications.gc.ca/collections/Collection-R/ LoPBdP/PRB-e/PRB0221-e.pdf (accessed 22 February 2017).

Stilborn, J. (2003). Canadian intergovernmental relations and the Kyoto Protocol: what happened, what didn't. Canadian Political Science Association Conference. Retrieved from www.cpsa-acsp.ca/paper-2003/stilborn.pdf

The Canadian Press. (2002, 14 February 2014). Kyoto supporters puzzled by Canada's position on emissions treaty. Retrieved from http://forests.org/shared/reader/welcome. aspx?linkid=15473&keybold=rainforest+logging+human+rights

8   2003–2005

Undemocratic unpredictability

"During this process we did not release different options, different scenarios. It would have been a killer."

(Dion, 2014)

After Canada ratified the Kyoto Protocol at the end of 2002, some major changes occurred, especially in regard to the national climate process including stakeholders and the provinces. Central process structures and actors like the NCCP, the NAICC-CC and, finally, the NCCS ceased to function. A brief résumé of the developments might therefore be necessary to understand developments in the context of the democracy-climate nexus.

Since the NCCP ceased to function when the federal government announced its intention to ratify the Kyoto Protocol in 2002, the government used bilateral agreements as a major instrument to navigate Canada's federal system and to move forward on climate policy arrangements with the provinces between 2003–2005. A first draft for a memorandum of understanding was sent to the provinces in April 2003 (Macdonald, 2010). As a result, five memoranda of understanding were signed (with Nunavut, Prince Edward Island, Manitoba, Ontario and Newfoundland) between 2003–2005. A LFE group led by the federal government and including industry representatives, provinces and other selected stakeholders was formed in 2003. It was the main policy instrument of the 2002 plan and one of the centrepieces with which to reach the Kyoto target and to work out details on how to reduce emissions by large industry emitters. The first results of this instrument were a couple of agreements with specific industries and on principles for carbon trading. Simultaneously, CCME meetings continued to take place and also discussed climate policy issues. In December 2003, Paul Martin (Liberals) succeeded Jean Chrétien as PM. This happened during an election period, since Jean Chrétien retired before his four-year term ended. Paul Martin was not satisfied with the existing plan of 2002 and announced in his Speech from the Throne of 2 February 2004 that a new plan would be developed. After the elections in mid-2004, the Liberal government under PM Paul Martin became a minority government. Even though the period between 2002–2004 was

DOI: 10.4324/9781315228983-10

not a very active one in terms of developing and implementing climate policies, at the end of 2004 climate policy developments became more serious, with a Cabinet committee led by ECan Minister Stéphane Dion forcing through more comprehensive policy packages (Bramley, 2014).

These dynamics resulted in a *Notice of Intent to Regulate Greenhouse Gas Emissions by Large Final Emitters* (Department of the Environment, 2005) and the inclusion of the six GHGs in the Canadian Environmental Protection Act, 1999 (CEPA), which enabled the federal government to regulate them. The overall result of these dynamics was a new climate change plan called *Project Green. Moving Forward on Climate Change. A Plan Honouring our Kyoto Commitment.* Presented in 2005 (Government of Canada, 2005), this plan contains some aspects which are more ambitious than in previous plans, but also includes a reduction in the LFE target from 55 Mt CO_2 eq. (Government, 2002) to 36 Mt CO_2 eq. In 2005, Canada also hosted the COP 11 in Montreal with Stéphane Dion as president of the proceedings, which made 2005 a year within which much political attention was paid to climate policy. The House of Commons announced that there would be new elections in January 2006 due to a motion of no confidence on 28 November 2005, following a sponsorship scandal in the Liberal Party. The Liberals lost the election and Stephen Harper (Conservatives) became Canada's new PM.

What mechanisms linked democratic quality and climate performance? This chapter will demonstrate that a lack of democratic quality meant that democratic quality had almost no influence on climate performance in the case of Canada's Kyoto Protocol climate policy. Throughout the process, informal influence and the government's preferences dominated decision-making, which is why, in this case, the relationship between democratic quality and climate performance can be described as being representative of *undemocratic unpredictability*.

Preconditions: the importance of procedural general performance

As time goes by, implementation becomes increasingly important in comparison to the formulation of climate policies. The setting and maintaining of strategic priorities in terms of an ambitious 6 per cent target seems to contain a back-loop which deserves closer examination. Decisions made in the past are relevant in terms of building the framework within which implementation takes place and targets are set.

Canada's industrial oil and gas facilities increased so much after the Kyoto Protocol was agreed on in 1997 that for many politicians the Kyoto target became an unrealistic target which could not seriously be seen as an option for implementation (Confidential2, 2014). Additionally, the Kyoto Protocol was seen as a European idea, with targets for overall emissions instead of emissions intensity (Confidential2, 2014). Thus, the Kyoto target was probably already not being taken seriously by 2003–2005. A connection to missing responsiveness can be drawn in regard to an aspect which we have already identified in the previous time frames. Namely, that the PM's decision in Kyoto had not been related to a sound democratic process, in which participants and politicians would have felt that they were part of the decision or at least that they had been consulted and that their voices had been heard. Since there had been no such process structure, the lack of responsiveness cast a long shadow over proceedings, which made the target appear to be unrealistic, "European" and something which many actors in Canada did not see themselves being able to implement.

However, the Canadian government had agreed to the target. And, in terms of the credibility of the government's commitment to policies and the coordination of conflicting objectives into a coherent policy, the government's departments had an important part to play. The two most important departments were ECan and NRCan. As in previous time frames, NRCan had close ties to the oil and gas industry and ECan to ENGOs, which resulted in fights between the two departments (Confidential4, 2014). According to a confidential interview partner, this conflict was one of the main reasons why implementation failed, since a consensus on moving forward between ECan and NRCan would have been necessary to do so (Confidential4, 2014). Nevertheless, on paper at least, climate change plans were developed. Whether they were plans which could be implemented and whether they included clear definitions of how implementation could succeed seems to be questionable. While the confidential interview partner could find commitments and was "under the impression that there was a plan because that was what we were told", the situation was actually quite different, since "when we started digging to find the plan, there was nothing" in terms of how the commitments would be implemented (Confidential4, 2014). Instead, there was only "a lot of lip service, anecdotal or isolated initiatives" (Confidential4, 2014).

So, even though there were written plans and specific commitments, the plans displayed no coherent way of implementing the policies and programmes required to reach the 6 per cent target. In regard to a target which could be realistically implemented in the provinces, Stéphane Dion, Minister of Intergovernmental Affairs 1996–2003 and Minister of the Environment 2004–2006, mentions that the constitutional shared jurisdiction of climate change meant that "it's better to have a policy that's less powerful but doable" (Dion, 2014). Whether his plan actually was more doable could not be further examined as the change of government in 2006 meant that it was never implemented. However, in Dion's opinion, the involvement of the provinces was a precondition for implementation, necessitated by the characteristics of the Canadian constitution and its executive federalism. The government therefore signed memoranda of understanding with several provinces, since it was not fully confident of having the power to regulate GHG emissions with policy-making against the provinces, as this would require considerable investment of political capital (Bramley, 2014). Due to these circumstances – the constitutional need to cooperate and the desire to economize on political capital – executive federalism demanded collaboration.

However, the government did not do a very good job of putting its "house in order". It seems that Canada failed to fulfil certain dimensions of procedural general performance in the second time frame, since "[e]ver-shifting responsibilities between federal departments and ministers, turnover of key personnel, and changes from plan to plan . . . caused delays and a loss of momentum" (CESD, 2006b, p. 9). In regard to the 2002 climate change plan, "a number of people, who were actually listed on the list of people responsible for things, didn't know that they were responsible" (Bennett, 2014). The government cut back on programme staff during the 1990s to control the budget deficit and thus no longer had the personnel capacity to implement the plan, resulting in years of restaffing (Bennett, 2014). The impression of one ENGO was that every time they met with NRCan "the person we meant to meet was in a different office because they kept re-arranging everything to squeeze more people in" (Bennett, 2014). It was probably much harder for the departments to introduce a (democratic) policy process for the implementation of climate change plans in these circumstances.

Overall, it seems to be pretty clear that some of the aspects of procedural general performance which are seen as preconditions for a democratic climate policy process were present. However, these aspects only existed in a very incomplete fashion. Similarly, in the absence of sufficient cooperation with the provinces and a plan capable of implementing policies which would achieve the Kyoto target, it seems unlikely that putting understaffed departments in charge of the organization of a democratic climate change process was ever likely to turn out to be a resounding success.

Accountability: incomplete with almost no influence

Previous time frames identified that accountability in the context of ministerial accountability did exist, but was democratically incomplete in that it failed to ensure control of decision-makers. For example, a detailed review of Canada's climate policy-making, undertaken in the form of the Report of the Commissioner of the Environment and Sustainable Development (RCESD) (2006) to Parliament, identified "weaknesses in the government-wide system of accountability":

> "Coordinating committees and mechanisms that once existed have been phased out and have not been replaced. A lack of central ownership, clearly defined departmental responsibilities, integrated strategies and ongoing evaluation systems all point to problems in the government's management of the climate change initiative. Since 1997, the government has announced over $6 billion in funding for initiatives on climate change. However, it does not yet have an effective government-wide system to track expenditure, performance and results on its climate change programmes. As a result, the government does not have the necessary tools for effective management, nor can it provide parliamentarians with an accurate government-wide picture on spending and results they have requested."
>
> (CESD, 2006b, p. 10)

Due to a lack of accountability structures, it was almost impossible for parliamentarians, as democratically legitimated actors, to control which decisions were made. In such a setting, it is neither possible to trace back decisions to decision-makers nor is it possible to control them. Moreover, the non-availability of an "accurate government-wide picture on spending and results" makes it almost impossible to evaluate the precise influence of this dimension of democratic quality on any concrete policy instrument or programme. Consequently, for the Committee on the Environment and Sustainable Development GHG reduction was "ad hoc, lacked an overall strategy and did not have an accountability framework" (CESD, 2006a, p. 10). Even ECan itself admitted that it found "no central ownership" (CESD, 2006a, p. 10). Since this lack of accountability was "of the government's own making" it seems doubtful whether the government really had a genuine interest in establishing accountability structures, since that would have restricted its room for manoeuvre (CESD, 2006b, p. 11).

These circumstances demonstrate once again that no functioning control over the decision-makers existed, which allowed them to make their decisions quite freely. Attempts, like those of the Treasury Board Secretariat, were made to establish a more extensive system of accountability, especially in terms of procedural general performance and democratic quality, but these never developed into comprehensive plans. Subsequently, at the end of the time frame, there was still no mechanism with which to adequately report on and manage climate change implementation (CESD, 2006b, p. 48). Consequently, the RCESD made two recommendations: (1) to track expenditure and performance in light of agreed targets and to report this information to Parliament and a broader public; (2) to constantly monitor the performance of all programmes in order to know how successful they were and with a view to retaining and improving the established programmes (CESD, 2006b, p. 15).

Taking a look inside government to try to figure out whether any forms of accountability existed, it becomes clear that final decision-making and policy packaging rested with a Cabinet committee (Confidential5, 2014). The Reference Group of Ministers on Climate Change Cabinet committee, led by Stéphane Dion, started to implement comprehensive policy packages in 2004 (Bramley, 2014). Thus, in the end, climate change policy-making fell overwhelmingly within the remit of ECan (Bennett, 2014). Bearing this in mind together with the accountability structures from the previous time frame it becomes obvious that the phasing out of the NCCS, the NCCP and JMMs led to a centralization of accountability within this Cabinet committee and ECan after Stéphane Dion became minister. This means that there were even less possibilities for actors outside the government to intervene in the policy-making process or to control decision-makers within the Cabinet. When accountability exists, political decision-makers can be held accountable for their actions by referring to the targets agreed upon and plans can be developed to ensure responsiveness. Where there is no accountability, politicians will be able to evade democratically legitimized actors and the broader public and will not be forced to implement previous agreements.

Another side of accountability became increasingly obvious the more the process developed. The interconnections between accountability and responsiveness were, by this point, becoming increasingly important, as the government had to take into account more and more past decisions. According to John Bennett, the second government under PM Martin was the first one to clearly state in public that it would reach the 6 per cent target (Bennett, 2014). While Martin and Dion probably were the first in government to see the Kyoto target as binding, their room for manoeuvre was tighter than for previous governments, as the target had been decided upon some years previously. Speaking at that time, Dion said that "a lot of decisions have been dismissed" and that these could no longer be revisited during his time as minister, therefore, he had "to figure out, well, how can we reach our Kyoto Protocol target with all these straitjackets" (Dion, 2014).

This, when assessing democratic quality, brings us to the question of whether decisions made in the past are to be considered permanently binding going forwards. Can governments be held accountable for decisions made by past governments and should it be possible in a democracy to reverse decisions once made? A democratically sound argument could posit that decisions are only binding for future generations when they are made in a fully democratic policy process structure which itself includes the voices of future generations. Otherwise, particular interests may dominate undemocratic decision-making and there seems to be no legitimate reason why such decisions should then be considered to be binding, nor why politicians of later governments should have to respect these decisions. Another line of this same argument could be that decision-makers require special mechanisms and/or a high degree of accountability during the early stages of a policy process, since their decisions will, due to path dependencies, restrict the room for future action. However, between 2003–2005, there were only limited opportunities to hold decision-makers accountable for the targets which had been set. More or less the only options, besides the aforementioned questions which could be raised by a parliamentary committee, were elections and, for societal actors like NGOs, public criticism (Bennett, 2014).

Overall, some tendencies can be detected in relation to accountability: broad weaknesses existed in accountability structures; decision-making and important aspects of accountability moved up to Cabinet level, which made it hard for actors outside the ministries to hold decision-makers accountable; and responsiveness became increasingly important, as the room for manoeuvre was starting to decrease. This raises the question of whether democratic decisions should be reversible. The influence of the democratic dimension of accountability on climate performance is very much the same as in previous time frames: when mechanisms of accountability to hold decision-makers accountable for their decisions do not (other than in the case of elections) exist, then decision-makers can very much do what they want. Incomplete accountability does not influence climate performance, since politicians in favour of climate protection can make even more ambitious decisions than those previously agreed, while politicians with no interest in climate protection can ignore previously agreed targets. Yet, precisely which actors were included and could have provided insight into the decision-making processes?

Inclusiveness: informality raises unpredictability

Even though openness and fairness of access should guarantee the involvement of a plurality of actors, the way actors were included in the climate policy process between 2003–2005 appears to have been very informal in comparison to the previous time frame, when a quite formalized NCCP took place. Basically, two rather informal ways of exchange existed: those requested by different actors and consultations to which ECan invited participants (Confidential5, 2014). As no specific criteria for selection were applied, the door to informal involvement was fairly open (Confidential5, 2014). Sometimes, ECan also tried to reach out actively but unsystematically by "taking a list that they used to have and sending out a mass email to a whole lot of people" (Dillon, 2014).

In terms of openness, the process seems at the first glance to have been very inclusive, since every actor was able to contact the ministry. Such openness could, however, be used much more effectively by well-organized actors than by those with less resources. There is also no guarantee that the ministry engaged with all actors in the same way. Moreover, it remains unclear whether the list ECan used for invitations was completely unbiased and, since it was probably a pre-existing list, if it was also able to reach out to new actors.

In a setting where involvement is organized rather informally and ministries are thus as important as government institutions consulting with actors outside government, the role of officials becomes increasingly important. Mentioning that he almost exclusively met with three specific groups, Dion states that he "was merged by people willing to meet me" without being able to refer to any criteria which determined who he met (Dion, 2014). He does, however, identify three major groups which he, at the time, stated "are after you all the time, all the time": NGOs, lobbyists and politicians (Dion, 2014). So, out of a much wider variety of actors, there appear to have been at least three groups which were included in the process and were able to speak to the minister himself. Other relevant and affected groups were probably excluded from these high-ranking informal inclusion processes, since Dion simply did not "have enough time to speak to all of them" (Dion, 2014).

Overall, inclusiveness was organized in a very informal way. To some extent, it seems as if actors could get in contact with ECan quite openly. However, only a few interests made it up to the minister through the department and its officials (see Dion's quote "I was merged"). Since no criteria or guidelines existed which made the whole selection procedure traceable, the selections made inside ECan could be biased either way. Therefore, as was the case with accountability, one can say that without clear structures of inclusiveness, the influence of those actors who were informally involved was unpredictable and very much depended upon the minister and his officials. Yet, how exactly did those informally involved influence decision-making?

Participation: informal with unpredictable positive influence

Participatory structures should enable democratically involved actors to influence decision-making in a democratic way. That both the selection procedures and the degree of inclusiveness involved were characterized by totally insufficient levels of democratic quality has already been explained above. What now has to be analysed is what participatory structures without any formal mechanisms of inclusiveness look like and how they influence climate performance.

Unsurprisingly, the participatory structures were informal and lobby based, since every actor undertook its own consultations (Confidential2, 2014; Confidential4, 2014), meaning quite simply that nothing resembling a process took place. From early 2003, the level of informality in the policy process increased, with people individually meeting officials, ministers and politicians to lobby for their causes (Bramley, 2014). When Stéphane Dion started work on a new climate change plan, he relied heavily on the informal involvement of ENGOs, meeting with them "one on one" (Bramley, 2014). Participation was at that time restricted to proceedings within the department, e.g. ECan invited people to comment on a draft plan, but they were not allowed to take the draft plan outside the room, while the whole consultation process once again occurred on a one-off basis (Bramley, 2014). The influence of actors outside the government itself was only possible when the government published a Notice of Intent to regulate industrial GHGs in the *Canada Gazette* Part One, which created a formal opportunity to comment via a written statement (Bramley, 2014). Thus, at a time when the government had already identified its position on a climate change plan, the only formal possibility of consultation was the one endorsed by the Notice of Intent. Nothing more than what was required by law was done in terms of carrying out a formal participation process.

Since Dion himself was very much in favour of active climate change policies, it would appear informality helped ENGOs to influence climate policy-making more than they had done in previous and would do in coming years. John Bennett's insights provide a more vivid impression of how ENGOs were able to influence climate policy-making. He explains that he had extremely close connections with the government and "used to meet with a policy advisor for that minister, the environment minister, at least once a week and there were, literally, hundreds and dozens of meetings" which he went to (Bennett, 2014).

These connections were so close that discussions were held to determine at what point what sort of public support or criticism by the ENGO community would help to develop active climate policies further and support the minister in the Cabinet (Bennett, 2014). The influence was so intense that a programme of home inspection was also favoured and introduced by Bennett, becoming an effective policy. The programme was his "own personal campaign inside the process" and they designed it in "exactly the way we wanted it" with "hundreds and millions of dollars that was going to be spent on [it]" (Bennett, 2014). Bennett suggests that the ENGOs were the most influential actors between 2003–2005, with the Conservative government which succeeded the Liberals in 2006 naming the executive director of Sierraclub as the "principal author of the climate change plan Dion produced" (Bennett, 2014). An official from ECan who was also involved in climate policy-making for many years suggests that the 2005 plan was very much in favour of the ENGOs' point of view (Confidential5, 2014).

However, there were also other forces which may not have had the same strength of influence on the minister of the environment, but which had the ear of his colleague in Cabinet, the minister of natural resources. For example, the CAPP tried to convince the minister not to move too quickly on climate change while being very discrete in public (Confidential4, 2014). Parliament, which, in such an informal setting of participation structures, was probably the most democratically legitimate actor, did play a minor role in terms of influencing climate performance, since it had responsibility for the reporting procedures in its committees, however, it was mainly restricted to trying to influence public opinion, without any really substantial or direct influence upon climate performance (Confidential5, 2014).

In the informal setting between 2003–2005, it seems as if the priorities of the minister of the environment, who had the lead on the climate file, probably ensured that the ENGOs had the highest levels of influence, while the oil and gas industry tried to push its perspectives through its contacts in NRCan. Parliament meanwhile looked to influence public opinion, without having much of a direct impact upon policy-making.

However, access to the greatest influence in such overwhelmingly informal participatory structures came through the PM. The PM, in a form of responsiveness to the previously agreed minus 6 per cent target, wanted to ensure that Canada met the target and, according to Kraft Sloan, who met him on several occasions to discuss climate politics, stated that "whatever Canada was going to negotiate, we are going to meet those targets" (Kraft Sloan, 2014). Therefore, the PM very much enforced and thus accelerated the process in terms of the government's capability to set strategic priorities. He phoned Dion asking why the climate change plan was still not ready and created a Cabinet committee which had to work out a climate change plan, putting intense pressure upon it during the course of its work (Dion, 2014). Finally, the 2005 climate change plan was a centralized issue that was enforced by the PM; at the end "it was more the prime minister's plan than it was the environment minister's plan" (Confidential5, 2014). Like Dion, the PM also consulted closely with a small group of NGOs, especially with the Sage Foundation (Confidential5, 2014). Although the PM clearly did set strategic priorities, maybe these strategic priorities were to some extent set in a fashion which conflicted with truly democratic participatory structures. Perhaps, therefore, there needed to be a well-designed approach, which describes how both can be brought together in a sound manner. However, on this occasion, the setting of priorities was not brought in line with any sort of democratic participatory structures, e.g. there was no room for considered judgement and, instead, individual actors directly consulted with the ministers and the PM. Nevertheless, for the first time, it seems as if a Canadian PM really undertook steps in the process in terms of being interested in working out a plan for implementation and actually reaching the minus 6 per cent target.

Looking at the finalized plan itself in regard to participatory structures, it says that provinces, territories, aboriginal people and stakeholders would be engaged in the Large Final Emitters GHG Protocol and development of regulations, the Climate Fund mandate, the creation of offset system rules and the development of the partnership with the provinces and territories (Government of Canada, 2005, p. 46). The plan also stated, very cursorily, that a public engagement mechanism would be developed (Government of Canada, 2005, p. 46). Thus, hints as to involvement and participation existed in a rudimentary form, but only in Annex 6 of the plan, which indicates that they were probably not a central element of the plan. In the end, probably at least partially as a result of the change of government in 2006, there is no suggestion that any structure of engagement was actually applied.

Even though in terms of democratic quality it might no longer be deemed significant, since inclusiveness and participation have to be ranked as pretty low, some sort of transmission belt seems to have existed at the ministerial level, where, in ECan's climate change bureau, domestic and international parties worked together and reported to one director general (Confidential5, 2014). Such a transmission belt should have been advantageous, but would only have been relevant in terms of democratic quality, were it, for example, backed up by corresponding participative elements.

In terms of their interrelations with other dimensions, participatory structures rely on inclusiveness and have to be brought in line with the setting of strategic priorities as an element of procedural general performance. Moreover, it seems that informal settings enable particular interests to become much stronger than they would probably be in a more formal setting. Informal participatory influence could influence climate performance in a variety of directions, depending on the preferences of the government, since the PM clearly enforced direction and the Cabinet had to work out a climate change plan. Therefore, in the case of the third time frame and the 2005 climate change plan, it seems to be obvious that informality led to a lack of participatory structures actually having a positive influence on climate performance. However, the influence of non-existent participatory structures was almost indiscernible, with the consequence that climate performance came to depend on other circumstances outside the standard democratic processes. In the end, the climate change plan which was developed was not implemented due to a change of government in 2006 and it is therefore impossible to analyse its implementation and influence upon GHG developments. However, was the public aware of these developments?

Transparency: unintended

Informality existed almost throughout the process in terms of inclusiveness and participation and these are, as the previous time frames indicated, very much interrelated with transparency. A closer look at transparency and the question of whether access, traceability and explanation of all relevant information at the different stages of the policy process between 2003–2005 ensured transparency might be informative to see what impact transparency had.

The CESD characterized the mechanisms to ensure transparency within this time frame as "not sufficiently accurate for management and reporting purposes" (CESD, 2006a, p. 13). Thus, the basic task of providing information through reporting was not fulfilled. More precisely, in regard to the 2002 climate change plan, the federal government announced that it would publish reports every two years to outline the plan's success and evolution, yet they did so only once in June 2003, while the website only provided general information (CESD, 2006a, p. 14). Thus, relevant information was neither accessible nor was the process traceable.

Parliamentarians also felt that the official information they received left them poorly informed. They needed connections to people outside Parliament, who were better connected to the bureaucracy or had some form of direct contact with people within the departments who provided them with "brown envelopes" (Kraft Sloan, 2014). Even though information was provided, it was, as an example demonstrates, not clear whether the information was correct (CESD, 2006b, p. 13): in March 2005, a parliamentarian asked how much of the announced $3.7 billion in climate change funding available between 1997–2003 had actually been spent on preparing to meet the Kyoto Protocol target. The Treasury Board Secretariat prepared a summary, indicating that $1.6 billion had been allocated. The CESD tried to recalculate this number, but was unable to do so, even though the Treasury Board Secretariat provided information. In the end, the secretariat explained the difference of $250 million by citing a double-counting error made during calculations for the summary.

Moreover, probably the most important aspect in terms of access and traceability of relevant information can be seen in the way the business as usual scenario for the 2005 climate change plan was calculated. Since the 2002 plan committed to a 55 Mt CO_2 eq. reduction target, the only way to change anything was to negotiate the reference number. Thus, there were basically two ways to influence the actual reductions: by negotiating the reductions or the starting point for the reduction. Consequently, in 2003 and 2004, the oil industry tried to negotiate the business as usual level with the government (Bramley, 2014). An advisor to Stéphane Dion and officials from ECan told Matthew Bramley that Mike Beale and Rick Hyndman from the oil and gas industry, who also talked to Bramley about the same matter, were working on the business as usual scenarios (Bramley, 2014). Hyndman worked on a regular basis, one day every week or every two weeks, at ECan in Ottawa, "helping" ECan officials on details of regulations and the business as usual scenario (Bramley, 2014). Hyndman, for instance, proposed that the industry could measure from a 2000 baseline in regard to the 45 Mt target of the 2005 plan. This would have been equivalent to a 39 Mt CO_2 eq. target on the baseline of the 2002 plan, which initially committed to a 55 Mt CO_2 eq. target, thus obviously softening the target. Bramley said that "a lot of those things were going on" (Bramley, 2014). Officials told Bramley that they were not willing to publish the calculations of the business as usual scenario, since it would have undermined negotiations with the gas and oil industry, to whom they were however showing details (Bramley, 2014). Bramley felt that "this was a good example, both of [the] lack of transparency and of favouritism to certain stakeholder groups", which is why he submitted an access to information request to understand the way the business as usual projection had been calculated (Bramley, 2014).

That Bramley knows of these circumstances is only due to the fact that he received information from an advisor to Dion. Otherwise, it might well have been impossible to discover that such a completely non-transparent mode of influence existed, which was quite sly and, for people not closely involved in the process, completely non-transparent. That fatal lack of transparency ultimately had a negative influence on climate performance, since Canadian industry was able to reduce reductions. Yet, as in the informal participatory structure, a counterfactual argumentation in terms of missing transparency somehow suggests a level of unpredictability, since, under different circumstances, the ministry could, for example, have chosen a person working at an ENGO to recalculate the business as usual scenario, with a completely different influence on emissions reductions subsequently being endorsed. However, perhaps resource rich actors, like the oil and gas industry, were able to more efficiently lobby in informal settings. The influence of such informal settings would thus be unpredictable or negative.

Stéphane Dion explained the government's attempt to provide as little information as possible as being a necessary step towards developing an ambitious climate policy. The release of different options and scenarios would, in his view, have "been a killer" (Dion, 2014). Since the NRCan minister allowed Dion a lot room on the climate file and their bureaucracy realised that Dion wanted to develop an ambitious plan, they became concerned. And, even though he has no definitive proof of such, Dion suggested that they therefore leaked information, since "they hated the plan" (Dion, 2014). Thus, specific details found their way out, even though the process was not intended to be transparent. This is not to say that a plan developed in such a way could not be ambitious, however, it was certainly not developed in a highly democratic fashion.

A lack of democratic quality leads to results which fall overwhelmingly short of democratic embeddedness. This leads to unpredictability in regard to the influence on the output targets in climate change plans, which itself probably has a negative impact upon outcomes such as actual GHG emission reductions. Whether the implementation of the secretly developed 2005 climate change plan would have led to significant reductions, e.g. by not involving allowing to participate or informing and explaining information in a transparent way to the broader public who would have had to make the most significant changes in terms of their lifestyles, etc., is questionable and cannot be definitively answered due to the change of government in 2006.

Results: unpredictability through a lack of democratic quality

Even though the reductions which were expected and enforced by different programmes between the 2002 and 2005 climate change plans changed (e.g. the decrease in expected LFE reductions from 55 to 45 Mt CO_2 eq. with 9 Mt CO_2 eq. purchasable through GHG credits), the overall goal mentioned in both plans remained the same: minus 6 per cent in relation to 1990 levels. However, the gap between actual GHG emissions and the targeted emissions grew steadily. As calculations demonstrate, even the 2005 climate change plan, despite being seen as very ambitious by many interview partners, would have fallen far short and only led to reductions of around 85 Mt CO_2 eq. by 2010, as opposed to the 270 to 300 Mt CO_2 eq. which would have been needed (Simpson, Jaccard, & Rivers, 2008, pp. 182–185).

In terms of the influence of democratic quality on climate performance, the third time frame provides new insights. It seems as if the generally very low democratic quality during climate policy-making between 2003–2005 led in the end to a very ambitious 2005 climate change plan, since, behind the secrecy, informality and insufficient transparency, the PM and his minister of the environment were very much in favour of ambitious climate change policies (Bennett, 2014; Confidential5, 2014). However, the plan was never implemented, as there was a change of government in 2006. Yet, what could nonetheless be observed was the positive influence which a lack of democratic quality had on climate performance. That is to say, the positive influence democratic quality had on climate policy output in the form of an ambitious climate change plan, this did not however stretch to the climate policy outcome, since emissions ultimately failed to fall. However, the likelihood of such an undemocratically developed climate change plan succeeding without the involvement of the broader public (which would ultimately have had to accept the policies and to have behaved as required for a reduction in GHG emissions to occur) is not the only questionable factor. It is also debatable whether the proposed policies would have been strong enough, because, as we have seen above, none of the targets looked likely to reach those agreed on in the Kyoto Protocol (Smith, 2008, p. 47).

As comments on other time frames on the democracy-climate nexus demonstrate, the understanding of what democratic quality is and how it might interrelate with climate performance was only marginally considered by those involved. A confidential interview partner did to some extent display a limited understanding of the overall influence of democratic quality on climate performance, arguing at the time that "it is not about democracy because we are a democratic country" and stating that it was more a matter of the "political willingness", which politicians would have had to have shown (Confidential4, 2014). Stéphane Dion instead argued that climate change is quite a difficult task for democracies, which is especially complicated by the free-riding effect, and that this is why he favours a common global price and thus a market solution (Dion, 2014).

However, for the practitioners involved in the policy-making process between 2003–2005, the interrelation of different dimensions does not appear to have been self-evident. In order to assess this further, more precision is needed in terms of the influence of the several dimensions of democratic quality on climate performance.

To sum up, two central findings exist in the time frame 2003–2005. The first finding is quite similar to the findings of the previous time frame: several aspects of procedural general performance are dependent on specific circumstantial preconditions for democratic quality. To some extent, it is necessary for a body of staff to exist, which does not change too often, as this leads to destabilizing circumstances and makes it harder for governmental departments to deal with how Canada's federal structure is negotiated to reach a solution. As simple as it sounds, without sufficient and knowledgeable staff members, nobody can initiate a successful democratic climate policy process. The second finding involves the complicity of four dimensions which, taken as a whole, led to *undemocratic unpredictability*. First, accountability was incomplete. In the previous time frame, there had been incompletely established mechanisms of accountability, which in this time frame had ceased to exist, therefore, there were no means with which to hold decision-makers inside the government accountable and even parliamentarians did not receive enough information to hold the government accountable. In such a setting, insufficient accountability has almost no influence on climate performance, since everything depends on the preferences of the Cabinet. Thereafter, climate performance depends on circumstances other than those within the democratic process, which itself leads to unpredictability. Secondly, democratic inclusiveness was non-existent, while informal ad-hoc involvement dominated proceedings. Openness and the access of relevant and affected actors were not ensured. Yet, once again, this lack of democratic inclusiveness had no influence upon climate performance, as everything depended on ministerial officials and ministers who talked to those people they wanted to talk to, without any sort of formalized structure for engaging different actors. Thirdly, the participatory structures were also far from being democratic and failed to enable the actors involved to influence decision-making with responsive results based on considered judgement, etc. Instead, participation was informal but ambitious in terms of active climate policies. Intense lobbying characterized the way certain actors tried to influence policy-making, in particular, ENGOs seem to have been intensively consulted by ECan. In a similar fashion to inclusiveness, such a secretive and undemocratic participatory structure allowed specific interests (from both pro and anti-climate change fractions) to influence policy-making. And, this is why this dimension's insufficient participation also led to unpredictability, with a positive influence on output and, in all likelihood, a negative influence on the outcome of Canada's climate performance between 2003–2005. Fourthly, transparency was officially unintended, since the government believed that an ambitious climate change plan could be talked to death. Such a lack of transparency either failed to influence or had an ambiguous influence on climate performance. On the one hand, a relatively ambitious climate policy plan was developed, but, on the other hand, direct behind the scenes lobbying influence was exerted, which led to changes in the business as usual scenario. Thus, an absence of accountability, inclusiveness, participation and transparency formed an undemocratic complicity leading to a number of different types of unpredictability in the influence these dimensions exerted upon climate performance.

Overall, the influence of insufficient democratic quality on climate performance during the third time frame is neither clearly positive nor negative. It can best be described as being characterized by *undemocratic unpredictability*, since the direction of the influence being exerted was determined solely by the preferences of the government and by informal forces which could have been either for or against ambitious climate policies.

References

The access date of all material retrieved from the Web is 5 June 2015 unless otherwise specified.

Bennett, J. (2014). Interview on Canada's Kyoto Protocol Process/Interviewer: F. Hanusch.

Bramley, M. (2014). Interview on Canada's Kyoto Protocol Process/Interviewer: F. Hanusch.

CESD. (2006a). *Report of the Commissioner of the Environment and Sustainable Development.* Chapter 1. Managing the Federal Approach to Climate Change. Retrieved from www.oag-bvg.gc.ca/internet/docs/c20060901ce.pdf (accessed 22 February 2017).

CESD. (2006b). *Report of the Commissioner of the Environment and Sustainable Development. The Commissioner's Perspective – 2006 – Climate Change – An Overview. Main Points – Chapters 1–5.* Retrieved from www.oag-bvg.gc.ca/internet/docs/c20060900ce.pdf (accessed 22 February 2017).

Confidential2. (2014). Interview on Canada's Kyoto Protocol Process/Interviewer: F. Hanusch.

Confidential4. (2014). Interview on Canada's Kyoto Protocol Process/Interviewer: F. Hanusch.

Confidential5. (2014). Interview on Canada's Kyoto Protocol Process/Interviewer: F. Hanusch.

Department of the Environment (2005). Notice of intent to regulate greenhouse gas emissions by large final emitters. Retrieved from http://publications.gc.ca/gazette/archives/p1/2005/2005-07-16/pdf/g1-13929.pdf#page=7 (accessed 22 February 2017).

Dillon, J. (2014). Interview on Canada's Kyoto Protocol Process/Interviewer: F. Hanusch.

Dion, S. (2014). Interview on Canada's Kyoto Protocol Process/Interviewer: F. Hanusch.

Government of Canada. (2002). *Climate Change Plan for Canada.* Retrieved from http://manitobawildlands.org/pdfs/CCPlanforCAN27Nov02.pdf (accessed 17 February 2017).

Government of Canada. (2005). *Project Green. Moving Forward on Climate Change. A Plan for Honouring Our Kyoto Commitment.* Retrieved from http://publications.gc.ca/collections/Collection/En84-15-2005E.pdf (accessed 17 February 2017).

Kraft Sloan, K. (2014). Interview on Canada's Kyoto Protocol Process/Interviewer: F. Hanusch.

Macdonald, D. (2010). Federal CC Action Consolidated Chronology May 2010. Unpublished paper.

Simpson, J., Jaccard, M. K., & Rivers, N. (2008). *Hot Air: Meeting Canada's Climate Change Challenge.* Toronto: Emblem/McClelland & Stewart.

Smith, H. A. (2008). Political parties and Canadian climate change policy. *International Journal, 64*(1), 47–66.

9 2006–2012

Democratic weakening and climate change as a shield issue

"I believe I made change. No one has to convince Canadians who see the Arctic ice cap disappearing that the climate is not changing."

(Kent, 2014)

"I think the philosophy is: we are elected into power, and therefore we can do what we want until the Canadians throw us out."

(Vaughan, 2014)

Shortly after Stéphane Dion announced the new Project Green climate change plan in 2005, Canadians elected a new government. In January 2006 the Conservative Party of Canada formed a minority government with Stephen Harper as the new PM. Since he opposed most of the climate policy activities of the previous Liberal governments, many changes can subsequently be identified in the climate policy-making and the policy process design of this time frame. Basic information on the developments of the years 2006–2012 has to be provided to research the democracy-climate nexus in this time period.

A Canadian Alliance Party (which later merged with the Progressive Conservative Party to form the Conservative Party) fundraising letter from 2002 offers insights into an understanding of Harper's basic opposition to the climate policy of the previous government and the Kyoto Protocol. The letter states the following about the Kyoto Protocol:

"- It's based on tentative and contradictory scientific evidence about climate trends.

- It focuses on carbon dioxide, which is essential to life, rather than upon pollutants.

- Implementing Kyoto will cripple the oil and gas industry, which is essential to the economies of Newfoundland, Nova Scotia, Saskatchewan, Alberta and British Columbia.

- As the effects trickle through other industries, workers and consumers everywhere in Canada will lose. There are no Canadian winners under the Kyoto Accord.

DOI: 10.4324/9781315228983-11

- The only winners will be countries such as Russia, India, and China, from which Canada will have to buy 'emissions credits.' Kyoto is essentially a socialist scheme to suck money out of wealth-producing nations."

(Sanger & Saul, n.d., pp. 281–282)

Consequently, in the 2006 elections, Harper promoted a "made in Canada plan" instead of following the Kyoto Protocol approach. After it was elected, the government said it would neither meet the commitments nor withdraw from the Kyoto Protocol. The government reduced funding for climate change programmes by around 40 per cent, which meant that much research was discontinued, many of the programmes which had been initiated, like the LFEs or the EnerGuide home programme, were stopped and the new Project Green programmes were not implemented (Parliament, 2007b, p. 8). In 2006, the government also introduced the Clean Air Act, which was criticized by the opposition as being low on specifics and far too weak. The Clean Air Act aimed to focus on action to reduce air pollution and GHGs by creating a Clean Air Part in the Canadian Environmental Protection Act, regulating vehicle fuel efficiency and setting energy efficiency standards (Government, 2006a). The opposition in Parliament was not satisfied with proceedings and introduced the KPIA (Parliament, 2007a) (which came into effect in June 2007) to force the government to proceed more ambitiously on the climate file by binding it to the production of a yearly updated plan, laying out how it intended to reach the Kyoto target.

At the beginning of the Conservatives' legislative period, climate change became an issue of public interest, because the broader public also felt that the government was falling far too short with its environmental policies (Macdonald, 2011, p. 129). Programmes under the label "ecoAction", most of them quite similar to the ones which had previously been stopped, were introduced in 2007, focusing on a combination of clean air and climate change. They focused on reducing motor vehicle emissions, increasing the number of energy efficient products and improving indoor air quality (Government of Canada, 2007a, p. 2). Further details were included in the *Regulatory Framework for Air Emissions* (Government of Canada, 2007a), which was released in 2007. A new climate plan called *Turning the Corner. Taking Action to Fight Climate Change* was announced in 2008 (Government of Canada, 2008). Its aim was to force industry to reduce GHGs via a carbon emissions trading market with a carbon offset system and a market price for carbon (Government, 2008, p. 2). The Conservatives basically tried to reduce GHGs with a regulatory framework based on intensity targets, which, as a long-term target, included the reduction of GHGs to rates 20 per cent below 2006 levels by the year 2020. Nevertheless, only a few of the proposed objectives were implemented and the government was only able to reach an agreement on emissions reductions with a small number of sectors.

At the same time, as a reaction to the KPIA, the government also published a report entitled *Cost of Bill C-288 to Canadian Families and Business* (Government of Canada, 2007c), in which they laid down the high costs of meeting the Kyoto target from the perspective of the government. It would appear Harper had changed his view on climate change, stating, in 2007, that it was "perhaps the biggest threat to confront the future of humanity today" (Harper, 2007). Nevertheless, in 2007, the government joined the widely decried and US led Asia-Pacific Partnership on Clean Development, which proposed voluntary emissions targets.

In the 2008 elections, the Conservatives were again able to form a government. With Stéphane Dion, the Liberals had at this time a prime ministerial candidate who explicitly proposed an eco-friendly programme called *Green Shift* (Liberal Party of Canada, 2008), which included a carbon tax. The electorate voted (also because of other policy issues) against the Liberals' green programme and in favour of the Conservatives. Subsequently, even though the plans enforced by the KPIA were developed, climate change became very much a non-issue and nearly non-existent. Finally, the last action of the government in regard to the Kyoto Protocol policy process was the withdrawal from the first implementation period of the UNFCCC, announced in December 2011. It justified its decision with reference to the $14 billion in penalties, which it expected to have to pay as a result of the great gap between the minus 6 per cent target and actual emissions (Curry & McCarthy, 2011).

However, which mechanisms linked democratic quality and climate performance? The results demonstrate that a government which was not in favour of active climate politics threatened democratic quality. The overall influence of insufficient democratic quality on climate performance seems to have either been non-existent or negative between 2006–2012. These findings support the suggestion of the exponential influence of dimensions of democratic quality on policy performance.

Procedural general performance: unfulfilled preconditions

Certain aspects of procedural general performance already played relevant roles as preconditions for the influence of democratic quality on climate performance in previous time frames and it seems as if this was also the case between 2006 and 2012.

A preliminary precondition that comes up in this time frame, but is, of course, probably also relevant in the previous time frames, is a certain level of climate education amongst decision-makers and/or politicians. As simple as it sounds, politicians must understand climate change in order to recognize it as an important policy field, because they must at least be able to estimate what sort of policies would work. According to Bramley, many did not have this knowledge, "most influential opinion leaders in the country mostly have a very poor understanding of climate change and of what to do about it" (Bramley, 2014). Thus, governmental capability in the sense of accepting, learning from and innovatively applying new knowledge in policy relevant issues like climate change is an important requirement.

Another closely related precondition is also associated with governmental capability, more precisely the setting and maintaining of strategic priorities. When the government does not understand or see climate change as a priority issue which has to be dealt with, it will not initiate a (democratic) policy process to find solutions in the climate policy field. The Conservative government distinguished between sword issues, which are issues a government uses to achieve gains through offensive actions, and shield issues, which are issues on which a government just tries to protect itself from losing any more support (McLaughlin, 2014). Obviously, climate change was a shield issue for this government (McLaughlin, 2014). So, the government set strategic priorities, but climate change was not one of them. The existence of governmental capability in this regard had a negative impact on climate change policies. That such priorities did not exist can also be seen in the way in which the government organized its departments to deal with climate change. They were steadily reorganized and competencies were either unclear or completely divided under different assistant deputy ministers, leading one commentator at the time to remark that "it's all quite diffused" (Confidential5, 2014).

Thus, the government neither ensured stability through organizational changes nor did it apply effectiveness and efficiency in the form of making efficient use of available resources. In such circumstances, it seems highly unlikely that the departments involved would have had the capabilities to provide support for a climate policy process and to build transmission belts between different branches and policy levels, let alone to initiate a democratic policy process. Again, as simple as it sounds, in the absence of a climate policy process, there cannot be a democratic policy process and thus this cannot influence climate performance in any form whatsoever, be it positive or negative. The inefficient use of available economic and human resources was also identified by the CESD, which at that time recognized that "the government has not established a governance structure that sets out clear roles and responsibilities, quality assurance systems for reporting on greenhouse gas reductions achieved, and financial and performance reporting systems and mechanisms for evaluating the climate change plans" (CESD, 2011, p. 16).

Overall, it seems as if the government did not understand climate change and subsequently it neither set a strategic priority on climate policy-making nor did it establish any departmental organization to deal with climate change or seek to implement any form of governance structure. The existence of a democratic climate policy process is not very likely in such circumstances. Without moving too deep into an overall conclusion of all the time frames, it seems obvious that three out of the four time frames identified certain aspects of procedural general performance as a precondition for a climate policy process to start. Only an existing policy process can influence climate performance. So, what influence do accountability structures for climate performance have in such circumstances?

Accountability: unpredictability and negative influence

The 2005 COP took place in Montreal, and the new Canadian environment minister, Ambrose, became president of the COP in 2006, when the Conservative government took power. However, after some criticism, John Baird replaced her and finally the PMO took complete control of decision-making on the climate change file, while ECan only continued to work on minor operational issues (Confidential6, 2014; McCarthy, 2014; McLaughlin, 2014; Slater, 2014). Consequently, ECan, a department which had already had less influence than others, became even less important in terms of climate change, while the PMO and other actors, such as the Department of Finance, NRCan and provinces like Alberta, Saskatchewan and British Columbia, became more important (Confidential2, 2014; Simpson, 2014).

Although ostensibly relevant institutions like the CCME or JMM still existed, they were not mentioned by one interview partner or in any documents, which means that even the formalized structures of executive federalism were no longer deemed to be relevant. Climate change policy-making and decision-making was centred on the PMO and a few other actors; it was, so to speak, a PM dominated executive selectionism. Already at the beginning of his term in office, *The Globe and Mail* journalist Jeffrey Simpson, who had previously called Jean Chrétien's government a "friendly dictatorship" due to the wide-ranging rights of the PM, described the way Stephen Harper governed as a "Sun King government", in which "absolutely everything revolved around him, his message, his persona" (Simpson, Jaccard, & Rivers, 2008, p. 102). Even though the historical comparison is questionable, the differentiation Simpson makes between Jean Chrétien, whose way of governing the climate file was described as making use of the prerogative in the first time frame, and Stephen Harper, who made extensive use of the prerogative, might be correct. The way power was concentrated and the lack of accountability under Harper seems to have been even more distinctive than it was under Chrétien, who at least left his environment ministers room to develop a climate policy process.

Probably the most important decision in regard to the Kyoto Protocol process was Canada's withdrawal from the process in 2011. According to the environment minister Peter Kent, he personally spoke to the Cabinet several times and to members of the BRICS (Brazil, Russia, India, China and South Africa) and the Major Economies Forum and held the position at the beginning of COP 17 that "if there was no change in the attitude of major emitters – both developed and developing countries – we would exercise the withdrawal" (Kent, 2014). It appears that there was no formally structured process which led to the withdrawal, instead it was a decision which arose within the Cabinet and through talks with other countries. Thus, there was no structured process, rather it was a decision taken very much inside the closest circles of the government. Nevertheless, Kent did talk to certain groups, like his deputy minister, bureaucrats, public servants, scientists, the provinces, international counterparts, NRCan, the Caucus and the Cabinet, which might have influenced his view, but, interestingly, no civil society representatives were part of these talks (Kent, 2014).

At the same time, the framework within which Kent was acting had already been limited by the recommendations of his predecessors and the GHG developments of previous years:

"My predecessors had made recommendations that there was a, you know, that there was a point where we needed to/because the previous government which had originally signed Kyoto had done nothing in emissions of increased 35 per cent because during our term even after signing Copenhagen the reality of our Kyoto obligation was looming. I think that's what brought us to the decision."

(Kent, 2014)

Thus, analysing Kent's explanations, the decision to withdraw was taken inside government and, although he names a couple of other actors (civil society aside), this seems only to be a list of people he talked to about climate change, as opposed to any suggestion of his having consulted in a structured and in-depth fashion on the question of withdrawal. Similarly, the limiting framework for action left by his predecessors indicates that the decision to withdraw was already in the minds of the government before Kent arrived as environment minister. A high-ranking public servant of ECan also takes the view that there was not "a lot of debate" within the government about "whether they should withdraw" and that the decision was pretty clear at the political level (Confidential6, 2014).

Although in the form of the Cabinet, the PM and the minister of the environment, democratically elected politicians decided on the climate file, vertical accountability (in terms of tracing back decisions more precisely) was not ensured due to the lack of involvement of actors outside government, such as, for example, civil society representatives. In terms of democratic quality, what is even more relevant is that there was – beside elections – absolutely no control over the PM as the primary decision-maker. It is therefore unclear whether and by whom the PM was informally influenced when making his decisions on the climate file.

Since the decision to withdraw from the Kyoto Protocol process was a decision which lowered climate performance in terms of both output and outcome and the degree of accountability was very low, we can expect that the lack of accountability might have had a negative impact on climate performance. Without any control over decision-making the government can more or less do what it wants. And, while Chrétien used the lack of accountability to make climate relevant decisions which were even more ambitious than would otherwise have been possible, Harper made use of the same circumstances to make decisions on climate performance which were much less ambitious than existing accountability structures would probably have allowed for. Thus, insufficient accountability has no influence on climate performance, as this then depends on the preferences of the government and the PM in power.

One of the groups which recommended more accountability and saw itself as a representative of Canadian citizens was an ENGO. According to Olivastri, the role of Friends of the Earth became "one of requiring accountability from our government on behalf of the citizens" (Olivastri, 2014). Since such groups exercise accountability over their decision-makers, inclusiveness and participation become important in regard to their influence on climate performance.

Inclusiveness and participation: elected irresponsibility in a mantle of democracy

During the last time frame, 2003–2005, inclusiveness and participation were, in a democratic sense, almost non-existent. It seems as if both dimensions merge together in circumstances within which they are not particularly distinct: where no open and fair access is guaranteed, democratic participatory structures are unlikely and informal inclusion stands for a way of access which is close to direct influence upon decision-makers. However, if that is the case, which mechanisms linked democratic quality and climate performance from 2006–2012? To provide an answer to this question, this section proceeds by: (1) explaining the general approach of the government; (2) looking at the way biased involvement existed; (3) analysing why there was no room for considered judgement; (4) detecting the specific influence certain actors had in such a setting; (5) explaining the role of Parliament, especially in terms of implementing the KPIA; and (6) providing a brief insight into the non-responsive transmission belt before drawing a conclusion on inclusiveness and participation and their influence on climate performance.

(1) According to official government documents, "extensive consultations were undertaken", with the provinces and territories, industry representatives, aboriginal groups and health and environmental organizations regarding a proposed regulatory framework as their main approach for dealing with climate change (Government, 2007b, p. 7). The government also mentioned consultations with the provinces, industry representatives and environmental organizations when determining the terms of the *Turning the Corner* climate change plan in 2008 (Government, 2008, p. 2).

As far as the significance of these statements can be determined through the interviews carried out, the reality of inclusiveness and participation looked somewhat different to that suggested by government sources. The basic approach actually applied by the government did not have much to do with "extensive consultations". Instead, apart from a handful of exceptions, public consultations did not take place (Vaughan, 2014). Besides the formal *Gazette* process (and the government also did not let anyone know what the outcome of the comments resulting from this 60-day period was), the government did not actively involve the public in the policy-making process, which contrasts with the actions of Chrétien government (Olivastri, 2014; Vaughan, 2014). Even though web-based consultation was announced, the announcement seems to have been some sort of window dressing, since no influence can be detected (Vaughan, 2014). While the government did not consult with a broader public, it did occasionally consult with some selected individuals and, on one occasion, with a tripartite group which recommended consultations (based on an initiative of industrial representatives, the provinces and several NGOs), but otherwise most interaction seems to have taken place in the form of lobbying (Bramley, 2014). Consequently, the government did not come together with other groups, as had been the case during the table process, and consultations became "more individual" (Dillon, 2014).

To get a more precise picture of how specific programmes (components) were developed, a public servant's description of the most important steps in the government's attempts to regulate the coal-fired electricity industry seems insightful, since the process resulted in the passage of regulation. The main programme was developed inside the formal structure as recommended by law, but nothing more than was required was done in terms of involving and ensuring the participation of actors, with many more informal meetings taking place with the provinces and corporations than with NGOs (Confidential6, 2014). The process proceeded as follows: after the government decided to regulate the sector, it published its intentions in the *Canada Gazette*; this was followed by informal bureaucratic negotiations, focusing on the technical aspects of regulation with the participation of interested parties, such as corporations, the provinces and NGOs (all of which also contacted ministers and the PMO at the political level); a draft regulation was then once more published in the *Canada Gazette* with a formal commentary period announced and public servants analysed these comments and made the changes they wanted to make; a Regulatory Impact Analysis Statement then sought the approval of the Cabinet, after which the final regulation was published in the *Canada Gazette* (Confidential6, 2014). During this process, the government chose to focus its informal discussions on consultations with industry and provinces instead of NGOs (Confidential6, 2014).

Having a look at the process structure from the point of view of democratic quality and its potential influence on climate performance, two preliminary conclusions on the general approach of the conservative government in regard to inclusiveness and participation can be drawn. First, the formal criteria of the *Gazette* process were complied with. The *Gazette* process itself is, however, only a formal law-making act, which does not reflect the full range of democratic possibilities for inclusiveness and participation, which, from a democratic quality perspective, would be possible. Secondly, the only way other actors were consulted and could influence the process was informal and probably biased. From all the evidence obtained so far regarding the general approach of the government, it seems that the provinces and corporations were more often informally consulted than the NGOs and, due to their preferences, they probably had a negative impact upon climate performance.

(2) Which actors were included and how? Peter Kent decided between meeting "Campaign NGOs" that "raise money by scaring the public" on the one hand and a middle range of NGOs on the other (Kent, 2014). Kent met with them on request in smaller or larger groups, but he cannot provide details of or a structure for these meetings (Kent, 2014). There is simply no identifiable structure, which suggests how these actors could have been involved and helped to participate. In this sense, Kent's statement fits into the broader picture that begins to develop in terms of a government which neither included external actors nor enabled their participation. The government "increasingly took on the mode of not consulting environmental groups and rather dismissing them", since they were not part of its political coalition, while business certainly "became more aware . . . of the file" (McLaughlin, 2014). According to Shawn McCarthy, bar the oil industry

and the conservative electoral base centred around Calgary, no other important groups were involved in the process (McCarthy, 2014).

A process which ensured open and fair access for ENGOs, involving relevant and affected actors, was not systematically applied, instead there was a preference for consulting with industry as one of the affected and relevant groups. According to a confidential statement by a senior high-ranking official, similar evidence can be found in regard to the regulatory approach, where many bilateral negotiations took place with the provinces and industry, but "other groups were not included in the same way" (Confidential6, 2014). This is problematic in the view of that confidential interview partner and their involvement in the regulatory approach, as it "detracts from the social licences, [the] social acceptability of regulations", since not all interested parties had the opportunity to participate. And, this is why this particular interview partner believes "that [in future] we could have better outcomes if we had a more inclusive process" (Confidential6, 2014).

Thus, besides the executive, regulators and industry, no other actors were involved in what were mostly informal negotiations under the Conservatives. In this context, the suggestion made by an expert deeply involved in the process that a more inclusive process could have produced better outcomes is quite insightful in terms of the (positive) influence of inclusiveness upon the form of regulations and climate performance is. However, it wasn't just ENGOs which weren't really included in climate policy-making. For example, Kent only met with First Nation and aboriginal groups on an ad hoc basis, doing no more than was needed and requested by law, since there is an obligation to consult.

FH: So, you involved these actors [First Nations and aboriginal] in . . .
PK: Oh, some of them.
FH: . . . on an ad hoc basis depending on the issue that was under debate?
PK: Exactly. . . . There is an obligation to consult, we also have an obligation to finance, to underwrite the costs of the meeting, of either bringing the First Nations leaders to Ottawa or gathering them in different places across the country.

(Kent, 2014)

Thus, Kent met with such groups as formally requested and also talked to actors which did not share the same views. However, talking to such groups is quite different from including them in a participative process which actually allows them to influence policy-making.

(3) Even though meetings with other actors were not numerous, it is, in regard to the democracy-climate nexus, useful to detect whether the types of meetings and the participatory structures they adopted allowed for considered judgement enabling deliberation. ENGOs claim that when they met with the minister of the environment, John Baird, "he just yelled at us" (Bennett, 2014). According to Bennett, there was no discussion, instead it was a meeting at which Baird identified which of the people attending were Liberals and "that was the discussion" (Bennett, 2014). It seems as if a deliberate setting was not provided, instead Baird

stated that he had no interest in any form of consultation with civil society. In describing the situation, Bennett stated that they had the feeling that in such meetings "the door just snaps shut" (Bennett, 2014). In a similar vein another ENGO representative felt that the way civil society was briefed was insufficient, since "you'd be told something and you would not have any time to discuss or provide input and that's it" (Olivastri, 2014). Annual meetings with the minister were deemed to be little more than "dog and pony shows", with "somebody trotting out the Government line and that's it" (Olivastri, 2014). There was "no discussion or debate or input" (Olivastri, 2014). A "dog and pony show" can be ranked as the weakest democratic form of absent considered judgement, since it only consists of one-way information. Deliberation was simply non-existent and considered judgement impossible, not only because the government did not enable an adequate atmosphere and/or setting for discussions but also because such preconditions as open and fair access in terms of inclusiveness were not guaranteed, leading to a process which failed to hear all voices and arguments.

The only slight tendency in terms of establishing a room for discussion was the launch of a web-based consultation format by the Treasury Board. However, in the end it seems to have been more about window dressing than practical interaction, since the structure was not responsive and did not initiate a debate, acting instead like some sort of black box, where nobody knew what kind of influence their written statement was likely to have. According to commentators, such an approach represents a form of "consultative process but nobody is actually listening" (Vaughan, 2014).

As a reaction to these circumstances, various stakeholders, including industry, asked the PM for broader consultation as early as 2007/2008. These requests led to the creation of a Multi-Stakeholder Discussion Group on Greenhouse Gases and Air Pollution Consultation, the so-called Tripartite Group (rcen, n.d.). However, this group failed to return significant results, as dialogue only occurred at one meeting, since federal officials withdrew from the group in September 2008. Subsequently, this attempt at consultation did not lead to any sustainable structures of inclusiveness and participation (Bramley, 2014; rcen, n.d.).

So, where could inclusiveness and participation and its influence on climate performance be found in this process? The general approach of doing only as much as required (through, for example, the *Gazette* process and informal consultations) represents a low level of democratic quality, which might have had a negative impact on climate performance. And, a closer look at the biased selection procedures, which favoured industry and business, points in the same direction. Since any room for considered judgement and deliberation was completely lacking, the preferences of the government and the actors they included from the oil and gas industry dominated climate policy-making. It could be counterfactually argued: had the government informally involved ENGOs instead of the oil and gas industry in similar circumstances (i.e. without room for considered judgement and deliberation), then the influence of these procedures upon climate performance could have been positive and this is why overall the absence of deliberation can be seen to have no influence on climate performance.

(4) However, a closer look at which actors had what kind of influence in such a setting might shed more light on the democracy-climate nexus, since the non-existent structures of inclusiveness and participation allowed some actors to influence decision-making more significantly than others. In such circumstances, it is particularly difficult for weak and marginalized actor groups with legitimate interests to gain influence. First Nations and aboriginal groups were also not included; at least there is no evidence to suggest that they were consulted on a systematic and regular basis. Even though they did not have much financial or personnel resources and were unable to participate, they do have some constitutional rights which allowed them to influence policy-making, e.g. by stopping the Mackenzie Valley pipeline, favoured by members of the Conservative Party (Confidential2, 2014; Confidential6, 2014).

As an actor group, scientists were responsible for raising initial awareness in the context of the democracy-climate nexus. Without climate science informed democratic decision-making is impossible. And, since climate scientists' lost avenues of expression and the financing of research projects under the Conservative government, they started to seek influence through their Death of Science demonstrations. However, in the end, their influence on any primary offices was not really noticeable (Vaughan, 2014). Even though they were not able to influence climate policy-making, they at least made their circumstances public, while climate change deniers like the Friends of Science were instead able to speak directly to the PM (Stone, 2014).

Scientists were not the only actor group which the government tried to undermine. The government also limited its (financial) support and started to intensively control ENGOs and environmental networks through the Canadian Revenue Organization. One good example of this is the Canadian Environmental Network, which originally brought together around 70,000 small groups, but disappeared after the federal government discontinued their funding. Larger ENGOs like Friends of the Earth also spent a lot resources and time on the CRA investigations, circumstances which Vaughan describes as "using state labours to intimidate groups that took a contrary view [to the government]" (Vaughan, 2014). Thus, ENGOs were not very influential at all after the Conservatives took power (Olivastri, 2014). This impression can be enriched by insights from officials who worked under the government, stating that the influence of (E)NGOs was low, especially in comparison to the oil and gas industry, which was much more influential (Confidential5, 2014; Confidential6, 2014).

Thus, even though almost all other actors were unable to influence climate performance in the given setting, "the biggest overall influence . . . based on the policies that have been introduced or the policies that have not been introduced is clearly the oil and gas industry" (Souza, 2014). Since the CAPP had very strong and direct contacts with the PMO, it was able to influence coal fire regulation in the interests of its members, e.g. it weakened the first proposal of 375 parts per million to 450 parts per million (Vaughan, 2014). The oil and gas industry was unquestionably able to strongly influence climate policy-making, as evidenced by various interview partners. However, it seems as if there was no obvious corruption in the form of payments or the like. As some interview partners, such as Shawn McCarthy, journalist at *The Globe and Mail*, Scott Vaughan and Matthew Bramley, mention, the closest thing they would relate to corruption is the very tight relationship and influence of the oil and gas sector on the government. Nevertheless, there are, to some extent, legitimate reasons for consulting with the oil and gas sector. It is undoubtedly a relevant and affected actor in terms of its importance for the Canadian economy, but it is not the only actor which should be involved and able to influence climate performance.

Another reason for the strong influence of the oil and gas sector is its interconnection with eastern Canada, being the region where the Conservative Party and most of its voters are based (Bennett, 2014; Confidential2, 2014). Therefore, an argument could be made that as part of the parliamentary system the Conservative Party simply represented its supporters, who were in favour of a friendly policy approach to the oil and gas industry. Thus, it is obvious that Parliament, as a representative method of participation, does not necessarily have a positive influence on climate performance, particularly when specific interests are used for informal consultation with defective inclusiveness and one particular interest is favoured over other legitimate interests.

Overall, it seems as if there are two strong and one weak group of actors which were able to use the non-existence of democratic inclusiveness and participatory structures to influence climate performance:

> "One, the Government and its political view, so the Caucus and the party. Two, the business community saying: 'Wait a second here.' So, a cautionary note. And, three, the environmental community pushing so hard but not giving any credit to the government, right? So, in other words: being on the other side. So you put those three things together and you do not have a lot of enthusiasm for acting."
>
> (McLaughlin, 2014)

Comparing the influence several actors had on climate performance, the informal influence of the oil and gas industry between 2006–2012 was probably stronger than the influence ENGOs had on ECan and thus on policy-making between 2003–2005. The main message remains important: the lack of structured inclusiveness and participatory structures had neither a positive nor a negative impact on climate performance, instead everything was determined by the government's preferences.

(5) Having explained inclusiveness and participation and their influence on climate performance from many aspects, one of Parliament's moves was probably the most important democratically legitimated attempt in terms of representative participation trying to push climate performance. Right at the beginning of Conservative government's legislative period, when it was only a minority government, Parliament reacted in the climate policy field by passing the KPIA – an interesting initiative for the democracy-climate nexus. As already mentioned, the parliamentary opposition was dissatisfied with the proceedings of the

government and introduced the KPIA (C-288), which came into effect in June 2007. Its purpose was "to ensure that Canada takes effective and timely action to meet its obligations under the Kyoto Protocol and help address the problem of global climate change" (Parliament, 2007a).

This act forced the government to prepare a yearly climate change plan listing the measures to be undertaken and the contributions required of the main sectors of the economy to meet the Kyoto Protocol target of minus 6 per cent as well as a projected timeline. Each climate change plan had to be tabled in Parliament. Reviews by both the National Round Table on the Environment and the Economy (NRTEE) – to check whether the measures would actually achieve the proposed GHG reductions and whether the Kyoto Protocol target could be met – and the CESD – to check how the plan was being implemented and whether the Kyoto Protocol target could ultimately be met – were meant to ensure that the plans actually led to GHG reductions. In the end, six climate change plans were produced between 2007–2012.

Being the result of an elected parliament as a form of representative participation, the question is whether and how the act influenced climate performance. Even though emissions dropped between 2007–2011 from 749 Mt CO_2 eq. to 702 Mt CO_2 eq. (or from 22.7 to 20.4 t CO_2 eq./capita), this effect must be seen in relation to the world financial crisis, while the effect of the reductions reported in the climate change plans required by the KPIA were minimal. However, there are mixed views on whether the KPIA had an influence on climate performance. Peter Kent clearly states that his government fulfilled the demands on reporting, but disagreed with and had no intention of meeting the, in his view, inconsistent Kyoto Protocol. He assumes that his climate policy approach was the right way of going about things and that is why he stated "I believe I made change" (Kent, 2014).

The official reaction of the government demonstrates that it classified the KPIA as inadequate, since it would have had a tremendous impact upon industry and the behaviour of Canadians. To underline its position, the government prepared a report entitled *The Cost of Bill C-288 to Canadian Families and Business*, which concludes, inter alia, that the KPIA is "an unbalanced approach that would plunge the Canadian economy into recession and dramatically lower the living standards of workers and families", since the "necessary changes to the Canadian economy would result in a decline in GDP of over 6.5% from expected levels in 2008" and so on (ECan, 2007).

Even though the concrete numbers estimated in terms of the economic impact were questioned afterwards, the government's direction was pretty clear: the KPIA and the minus 6 per cent goal could not be implemented. John Godfrey comes to a conclusion that goes hand in hand with the insights provided by Peter Kent and the report, expressing the opinion that the KPIA had no impact because it had not previously been negotiated with the government. It simply "was a source of embarrassment for the government, but it certainly didn't make them reconsider their position on climate change or change anything" (Godfrey, 2014). As a consequence, there was no coordination between different federal departments in regard to the KPIA (Vaughan, 2014). The reductions achieved by the climate change programmes were minimal and far from being sufficient to reach the Kyoto target, e.g. between 2008–2009 reductions totalled only 6 Mt CO_2 eq., while over 800 Mt CO_2 eq. would have been needed between 2008–2012 (CESD, 2012, p. 22).

Thus, the environment minister clearly stated that he did not make any policies in accordance with the KPIA, since the government was in favour of a different approach and other sources indicate that its final influence on GHG reductions was therefore marginal. However, Kent also stated that the government fulfilled its reporting obligations, which may have provided a form of influence on climate performance. Transparency and publicity increased, since enforced reporting held the government accountable to a certain degree; "it did bring the issue into the public" and "got people talking about climate change" (McLaughlin, 2014; Souza, 2014).

Moreover, the reports of the NRTEE and the CESD also adjudged the climate change plans and their implementation to have had an influence on climate performance by recommending improvements on measures in many instances, like effective dates of measures and expected emission levels per year; all calculations or describing measures which would have helped enable Canada to meet the Kyoto Protocol target (CESD, 2011, pp. 20–21). Similarly, the NRTEE reported these shortcomings and, according to David McLaughlin, calculations and measurements improved due to the NRTEE reviews, especially on modelling and forecasting (Bramley, 2014; McLaughlin, 2014). Equivalent information can be found in the RCESD. While in 2009 and 2010 reporting was very much incomplete (CESD, 2009, p. 58; 2011, p. 16), the 2011 plan was "more explicit than previous plans published" (CESD, 2012, p. 16).

To draw a conclusion regarding the KPIA, it seems it informed climate policy-making and was able to make policy-making more transparent. It initiated public debate and thus politicians could be better held accountable in terms of public pressure, which might eventually have had some indirect influence. However, the government seemed to be particularly unaffected by yearly publicity. It simply fulfilled its reporting requirements, but made no attempt to change policies or to introduce new instruments which might have led to GHG reductions as a result of the KPIA. Thus, it would appear the KPIA had an influence on transparency, but not on substantial policy, at least not directly (Bramley, 2014). The influence of the KPIA as the initiative of an elected parliament was ultimately quite marginal and this is why only a very weak positive influence on climate performance can be detected.

The KPIA was, of course, the most significant way the parliament as a representatively legitimated mechanism of participation tried to influence climate performance. However, a brief look at activities other than those of the KPIA is necessary to reach a comprehensive view of the influence Parliament had on proceedings. At least two other attempts are worth mentioning: first, bill C-474 as an approach to establish a holistic sustainable development strategy on many issues, including but not specifically about climate change. The bill was introduced by

John Godfrey, who was focused on reaching results and thus cooperated with the government, which was, according to him, "the right way to go given the government of the day" (Godfrey, 2014). However, even though there might have been some (long-term) effects on other environmental policy fields, there does not seem to have been any influence on climate performance, e.g. the CESD does not even mention the bill in its reports on climate change.

Another attempt can be seen in bill C-377 which would have laid out long-term reduction targets for 2020 and 2050 and thus was directly related to climate change. However, the Senate killed the bill after it was passed by Parliament during the Conservative minority government in 2007. As a matter of democratic quality, it is questionable whether the Senate, which is not democratically elected, should be able to kill a bill. While the Westminster system in Britain has removed the rights of its equivalent chamber to kill a bill approved by Parliament, the Canadian system still allows this. Thus, the Senate, whose members are in fact appointed by the PM, is of course much less democratically legitimated than the House of Commons. Therefore, a less democratic part of Parliament killed a bill which had passed through the more democratically legitimated part of Parliament and could have had a positive influence on climate performance. In this case, less democracy had a negative impact on climate performance. Nevertheless, it can be summarized that Parliament was quite active in the 2000s, especially after the election of the new government in 2006 (Cleland, 2014). At the same time, the influence it had was quite limited. The explanation can probably be found in a government which tried and was able to turn its shield issue (climate change) into a non-issue, which nobody spoke about or had an influence upon, with as few debates as possible in Parliament (Simpson, 2014). Consequently, the Standing Committee on the Environment and Sustainable Development became more and more dysfunctional:

"So, I had several meetings behind closed doors with members of parliament and they would say to me the science was wrong, one member said to me that this was a socialist plot, the climate change was a socialist plot; another one said that it was sun spots. So, these are Canada's elected officials. So, because of that when you got into the committee, the committee got absolutely dysfunctional. I found it a distinctly unpleasant experience because they would be attacking our work as being biased."

(Vaughan, 2014)

Clearly, the preferences and understanding which were required to make Parliament a place which discussed and influenced climate performance were lacking. The democratic power of Parliament is thus strongly dependent on the PM and the government in power. Overall, it is a mixed picture of insufficient attempts by Parliament to legislate to reduce carbon emissions without much evidence that it actually influenced climate performance in a specific or significant way (Confidential2, 2014).

So, what insights can we take away in terms of the climate-democracy nexus? Representative representation in the form of Parliament fulfilling certain aspects of democratic quality has neither a significant positive nor negative impact on climate performance in the Canadian case; indeed, it becomes quite irrelevant when the government in power does not let it influence climate policy-making. Despite its rights, the opposition is simply too weak, since it is not even able to influence the actions of a minority government.

(6) Even though domestically no democratic consensus was reached on how to deal with climate change, the existence of a transmission belt connected to the international level could indicate that responsiveness would have been guaranteed, had such a consensus existed. However, the national-international connections were also not characterized by high democratic quality. And the transmission belt, which, in the previous time frames, had already been identified as being weak, had by this point ceased to exist. Similarly, the ministerial setting did little to ensure responsiveness, since the responsibility for national and international climate policy-making was organized by different branches and participation within delegations was closed to actors outside the government (Confidential5, 2014; Dillon, 2014). The fragile link which had previously existed, had, therefore, by this point, disappeared. Subsequently, the ministerial level was unable to build a departmental transmission belt and no attempt at democratic foreign or intermestic policy-making can be detected.

To summarize the findings in regard to the democratic quality dimensions of inclusiveness and participation, a brief look at the different aspects might be helpful and should enable us to come to a conclusion on the overall influence of democratic quality on climate performance. The general approach showed that the absence of democratic quality might have had a negative impact on climate performance, more precisely, involvement was very biased and preferred actors with a preference for delaying action. Considered judgement was absent and this is why everything ultimately depended on the government's preferences and a lack of deliberation thus led to unpredictability. The influence of the oil and gas industry was, unsurprisingly, significantly high in the informal setting, Parliament was unable to force the government to take action on climate change and there was no responsive transmission belt. Thus, to set these findings in the context of inclusiveness and participation in the democracy-climate nexus, it can be concluded that the general approach, biased selection and structures of influence massively lacked democratic quality and had a negative impact upon climate performance, while an absence of structures of considered judgement had no influence on climate performance and the non-existence of a responsive transmission belt left everything up to the government. Parliament, as a democratically legitimized actor characterized by relatively high democratic quality, had no influence on climate performance, even though it tried hard to do so. Thus, even though each finding and each indicator has to be analysed separately, the dimensions of inclusiveness and participation between 2006–2012 show that a lack of democratic quality had a negative influence upon proceedings or led to unpredictability, while high democratic quality, in terms of Parliament, was unable to influence climate performance positively, even though it tried to do so. In the end, the government acted without breaking the law but in the belief that it could do whatever it wanted, since it had been elected. In terms of climate change, one can call it a government of *elected irresponsibility*.

The KPIA seems to have had a slight positive influence upon transparency, but the government never attempted to follow the KPIA in its goal to reach the Kyoto target. The question is now whether it was able by law to force the government to actually implement policies which would have been required to reach the Kyoto Protocol target.

Independence: no interference in policy-making

Independence as a dimension of democratic quality is guaranteed through the rule of law. One of its indicators is open and free access to the judiciary or neutral courts which are not interrelated with the executive or the legislative ensuring they are free to judge objectively.

Generally speaking, whether the federal government has the constitutional power to regulate GHGs is an open question, since, as yet, there has been no final court decision. Asking environmental lawyer Hugh Wilkins, who was involved in the KPIA case, what a final decision on the allocation of responsibility in regard to climate change would look like, he suggests that responsibility would likely end up shared between the federal and provincial governments, since climate change is so extensive and interlinked with other issues that it is doubtful whether one level of government would have exclusive jurisdiction (Wilkins, 2014).

Even though a final decision regarding the question of responsibility is outstanding, Friends of the Earth brought up a concrete court case (Federal Court) in relation to the KPIA in 2008 (Federal Court, 2008). The parliamentary opposition passed the KPIA against the Conservative minority government. Basically, its purpose was to force the government to publish and implement climate change plans to actually meet the Kyoto Protocol target. Since the ENGO Friends of the Earth had the impression that the government was not complying with the act, it pursued a judicial review in 2008 based on the assumption that the government was ignoring the rule of law as well as the will of Parliament that the government comply with the act. The court heard the case, but dismissed it. More precisely, the issue was whether

"section 5 of the KPIA imposed a justiciable duty upon the minister to prepare and table a climate change plan that is Kyoto compliant and sections 7, 8 and 9 of the KPIA imposed justiciable duties upon the GIC to make, amend or repeal environmental regulations within the timelines therein stated."

(Federal Court, 2008, p. 2)

The court decided as follows:

> "While the failure of the minister to prepare a climate change plan may well be justiciable, as evidenced by the mandatory term "shall" in section 5 of the KPIA, an evaluation of its content is not. The word "ensure" found in section 5 and elsewhere in the KPIA is not commonly used in the context of statutory interpretation to indicate an imperative. . . . That the words "to ensure" used in section 5 reflect only a permissive intent is also indicated by the use of those words in section 7 dealing with the authority of the GIC to pass, repeal or amend environmental regulations. If section 7 of the KPIA does not create a mandatory duty to regulate, it necessarily follows that all of the regulatory and related duties described in sections 8 and 9 of the KPIA are not justiciable if the GIC declines to act. . . . Parliament has, with the KPIA, created a comprehensive system of public and parliamentary accountability as a substitute for judicial review."
>
> (Federal Court, 2008, pp. 2–3)

Thus, the court ruled that the KPIA was not an act which was suitable for judicial review. According to the court, only the phrasing of the KPIA was mandatory, Parliament had established review mechanisms of accountability outside judicial review and concrete regulations and the content of the climate policy decision was outside the realm of judicial review.

Wilkins, who worked as a lawyer for Friends of the Earth in that case, had, of course, a different interpretation regarding the act, arguing that the judges thought that the act was an abolition of parliamentary democracy, since it was passed by the opposition during a minority government, while Wilkins and Friends of the Earth saw the language as mandatory based on the minutes of Parliament's debate around the KPIA (Wilkins, 2014). Since the Supreme Court did not hear the case made by the Friends of the Earth, Beatrice Olivastri, CEO of Friends of the Earth Canada, argues that it was not possible to test the broader principle of law in terms of forcing the government not only to produce a plan but also to implement that plan (Olivastri, 2014).

There are almost no insights regarding the climate-democracy nexus. It seems as if the court ruled, even though not satisfying Friends of the Earth, in an independent way. Hugh Wilkins was also unable to identify any form of corruption (Wilkins, 2014). The influence such open access (besides the Supreme Court, which could have made a decision with far-reaching implications) had, however, did not lead to any changes in Canada's climate performance. The reasons for this might be mixed; it is possible that a differently phrased KPIA might have led to another judgement, etc. At the same time, the legislative was to some extent weakened by the judgement and the executive strengthened, which could weaken democracy. It seems it is almost impossible to draw any conclusions based on this one case regarding the (in)direct influence of an obviously functioning judiciary (as an indicator of independence) on climate performance. More empirical evidence is necessary. The CESD, which followed the process very closely, was also unable to identify any impact which the case might have had (Vaughan, 2014).

There might have been another attempt to gain indirect influence though. By bringing the case to court, Friends of the Earth acquired some media aware-ness and climate policy was debated in public. Indeed, one of John Godfrey's main impressions was that Friends of the Earth was trying to get media atten-tion and didn't really expect to win or to be able to force the government to act (Vaughan, 2014). Of course, Wilkins and Olivastri argue against this, stating that they thought they could win the case and would not have invested resources without the possibility of winning (Olivastri, 2014; Wilkins, 2014). However, nobody, including the three journalists who functioned as interview partners, mentioned the case in regard to any influence upon climate performance. There-fore, it probably must be concluded that it also had no indirect influence on climate performance.

The same can be said about a second Federal Court case which came up in 2012, after Canada had announced its withdrawal from the Kyoto Protocol in 2011 (Federal Court, 2012). The application was made by Daniel Turp (Professor at the University of Montreal) and supported by various others. He argued that the government had surpassed its competencies in foreign affairs in withdrawing from a treaty passed by Parliament and thus violating the separation of powers against the rule of law. The suit was dismissed. Here, the suggestion is also made that the power of Parliament was probably weakened. However, access to the judiciary was free and an influence on climate performance cannot be identified.

Both cases could, counterfactually, have had a positive influence on climate performance had the court decided differently. Nevertheless, in terms of demo-cratic quality and its connection to a democratic interpretation of the rule of law, the question is not so much how the court ruled, but whether it decided neutrally and access to the court was free. The only very small point that could be made is perhaps the negative influence the judgements had on the power of Parliament, which probably felt quite helpless in terms of enforcing climate policy, even though a majority of parliamentarians (in terms of the KPIA) had tried to vote in favour of enforcement. Yet the tendency is very weak and further evidence for this thesis might be necessary. Free access to courts and the rule of law do not seem to have influenced climate performance, at least the empirical cases do not show any clear tendencies in this respect.

However, the KPIA (as the most important parliamentary attempt to enforce the reduction of GHGs and the most important case in terms of independence) also plays an important role in transparency, since it enforced reporting about cli-mate change. Whether this enforcement had an impact on climate performance must therefore be analysed.

Transparency: minimal requirements adhered to

In a fully transparent policy process, access, traceability and the explanation of relevant information should be guaranteed. According to Peter Kent, the gov-ernment was quite transparent and he provides the example of a monitoring programme overseeing the oil and gas industry in Alberta, where the industry paid for the establishment of monitoring and the results were posted and made available (Kent, 2014). However, one small programme is not representative of the government's overall approach regarding transparency, which seems to have been much more lacking in transparency than Kent suggests. We have already seen how the main way the Conservative government used to get into contact with certain actors was based on lobbying and how this left others outside these channels with almost no access to information on how the government was proceeding with its policy planning (Bennett, 2014). Consequently, even parliamentarians were not appropriately informed, but, although the government was suppressing information, parliamentarians "had ways of finding out" the level of emissions (Godfrey, 2014). A clear indicator that the government was not interested in granting parliamentarians the provision of transparent information from an objective source is the fact that they did not invite the CESD to join the Committee of the Environment and Sustainable Development, which had previously been a quite common occurrence (Godfrey, 2014). Subsequently, a former deputy minister of ECan between 2010–2012 concluded an article as follows: "Finally, even strategic regulatory processes need some clearly defined ground rules, if only around transparency. In the long-run it is in no one's interest, even the currently politically influential, to have weak processes for formulating regulations" (Boothe, 2013, p. 369).

Transparency of information is also a precondition for publicity and a functioning democracy needs an informed public and people who understand what they are voting on. The government was, however, probably not that interested in informing the public about climate change. Instead, it provided information in a minimalist fashion, doing no more than what was strictly required by law. According to Matthew Bramley, in Canada one of the biggest problems and certainly a disadvantageous precondition might be that the "public understanding of climate change is very low" and that the public is "unwilling to take guidance from experts" (Bramley, 2014). However, a government which acts transparently would provide information about climate change for its citizens and not hold back information nor question the legitimacy of scientific information. Yet, the Conservative government eliminated organizations producing transparent information, such as the NRTEE, as well as climate research in federal government institutions and at universities, all of which could be seen as "a kind of organized effort to limit the amount of information going in to the public [realm]" (Confidential2, 2014).

At this point, transparency is very much interrelated with publicity. When no transparent information exists, the media cannot do its job and work in a free public sphere. The government provided the CESD with all the information it asked for, but otherwise provided as little information as required by law, applying tricks like tabling information when nobody was looking or ensuring that reports disappeared shortly after they were published online (Vaughan, 2014). Beatrice Olivastri had almost the same experience and notes a decline in transparency around the mid-2000s, with a government which only fulfilled the minimum legal requirements and let historical information disappear (Olivastri, 2014). Jeffrey Simpson describes the government's efforts as a systematic effort "to restrict to the greatest extent possible debate" about climate change (Simpson, 2014). Peter Kent, aware that the government's efforts were being criticized, defends the approach taken, arguing that the UNFCCC criteria were always fulfilled and he simply "didn't grant interviews very often" (Kent, 2014).

However, there was also some controversy about transparency in relation to scientists employed by the government and their ability to speak in public. In Kent's view the problem rests with inadequate journalistic work:

> "The controversy of muzzling scientists developed in my first few months when we had a report, not to do with CO_2, but to do with ozone. . . . [O]ne journalist, followed by several others, called on a Sunday afternoon and demanded access to the scientists who had authored the ozone report. And the media, the person responsible for media said: 'Well,' you know, 'it's Sunday afternoon.' . . . So, the decision was taken at that time to let the paper stand on its own and there was a feeling . . . [T]here has been a reluctance with a number of journalists who represent mainstream journalistic publications or agencies in the daytime but who go on the blogger sphere at night and rent and rape in very partisan ways."
>
> (Kent, 2014)

Kent's statements demonstrate that he had no interest in giving interviews, the government was not proactive in providing transparency, free speech on the Internet by bloggers is criticized and scientists came under certain rules which limited their freedom of expression about what they were allowed to state in public, since they needed permission to speak from the press secretariat. Observations made by Mike de Souza, a journalist from the *National Post*, who worked intensively on climate issues during the Conservative government, describes an atmosphere in which scientists felt afraid:

> "And, yes, it changed the way scientists could do interviews, created some bureaucracies for them, paperwork, created conditions where they were discouraged from giving interviews. Even if they got approval, the hassle of getting the approval was so much that they did not want to. And, they created a climate, the scientists themselves told us this, where they were afraid to talk about their work and about what tax payers were paying for."
>
> (Souza, 2014)

Jeffrey Simpson sees a "systemic campaign" by the government in which only ministers spoke to the public, which had a "dampening effect on public opinion". Simultaneously, he assumes that the media didn't show enough interest in the reports which were being produced (Simpson, 2014). Thus, hindering the transparency of science weakened a precondition for an informed public and portrays another way in which government acted with *elected irresponsibility* in terms of climate change. However, it also shows that the absence of transparency manifested a status quo in terms of climate performance and emissions development, since the broader public subsequently neither better understood climate change nor the need for everybody to take action. Informed decisions, by politicians and/ or the broader public, are unlikely in such a setting.

Nevertheless, it seems the KPIA improved transparency even though it had no direct impact on the government's climate policy-making. Matthew Bramley assumes a big jump in transparency and suggests that a permanent institutionalized body reporting in the way that the CESD and the NRTEE did in keeping with the KPIA's requirements could help to make transparency a permanent source of positive influence on climate policy-making (Bramley, 2014). He recommends a climate change institution like the Committee on Climate Change in the UK, since regular reporting would simultaneously improve both transparency and accountability (Bramley, 2014). The former chair of the NRTEE was also frustrated by the amount of accessible information and suggests that the KPIA at least made some documentation public, while, overall, there was a tremendous lack of transparency (McLaughlin, 2014). McLaughlin states that he often had to rely on reports from American and European institutes, as there were no central databases on energy and economic data in Canada (McLaughlin, 2014). Thus, it seems that the government fulfilled the requirements of the KPIA and the UNF-CCC, but "they did so grudgingly in a minimalist fashion" (McCarthy, 2014).

So, taking into account the KPIA's efforts at enforcement, what was the overall influence of absent transparency on climate performance? It seems that merely fulfilling the minimal legal requirements while almost systematically restricting public debate about climate change (by making it harder for scientists to speak freely to the media, etc.) had a negative impact on climate performance. An informed citizenry which has access to relevant information can be the first step to understanding why active climate policies are needed and can help to hold the government accountable. The picture that seems to emerge from this time frame is of minimal democracy which only fulfilled its legal obligations in relation to transparency. Consequently, Matthew Bramley suggests that "even when good things happen like more transparency, it still is not enough to get over these tremendous obstacles" (Bramley, 2014).

As a consequence of its difficult relationship with transparency, the government worked on having fewer institutions which would produce transparency and therefore a look at the stability dimension is necessary, in order to detect its potential impact on the democracy-climate nexus.

Stability of democratic institutions: win-win situations

In a democracy, it is important that policy processes are embedded in stable democratic structures. Certain institutions guarantee such a kind of stability as a precondition for a functioning and high quality democracy. In Canada, two of these institutions are the CESD and, to some extent, the NRTEE. Since they were able to work quite freely during the first three time frames, their importance has already been recognized and their work honoured. However, under circumstances as complicated as those surrounding climate policy-making under the Conservative government, their existence becomes even more important.

There is one notable difference between the two institutions: while the CESD evaluates the work of the government for Parliament, so that Parliament and a broader public can hold the government accountable, the government announces the members of the NRTEE, which evaluates policies and also provides more concrete instructions on how to combine the environment and the economy through closer dialogue with the government. With their work in ensuring that policy-making is transparent, evaluating achievements and providing recommendations, these two institutions constitute preconditions for a policy process which is embedded in stable democratic structures. Thus, such institutions are an important element of democracies, since they are not only able to ensure the criteria of general systematic performance, such as effectiveness and efficiency, but also guarantee that policies are made in a transparent way, so that the (broader) public is well informed and policies are responsive to previously agreed targets, etc.

Even though these two institutions existed, Matthew Bramley identifies a lack or weaknesses of such institutions in terms of climate policy-making, since, in his view, too few strong institutions existed, which were able to hold the government accountable (Bramley, 2014). Moreover, the CESD is a commissioner of the environment, not of climate change, and thus no guarantee exists that he or she will report on climate change. Since climate change is such a complicated issue to deal with, institutions are required which "get to the bottom of the issue" when the media is unable to do so and both NGOs and opposition parties lack the resources to do so (Bramley, 2014). In terms of democratic quality, it is reasonable to note that the Canadian Parliament is, in the view of somebody deeply involved in and closely following climate policy-making, not adequately equipped, especially in comparison to the resources allocated to the government. Our investigation of the independence dimension has already identified suggestions of Parliament's weaknesses in comparison to the executive and it seems that these findings are confirmed in this regard. Parliament appears to be too weak to control a well-equipped government and this is why democratic stability in terms of a balance of powers is threatened. Therefore, institutions like the CESD and the NRTEE become even more important. However, even though they deal with climate change from time to time, they are not institutions which focus on climate change. Due to these two shortcomings, Bramley proposes a permanent institution which deals with climate policy in the form of an Office of Parliament (similar to that of the environment commissioner or the auditor general), since "at key moments in Canadian political life, when the government gets held to account in a really powerful way, very often it is because the Auditor General has reported" (Bramley, 2014). A new climate change institution, with a legal mandate and a level of independence could "give members of parliament a richness, a depth of information of analysis that they simply do not have at the moment" and help NGOs and the media to improve accountability (Bramley, 2014).

It seems Bramley identified a quite important aspect in terms of democratic stability and its potential influence on climate performance during a policy process which came to the public attention during this fourth time frame, when the NRTEE and the CESD became essential, due to, amongst other reasons, the

KPIA. It also became clear that there was no institution which ensured that the work done by the NRTEE and CESD during the KPIA would also be available afterwards. The creation of an Office of Parliament, e.g. a commissioner of climate change, would probably increase democratic quality by providing a stable democratic institution and information with which parliamentarians, citizens, NGOs, businesses, etc. could hold the government accountable. At the same time, it could enforce climate performance by providing suitable evaluations of how climate policies could be made in a more effective manner, etc.

However, developments at the end of the fourth time frame point in the opposite direction. The NRTEE was suspended by Peter Kent in 2012, since it "was created before the internet, when there were few such sources of domestic, independent research and analysis on sustainable development", whereas, in 2012, enough institutions, like the NRTEE, existed which provided information (Visser, 2012). One of the main underlying reasons why the NRTEE was suspended seems to be that the government was against a price on CO_2, which had been proposed in several NRTEE publications. According to a member of the NRTEE, Robert Slater, the government used its prerogative in an inadequate way:

FH: Maybe you can, as I know that you were part of the National Roundtable, maybe you can give me some insights into that issue. Why did it end up in the way it ended up?

RS: Well, I have no clue. No one ever told us. So, there was no discussion, right? This was the government again demonstrating it has the prerogative to make these sorts of decisions.

(Slater, 2014)

The government seems to have used its prerogative in terms of climate change quite intensively, controlling environmental assessments in general, which could have enriched an informed public. Instead, the government made use of its prerogative as an elected government as much as possible with the philosophy "We are elected into power and therefore we can do what we want until the Canadians throw us out, so you know, environmental assessments: who cares, let's cut the act, we have the power to cut the act" (Vaughan, 2014). Not surprisingly, with the government being able to use its prerogative so intensively, which of course has to be seen as a democratic weakness in the Canadian parliamentary system, it had no need to respect or make use of the findings and recommendations provided by the NRTEE, which is why the reports ultimately only had a very limited influence (Confidential2, 2014). The only impact the NRTEE might have had was on improving the measurements and modelling of the climate change plans under the KPIA.

So, what do these findings in terms of the stability of democratic institutions tell us about the potential influence of democratic quality on climate performance? It can be estimated that stability and the existence of democratic institutions such as the CESD are of crucial importance for the democracy-climate nexus. They provide systematic information which a wide range of actors, such as industry representatives, NGOs, parliamentarians or the broader public, would not be able to analyse on their own. In a democracy, an informed citizenry can only actively engage, participate, deliberate and elect if it is provided with all necessary information. Otherwise, the executive cannot be held accountable. In the Canadian case, there seems to have been an imbalance, since the executive was able to use its prerogative in quite an extensive way. In the absence of a government which shows interest in such institutions as the CESD or the NRTEE, it is unlikely that said institutions will have much influence. It could be counterfactually argued: if the anticipated Office of Parliament in the form of a commissioner of climate change, as proposed by Matthew Bramley, were to exist, it would be able to do significant work, which would be relevant for both democratic quality and climate performance. Such a commissioner could provide a hinge between democratic quality and climate performance. The reports prepared by the CESD over the years on climate change clearly point in this direction. They were often mentioned as a legitimate source of information in the interviews, while the importance of the CESD was underlined and supported. It can therefore be concluded that more or stronger democratic institutions along the lines of the CESD (with its stability in terms of no destabilizing circumstances on financing, personnel or even suspensions, such as was the case with the NRTEE) and clearly defined responsibilities can create a win-win situation for democratic quality and climate performance. The influence of more stable democratic institutions on climate performance has therefore to be evaluated as positive.

Whether such institutions exist and provide analysis and information is one important aspect, but actors also have to be able to talk freely about their analyses and this is why liberty plays an important role.

Liberty: muzzling ENGOs and climate science

Associational and organizational rights and their practical application enable autonomy and guarantee liberty. Therefore, organizations, whether strong or weak, must be able to act and express themselves freely, without being influenced by or dependent on third parties, or being excluded from the process. Moreover, individuals must also be able to make use of their political and civil rights to state their views on the issues under consideration.

Between 2006–2012, the evidence suggests that the government more or less systematically weakened liberty – especially in regard to (E)NGOs and (climate) science – which could have lead to a less informed and freely articulating public and less or uninformed engagement in climate policy-making, resulting in less climate performance. The weakening of NGOs and particularly ENGOs can be identified in regard to a number of conditions.

(1) Already at the beginning of its term of office, the Conservative government clearly demonstrated to ENGOs that it intended to restrict their ability to speak freely and express their concerns and ideas. In 2007, when the government announced the *Turning the Corner* climate change plan, it invited media and ENGOs at the same time, but to different places, in Toronto

(Bramley, 2014). After a brief announcement by the government, ENGOs realized that they had been invited to a different place than the media and tried to get to where the media was, but arrived too late, reaching the location just as most media outlets had already finished their reporting (Bramley, 2014). Thus, the ENGOs were unable to speak to journalists before most of them had already determined their stories, which Bramley describes as "a deliberate strategy by the government communications people to prevent NGOs commenting on the announcement" (Bramley, 2014). In terms of liberty, ENGOs were hindered in their ability to express themselves by the government and, consequently, were unable to communicate their opinions freely in Canadian media.

Another even more tactical and long-term strategy to immobilize ENGOs in their work and their mode of expression can be seen in the way in which the Canadian Revenue Agency (CRA), which is the federal agency dealing with federal taxes, started increasingly auditing those groups that were not in line with views expressed by the government. The CRA conducted audits to see whether the audited organizations were approved to be charities. Charities are only allowed to spend 10% of their money on so-called political activities, which are those that seek to "further the interests of a particular political party; or support a political party or candidate for public office; or retain, oppose, or change the law, policy or decision of any level of government in Canada or a foreign country" (CRA, 2014).

The government had the feeling that certain organizations, which were official charities, were spending more than 10% on political activities and were maybe being financed by foreign sources in what they considered to be an illegal way. Of course, these organizations could have chosen to not have been classified as charities and thus spent as much of their time and resources on political activities as they would have liked, however, many of the organizations concerned (i.e. climate change charities, representing relevant and affected actors, such as civil society and/or specific environmental needs) did not have as strong financial backgrounds as other actors participating in the same political arena, such as businesses and industry. Therefore, it seems to be reasonable to expect that such organizations are enabled by providing such resources as tax subsidies, which help them to speak and express their concerns freely without being too dependent on third sources.

While an audit is a completely legitimate element to evaluate the status of a charity, it seems as if these audits were used as instruments to weaken actors the government disagreed with. The environment minister identifies the main reason for the increase in audits by claiming that "supposedly charitable organizations" were not charities, since the funding they received through international foreign funds were used to allow them to engage "more in political activities" (Kent, 2014). This, he says, is why he "suggested that our Canada Revenue Agency investigate to see whether some of these charitable authorizations for NGOs were actually being improperly used" (Kent, 2014). Moreover, the environment minister described problems he had in his own constituency as another reason for carrying out the audits:

"A lot of the ENGOs are most active in environmental defence. I had a lot of problems with their opposition to our climate change policy was to threaten to import campaigners, canvassers, door-to-door canvassers from across the country and from the United States to knock on doors in my constituency to defeat me. And, when I suggested that the environmental defence charitable status be investigated for political activism, they stopped."

(Kent, 2014)

Besides the obvious fact that Kent used audits to limit the freedom of speech of those who were opposed to his environmental views, another problem exists. The main difficulty for (small) ENGOs is often the fact that they have limited personnel numbers and thus the effort of responding to the audits and answering the CRA's questions meant that many were unable to work on anything else (Bramley, 2014; Wilkins, 2014). At the time, Bramley concluded that "the government is basically bullying small organizations with threats of financial consequences because of what those organizations are saying (. . .) it is a limitation of the freedom of speech" (Bramley, 2014). An example is Friends of the Earth, which found it frightening to be audited (Olivastri, 2014). According to Beatrice Olivastri, Friends of the Earth was audited because someone from Alberta was annoyed that they "would be suing the government" and enforced the audit (Olivastri, 2014). Quite insightful is the context in which the audit started, which was in direct connection to the KPIA case brought to the Federal Court by Friends of the Earth (Olivastri, 2014). Thus, there is a quite direct relation between acting against a certain decision of the government before the court and being audited. In the end, however, the KPIA case was deemed to not be a political activity (Olivastri, 2014). Thus, the line applied to distinguish between political and other activities seems to be very thin, since "if you say that oil sands are bad that can be legally construed as lobbying and therefore you are under investigation and therefore you are intimidated" (Vaughan, 2014). Finally, in 2012, the CRA was provided with $8 m to launch political activity audits, which were as NRCan Minister Joe Oliver stated, initiated to audit "environmental and other radical groups" over a period of two years (Beeby, 2014).

Besides audits by the CRA, the government simply stopped funding certain civil society groups with long traditions in Canada. Since many of these organizations were unable to find alternative sources for funding their work on a short-term basis, they "became weaker simply because they could not afford to have good scientists and, you know, experts working with them" (Confidential4, 2014). A good example might be the Canadian Environmental Network, which, at very short notice, was informed that ECan would not enter into a new contribution agreement with the network. The Canadian Environmental Network functioned as the umbrella organization which worked to include small groups which were usually marginalized due to their geographic circumstances by inviting them to a yearly caucus (McDiarmid, 2011). Scott Vaughan characterizes the actions taken by the government to systematically limit the funding of such groups as the Canadian Environmental Network (which subsequently was only to continue to exist in the form of a website), as "using state labours to intimidate groups that took a contrary view to you [the government]" (Vaughan, 2014). Thereby, the government silenced voices it disliked.

Overall, the strategy to audit and limit the financing of ENGOs seems to have worked out in the way the Conservative government intended. The limitation of freedom of speech and the disabling of free expression clearly limited liberty. And, such types of limited liberty have a negative effect on climate performance, since those voices influencing public discourse through information translated to the broader public etc. are subsequently not as active as they were before and ambitious climate policies and their implementation are less likely.

(2) The second systematic weakening of liberty affects (climate) science. The relationship between democracy and climate change is an important one, particularly in regard to considered judgement. Science and the acceptance of its results are of crucial importance, if a state is to build an informed public sphere which is, on the basis of scientific information, able to hold the government accountable or to find new and innovative democratic ways of problem-solving. However, Peter Kent assumes that, in Canada, "as in every government there are sceptics and deniers" (Kent, 2014). Whether every government includes sceptics cannot be proved, however, such politicians are, of course, sceptical about the need for climate change research. Unsurprisingly, a broad range of scientists felt that the government used the reduction of the financial deficit as legitimation for systematically reducing funding in areas where scientific findings opposed its views (Confidential4, 2014). One example in regard to climate change research is the prominent Polar Environmental Atmospheric Research Laboratory. Even though its year-round research was ensured by new funding in 2013 – probably due to public pressure and pressure from the worldwide scientific community – it was ultimately forced to close, since the government didn't provide enough funding in 2012 and actually shut it down for some months (CBCNews, 2012, 2013). The government thus acted in the same way as it had with the CRA audits of civil society groups. Pressure and funding reductions were broadly reported in the news, with documentaries like *The Fifth Estate – Silence of the Labs* (CBC, 2014) and scientific journals stating that "[s]cientific expertise and experience cannot be chopped and changed as the mood suits" (*Nature*, 2012a (quotation); 2012b; O'Hara, 2010). Nevertheless, it can be noted that the media was able to act in a free public sphere, which raised public awareness and, in the end, seems to have influenced changes in spending, e.g. for the Polar Environment Atmospheric Research Laboratory (PEARL). However, the role of climate scientists nonetheless changed and their influence seems to have been reduced, as "they were eliminated from all the departments" and thus "slowly the Conservative government got rid of all the scientists especially in the climate change area" (Confidential4, 2014).

Another aspect of weakening scientific voices in public was the new and more restrictive rules on media access for scientists working in departments. While it was common for journalists to have relatively quick and direct access to scientists working in departments, receiving responses within a few hours, the time between a request for an interview with a scientist and an interview being granted became much longer, often taking up to several weeks (Vaughan, 2014). According to a senior official, the new more restrictive rules relating to scientists speaking to the media were a result of the fact that scientists as well as other public servants had to support the elected government and public disagreement would have been unethical (Confidential6, 2014). Journalists, according to the senior official, would have asked questions to try to find disagreements between scientific work and the government's decisions, even though the government would have to take factors other than science into account when making decisions (Confidential6, 2014). In the end, "this runs into a problem because people outside the Government think that for some reason the same rules that apply to all other public servants don't apply to scientists who are public servants", which would be "not consistent with the Westminster parliamentary system" (Confidential6, 2014). Consequently, the government decided that contact with the media would have to be managed at the political level. In terms of the scientists' freedom of speech, the presentation and explanation of scientific results is always democratic, not only because scientists have to be enabled to speak freely, but also because they produce relevant data for evidence-based decision-making and an informed citizenry, which must be enabled to hold the government accountable.

However, even though Peter Kent and a senior official claim that they encouraged scientists to publish journal articles and present them to the public, investigations point in another direction: media coverage of climate change science actually reduced by 80 per cent in the first year after the release of Ecan's new press guidelines (Souza, 2010). Moreover, and highly relevant for liberty as a dimension of democratic quality, a survey undertaken by the Professional Institute of the Public Service of Canada (PIPSC, 2013) in 2013 showed that 90 per cent of federal government scientists felt that they were not allowed to speak freely to the media, that 24 per cent had been asked to exclude or alter information for non-scientific reasons and that 37 per cent had been prevented from speaking to the media at some point in the previous five years. These numbers clearly demonstrate that scientists working for the government were not able to speak freely, indeed, that their opinions were suppressed and the public was deprived of scientific knowledge which was necessary to control the government and to engage in considered judgements.

Scientists were not satisfied with the developments and, even though traditionally "Canadians are not as expressive as perhaps people in other countries are" (Wilkins, 2014), in 2012 they went to Parliament Hill and chanted "no science, no evidence, no truth, no democracy", "death of science", etc. (Star, 2012). The slogan "no science, no evidence, no truth, no democracy" seems, due to the logic it subsumes, to be of interest for the democracy-climate nexus. Activists take the sequence portrayed in the slogan quite literally, pointing out that attacks on science can be seen as attacks on democracy itself, since scientific facts hold political power accountable and scientists should thus always have the possibility to communicate freely (Linnitt, 2013). Thus, as the main argument, it can be said that without research and scientifically produced information being available to both members of the public and experts, informed decision-making becomes impossible.

To sum up, we will look at the consequences of the aforementioned developments in the ENGO and science sectors for civil society funded organizations, which, like Evidence for Democracy (E4D), tried to explain and stand up for the relationship between functioning democracy and science (E4D, 2015). Some ENGOs, like the David Suzuki Foundation, withdrew from the federal level of government (since they felt they could no longer work effectively there), changed their strategies and tried to work through provincial governments (Bennett, 2014). The scientific advisory organization NRTEE (which we know was closely related to the government, since it published information on its members) was also suspended. One of the main tasks of the NRTEE had been to support public policy discussion by providing data and research in an innovative way (through modelling, etc.) and bringing people together to reach consensus on contentious issues. However, "the dilemma with that is that the government wasn't in the mood for different solutions", so nobody in the government was listening any more (McLaughlin, 2014).

If we look at all the developments in science (where the government shut down important climate change research programmes, scientists were not allowed to speak freely, protests linked science and democracy and the NRTEE was suspended) and in the ENGO sector (where obstacles were laid to prevent ENGOs in speaking to the media and CRA audits were used to silence ENGOs) in regard to liberty as a dimension of democratic quality, then it is difficult to argue that the elected government was using its prerogative in a democratically legitimate way to set priorities. The government's whole approach seems to have been much more systematic. It clearly limited liberty by disabling freedom of speech and expected that this would reduce the need to actively engage in climate policy-making and implementation. This goes very much hand in hand with the government's strategy to make climate change a shield issue. Thus, it has to be concluded that a reduction in liberty led to a reduction in climate performance. The public were not sufficiently informed about climate change and therefore nothing happened. It also seems that the relationship between the media, ENGOs and science came under significant pressure between 2006–2012. However, a closer look is necessary to get more insights and to discover whether and how publicity influenced climate performance.

Publicity: only by the grace of the government

Publicity is ensured by a free public sphere, which makes it more likely that issues raise public awareness and are debated and enables the public to hold the government accountable, be informed and be able to participate in considered judgements. So, what kind of publicity existed between 2006–2012 and how did it influence climate performance?

A first indicator regarding publicity is whether and how the government supported public debate on climate change through the provision of information and information outreach, public education, explanation of scientific results, etc. Simply put, in a democracy the government has to explain how and what it decides on. A highly democratic government is characterized not only by being required to answer questions (e.g. through Parliament during PM's questions) but by actively informing the public about policy issues and decisions under consideration. And, to some extent, Peter Kent shows awareness of the complexity of climate change meaning that it requires explanation, when arguing that "complicated issues mean digesting great amounts of information and conflicting information and conflicting theories" (Kent, 2014). Yet, although seemingly aware of these circumstances, the government does not appear to have applied an approach in accordance with this theory. The CESD notes, inter alia, that it was completely unclear which parts of the government were responsible for the implementation, measurement and reporting of the climate plans published and thus, in terms of responsiveness, there was no comprehensive reporting on or translation of policy and science to the public (CESD, 2011, p. 35). The government would simply make a plan public and then, in the words of Bramley, "they forget about it and hope the public forgets about [it]" too (Bramley, 2014). Moreover, information provided for the national report to the UNFCCC in 2010 was far more general and unspecific ("Canada continues to educate and raise public awareness on the subject of climate change, and recognizes that permanently changing behaviours and instilling a low-emissions mindset throughout society is a long-term process") than for the previous national report to the UNFCCC in 2006 (Government, 2006b; 2010, p. 140). Additionally, the aforementioned muzzling of scientists, through rules which made it much less likely that scientists would be available for interviews, points in the same direction. The government did not enable a free public sphere which was equipped with all necessary information and to which governmental policy-making or scientific results were explained. Thus, it could be said that "the climate change argument has led a lot of people to make a decision one way or the other without really basing that on science and facts" (Kent, 2014), which itself could at least be partially explained by insufficient publicity, since the government did not help to enable the public to make an informed choice.

Nevertheless, in regard to a second indicator of publicity, the media itself had a responsibility to raise public awareness and to control the government. People had to be engaged "because it is about making choices and about making sensible choices" and, even though the government was not very active in this regard, the media was able to do its work and contemporary witnesses stated "there are a number of people in the media that are trying" (Dillon, 2014). However, was the way the media worked on climate policy-making characterized by democratic circumstances, such as an unrestricted plurality of informed media reporting and did it influence climate performance? Besides the almost trivial circumstance that certain newspapers were more in favour of active climate policies, such as *The Globe and Mail*, than others, such as the *National Post*, the picture seems to have been quite diverse. There were specialized environmental reporters, like Mike de Souza, Jeffrey Simpson, Margo McDermitt and Louis-Gilles Francoeur, working for different newspapers, but all trying to educate and provide in-depth reporting on climate change issues (Bramley, 2014; Confidential5, 2014; Vaughan, 2014). Such people are described as people who "really get to understand the issue" (Bramley, 2014). The influence of these journalists was positive, but quite limited. It was not a case of a general "organized effort from the media to try and make the government accountable for its Kyoto obligations, which were signed and ratified" (Confidential2, 2014). For example, on the other side of the spectrum, there were journalists with "an unacceptably poor understanding of the issue" of climate change, who nevertheless reported on it. Such journalists could easily be found in radio and TV stations as well as in newspapers in the form of editorial and opinion writers (Bramley, 2014; Confidential5, 2014). Moreover, from 2006–2012, the media still adopted a binary view with pro and anti-climate change positions. Such a setting, which focused on publicizing different opinions, made the debate more divisive and failed to highlight the lack and low quality of policy (Confidential5, 2014). Another example of how reporting on climate change was not always as focused as it could have been is the carbon tax, which was not so much analysed in terms of whether it would have been a good policy but in terms of whether it was a sellable idea (McCarthy, 2014). Furthermore, as a study shows, the debate seemed to be centred around Canada itself, with the media not really looking outside of the box and focusing on national "solutions to what is actually a global problem" (Konieczna, Mattis, Tsai, Liang, & Dunwoody, 2014). Overall it seems media reporting was in fact fairly diverse, which indicates a reasonably free public sphere. However, bar some exceptions, the media did not report in an evidence-based high quality manner nor did it raise sufficient public awareness to hold the government accountable or open a debate on the government's climate change shield issue. Yet, there might have been reasons for this: without a government forcing climate change policies by setting strategic priorities and enabling public discourse about the issue, it seems to have been hard for the media to hold the government accountable on an issue which was as complex as climate change and not traditionally associated with the media sphere. The most serious problem was that in Canada this combined with a strong oil industry golden goose, which would have had to have been killed (McCarthy, 2014). On the whole, it seems there were circumstances (such as the complexity of climate change, the government setting strategic priorities, a lack of knowledgeable journalists. etc.) which restricted the influence of media pluralism on climate performance to a few cases where the circumstances were more advantageous.

So, can any more concrete examples be identified of the degree to which publicity as a dimension of democratic quality had an influence on climate performance? The years 2006–2007 are insightful in this case. At this time, climate change became a big issue in Canada due to publications and events like the release of the IPCC and Stern reports and the occurrence of Hurricane Katrina, which, shortly after the Conservatives took power, led to an increase in public awareness about climate change through the reporting of these events in the media. In the end, that whole discourse changed public opinion, led to public concern and interest and pushed the government to announce the ecoAction programmes. However, these programmes were not very significant and did not significantly reduce GHG emissions (Bennett, 2014; Souza, 2014). Considering the whole time frame from 2006–2012, it is clear that the government felt the need to somehow act seriously, so that the public would be satisfied. Around 2006/2007, this action came in terms of announcing a plan, but thereafter not much happened, with no real attempt to implement the plan nor any significant GHG reductions. Similarly, with the start of the financial crisis in 2008, both the public and the media became much more interested in other big problems (McCarthy, 2014). Thus, the media and the public often take note when policies are announced, but do a poor job when it comes to holding the government accountable for their implementation. So, there is a weakness or a gap in terms of public attention focusing on announcements vs. implementation. This leads to reporting, and thus any possible influence, being much more intensive around announcements than around implementation (Bramley, 2014). From 2006–2012, both media reporting and public awareness were too inconsistent to have much influence in addition to which the government was not prepared to allow much influence to be brought to bear (Godfrey, 2014; Souza, 2014). Consequently, after 2007, publicity had, on the whole, no influence on the government's climate change policy. Peter Kent himself states that "it certainly didn't affect our decision-making processes and . . . the sector-by-sector regulation" (Kent, 2014). In the end, the problem remains that the public often cannot and does not follow policy issues in detail, which seems to be even more challenging in regard to such a complex issue as climate change (Souza, 2014). A survey undertaken in 2013 clearly demonstrates these complications by showing that people did not know that Canada had withdrawn from the Kyoto Protocol: when asked whether Canada was still part of the Kyoto Protocol 41 per cent responded with "no" and 33 per cent with "yes", with the remainder being unsure (Souza, 2013).

Overall, three findings exist: first, the government did not proactively inform and educate the public and/or media; secondly, certain preconditions were in place which allowed the media to make use of a free public sphere; and, thirdly, the only concrete example of influence can be seen in the public pressure in 2006/2007, which resulted in the announcement of ecoAction. What follows from these findings? It can be concluded that the influence of publicity is quite limited when the government in power is not willing to cooperate. Without this precondition, publicity is a dimension which to some limited extent can keep the issue alive (McCarthy, 2014), but, without politicians being able to be held accountable, this publicity has almost no influence on climate performance. Thus, even though an apparently free public sphere exists, it is highly dependent on the government's willingness to share information and only continues *by the grace of the government*. When no procedures exist to ensure that the government explains, educates and informs the public, then the media is unable to do this job alone. Moreover, in the absence of interest from government, journalists or the broader public, the *announcement-implementation gap* exists, with not enough attention being paid to the implementation of initial announcements. Thus, publicity has no influence on climate performance as long as the verification of the implementation of announced policies does not receive the same media attention as the announcement itself.

An open question would be whether a mechanism of another form of publicity is imaginable, which could close the *announcement-implementation gap* and remove the dependence on the *grace of the government*. Maybe an answer could be found in a regulation or law which enforces the government to announce its performance on implementation more prominently and more regularly. Such a task would be closely connected to the pre-existing CESD and helps to demonstrate its importance for the democracy-climate nexus.

Results: no interest in the democratization of democracy

The findings on the manifestations of the dimensions of democratic quality and their influence on climate performance between 2006–2012 are quite numerous and have to be compiled and contextualized in order to make more fundamental assumptions about the democracy-climate nexus.

Interview partners: the need for democratic tools and their application

The understandings of the democracy-climate nexus made by actors directly involved in the process from 2006–2012 form the first point of reference for interpretation. A confidential interview partner working at ECan described the whole climate policy-making process as being a "revolving cycle of develop a plan, announce a plan, throw the plan in the garbage, develop a new plan, announce that plan, throw it in the garbage and repeat to the point now where much, much time has passed" (Confidential5, 2014). In general, Scott Vaughan, CESD 2008–2013, describes the "democratic" processes of public policy-making as "often irrational and messy and non-linear", since the process was, according to him, neither based on considered judgement nor responsive (Vaughan, 2014). More precisely, Scott Vaughan sees the Kyoto Protocol process in Canada as a "classic example of a democratic deficit", characterizing the process as "absolutely not" transparent and arguing that the government not only did not try to engage with Canadians on climate change policies, but, on the contrary, was "quite extraordinary in harassing Canadian civil society" with the existence of "an absolutely direct correlation between taking a very strong stand on climate and oil sands" and being audited by the Canadian Revenue Agency (CRA) (Vaughan, 2014). In Vaughan's view "you cannot have good public policy without public input and public participation" and the public must at least "get a sense that I have been engaged, I have been listened to" (Vaughan, 2014). Vaughan's standpoint assumes a negative impact of diminished democratic quality on climate performance.

According to other interview partners, another key question for the democracy-climate nexus is whether the government represents the preferences of the voters. The journalist Shawn McCarthy argues that everybody knows where the government stood in regard to climate change, but it was nevertheless elected (McCarthy, 2014). The former environment minister Peter Kent argues "if [a] general election occurs [and] Canadians think we perform badly then democracy will have a chance to select somebody else" (Kent, 2014). These assumptions sound as simple as they do logical, but perhaps they are nonetheless unreasonable. Contrary views are expressed by Scott Vaughan, arguing that people who were concerned about climate change had given up on Ottawa and become engaged elsewhere, while journalist Mike de Souza presents the following analysis of withdrawal:

> "The public opinion polls show Canadians want something and the government is doing something else. It is doing some things they want but not everything, which can happen on a variety of issues. When the government decided to pull out of Kyoto as a majority government this issue was not debated during the election campaign preceding that. There was not a debate in Parliament on the government's decision to pull out of the Kyoto Protocol. So, should Parliament debate when a government wants to enter or pull out of a treaty? Most people who support democracy would say yes."
>
> (Souza, 2014)

In the end, the climate change debate is, of course, also a debate about how to handle the short-term preferences of current voters, who are probably often more in favour of the jobs saved by the oil and gas industry than acting on climate change. In comparison, the political legacy handed down to and the preferences of future generations are – as in almost every state worldwide – inadequately represented in Canada's current political system. Moreover, the analysis by Mike de Souza highlights another potential weakness in the Canadian system of democracy: the power of the prerogative, which can be used in a quite extensive way without coming into conflict with any laws. The power of the prerogative basically allows the government to say, "we are elected into power, and therefore we can do what we want until the Canadians throw us out" (Vaughan, 2014). The government "can actually shut down the debate on an issue just by not debating [it]" and it did so on climate change (Bennett, 2014). The power of the prerogative in the context of the analysis of the democracy-climate nexus seems to be problematic: on the one hand, a government needs legitimation to govern through its election and needs (in terms of procedural general performance) the capability to set and maintain strategic priorities, etc., while, on the other hand, the prerogative is a double-edged sword which allows a government to negate a policy issue like climate change. A mechanism which balances the need to set strategic priorities and the possibility to negate a policy issue does not exist but would be an asset for Canadian democracy. In terms of the democracy-climate nexus, the prerogative is a factor of uncertainty: while PM Chrétien used it to set very ambitious targets, PM Harper applied it to the negation of climate change debates. In both cases, the influence on climate performance was negative. It can be concluded that the prerogative is a problematic tool of the Canadian government, with low democratic quality, which overwhelmingly has a negative influence on climate performance.

Interview partners also identified a "lack of democratic tools" (Vaughan, 2014) in terms of the absence of a "mechanism or process or the political engagement to bring players around the tables to figure out the best way of doing this" (McLaughlin, 2014) and to build consensus (Confidential6, 2014). Thus, the way in which the interview partners interpreted the developments between 2006–2012 point in a direction which at least partially explains the weak climate performance through a lack of democratic quality and a focus on the two-edged prerogative and the absence of the necessary democratic tools to deal with climate change.

Findings and intrepretation: no democratic quality, no influence

The results of the analysis in the time frame from 2006–2012 include seven findings. The first finding can partially be seen as a repetition of the previous time frames: to start a (democratic) policy process, certain preconditions of general systematic performance are necessary. Between 2006–2012, these preconditions were overwhelmingly absent: many politicians in the government did not understand climate change sufficiently, the strategic priorities chosen by the government did not include climate change and there was either a lack of governing structures or these were repeatedly undergoing various processes of reorganization. In the absence of these preconditions, a (democratic) policy process was not very likely. A far-reaching implication of this and previous findings can be found in the following assumption, which will be further analysed in the overall conclusion: it seems that general procedural performance ensures that certain policy issues are either implemented or hindered in their implementation, but general procedural performance cannot ensure that the right things are done, while procedural democratic quality ensures that, whether policy issues are implemented or hindered in their implementation, nonetheless the right things get done. Secondly, mechanisms to ensure horizontal accountability were once again absent. PM Harper often acted by making extensive use of the prerogative in regard to climate change. The detected influence on climate performance between 2006–2012 is negative, while, in previous years, the influence led to unpredictability. Since there was a lack of transparency, inclusiveness and participation, these elements were unable to interrelate with and ensure accountability. The great importance of the stability of democratic institutions forms the third finding. Institutions like the CESD provide important analysis and evaluation, not only for Parliament, civil society and citizens but also for the government. They function as links between democratic quality and climate performance, simultaneously improving both spheres. A to-be established office for a commissioner of climate change could come to be an essential mechanism for the transmission of information. The influence of the stability of democratic institutions on climate performance is positive. The fourth finding exists in the context of inclusiveness and participation. The degree of both dimensions was very low in this time frame: inclusiveness was biased, the *Gazette* process was almost the only formal means of participation, considered judgement did not take place, Parliament tried (through the KPIA) to influence and impact upon climate relevant policies and was centred around the oil and gas industry and the Conservative electorate. Taking into account the negative impact of biased selection and informal structures of influence combined with a lack of considered judgement and responsiveness and the non-existent influence of Parliament, a tendency can be identified for the absence of democratic quality to have either no or mostly negative influence on climate performance. Closely related to the informal character of inclusiveness and participation, the threats posed to transparency form a fifth finding. While the KPIA did lead to some improvements, the government only did the absolute minimum in fulfilling its legal requirements, but was in no way proactive and instead tried to restrict every public debate and to avoid having an informed public on climate change. Without transparency, the public is unable to hold the government accountable. Insufficient transparency influences climate performance negatively. The threatening of liberty has to be seen as a sixth finding. The government muzzled ENGOs and climate scientists to reduce their scope of action. The government systematically limited freedom of speech to reduce the need to engage in climate policy-making and implementation. Thus, some voices, usually those in favour of active climate politics, were kept silent. The constraints on liberty have a negative influence on climate performance. That publicity existed only *by the grace of the government* is the seventh finding. The government's willingness to share information, engage and cooperate with the public builds a precondition for high publicity. The government instead applied no procedure to explain, educate, etc., so that media would have been able to have done its job more easily. Moreover, the media and the public failed to recognize the existence of an *announcement-implementation gap*. Limited publicity has no influence on climate performance.

The government in place between 2006–2012 does not seem to have been interested in democratizing Canadian democracy. The overall influence of an absence of democratic quality on climate performance appears to have been either non-existent or negative.

References

The access date of all material retrieved from the Web is 5 June 2015 unless otherwise specified.

Beeby, D. (2014). Timeline. Canada Revenue Agency's political-activity audits of charities. *CBC News online*. Retrieved from www.cbc.ca/news/politics/canada-revenue-agency-s-political-activity-audits-of-charities-1.2728023

Bennett, J. (2014). Interview on Canada's Kyoto Protocol process/Interviewer: F. Hanusch.

Boothe, P. (2013). Making good regulations. *Canadian Public Policy – Analyse de Politiques*, 39(3), 359–370.

Bramley, M. (2014). Interview on Canada's Kyoto Protocol process/Interviewer: F. Hanusch.

CBC. (2014). *The Fifth Estate – Silence of the Labs*. Season 39. Retrieved from www.cbc.ca/fifth/episodes/2013–2014/the-silence-of-the-labs (accessed 23 February 2017).

CBCNews. (2012). High Arctic research station forced to close. *CBC News online*, 28 February. Retrieved from www.cbc.ca/news/technology/high-arctic-research-station-forced-to-close-1.1171728

CBCNews. (2013). High Arctic research station saved by new funding. *CBC News online*. Retrieved from www.cbc.ca/news/technology/high-arctic-research-station-saved-by-new-funding-1.1360779

CESD. (2009). *Report of the Commissioner of the Environment and Sustainable Development*. Chapter 2. Kyoto Protocol Implementation Act. Retrieved from www.oag-bvg.gc.ca/internet/docs/parl_cesd_200905_02_e.pdf (accessed 23 February 2017).

CESD. (2011). *Report of the Commissioner of the Environment and Sustainable Development*. Chapter 1. Climate change plans under the Kyoto Protocol Implementation Act. Retrieved from www.oag-bvg.gc.ca/internet/docs/parl_cesd_201110_01_e.pdf (accessed 23 February 2017).

CESD. (2012). *Report of the Commissioner of the Environment and Sustainable Development*. Chapter 2. Meeting Canada's 2020 climate change commitments. Retrieved from www.oag-bvg.gc.ca/internet/English/parl_cesd_201205_02_e_36774.html (accessed 23 February 2017).

Cleland, F.M. (2014). Interview on Canada's Kyoto Protocol process/Interviewer: F. Hanusch.

Confidential2. (2014). Interview on Canada's Kyoto Protocol process/Interviewer: F. Hanusch.

Confidential4. (2014). Interview on Canada's Kyoto Protocol process/Interviewer: F. Hanusch.

Confidential5. (2014). Interview on Canada's Kyoto Protocol process/Interviewer: F. Hanusch.

Confidential6. (2014). Interview on Canada's Kyoto Protocol process/Interviewer: F. Hanusch.

CRA. (2014). Political activities. Retrieved from www.cra-arc.gc.ca/chrts-gvng/chrts/plcy/cps/cps-022-eng.html#N10230

Curry, B. and McCarthy, S. (2011). Canada formally abandons Kyoto Protocol on climate change. Retrieved from www.theglobeandmail.com/news/politics/canada-formally-abandons-kyoto-protocol-on-climate-change/article4180809 (accessed 23 February 2017).

Dillon, J. (2014). Interview on Canada's Kyoto Protocol process/Interviewer: F. Hanusch.

E4D. (2015). Evidence for Democracy. Retrieved from https://evidencefordemocracy.ca

Federal Court (2008). *Friends of the Earth v. Canada*, 2008 FC 1183, [2009] 3 F.C.R. 201 (2008). Retrieved from http://commonlaw.uottawa.ca/15/index.php?option=com_docman&task=doc_download&gid=3993 (accessed 23 February 2017).

Federal Court (2012). 2012 FC 893. Retrieved from www2.ecolex.org/server2.php/libcat/docs/COU/Full/En/COU-159630.pdf (accessed 23 February 2017).

Godfrey, J. (2014). Interview on Canada's Kyoto Protocol process/Interviewer: F. Hanusch.

Government of Canada. (2006a). *Canada's Clean Air Act*. Retrieved from http://publications.gc.ca/collections/Collection/En84-46-2006E.pdf (accessed 17 February 2017).

Government. (2006b). *Canada's Fourth National Report on Climate Change*. Actions to meet commitments under the United Nations Framework Convention on Climate Change. Retrieved from http://unfccc.int/resource/docs/natc/cannc4.pdf (accessed 22 February 2017).

Government of Canada. (2007a). *EcoAction*. *Action on Climate Change and Air Pollution*. Retrieved from www.ec.gc.ca/doc/media/m_124/brochure/brochure_eng.pdf (accessed 17 February 2017).

Government of Canada. (2007b). *Regulatory Framework for Air Emissions*. Retrieved from https://www.ec.gc.ca/doc/media/m_124/report_eng.pdf (accessed 22 February 2017).

Government of Canada (2007c). *Cost of Bill C-288 to Canadian Families and Business*. Retrieved from www.ec.gc.ca/doc/media/m_123/report_eng.pdf (accessed 22 February 2017).

Government of Canada. (2008). *Turning the Corner*. *Taking Action to Fight Climate Change*. Retrieved from http://publications.gc.ca/collections/collection_2009/ec/En88-2-2008E.pdf (accessed 17 February 2017).

Government of Canada. (2010). *Fifth National Communication on Climate Change*. Actions to Meet Commitments Under the United Nations Framework Convention on Climate Change. Retrieved from http://unfccc.int/resource/docs/natc/can_nc5.pdf (accessed 23 February 2017).

Harper, S. (2007). Prime Minister Harper calls for international consensus on climate change (Press release, 4 June 2007). Retrieved from http://news.gc.ca/web/article-en.do?crtr.sj1D=&mthd=advSrch&crtr.mnthndVl=&nid=311779&crtr.dpt1D=&crtr.tp1D=&crtr.lc1D=&crtr.yrStrtVl=2008&crtr.kw=&crtr.dyStrtVl=26&crtr.aud1D=&crtr.mnthStrtVl=2&crtr.yrndVl=&crtr.dyndVl= (accessed 23 February 2017).

Kent, P. (2014). Interview on Canada's Kyoto Protocol process/Interviewer: F. Hanusch.

Konieczna, M., Mattis, K., Tsai, J. Y., Liang, X., & Dunwoody, S. (2014). Global journalism in decision-making moments: a case study of Canadian and American television coverage of the 2009 United Nations Framework Convention on Climate Change in Copenhagen. *Environmental Communication – A Journal of Nature and Culture*, 8(4), 489–507.

Liberal Party of Canada (2008): *Green Shift*. Retrieved from https://www.poltext.org/sites/poltext.org/files/plateformes/ca2008lib_plt_eng._05012009_111617.pdf (accessed 22 February 2017).

Linnitt, C. (2013). Harper's attack on science: no science, no evidence, no truth, no democracy. See more at *Academic Matters*. *The Journal of Higher Education* (May 2013). Retrieved from www.academicmatters.ca/2013/05/harpers-attack-on-science-no-science-no-evidence-no-truth-no-democracy

Macdonald, D. (2011). Harper energy and climate change policy: failing to address the key challenges. In C. Stoney & G. B. Doern (Eds.), *How Ottawa Spends 2011–2012: Under the Knife (Again!)* (pp. 127–143). Montreal: McGill-Queen's University Press.

McCarthy, S. (2014). Interview on Canada's Kyoto Protocol process/Interviewer: F. Hanusch.

McDiarmid, M. (2011). Environmental network forced to close doors. Retrieved from www.cbc.ca/news/politics/environmental-network-forced-to-close-doors-1.993825

McLaughlin, D. (2014). Interview on Canada's Kyoto Protocol process/Interviewer: F. Hanusch.

Nature. (2012a). Death of evidence. *Nature*, 487(7407), 271–272.

Nature. (2012b). Frozen out. *Nature*, 483(7387), 6.

O'Hara, K. (2010). Canada must free scientists to talk to journalists. *Nature*, 467(7315), 501.

Olivastri, B. (2014). Interview on Canada's Kyoto Protocol process/Interviewer: F. Hanusch.

Parliament. (2007a). *Kyoto Protocol Implementation Act: Implementation and Consequences*. Retrieved from www.parl.gc.ca/Content/LOP/ResearchPublications/prb0740-e.pdf

Parliament. (2007b). *An Act to Ensure Canada Meets Its Global Climate Change Obligations under the Kyoto Protocol (Bill C-288)*. Retrieved from www.parl.gc.ca/HousePublications/Publication.aspx?Language=E&Mode=1&DocId=3066127 (accessed 23 February 2017).

PIPSC (2013). *The Big Chill. Silencing Public Interest Science, a Survey*. Retrieved from www.pipsc.ca/portal/page/portal/website/issues/science/pdfs/bigchill.en.pdf

rcen. (n.d.). Multi-stakeholder discussion group on greenhouse gases and air pollution. Retrieved from http://rcen.ca/public-participation/multi-stakeholder-discussion-group-on-greenhouse-gases-and-air-pollution

Sanger, T., & Saul, G. (n.d.). The Harper government and climate change. In T. Healy (Ed.), *The Harper Record*, 281–298. Retrieved from www.policyalternatives.ca/sites/default/files/uploads/publications/National_Office_Pubs/2008/HarperRecord/The_Harper_Record.pdf (accessed 23 February 2017).

Simpson, J. (2014). Interview on Canada's Kyoto Protocol process/Interviewer: F. Hanusch.

Simpson, J., Jaccard, M. K., & Rivers, N. (2008). *Hot Air: Meeting Canada's Climate Change Challenge*. Toronto: Emblem/McClelland & Stewart.

Slater, R. (2014). Interview on Canada's Kyoto Protocol process/Interviewer: F. Hanusch.

Souza, M. D. (2010). Climate-change scientists feel "muzzled" by Ottawa: documents. Retrieved from www.canada.com/technology/Climate+change+scientists+feel+muzzled+Ottawa+Documents/2684065/story.html#__federated=1

Souza, M. D. (2013). Most Canadians don't know Stephen Harper withdrew from Kyoto climate agreement, says poll. *canada.com*. Retrieved from http://o.canada.com/news/national/most-canadians-dont-know-stephen-harper-withdrew-from-kyoto-climate-agreement-says-poll

Souza, M. D. (2014). Interview on Canada's Kyoto Protocol process/Interviewer: F. Hanusch.

Star, The. (2012). Scientists march on Parliament Hill to protest research cuts. Retrieved from https://www.thestar.com/content/dam/thestar/news/canada/2012/07/10/scientists_march_on_parliament_hill_to_protest_research_cuts/scienceprotest.jpeg

Stone, J. (2014). Interview on Canada's Kyoto Protocol process/Interviewer: F. Hanusch.

Vaughan, S. (2014). Interview on Canada's Kyoto Protocol process/Interviewer: F. Hanusch.

Visser, J. (2012). John Baird happily admits Tories didn't like axed environment watchdog's advice. *National Post online*. Retrieved from news.nationalpost.com/news/canada/john-baird-happily-admits-tories-didnt-like-axed-environment-watchdogs-advice#__federated=1

Wilkins, H. (2014). Interview on Canada's Kyoto Protocol process/Interviewer: F. Hanusch.

10 Discussion analysis II

Linkages between democratic quality and climate performance

"Did the democratic process shape the thing? Unquestionably! Unquestionably!"
(Cleland, 2014)

The case study asks what mechanisms linked procedural democratic quality and climate performance. Results in the form of the mechanisms explored indicate that decreasing levels of procedural democratic quality negatively influence climate performance. Hence, the findings point in the opposite, but logically same, direction as we saw in analysis I, thus verifying the positive trend detected there. The linking mechanisms identified between procedural democratic quality and climate performance even indicate that with increasing levels of democratic quality the positive influence becomes stronger and more predictable. This assumption is based on the observation that dimensions of procedural democratic quality form mechanisms where they influence each other, and thereby climate performance, positively. For example, transparency ensures accountability, which requires higher levels of inclusiveness and participation, resulting in more responsiveness and less dominance of particular interests, etc. Minor caveats seem only to exist very occasionally at an intermediate stage, when one democratic dimension requires other dimensions, but the partnering dimension does not exist (e.g. well-organized inclusiveness might, in the absence of participatory structures, immobilize decision-making rather than facilitating it). Thus, there is a positive kind of self-enhancement of the existing dimensions of procedural democratic quality, which increases their ability to produce desired and intended climate performance as theorized by the concept of democratic efficacy. The concept can be advanced by both a detailed and a generalized model of mechanisms of influence and hypotheses defining further developments on the way to a middle range theory.

To reach these findings, expert suggestions on a potential redesign of the policy process and the democracy-climate nexus are investigated, the results of the four time frames are condensed and analysed and, lastly, the findings are discussed and generalized.

DOI: 10.4324/9781315228983-12

Expert opinions

Based on the experiences of people involved in Canadian climate policy-making, one can generate interpretative knowledge through specific interview questions. First, based on their experiences and knowledge of the process, experts were asked how they would design Canada's Kyoto Protocol process, assuming they were in the mid-1990s with the knowledge of 2014 and in the position to do so. The experts recommended a variety of approaches. The proposals included the expansion of political capital to mobilize constituencies in combination with the presentation of a plausible plan (Simpson, 2014), formal stakeholder consultations leading to a target combined with penalties and incentives (Confidential4, 2014), a transparent small working group followed by public consultations with a quick implementation phase (Confidential5, 2014), a legally binding process to set legally binding targets in connection with an institution designed to hold the government accountable (Bramley, 2014) and leadership initiating a broad citizens' platform for the development of a common goal and a plan with the spirit of trial and error (Confidential1, 2014). This broad range of answers indicates that even the experts can only partially provide compatible answers to the problems which occurred during the process. Thus, no dominating design with particular links to the influence of democratic quality on climate performance becomes evident.

Secondly, there are also diverse answers to the influence of the generation of interpretative knowledge on democratic quality and its influence upon climate performance in Canada. Jeffrey Simpson argues that Canadian democracy had a negative impact on climate performance and that there were several reasons for this (Simpson, 2014). First, the powerful PM had to invest political capital and financial resources to move forward on the Kyoto Protocol, which he did not. Secondly, as the PM was not fully engaged, the Caucus and the civil service also did not become fully engaged. Thirdly, even if the federal government had wanted to move forward, it wouldn't have been able to do so without the provinces. Simpson argues that these democratic conditions ensured that no coherent national approach was able to develop (Simpson, 2014). F. Michael Cleland argues that the democratic process "unquestionably" shaped climate performance (Cleland, 2014). Yet, even though parliamentarians took an active role in pushing for the implementation of the Kyoto Protocol, the file had little traction beyond Parliament. According to Cleland, the problem for the democratic process was that climate change was "so abstract and kind of long-term in its nature that it was just very difficult for a lot of people to get the hazard" (Cleland, 2014). Shawn McCarthy's arguments also focus on a lack of leadership and salesmanship, which he feels would have been necessary to persuade people that they had to pay a price for future benefits (McCarthy, 2014). He sees climate change as one of those problems to which democracies are not able to apply a long-term view (McCarthy, 2014). Referring to lines of democratic theory and stating that a government should represent the values of society, Robert Slater finds one of those values in the fact that society wants to ensure stability and security over generations (Slater, 2014). To ensure these values, government institutions should deal with the common property interest. Since collective interests are threatened by the global problems posed by climate change, "it is not the matter of whether the government elects to do something, it has a fundamental obligation to do something", especially for a country that has stewardship over the second largest land mass and thus has responsibility on a global scale (Slater, 2014). John Stone argues that the democratic mechanism of a national debate on climate change was necessary, yet this did not take place, since no PM invested his leadership in stimulating such a debate, resulting in a lack of information and engagement (Stone, 2014). According to Stone, Canada was "not taking full advantage of . . . [its] democratic opportunities, which is sad when you think about it" (Stone, 2014).

So, what can be concluded from the arguments provided? Absent leadership on the climate file is often mentioned, as is the fact that climate change is a complex problem. Calls for a "leadership democracy" appear to function as the only way out for those who do not see how contemporary democratic structures could deal with climate change and thus rely on eco-dictatorship tendencies. While these views demonstrate a restricted understanding of democratic quality, reduced to the current system of democracy applied in Canada, it only scratches the surface of the democracy-climate nexus. This position is unable to take into account the possibility of further options of democratic quality which did not feature in Canada's Kyoto Protocol process. Here, Slater and Stone's analyses seem to offer far more insight. Slater argues that the collective interests of Canadian society, such as security and stability, demand that the problems caused by climate change be faced. The government has an obligation to act, in part because it has a global responsibility. The connection which is drawn is thus procedural and ethical at the same time. Canada does not seem to be democratic enough to represent the long-term interests of the collective and to introduce the future to the present. The argument made by Stone that democracy was "not taking full advantage of its democratic opportunities" seems to be central for the Canadian case as a whole in regard to the democracy-climate nexus. As was identified in the various time frames, the democratic opportunities to deal with climate change were generally applied only partially or not at all, while, at the same time, an *exponential influence of the dimensions of democratic quality on policy performance* is assumed.

Even though these considerations provided useful insights into the influence of democratic quality on climate performance as interpreted by those involved, a systematic condensation, analysis and discussion of findings in line with the methodological design developed is necessary. As the four time frames demonstrated, knowledge of the distinctive elements of a democracy and thus the understanding of what democratic quality stands for often only rudimentarily exists in the expert's analysis.

Condensation of the empirical findings

Narrowing the findings of the four time frames down with a focus on the mechanisms which link democratic quality and climate performance, the following can be asserted. When Chrétien made use of the prerogative to establish an ambitious climate policy target in 1995–1997, the overall democratic quality of the climate policy process could be characterized as low. Accountability structures were almost non-existent and this resulted in climate policy-making being entirely in the hands of the PM. Inclusiveness and participation were very informal, without the involvement of the broader public but with *enlightened officials* who claimed to know in advance what everybody would want to say. Interrelations between inclusiveness, participation and accountability did not succeed since the actors were insufficiently included, with minimal participation in decision-making and thus no control over the decision-makers. Without the existence of these dimensions, policy-making was unpredictable and solely dependent on the government's preferences. A lack of inclusiveness and participation on the way to Kyoto also resulted in a particularly undefined and non-binding negotiation mandate. These two dimensions were also absent in regard to efficiency and effectiveness, since the credibility of the government's commitment to policies and their ability to navigate between conflicting objectives to reach a coherent policy was subsequently diminished. These circumstances might have influenced climate performance indirectly and negatively. Thus, empirical insights from 1995–1997 show the first evidence that low dimensions of democratic quality lead either to an indirectly negative influence or have no impact on climate performance at all.

The consequence of having no transmission belt between the national and the international levels was that the federal government had to ensure a certain kind of *ex post facto responsiveness* in the form of the NCCP, which was established after the COP in Kyoto in 1998 and sought to bring the provinces and territories and other actors which had not been included in the minus 6 per cent target back into the process. The years 1998–2002 were important for the democracy-climate nexus as they saw intense discussions at the national and federal level, yet these ultimately ended in futile consultations. At the national level a precondition existed in terms of governmental capability, efficiency and effectiveness by defining a management role for the NCCS and a purpose for the NCCP. Even though options were produced and people educated, the overall influence of the NCCP seems to have been negative: high inclusiveness without any precise participation immobilized decision-making rather than facilitating it, since the participants' views had become even more conflicting by the end of the process than they had been at its beginning. Thus, the NCCP experiment had a negative impact upon climate performance. However, the overall influence should not only be measured in terms of whether higher or lower democratic quality had a positive or negative influence on climate performance. Instead, interdependencies and interrelations characterized the type of influence: while inclusiveness alone had a negative impact, there is a sound argument to assume that this would have commuted into a positive influence had suitable participatory structures existed.

Almost the same applies to *explaining transparency* and *publicity*. At the federal level, procedural general performance in the form of capability, efficiency and effectiveness was again a precondition for the (democratic) policy process.

Simply put, the government initiating a process has to plan that process democratically, so that an influence on climate performance is possible, yet the differences between NRCan and ECan proved insurmountable in this regard. A democratic process needs to be both intended and designed to be democratic, which was a challenging task in Canada, since officials were neither trained in nor aware of what an adequate democratic policy process design would look like. This can be seen at the national level, where the inclusiveness of stakeholder sessions was reasonably well organized, yet there was a complete lack of participatory structures, as the government had already decided which option it preferred. However, an active Parliament equipped with sufficient resources (like transparency and information) could have produced public pressure, controlled decision-making and (counterfactually) been a veto player. At the same time, accountability, e.g. in terms of a transmission belt between the PM and relevant and affected actors and the public, was postponed till a future date.

The most important finding from 1998–2002 is the way in which dimensions of democratic quality are interrelated. If more democratic dimensions are substantially present, then their interrelations can succeed and exponentially increase their combined influence upon climate performance. Otherwise, the existence of one dimension without interrelations with its counterpart dimension/s can lead to a negative influence, as seen in regard to inclusiveness without participation. This circumstance, where not the additive sum but their interconnection characterizes the overall influence, can be described as the *exponential influence of interrelated dimensions of democratic quality on climate performance*.

Between 2003–2005, elements of procedural general performance, like a realistic target, staff with expertise and cooperation between NRCan and Ecan, appeared to be necessary preconditions. Thus, democratic quality in a functioning policy process relies on certain sound circumstances. Even though the government was ambitious, it was not ambitious in reaching its targets in a very democratic way, e.g. it stated that it did not want too much transparency. An *undemocratic complicity* of absent accountability, inclusiveness, participation and transparency led to unpredictability. The influence of insufficient democratic quality on climate performance was neither clearly positive nor negative, but can be described as *undemocratic unpredictability*, since the direction of influence was entirely determined by the preferences of the government and informal forces which may or may not have been in favour of ambitious climate policies.

The years 2006–2012 stand for a weakening of democracy, observable in, for example, the composition of delegations. When, as in 2006–2012, democracy is threatened by *elected irresponsibility* and an extreme use of the prerogative by the PM certain democratic dimensions seem to function as basic ground rules: liberty ensured that rights for free speech existed despite climate science and ENGOs having been muzzled, independence guaranteed the rule of law and access to the judiciary and democratic stability ensured basic proceedings and institutions, for example, in the form of CESD reports. The overall influence of this lack of democratic quality on climate performance seems to have been either non-existent or negative. These findings fit in with the proposed *exponential influence of interrelated dimensions of democratic quality on climate performance* and are able to refine it: low democratic quality has either no or negative influence upon climate performance, leading to unpredictability. Since no evidence could be found that low democratic quality leads to high climate performance, especially output, an exponential negative influence of the missing dimensions of democratic quality on climate performance can also be assumed. Moreover, the importance of procedural general performance as a precondition can also be seen in the fourth time frame: many politicians did not understand climate change (capability), the government did not set climate change as a priority (capability) and there was an absence of governance structures, while reorganizations took place (stability, efficiency and effectiveness).

Overall, four formative events for the democracy-climate nexus can be identified: first, the acceptance of a minus 6 per cent target at Kyoto without a democratic process leading to a binding negotiation framework; secondly, the missed chances at an inclusive but not participative NCCP which immobilized views; thirdly, the ratification of the minus 6 per cent target despite still not having formed any consensus; and, fourthly, a tremendous weakening of democratic quality, and thus climate performance, under the Conservative government through measures such as the limitation of freedom of speech for climate scientists and ENGOs. As John Stone puts it, Canada was both failing to take full advantage of its democratic opportunities and lacking the democratic elements which could have made the use of the democratic opportunities which influence climate performance more likely (Stone, 2014).

Observing the individual dimensions over the four time frames, differences can be detected in the ways in which they influence climate performance. Observations of the influence of accountability on climate performance existed in every time frame. A determining factor in its influence was the strong prerogative of the PM. A mostly positive influence of accountability on climate performance could (counterfactually) be identified, particularly, when accountability worked in interrelation with other dimensions and ensured predictability. Independence, instead, includes only one case (KPIA) and no tendencies towards either a positive or a negative influence. Although only one observation was made for stability, it is a substantial one: democratic institutions like the CESD are of crucial importance for democratic quality and climate performance. The existence and stability of such institutions creates win-win situations. Inclusiveness, however, is one of the two dimensions which had a negative influence on climate performance on at least one occasion. The reason for this lies in its interrelations with other dimensions, especially participation. Inclusiveness is a precondition for a functioning participative process, enabling all relevant and affected actors to influence decision-making, yet without participatory structures the views of those involved in a process can become even more diverse and immobilize decision-making. Participation therefore requires inclusiveness and has to include mechanisms to reach consensus. Parliament, as a form of representative participation was, insofar as it had access to information, etc., quite active in influencing climate performance positively. Transparency was interrelated with participation, but also with publicity. While too much transparency might in some cases kill an ambitious climate change plan, it is necessary to inform Parliament and the broader public adequately, so that positive influences can evolve. Creativity seems to be the only dimension to emerge with a solely negative observation: the NCCP experiment failed at least partially. Counterfactually argued, the experiment was not designed appropriately and could have had a positive influence, but experiments always have the potential to fail and maybe that is one of the risks democracy has to live with. Liberty is another of the dimensions which are closely related to others: actors need to be involved and enabled through explanatory transparency and the publicity to speak freely. Furthermore, publicity has the potential to influence climate performance positively, e.g. through the explanation of scientific findings to the broader public.

To conclude, the findings are quite clear: a tendency can be detected that more democratic quality leads to better climate performance, while interrelations are of crucial importance and certain dimensions might, in isolation, even have a negative influence. Additionally, more democratic quality ensures more predictable policy-making, since decisions come to rely on more than the executive and informal sources of influence. Of special importance are the interrelations between dimensions. Liberty, stability, accountability and independence are likely to function as basic dimensions of democratic quality in a policy process: after the rule of law is established, actors must have both the possibility and the capability to express themselves in stable democratic structures with inbuilt accountability mechanisms. Regarding the design of policy formulation and implementation, the transparency, inclusiveness, participation and publicity dimensions and their interrelations seem to be the most important, structuring the centre of the process how democratic quality influences climate performance and including actors and the public. In addition to these factors, creativity, as the experimental dimension, allows new ways of establishing democratic processes.

The Canadian type of democracy detected in the Kyoto Protocol process from 1995–2012 is characterized by a strong prerogative, diminished accountability, partially well-organized inclusiveness, a lack of participatory structures (providing an obstacle to attempts to reach a consensus) and, overall, low degrees of democratic quality. The mechanisms this book has identified could counterfactually demonstrate an exponentially positive influence of democratic quality on climate performance, but the Canadian process was nonetheless one of missed opportunities with few findings on win-win situations like the work of the CESD. Therefore, it can also be concluded that undemocratically developed targets will neither get the legitimation nor the momentum to be translated into a climate change plan (output) and will doubtless not be implemented in the form required to reach sufficient GHG reductions (outcome).

Having summarized the findings of the Canadian case, a discussion is necessary about the implications for that case, on generalizations about the democracy-climate nexus and on further interpretations and research on the influence of democratic quality on policy performance in terms of democratic efficacy.

Verification of analysis I and advancement of the concept of democratic efficacy

The case study asked what mechanisms link democratic quality and climate performance. It then identified many of these interrelations. The following discussion explores the implications of the findings from the Canadian case, translates these insights onto a more general level for the democracy-climate nexus and advances the initially outlined concept of democratic efficacy.

The mechanisms explored in the Canadian case indicate that decreasing levels of procedural democratic quality negatively influence climate performance, which in turn implies that more democratic quality positively influences climate performance. Thus, the findings of analysis II verify the trends detected by analysis I. The mechanisms which have been identified as linking procedural democratic quality and climate performance even indicate that with increasing levels of democratic quality the positive influence becomes more predictable and stronger. This assumption is based on the observation that dimensions of procedural democratic quality form mechanisms with which they positively influence each other and, thereby, climate performance. For example, transparency ensures accountability, yet requires higher levels of inclusiveness and participation. These themselves both result in more responsiveness and minimize the dominance of particular interests, etc. Thus, there is a positive kind of self-enhancement of the existing dimensions of procedural democratic quality. Minor caveats seem only to exist very occasionally at an intermediate stage, when one democratic dimension requires other dimensions, but the partnering dimension does not exist (e.g. well-organized inclusiveness might, in the absence of participatory structures, immobilize decision-making rather than facilitate it). Comparing these insights with existing research literature on Canada's climate policy-making shows that these are new explanations. The existing literature only explains Canada's climate policy-making with factors like federalism, the structure of the Canadian economy, the country's closeness to and interrelations with the US, Canada's geography and a lack of political will and leadership. Without strengthening or rejecting those sources of influence, an additional and important factor influencing Canada's climate performance has to be added: democratic quality.

Based on the findings of this study, policy recommendations can be formulated. Looking at this case study's findings, some of the prominent shortcomings of the Canadian procedural democratic quality itself become obvious, such as the way the PM's strong prerogative is not supported by any corresponding accountability structures, the lack of strong democratic institutions which report on the output-outcome gap, a restricted understanding of democratic processes amongst officials, a lack of concepts upon which to build participatory consensus, faintheartedness in respect to democratic experiments and the informal influences of non-legitimized actors on policy-making. Arguments in favour of an eco-dictatorship or more leadership-orientated and authoritarian ways of policy-making can be rejected, e.g. Chrétien's use of the prerogative at Kyoto and the subsequent ratification did not lead to better climate performance, rather the contrary. At the same time, the potential to improve democratic quality, and thus climate performance, is obvious: Canada can build upon its partially well-organized inclusiveness; a climate change commissioner's office similar to the CESD could be instituted; officials could be educated in democracy; both ideal and pragmatic holistic democratic policy process designs can be developed, etc. Both lists could be continued, but the central message is clear: if Canada's climate performance is to be improved, then the country needs changes which are of a more fundamental nature than just another NCCP. A democratic renewal would be an important factor in the success of the climate file.

However, the ways in which the dimensions of democratic quality cause influence are much more complex than the simple thesis of more democratic quality leading to better climate performance is able to describe. A democratic process is not only about bringing everybody together in the same room, it also involves a well-arranged interaction of different dimensions forming mechanisms in need of certain techniques to find sound solutions under time pressure. While an elected executive guides direction, it needs renewed mandates in order to keep up to date with the challenges of the twenty-first century. As regards climate change, it seems procedural democratic quality has to be even better and include future generations, if it is to cope with such a long-term and complex issue. Thus, it appears to be justifiable to argue that the more long-term and more complex the policy issue under consideration, the more democratic the process dealing with solutions has to be, since decisions on such issues are hard to reverse. To advance democratic quality gradually, and thus to increase climate performance, new and more democratic forms of democratic predictability and efficacy are needed. Democracy has to be understood as a democratic process of steady renewal. To improve democracy and policy performance simultaneously, the focus has to be on win-win improvements, such as through, in Canada's case, the creation of a strong commissioner of climate change. Therefore, some existing elements of democratic theories (such as deliberation based on considered judgement leading to responsive results) will need to be fully applied, while, simultaneously, democratic experiments as proposed by pragmatism will have to be carried out to find new democratic institutions and/or tools, which through their approach and participatory structures create a positive attitude towards democratic interaction within the participants, encouraging them to move forwards together on common and accepted policy solutions (as was identified in the context of the NCCP) (Oulton, 2014). Such a process of democratic renewal might need to be backed by an institution which does not yet exist. Such an institution would have to be independent from executive, legislative and judicative bodies and focused on the renewal and democratization of democracy. Every policy field has its own lobby, but democracy is believed to stay and develop on its own. The challenges of the twenty-first century cannot be faced with the democratic institutions of previous centuries alone. Such new democratic tools and institutions must be as compatible as possible with procedural general performance without limiting their purely democratic momentum. Procedural general performance ensures that things get done, while democratic quality ensures that if things get done, they are also both right and legitimate. The findings on the exponential influence of interrelated dimensions of procedural democratic quality on general performance might be an indication that the two tasks could be accomplished simultaneously while at the same time ensuring more predictability.

Based on the findings of the Canadian case and their interpretation in the context of the democracy-climate nexus, the outline for the concept of democratic efficacy can be advanced. As an advancement of the initially outlined concept of democratic efficacy, which could not explain the mechanisms of influence in detail, a first draft of a more detailed, but, for the sake of generalization, nonetheless somewhat simplified model of the influences linking procedural democratic quality and climate performance can be developed. While the concept of democratic efficacy assumes that the ability to produce desired or intended climate performance improves concomitantly with increasing levels of democratic quality, the model of mechanisms represents the empirical translation, explaining, in particular, the black arrow of Table 3.5 in more detail. Based on the Canadian case and counterfactual argumentation, the model can be illustrated (see Figure 10.1).

This model assumes that procedural general performance can be a precondition for procedural democratic quality. Looking at procedural democratic quality in more detail, accountability, independence and stability seem to be preliminary dimensions which need to be present to guarantee liberty and inclusiveness. If these two dimensions are present, participation can emerge and participants may (in)directly (through procedural general performance) influence climate performance. At all stages, transparency and publicity influence the other dimensions and provide information, etc. Creativity emerges as an additional dimension

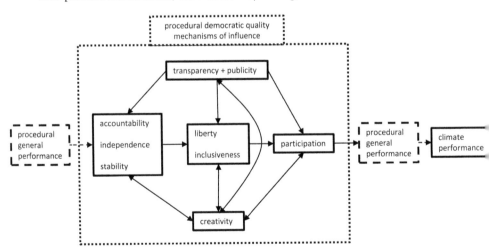

Figure 10.1 A model of the mechanisms of influence

when other dimensions are present to a certain extent, whereas undertaking experiments can influence the dimensions through two-way interaction. The dimensions of procedural democratic quality need other dimensions to exert a positive influence on climate performance. Thus, this model proposes democratic quality mechanisms of influence on climate performance which are quite complex and full of interrelations, but, to a certain extent, distinguishable in specific interconnected stages.

Moreover, the findings can be converted and generalized in the detected *exponential influence of interrelated dimensions of democratic quality on climate performance*. This is done to understand what effect the level of democratic quality might have on the kind of influence to be expected in regard to the model of mechanisms.

Figure 10.2 shows that the exponential increase in procedural democratic quality leads to an exponential increase in climate performance. This increase also leads to an increase in predictability: while low procedural democratic quality can, to a certain extent, be climate active under climate friendly leadership, only highly democratic processes positively influence climate performance in a predictable way. That means that it is not the additive sum of democratic dimensions but their interconnection that characterizes the overall influence they have. The concept of democratic efficacy in terms of the ability of democracy to produce desired and intended climate performance is thus underlined by empirical findings and further defined. However, the assumed influence is only projected,

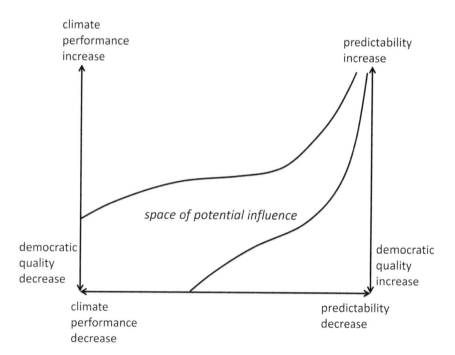

Figure 10.2 An illustration of the hypotheses

primarily based on counterfactual argumentation and, thus, currently a research gap in need of further redefinition.

Based on these interpretations and assumptions, hypotheses can be formulated, potentially leading to a further redefinition of the proposed model for future research. The hypotheses could be applied to other cases where a (democratic) policy process is meant to produce general substantive performance. The lack of a dataset on procedural democratic quality could, however, limit future efforts, as it means that any empirical modelling of the interactions and influences of different dimensions would currently either be impossible or only partially achievable. Future research therefore has the task of developing such comprehensive datasets and modelling their interactions and effects. The development of such a dataset might be a precondition for testing the hypothesis on a broader basis, for precisely tracing the process and for being able to distinguish between outputs and outcomes. Both the ascertainment tool developed and applied to the Canadian case and the developed model of the mechanisms of influence might function as starting points. The hypotheses to be researched are as follows:

1   *Exponential influence*: an exponential increase of procedural democratic quality (independent variable) due to interrelations between dimensions leads to an exponential increase in climate performance (dependent variable)
2   *Increasing predictability*: more procedural democratic quality (independent variable) leads to more predictability (dependent variable)
3   *Procedural general performance caveat*: the influence of procedural democratic quality (intervening variable) on climate performance (dependent variable) depends on the existence of procedural general performance (independent variable), which creates the context which enables a democratic policy process to occur.

Lastly, the assumed influence translated into hypotheses and the model of influences are two elements which advance the concept of democratic efficacy based on empirical evidence and counterfactual argumentation. These insights introduce further advancements of the general framework, the normative background and practical implications. Thereby, the concept of democratic efficacy gradually develops its very first outlines as a middle range theory.

The concept of democratic efficacy basically assumes that increasing levels of democratic quality improve the ability to produce desired and intended substantive general performance. Few studies have so far tried to argue in favour of such a concept as democracy has generally been seen as a static term and not in terms of the different democratic qualities. In other words, the unused potentials and possibilities of democracies have, as yet, not been taken into account. Instead, the limited Western representative style of democracies, which was established centuries ago, has become threatened and weakened by various forces and the often minimal levels of adaptation of democratic procedures, tools and institutions has been taken for granted. A scientific awakening is required, which takes possible developments into account (Hirschman, 2015). While some elements of democratic efficacy already exist – deliberation might be *one* of them (for limitations see, for example, Morrell, 2005) – others will have to be developed from scratch. Particularly at the regional and national levels the box of democratic efficacy tools is empty (for such processes at the more local level see, for example, the *Office for Future-Related Issues* (Vorarlberg, 2015), and for proposals at other levels see suggestions such as the idea of future councils (Leggewie & Nanz, 2013)).

The practical implications of the development and further definition of a concept of democratic efficacy need to be considered. It is surprising that democracies have created numerous institutions dealing with all kinds of topics, but no institution which focuses on the renewal of democracy itself. Thus, the main task of any independent (which does not belong to the executive, the legislative or the judicative), subsidiarily organized, democratic-efficacy institution would be to develop a permanently evolving modular policy process design, based on the principles of democratic efficacy. These circumstances might ensure an ongoing renewal and democratization of democracy which could be combined with efficacy. Such experiments can succeed, since "what many people call impossible may actually only be a limitation of imagination that can be overcome by better design thinking" (Buchanan, 1992, p. 21; Stoker, 2010; Stoker & John, 2009).

References

The access date of all material retrieved from the Web is 5 June 2015 unless otherwise specified.

Bramley, M. (2014). Interview on Canada's Kyoto Protocol process/Interviewer: F. Hanusch.

Buchanan, R. (1992). Wicked problems in design thinking. *Design Issues*, 8(2), 5–21.

Cleland, F. M. (2014). Interview on Canada's Kyoto Protocol process/Interviewer: F. Hanusch.

Confidential1. (2014). Interview on Canada's Kyoto Protocol process/Interviewer: F. Hanusch.

Confidential4. (2014). Interview on Canada's Kyoto Protocol process/Interviewer: F. Hanusch.

Confidential5. (2014). Interview on Canada's Kyoto Protocol process/Interviewer: F. Hanusch.

Hirschman, A. O. (2015). *The Essential Hirschman.* Princeton, NJ: Princeton University Press.

Leggewie, C., & Nanz, P. (2013). The future council. New forms of democratic participation. *eurozine.* Retrieved from www.eurozine.com/articles/2013-08-20-leggewienanz-en.html

McCarthy, S. (2014). Interview on Canada's Kyoto Protocol process/Interviewer: F. Hanusch.

Morrell, M. E. (2005). Deliberation, democratic decision-making and internal political efficacy. *Political Behavior,* 27(1), 49–69.

Oulton, D. (2014). Interview on Canada's Kyoto Protocol process/Interviewer: F. Hanusch.

Simpson, J. (2014). Interview on Canada's Kyoto Protocol process/Interviewer: F. Hanusch.

Slater, R. (2014). Interview on Canada's Kyoto Protocol process/Interviewer: F. Hanusch.

Stoker, G. (2010). Exploring the promise of experimentation in political science: micro-foundational insights and policy relevance. *Political Studies, 58*(2), 300–319.

Stoker, G., & John, P. (2009). Design experiments: engaging policy makers in the search for evidence about what works. *Political Studies, 57*(2), 356–373.

Stone, J. (2014). Interview on Canada's Kyoto Protocol process/Interviewer: F. Hanusch.

Vorarlberg. (2015). Büro für Zukunftsfragen. Retrieved from www.vorarlberg.at/english/vorarlberg-english/environment_future/officeforfuture-relatedis/officeforfuture-relate dis.htm

III

Synergy

11 Overall discussion

This book found that democratic quality tends to have a positive influence on the climate performance of established democracies. Detailed mechanisms have verified statistical trends and a concept of democratic efficacy which assumes that the ability to produce desired and intended climate performance increases concomitantly with democratic quality, thus robustly clarifying the finding.

These main insights were further developed through the book's research. In the introduction, the observation was made that established democracies differ greatly in their climate performances (see Chapter 1). One reason for this was seen in the extent to which the characteristics of climate change and the unintended consequences of democracy might contradict each other, e.g. some democracies perhaps find better solutions to overcome their short-termism and thus deal with the long time horizon of climate change better than others. Consequently, it was assumed that different levels of democratic quality might be an explanatory factor for differences in the climate performances of established democracies.

Previously, research was unable to explain this observation, since it was fragmented and focused on the autocracy-democracy divide. The main research question, which was identified to close that research gap, therefore asked: how does democratic quality influence the climate performance of established democracies? This research question was translated into three specific research needs (see Chapter 2). First, this book needed to find robust trends in democratic quality, which existed across established democracies and caused variations in climate performance. Secondly, it had to explore the detailed mechanisms inside democracies which verify the aforementioned trends. Thirdly, a generalizable approach had to be formulated, which could function as an explanatory link between democratic quality and climate performance. Collectively, the research required a conceptual framework based on an explanatory mixed methods design to provide a comprehensive answer in terms of identifying quantitative trends, verifying them through detailed mechanisms and developing a generalizable explanatory approach (see Chapter 3). Subsequently, analysis I estimated panel regressions based on the Democracy Barometer and the CCPI in order to detect trends (see Chapter 4). Analysis II investigated Canada's Kyoto Protocol process to explore

DOI: 10.4324/9781315228983-14

mechanisms which would verify the trends of the previous analysis and advance the initially outlined concept of democratic efficacy (see Chapters 5–9). While both analyses presented their findings separately, a comprehensive answer is now required. Such an all-inclusive answer is necessary to demonstrate how essential the findings of this book are for future research and to explore the variety of internal processes of democracies and thus deconstruct the understanding of democracy as a static entity by drawing more attention to the influence of different democratic qualities on climate and performance in other policy fields.

Thus, the purpose of the overall conclusion is to provide a comprehensive answer to the main research question by compiling the answers to the three research needs and interconnecting them alongside each other to demonstrate the synergy beyond individual analyses. Based on these insights, research gaps and policy recommendations can be formulated.

A mostly positive influence, explained by democratic efficacy

The findings on the three research needs are separated in various chapters, but need to be discussed alongside each other to generate synergy beyond individual analysis. The findings demonstrate that it is of crucial importance to distinguish and analyse established democracies, since different levels of democratic quality are an explanatory factor for differences in the climate performances of established democracies.

Mostly positive statistical trends

Analysis I addressed research need one. The question asked was: what influence does substantive democratic quality have on climate performance? The corresponding hypothesis assumed that higher levels of democratic quality positively influence climate performance. Therewith, the general assumption of the previously outlined concept of democratic efficacy was tested, which assumed that the ability to produce desired and intended climate performance rises with increasing levels of democratic quality. The empirical analysis applied panel regressions to the Democracy Barometer and the CCPI based on 193–326 country-years.

The results of the panel regressions allow, with one limitation, a concise confirmation of the hypothesis: as previously theorized, increasing levels of substantive democratic quality have a mostly positive influence on climate performance in established democracies. More precisely, the findings for the influence of democratic quality on overall climate performance, as measured by the CCPI, are positive and confirm the hypothesis. The same can be said in regard to output as measured by the climate policy component of the CCPI. The findings on the outcome variable, as measured by the emissions development component of the CCPI, also show a positive and significant effect, but face certain statistical restrictions, which means that they cannot be taken for granted. An explanation for the caveat regarding outcome might indicate that other factors have so far almost completely dominated outcomes (Bättig & Bernauer, 2009; Bernauer,

2013, p. 285; Bernauer & Koubi, 2009; Spilker, 2012, 2013). Thus, trends on overall climate performance, outputs and – with limitations – outcomes confirm the hypothesis and the concept of democratic efficacy.

Detailed mechanisms verify trends and advance the concept of democratic efficacy

Analysis II addressed research need two. The question examined was: which mechanisms link procedural democratic quality and climate performance? By answering this question, analysis II could, first, verify whether the trends detected in analysis I relied on detailed mechanisms inside democracies and, secondly, advance the concept of democratic efficacy by generalizing mechanisms. Canada's Kyoto Protocol process from 1995–2012 was chosen as a case study and investigated by process tracing.

The findings overwhelmingly verify the positive trend of analysis I and the concept of democratic efficacy. Furthermore, they advance the concept of democratic efficacy through a generalized model of mechanisms and a concretization of the positive influence becoming stronger and more predictable with increasing levels of democratic quality.

These findings rely on an in-depth investigation of the Canadian case. Between 1995–1997, the PM accepted a minus 6 per cent target in the Kyoto Protocol due to the competencies of a strong prerogative. Together with other democratic shortcomings, like mutually *enlightened officials* and the lack of a transmission belt between the national and international levels, low degrees of democratic quality seem to have generally had an indirect and negative influence upon climate performance. The result of not having a transmission belt between the national and international level was a certain kind of *ex post facto responsiveness*, which the federal government had to ensure in the form of an inclusive climate change process at the national level between 1998–2002. The process ended in futile consultations, characterized by high levels of inclusiveness, which, however, in the absence of any precise participatory structures actually immobilized decision-making rather than facilitating it. Participants' views were seen to have become even more entrenched as a result of the process than they had been at its start. However, the Kyoto Protocol was still ratified in 2002, despite the lack of consensus behind it. Counterfactually argued, the interrelations between dimensions could have been important: while inclusiveness alone had a negative impact, it is reasonable to assume that a positive influence would have existed, had there been participatory structures creating consensus. Looking at the time frame between 2003–2005, it emerged that democratic quality in a functioning policy process appears to rely on certain circumstances, such as a realistic target, staff with expertise and cooperation between the ministries involved in the process. During this time frame, the book also found that the effect of a lack of democratic quality on climate performance was more negative than positive and that this could be described by *undemocratic unpredictability*. This was due to the direction of influence, which was solely determined by the preferences of the government and informal forces, which could either be in favour of or against ambitious climate policies. The years 2006–2012 saw Canadian democracy weakened under the Conservative government through *elected irresponsibility*, which undercut the previous years' lowest democratic qualities, e.g. by limiting freedom of speech or muzzling ENGOs, with this all having a negative influence upon climate performance. During this time frame, the importance of procedural general performance (already identified as a precondition in previous years) became very obvious: many politicians did not understand climate change, the government did not make climate change a priority and there was a lack of climate governance structures. Without such preconditions, democratic quality can make hardly any use of its potential to influence climate performance positively.

Overall, the results mostly indicated that decreasing levels of democratic quality influence climate performance negatively. Thus, the findings point in the reverse but, logically, same direction as analysis I and thus verify the positive trend, which said analysis detected. Minor caveats only seem to exist in two regards and they pose no general limitations on the central pattern of a positive influence: first, dimensions of democratic quality sometimes have only an intrinsic value without having any influence on climate performance and, secondly, in certain situations, some dimensions require a partner dimension (such as in the case of inclusiveness and participation), if they are to show a positive influence.

Based on the process tracing of the Canadian case, it seems liberty, stability, accountability and independence function as basic dimensions of democratic quality in a policy process: the rule of law has to be established, actors must be able to express themselves and there have to be stable democratically accountable structures. Transparency, inclusiveness, participation, publicity and their interrelations come into focus for the process itself and the design of policy formulation and implementation. The icing on the cake is creativity, which is the experimental dimension, which enables new democratic processes and a democratization of democracy. These mechanisms can be generalized in a model of mechanisms to advance the concept of democratic efficacy.

Moreover, mechanisms indicate that the positive influence of democratic quality becomes more predictable and stronger the more it increases. The assumption is based on the observation that the dimensions of procedural democratic quality form mechanisms through which they have a positive impact both on each other and, subsequently, upon climate performance. For example, in order for transparency to ensure accountability, higher levels of inclusiveness and participation are required, which themselves result in more responsiveness and a reduction in the dominance of particular interests, etc. Thus, the existing dimensions of procedural democratic quality undergo a form of positive self enhancement, which increases their ability to produce the desired and intended climate performance, as theorized by the concept of democratic efficacy.

Thus, the mechanisms explored in the context of this book not only verify the trends seen in analysis I, and thereby confirm the concept of democratic efficacy, but advance these trends through a model of mechanisms and the hypothesis of a stronger and more predictable influence upon climate performance.

The concept of democratic efficacy as an outline of a middle range theory

While the concept of the quality of democracy asks: how well does democracy function? and is evaluated independently of its connections to general performance (such as climate performance), democratic efficacy asks: how do dimensions of democratic quality interact and what effect does this have on general performance? Subsequently, its analysis focuses on the mechanisms which explain how this influence comes about and how it can be generalized as a very first outline for a middle range theory. The concept of democratic efficacy assumes that the ability to produce the desired and intended climate performance rises concomitantly with increasing levels of democratic quality.

The reason that so far no studies have yet established such a concept might be because that democracy has, to date, mostly been understood as a static term and established democracies have subsequently not been identified on the basis of their democratic qualities. However, the concept of democratic efficacy is an analytical concept. The concept does not stand for a determined relationship which assumes that every improvement in democratic quality necessarily deterministically leads to an increase in general performance. Instead, it assumes that the ability of democracies to produce the desired or intended results in a diverse set of policy fields rises concomitantly with increasing levels of democratic quality. As the simplified diagram in Figure 11.1 demonstrates, the concept of democratic efficacy has to be understood as the arrow which explains how democratic quality influences general performance.

Such an explanatory concept relies on certain presumptions. At the level of individuals, it differs from many other approaches by drafting a concept which is applicable for empirical research. In simple terms, the approach of theories which assume a certain kind of individual actor and aggregate their behaviour to nation state levels – like the rational actor in collective action theories – is oversimplified and, due to phenomena such as emergence, academically unsatisfying (Cartwright, 2002a, 2002b; Kittel, 2006). Instead, it is important to recognize democracy as a mode of operation which, in an ongoing fashion, is created by and shapes humans. This mode of operation, or the democratic design, influences the ability to produce desired or intended general performances.

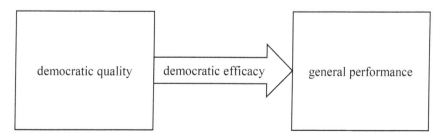

Figure 11.1 Democratic efficacy as an explanatory link

More precisely, it is presumed that the influence of democratic quality on general performance depends on the existence of its different dimensions and the interplay between them. The more dimensions of democratic quality are present, the better they can serve their main purpose of problem-solving and anticipating better futures. These assumptions rely on thinking about and practising democracy in a problem-solving manner: democracy was mostly theoretically devised and empirically implemented to solve common problems and to lead to better futures. Consequently, the concept of democratic efficacy expects that the ability to produce general performances, such as in regard to climate change, rises concomitantly with increasing levels of democratic quality. Based on the mechanisms detected in the Canadian case, the model of mechanisms represents the empirical translation of this expectation, outlining the arrow above in more detail.

This model assumes that procedural general performance can be a precondition for procedural democratic quality. Looking at procedural democratic quality in more detail, accountability, independence and stability seem to be preliminary dimensions which need to be present to guarantee liberty and inclusiveness. If these two dimensions are present, participation may be able to emerge and the resultant participants able to (in)directly (through procedural general performance) influence general performance. At all stages, transparency and publicity influence the other dimensions and provide qualities such as information. Creativity appears as an additional dimension when other dimensions have a degree of presence and the experiments it encourages can influence these dimensions as part of a two-way interaction. In the main, the dimensions of procedural democratic quality need other dimensions if they are to exert a positive influence on general performance. It is not the additive sum of democratic dimensions but their interconnections that characterize the overall influence. Due to the insights

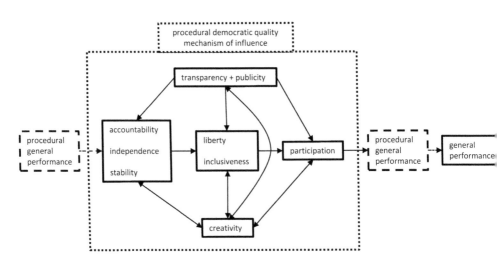

Figure 11.2 A general model of the mechanisms of influence

provided by the Canadian case, the influence which democratic quality has on general performance is hypothesized to become stronger and more predictable with increasing levels of democratic quality.

Based on these considerations, the concept of democratic efficacy can be seen as an outline for a middle range theory, which would offer an approach to general theory building, which would avoid universal answers and go beyond empirical facts alone to start to fill an important research gap (Cao, Milner, Prakash, & Ward, 2014, p. 293; Merton, 1949; Ziblatt, 2006).

Research gaps: think possibilistic

The findings of this book are relevant in the context of existing research. A recent article asked whether a more democratic world and a world successfully dealing with climate change are mutually compatible (Petherick, 2014). Even though this book provides no answers to the question of mutual compatibility, it can provide a partial answer: the more democratic democracies deal more successfully with climate change. Arguments recommending eco-authoritarian ways of governing climate change appear to be rejected. These insights could be demonstrated through empirical and conceptual evidence, and were merely anticipated in previous literature (see, e.g., Held, 2014; Stehr, 2013).

However, research gaps appear in the context of the two analyses, but they are not the direct result of the focus of my study. A first research gap detected in analysis I is the need for more and better indices. The Democracy Barometer is the only index which substantially distinguishes between democracies and provides data for a significant number of country-years. Alternative normative ideas, different to those the Democracy Barometer is based on, do not exist. Moreover, the CCPI is the only index providing reliable data on climate performance. In order to apply more robust checks and to clarify the limited findings on outcome, improvements in both the democratic quality and climate performance indices are necessary. Thus, a whole new research field emerges, which should pay attention to the differences between democracies, as, for example, measured by the Democracy Barometer, and their influence on general performance. Explanations of the different behaviours of democracies due to their democratic quality are currently in the fledgling stage.

Further research gaps derive from panel regression itself. Future research should pay attention to the divide between and within models since results indicate significant patterns such as the significant within effects of climate policy which move to between effects in relation to emissions development. Moreover, the results of certain control variables demonstrate that there seem to be some influences which have so far not been empirically taken into account, such as the ambivalent role of vulnerability. Vulnerability delivers significant results in most models, but the influence points in different directions.

Analysis II demonstrated that Canada's democratic quality influences its climate performance. While the case study demonstrated that some general debate takes place, there is almost no research which considers the role of democratic quality for general performance in Canada. Thus, there is a need to consider what influence democratic quality has in other policy fields. Moreover, analysis II demonstrated the need for a comparable approach to evaluate the democratic quality of a policy process. The indices considered in analysis I focus on the democratic quality of a nation state, but, for specific policy processes, different conceptualizations are necessary. This book developed such an evaluation. The approach proposed by this book might function as a starting point to advance comparable democratic quality evaluations of policy processes Thereby, the distinction of several dimensions of democratic quality remains crucial to understanding which components of a democracy have which kind of influence.

The concept of democratic efficacy is closely related to these considerations. The concept is primarily outlined in this book and, if further advances are undertaken, it may develop to a middle range theory. These advances include two aspects. First, the model of mechanisms of influence, explaining how dimensions of democratic quality interrelate and influence general performance, is outlined on the basis of one case study and counterfactual argumentation. It is more likely than unlikely that the interplay might have to be advanced or redefined. Hitherto, far too little has been known about how interaction effects, etc. work out. Secondly, three hypotheses can be formulated which investigate the kind of influence:

- *Exponential influence*: an exponential increase in procedural democratic quality (independent variable) due to interrelations between dimensions leads to an exponential increase in climate performance (dependent variable).
- *Increasing predictability*: more procedural democratic quality (independent variable) leads to more predictability (dependent variable).
- *Procedural general performance caveat*: the influence of procedural democratic quality (intervening variable) on climate performance (dependent variable) depends on the existence of procedural general performance (independent variable), which creates the context which allows a democratic policy process to occur.

Moreover, research gaps appear beyond the two analyses and the concept of democratic efficacy in the context of the book. These include the transmission belt between the domestic and the international level, which is especially important when the policy issue under investigation is not related to national borders, as is the case with climate change. Such research has to focus on questions such as what democratic foreign policy is and to what extent this influences a state's general performance. Furthermore, the proposed findings on the democracy-climate nexus are so far very much centred on the nation state, but democratic quality can also occur in other settings, e.g. transnational regions, etc. How and whether democratic quality influences general performance in such "new regions" is an open research question. Moreover, even though such agreements as the Kyoto Protocol define specific time frames in which certain reductions should be performed, an overall time pressure also exists in terms of global reductions which have to be reached to avoid dangerous climate change. The significance of a shrinking time frame in the context of planetary boundaries and dangerous earth system changes needs further research, so that we can discover what it means for the democratic procedures of formulating and implementing policies. It is, for example, unclear how democratic procedures can be accelerated without losing democratic quality. However, such research is closely related to the identification of practical alternatives.

Policy recommendations: democratize democracies

The fundamental practical implication is as simple as it is complex: overcome democratic shortcomings and thus democratize democracies to make them more efficacious. Empirical evidence demonstrates that the democratic quality of established democracies differs and that this circumstance has an influence on climate performance. Thus, there are democracies which are more capable of overcoming shortcomings, such as short-termism, than others. Calls for a leadership democracy seem to rely heavily on restrictive understandings of democratic processes. In all likelihood, the more long-term and complex the policy issue under consideration is, the more democratic the process dealing with solutions has to be, since decisions on such issues are hard to reverse. Therefore, new and more democratic forms of democratic efficacy and predictability are needed.

Generally speaking, it becomes obvious that the challenges of the twenty-first century cannot be tackled using the democratic institutions of previous centuries alone. It might therefore help a process of democratic renewal if one or more subsidiary organized institutions were to be created with the purpose of democratizing democracy. Such an institution, which is independent of executive, legislative and judicative influence, does not yet exist. It is an interesting anomaly that there appear to be lobbies for each and every policy field, yet democratic renewal seems to have no genuine lobby nor institutional backup; for a "long period we acted as if our democracy were something that perpetuated itself automatically" (Dewey, 1998 [1939], p. 341). Consequently, in the context of the concept of democratic efficacy, the main goal of such an institution is democratic efficacy through democratic renewal. Some first efforts pointing in that direction at the more local level might be the *Office for Future-Related Issues* (Vorarlberg, 2015) or the idea of future councils (Leggewie & Nanz, 2013).

However, the recommendation to democratize democracy is so abstract that it needs to be separated into many steps and made more imaginative. Some of these improvements can be exemplified through the Canadian case study. For example, prominent shortcomings in Canadian democracy are the PM's strong prerogative and the lack of corresponding accountability structures, the absence of strong democratic institutions which report on the output-outcome gap, restrictive official understandings of a democratic process, a lack of concepts with which to build participatory consensus, faintheartedness in regard to democratic experiments and inadequate informal influences on policy-making. At the same time, there is the potential to improve Canadian democracy and, subsequently, climate performance: Canada could build upon its inclusiveness which is well-organized in parts, a commissioner of climate change (similar to the CESD) could be installed, officials would have to be educated in democracy and a holistic demo-cratic policy process design could be developed based on the experiences made thus far.

Improvements in Canada and beyond should, in regard to the democracy-performance nexus, in the first instance focus on win-win situations, where dem-ocratic quality and policy performance can be improved simultaneously. Such win-win situations, like the CESD in Canada, can be derived from both theoreti-cal considerations and practical experiments. On the one hand, certain elements which already exist in democratic theories, like deliberation based on considered judgement leading to responsive results, need to be fully applied. On the other hand, democratic experiments proposed by pragmatism have to be performed simultaneously to find new democratic institutions or tools, which, through participatory structures and a certain attitude, create a positive atmosphere (Oulton, 2014) amongst the participants, enabling them to move forward together on common and accepted policy solutions.

Furthermore, democratic efficacy, as the ability of democracies to produce desired and intended policies, could also be supported by financial mechanisms at the international level to force cooperation through democracy. Analogous to support schemes in international development, where countries need to improve their governance structures to gain further support, a similar incentivization approach could be applied in terms of democratic quality and climate perfor-mance. Under this sort of scheme, countries democratizing their state of democ-racy would be viewed favourably when revenues from emission trading schemes and similar climate based economic instruments were distributed.

However, in the end, there might be not one single initiative which would improve democratic efficacy but many approaches, with improvements having to be introduced simultaneously, due to the complexity of both democracies and climate change.

References

The access date of all material retrieved from the Web is 5 June 2015 unless otherwise specified.

Bättig, M. B., & Bernauer, T. (2009). National institutions and global public goods: are democracies more cooperative in climate change policy? *International Organization*, 63(2), 281–308.

Bernauer, T. (2013). Climate change politics. *Annual Review of Political Science*, 16(16), 421–448.

Bernauer, T., & Koubi, V. (2009). Effects of political institutions on air quality. *Ecological Economics*, 68(5), 1355–1365.

Cao, X., Milner, H. V., Prakash, A., & Ward, H. (2014). Research frontiers in comparative and international environmental politics: an introduction. *Comparative Political Studies*, 47(3), 291–308.

Cartwright, N. (2002a). In favor of laws that are not ceteris paribus after all. *Erkenntnis*, 57(3), 425–439.

Cartwright, N. (2002b). The limits of causal order, from economics to physics. In U. Maäki (Ed.), *Fact and Fiction in Economics: Models, Realism, and Social Construction* (pp. 137–151). Cambridge: Cambridge University Press.

Dewey, J. (1998 [1939]). Creative democracy – the task before us. In L. A. Hickman, & T. A. Alexander (Eds.), *The Essential Dewey* (pp. 340–343). Bloomington: Indiana University Press.

Held, D. (2014). Climate change, global governance and democracy: some questions. In M. Di Paola, & G. Pellegrino (Eds.), *Canned Heat: Ethics and Politics of Global Climate Change* (pp. 17–28). New Delhi: Routledge.

Kittel, B. (2006). A crazy methodology? On the limits of macro-quantitative social science research. *International Sociology, 21*(5), 647–677.

Leggewie, C., & Nanz, P. (2013). The future council. New forms of democratic participation. *eurozine*. Retrieved from www.eurozine.com/articles/2013-08-20-leggewienanz-en.html

Merton, R. K. (1949). *Social Theory and Social Structure; Toward the Codification of Theory and Research*. Glencoe, IL: Free Press.

Oulton, D. (2014). Interview on Canada's Kyoto Protocol process/Interviewer: F. Hanusch.

Petherick, A. (2014). Seeking a fair and sustainable future. *Nature Climate Change, 4*(2), 81–83.

Spilker, G. (2012). Helpful organizations: membership in inter-governmental organizations and environmental quality in developing countries. *British Journal of Political Science, 42*, 345–370.

Spilker, G. (2013). *Globalization, Political Institutions and the Environment in Developing Countries*. New York: Routledge.

Stehr, N. (2013). An inconvenient democracy: knowledge and climate change. *Society, 50*(1), 55–60.

Vorarlberg. (2015). *Office for Future-Related Issues*. Retrieved from www.vorarlberg.at/english/vorarlberg-english/environment_future/officeforfuture-relatedis/officeforfuture-relatedis.htm

Ziblatt, D. (2006). Of course generalize, but how? Returning to middle range theory in comparative politics. *American Political Science Association – Comparative Politics Newsletter, 17*(2), 8–11.

12 Conclusion

This book has demonstrated that more democratic quality has a mainly positive influence on the climate performance of established democracies. The research results of the mixed methods design are robust and merge detailed mechanisms, verifying statistical trends. A generalizable framework which explains the results is the concept of democratic efficacy, which assumes that the ability to produce the desired and intended general performance increases concomitantly with levels of democratic quality.

So, different levels of democracy are indeed an explanatory factor for differences in the climate performance of established democracies and the democratization of democracies thus makes a solution to the challenges of climate change that little bit more likely. Admittedly, this is – to put it mildly – a complex task. Therefore, an even more important implication for further research is that, when redefining the concept of democratic efficacy, etc., its focus should not only rely on evaluations of contemporary democracies. Instead, new research should endeavour to think possibilistically and look to take plausible possibilities for the advancement of current democracies into account, even if these have not yet been empirically observed. Democracy has to be understood as an ongoing process with alternative futures and should be researched as such.

Practically speaking, the only "cure for the ailments of democracy is more democracy" (Dewey, 1984 [1927], p. 327). However, there is no guarantee that experimenting with the democratization of democracy will easily accomplish its objective, but only more democracy can introduce the future to the present, not less. And, "[e]ven if nothing else survives from the age of the democratic revolutions, perhaps our descendants will remember that social institutions can be viewed as experiments in cooperation rather than as attempts to embody a universal and ahistorical order" (Rorty, 1991 [1984], p. 196).

References

Dewey, J. (1984 [1927]). The public and its problems. In J. A. Boydston (Ed.), *John Dewey: The Later Works: 1925–1953* (Vol. 2, pp. 335–372). Carbondale: Southern Illinois University Press.
Rorty, R. (1991 [1984]). The priority of democracy to philosophy. In R. Rorty (Ed.), *Objectivity, Relativism, and Truth: Philosophical Papers*. Vol. 1 (pp. 175–196). Cambridge: Cambridge University Press.

DOI: 10.4324/9781315228983-15

Pragmatic afterword

Every piece of research is based upon certain presumptions of enquiry, which are explicitly presented to the public or are implicit in the way the research is done. In order to undertake comprehensible research, it is necessary to present the scientific presumptions of a study. The presumptions outlined in this afterword are mainly based on pragmatism. Since the pragmatic approach of enquiry or its revival started some ten years ago, the basic literature of this field is still in its early stages. However, every new or reinvented perspective of scientific presumptions of enquiry initially depends upon a small number of sources (Morgan, 2007, p. 48). The reason for choosing a pragmatic approach is that it seems to provide the best way of dealing with relevant problems in a world full of complexities and of leaving behind the research boundaries between different theoretical and disciplinary research traditions.

Charles Sanders Peirce's 1878 article "How to make our ideas clear", in which he formulated a pre-pragmatic notion of clear concepts, could be seen as the starting point of classical pragmatism (Peirce, 1878). William James was, however, the first one to actually use the term "pragmatism" in a lecture given in 1898. One of his central tenets was the claim that theories should be seen as instruments and not as answers (James, 1907). In the traditions of Peirce and James, John Dewey further developed the ideas of pragmatism and founded his own line of thought, which saw enquiry as the basis for social change (Dewey, 1938). Thereafter, Richard Rorty's *Philosophy and the Mirror of Nature*, published in 1979, reinvented pragmatism in regard to scientific debate (Rorty, 1979). Following the establishment of a very philosophically organized neo-pragmatism, this new approach diffused into other subjects, particularly the social sciences. As a result, political scientists came to recognize pragmatism in the 1990s and, in the 2000s, a couple of publications indicated that more and more researchers were beginning to turn to pragmatism as an appropriate approach (see, e.g. the special issue of the *Millennium* (31:3), a symposium on pragmatism in the *Journal of International Relations and Development* (10:1) and a forum in the *International Studies Review* (11:3)).

However, what is pragmatism in the context of this book's research? Pragmatism can be characterized "as an instrument to go about research with an appropriate degree of epistemological and methodological awareness" (Friedrichs,

2009, p. 646). This awareness is based on a consensus theory of truth, which outlines the reflexive practice of discursive scholarly communities. First and foremost, this ensures an intersubjective understanding of how to deal successfully with reality, but it also allows epistemological instrumentalism as a device for the generation of useful knowledge where thinking and acting are very much two sides of the same coin (Friedrichs & Kratochwil, 2009, p. 711; Hellmann, 2009, p. 641). Pragmatism commits to holism, pluralism, anti-dualism, anti-determinism, anti-scepticism and fallibilism (Festenstein, 2009, pp. 147–148). In political science, as elsewhere, theories are of most value as instruments and within practice, insofar as they are not mere intellectual exercises (James, 1907; Rorty, 1996). Therefore, the point of science is to become outdated, not to establish an impregnable theory.

The need for a pragmatic approach in current research results from, inter alia, inadequate debates about the meta-theoretical questions of political science. While research concerned with finding a common ground for ontology, epistemology and methodology is, of course, essential, social science research is probably too often more concerned with gaining a common meta-theoretical foundation, or arguing about it, than dealing with academically and practically relevant problems. The bone of contention in the contemporary meta-theoretical debate might rest in the seminal publication *Designing Social Inquiry*, in which the authors advocate the same logic of inference for qualitative and quantitative research (King, Keohane, & Verba, 1994). What followed was a huge debate about the positivist presumptions the authors presented (Brady & Collier, 2010). Studying research done outside the realms of the meta-theoretical debate, one can see that most research is organized pragmatically rather than precisely following proposed stylized steps (Friedrichs & Kratochwil, 2009, p. 710). Doubtless, the same is true the other way round for post-positivist research working in a postmodern fashion and leading, inter alia, to the accusation of a doubtful relativism (Rorty, 1996; Wolin, 2004). The positivist and post-positivist research traditions maximize different important values, like logical coherence on the one hand and scepticism about objective truths on the other, yet they often do a poor job in "the efficient and efficacious production of useful knowledge" (Friedrichs & Kratochwil, 2009, p. 702). Thus, the need for a pragmatic reorientation is assumed (Cochran, 2002; Kratochwil, 2009; Morgan, 2007, pp. 56–60).

Pragmatism provides research strategies which have implicitly influenced the conceptualization of this book. One of these research strategies was analytical eclecticism (Sil & Katzenstein, 2010a). The main idea of analytical eclecticism is to combine existing theories to enable them to suit more complex settings. By doing so, the goal is not to synthesize theories, which is almost impossible because of incommensurable epistemological and ontological views, but to find a common vocabulary and to recombine various theoretical approaches until they fit in, matching the world with words (Friedrichs & Kratochwil, 2009, pp. 708–709; Sil & Katzenstein, 2010a, pp. 17–18). Three criteria are characteristic of analytic eclecticism: taking problems of a broad scope, developing complex causal stories at the level of middle range theories and seeking pragmatic engagement in academia and beyond (Sil & Katzenstein, 2010b, p. 421). Thus, analytical eclecticism is an alternative to the "gladiator style of analysis", where one perspective goes forth and slays all the others, since it identifies different possibilities amongst the interacting explanatory factors producing the outcome (Checkel, 2001, p. 243). However, the combination of existing approaches proved insufficient to answer the question of whether democracy can deal with climate change. Thus, we come to abduction, which can be used if a researcher identifies a problem with a class of non-randomly occurring phenomena for which there is not yet a suitable explanatory theory (Friedrichs, 2008, p. 12; Friedrichs & Kratochwil, 2009, p. 714). Abduction tries to discover "new" and undiscovered connections, like those linking democracy and climate change in the Canadian case study. Its central concern is the orientation within a complex field. The third strategy which this study adopted, probably also as a result of the two other research strategies, was a mixed methods approach, which is often applied in pragmatic research (Johnson & Onwuegbuzie, 2004, p. 16; Tashakkori & Teddlie, 2003, p. 677). Mixed methods research is not purely preoccupied with the technical level, but instead tries to handle techniques pragmatically with regard to the research focus at hand, using methods from the whole spectrum, from qualitative to quantitative, to gain the most significant evidence possible. Thus, pragmatism forms the basis for the way this study's research.

References

The access date of all material retrieved from the Web is 5 June 2015 unless otherwise specified.

Brady, H. E., & Collier, D. (2010). *Rethinking Social Inquiry: Diverse Tools, Shared Standards* (2nd ed.). Lanham, MD: Rowman & Littlefield Publishers.

Checkel, J. T. (2001). Constructivism and integration theory: crash landing or safe arrival. *European Union Politics, 2*(2), 240–245.

Cochran, M. (2002). Deweyan pragmatism and post-positivist social science in IR. *Millenium, 31*(3), 525–548.

Dewey, J. (1938). *The Theory of Inquiry*. New York: Henry Holt and Co.

Festenstein, M. (2009). Pragmatism's boundaries. In H. B. Bauer, & E. Brighi (Eds.), *Pragmatism in International Relations* (pp. 145–162). London/New York: Routledge.

Friedrichs, J. (2008). *Fighting Terrorism and Drugs. Europe and International Police Cooperation*. London/New York: Routledge.

Friedrichs, J. (2009). From positivist pretense to pragmatic practice. Varieties of pragmatic methodology in IR scholarship. *International Studies Review, 11*(3), 645–648.

Friedrichs, J., & Kratochwil, F. (2009). On acting and knowing: how pragmatism can advance international relations research and methodology. *International Organization, 63*(3), 701–731.

Hellmann, G. (2009). Beliefs as rules for action: pragmatism as a theory of thought and action. *International Studies Review, 11*(3), 638–662.

James, W. (1907). *Pragmatism: A New Name for Some Old Ways of Thinking*. London/New York: Longmans, Green & Co.

Johnson, R. B., & Onwuegbuzie, A. J. (2004). Mixed methods research: a research paradigm whose time has come. *Educational Researcher, 33*(7), 14–26.

King, G., Keohane, R. O., & Verba, S. (1994). *Designing Social Inquiry: Scientific Inference in Qualitative Research.* Princeton, NJ: Princeton University Press.

Kratochwil, F. (2009). Ten points to ponder about pragmatism. Some critical reflections on knowledge generation in the social science. In H. B. Bauer, & E. Brighi (Eds.), *Pragmatism and International Relations* (pp. 11–25). London/New York: Routledge.

Morgan, D.L. (2007). Paradigms lost and pragmatism regained. Methodological implications of combining qualitative and quantitative methods. *Journal of Mixed Methods Research, 1*(1), 48–76.

Peirce, C.S. (1878). How to make our ideas clear. *Popular Science Monthly, 12*(1), 286–302.

Rorty, R. (1979). *Philosophy and the Mirror of Nature.* Princeton, NJ: Princeton University Press.

Rorty, R. (1996). Relativism: finding and making. In J.S. Niznik, & J.T. Sanders (Eds.), *Debating the State of Philosophy: Habermas, Rorty and Kolakowsky* (pp. 31–48). London: Praeger.

Sil, R., & Katzenstein, P.J. (2010a). *Analytical Eclecticism in the Study of World Politics.* Basingstoke/New York: Palgrave Macmillan.

Sil, R., & Katzenstein, P.J. (2010b). Analytical eclecticism in the study of world politics: reconfiguring problems and mechanisms across research traditions. *Perspectives on Politics, 8*(2), 411–431.

Tashakkori, A., & Teddlie, C. (2003). The past and future of mixed methods research: from data triangulation to mixed models design. *Handbook of Mixed Methods on Social and Behavioral Research* (pp. 671–702). Thousand Oaks, CA/London/New Delhi: Sage Publications.

Wolin, R. (2004). *The Seduction of Unreason. The Intellectual Romance with Fascism from Nietzsche to Postmodernism.* Princeton, NJ/Woodstock: Princeton University Press.

Appendices

Appendix A
Stata do file

```
version 12
dembarclimperf.dta

**prepare panel data**
encode country, gen(countrynum)
xtset countrynum year

*graphics*
xtline dembar, overlay
xtline CCPI, overlay
xtline policyCCPI, overlay
xtline emissiondevelopmentCCPI, overlay

*histograms*
hist CCPI
hist policyCCPI
hist emissiondevelopmentCCPI
hist dembar

*description of variables*
summarize CCPI emissiondevelopmentCCPI policyCCPI
summarize dembar
summarize oilgascoal income tradeopeness vulnerability urbans internetusers
    population14 population65 services

*scatter with mean and country names*
egen mCCPI = mean(CCPI), by(countrynum)
scatter mCCPI mdembar, mlabel(country)

*intraclass-correlation-coefficient*
xtreg dembar, mle
xtreg CCPI, mle
```

```
xtreg emissionlevelCCPI, mle
xtreg emissiondevelopmentCCPI, mle
xtreg policyCCPI, mle
xtreg oilgascoal, mle
xtreg income, mle
xtreg tradeopeness, mle
xtreg vulnerability, mle
xtreg urbans, mle
xtreg internetusers, mle
xtreg population14, mle
xtreg population65, mle
xtreg services, mle

*test on cross-sectional-dependence*
xtreg CCPI dembar, fe
xtcsd, pesaran abs
xtreg CCPI dembar, re
xtcsd, pesaran abs
xtreg emissiondevelopmentCCPI dembar, fe
xtcsd, pesaran abs
xtreg emissiondevelopmentCCPI dembar, re
xtcsd, pesaran abs
xtreg policyCCPI dembar, fe
xtcsd, pesaran abs
xtreg policyCCPI dembar, re
xtcsd, pesaran abs

*HHHHHHHHausman test*
xtreg CCPI dembar, fe
estimates store fixed
xtreg CCPI dembar, re
est store random
hausman fixed random

xtreg emissiondevelopmentCCPI dembar, fe
estimates store fixed
xtreg emissiondevelopmentCCPI dembar, re
est store random
hausman fixed random

xtreg policyCCPI dembar, fe
estimates store fixed
xtreg policyCCPI dembar, re
est store random
hausman fixed random
```

hybrid model
preparation of data for hybrid model: calculating a) country specific means over time and b) deviations of these means in every year
egen mdembar = mean(dembar), by(countrynum)
gen ddembar = dembar-mdembar
egen moilgascoal = mean(oilgascoal), by(countrynum)
gen doilgascoal = oilgascoal-moilgascoal
egen mincome = mean(income), by(countrynum)
gen dincome = income-mincome
egen mGDP = mean(GDP), by(countrynum)
gen dGDP = GDP-mGDP
egen mGDPgrowth = mean(GDPgrowth), by(countrynum)
gen dGDPgrowth = GDPgrowth-mGDPgrowth
egen mtradeopeness = mean(tradeopeness), by(countrynum)
gen dtradeopeness = tradeopeness-mtradeopeness
egen mvulnerability = mean(vulnerability), by(countrynum)
gen dvulnerability = vulnerability-mvulnerability
egen murbans = mean(urbans), by(countrynum)
gen durbans = urbans-murbans
egen mpopulation14 = mean(population14), by(countrynum)
gen dpopulation14 = population14-mpopulation14
egen mpopulation65 = mean(population65), by(countrynum)
gen dpopulation65 = population65-mpopulation65
egen mservices = mean(services), by(countrynum)
gen dservices = services-mservices
egen minternetusers = mean(internetusers), by(countrynum)
gen dinternetusers = internetusers-minternetusers

panel regressions with standard errors consistent with cross-sectional dependence
model 1 (small)
xtscc CCPI mdembar ddembar moilgascoal doilgascoal mincome dincome mvulnerability dvulnerability
xtscc emissiondevelopmentCCPI mdembar ddembar moilgascoal doilgascoal mincome dincome mvulnerability dvulnerability
xtscc policyCCPI mdembar ddembar moilgascoal doilgascoal mincome dincome mvulnerability dvulnerability

model 2 (broad)
xtscc CCPI mdembar ddembar moilgascoal doilgascoal mincome dincome mtradeopeness dtradeopeness mvulnerability dvulnerability murbans durbans mpopulation14 dpopulation14 mpopulation65 dpopulation65 mservices dservices minternetusers dinternetusers
xtscc emissiondevelopmentCCPI mdembar ddembar moilgascoal doilgascoal mincome dincome mtradeopeness dtradeopeness mvulnerability

dvulnerability murbans durbans mpopulation14 dpopulation14 mpopula-
tion65 dpopulation65 mservices dservices minternetusers dinternetusers

xtscc policyCCPI mdembar ddembar moilgascoal doilgascoal mincome dincome mtradeopeness dtradeopeness mvulnerability dvulnerability murbans
durbans mpopulation14 dpopulation14 mpopulation65 dpopulation65
mservices dservices minternetusers dinternetusers

Appendix B
Expert interview guidelines

Expert Interview Guidelines: Canada's Kyoto Protocol Process

1 Introduce myself and my research

As you may remember, I am a research analyst at the German Advisory Council on Global Change to the Federal Government and part of the research group Climate Change and Democracy at the Institute for Advanced Study in the Humanities in Essen, where I am doing my PhD. During my stay in Canada, I am working as a visiting PhD scholar at the University of Toronto's School of the Environment.

To start with, I would like to outline the main aim of my research. After that, I will start with concrete questions on Canada's Kyoto climate policy process. My main research question is "How does democratic quality influence climate performance?" Two concepts are important in this regard: democratic quality and climate performance. My understanding of democratic quality covers a couple of dimensions, such as participation (which actors are involved), or transparency (the way documents and reports are made public). As a second concept, climate performance can be divided into targets/decisions and GHG emissions/ implementation.

My thesis includes two empirical analyses. In a first step, I shall undertake quantitative analysis of democracies and their climate performance to see if statistical hints as to the relationship between these two elements can be found. In a second step, I shall focus on Canada's Kyoto Protocol process from 1995–2012, beginning with the preparation of the negotiations in Kyoto in 1997, going on to the following translation of Canada's reduction target into (federal/federal-provincial) climate plans and, finally, ending with the implementation of this reduction target up till the end of the first commitment period in 2012. Canada's Kyoto Protocol process forms a case study with which to research the concrete mechanisms between democratic quality and climate performance, e.g. whether and why more/ less transparency leads to better/worse climate policy. In regard to the Canadian case I have already read much of the secondary literature about Canada's climate policy and relevant documents, like the RCESD, climate change plans, national reports to the UNFCCC, etc. However, there is no complete or comprehensive documentation of the whole process which is available to the public and includes minutes of the most important meetings and decision-making processes. Therefore, I would like to speak to you as an expert with concrete knowledge about important parts of the process you participated in.

Before we start, I have to inform you that based on the rules for safeguarding good scientific practice at my institute: (1) your consent to give me an interview is voluntary and can be revoked at any time, (2) the interview will only be used for academic purposes in the context of my dissertation.

Based on these rules I also have to ask you: (1) if you agree to the interview being recorded (which would be a great help for me, as it would enable me to listen to it again when I am back in Germany) and (2) if you would you prefer to make an anonymous interview?

Start recording
It is DATE and I will now conduct an interview with XX. XX (did not) agree(d) that the interview can be recorded and (does not) need(s) its content to be published anonymously.

//10min

2 The experts present themselves
Even though I know some information about your involvement, it is important for me to ask a first brief question about your background.
- What was your formal position and what responsibilities did you have during what time period of Canada's Kyoto Protocol Process (formulation to implementation, 1995–2012)?

//5min

3 Stimulus question
- I would like to ask you to explain to me how the Kyoto Protocol formulation/implementation process was organized during your involvement.
- Based on what you remember, which were the particularly crucial phases and meetings during your involvement and why do you think they were so crucial?

//10min

4 Specific questions for different experts

Meta dimension	Empirical translation of dimensions	Main questions and possible sub-questions
control	decision-making is set up in clear lines of *accountability*	There are always phases in a process which have a decision-making character, i.e. when reduction targets or financial contributions were finally decided. Could you please explain to me who was involved in the final decision-making?
		Possible sub-questions:
		Was it always possible to trace back results to decision-makers?
		Were there mechanisms in place to make decision-makers accountable for their decisions?
		For me, accountability means the way in which control over decision-makers is ensured. Would you say that the way accountability was applied influenced the results of the policy process?

	judicial independence is guaranteed through the rule of law	Do you remember any conflicting issues during the process which were brought to court or which, from your point of view, should have been brought to court?
		Possible sub-questions:
		If there were conflicting issues: was judiciary access always open and free?
		Do you remember any form of corruption during your involvement?
		For me, the rule of law means that power is constrained by the law. Would you say the way the rule of law was applied influenced the results of the policy process?
	policy process is embedded in *stable democratic structures* and democratic institutions are equipped with sufficient resources	In what way did the influence of involved state institutions (federal-provincial coordination committees, NRCan vs. EnCan, Parliament, etc.) change over time?
		Possible sub-questions:
		How did the responsibilities of those institutions change depending on the government in power?
		Were democratically legitimated actors (MPs, etc.) accepted and supported by other relevant actors?
		For me, embeddedness in stable democratic structures means that state institutions are not subject to radical change in short time periods. Would you say that the way the climate policy process was embedded in democratic structures influenced the results of the policy process?
equality	openness and fairness of access guarantee the *involvement* of a plurality of relevant actors	During the process, many (governmental, non-governmental, business) actors were involved. Were you satisfied with the selection of those actors who were finally involved in the process?

Possible sub-questions:

Do you think that all relevant and affected actors/groups were involved in the process or was the selection of involved actors biased and incomplete?

How was the involvement of weak and marginalized actors ensured (i.e. aboriginal people)?

For me, involvement means that the access to the policy process is open and fair to a plurality of relevant actors. Would you say that the way involvement was organized influenced the results of the policy process?

participatory structures enable involved actors to influence decision-making

Participatory structures can allow different actors like citizens (direct), NGOs (intermediary), MPs and representatives of the provinces (representative) to participate. From your point of view, which sort of participatory structures were particularly significant for the purposes of the process?

Possible sub-questions:

Which actors were able to strongly influence decision-making in formal as well as in informal settings?

If you remember the meetings during your involvement, in what way did the discussions taking place influence the views of the actors involved? (Were the discussions full of conflicts; was there an exchange of arguments; did these arguments remain objective?)

In what way do the results of the decision-making processes represent the views of the actors involved?

access and traceability of all relevant information at all stages of the policy process guarantees *transparency*

Access to important information like minutes, documents, reports, etc. is an important part of a process being transparent to the actors involved and the public in general. Would you say that the process was transparent in this regard?

		Possible sub-questions:
		Did especially important meetings with decision-making character show a high involvement of actors, since they knew that these were the meetings at which decisions would be made?
		Did informal meetings take place? How were these informal meetings arranged and what did they decide?
freedom	competition, experimentation and innovation enable *creativity* and thus provide the potential for a more democratic policy process	For me, transparency means that the access and traceability of all relevant information is guaranteed at all stages of the policy process. Would you say that transparency (or a lack thereof) during the policy process influenced the results of the Kyoto process?
		Were there any discussions about how the Kyoto Protocol's formulation/implementation should be undertaken in the most democratic way with new and innovative democratic procedures or was the above carried out much like processes in other policy fields?
		Possible sub-questions:
		Would you say that new forms of democratic engagement were wilfully (not) applied or did they just happen?
		In what way was a free competition between actors and their ideas possible and how did this lead to more/less democratic elements in the policy process?
		For me, creativity means that competition, experimentation and innovation enable potentials for a more democratic policy process. Would you say that the way creativity was applied influenced the results of the policy process?
	associational and organizational rights enable autonomy and guarantee *liberty*	Do you remember any event during the policy process at which individuals or organizations were hindered in expressing themselves autonomously?

Possible sub-questions:

Do you remember any event at which organizations, especially those of weak and marginalized groups, were strongly influenced or restricted by third parties and/or excluded from the process?

Do you remember any event at which individuals were unable to make use of their political and civil rights to state their views about the issue under consideration?

For me, liberty means that associational and organizational rights enable autonomy. Would you say that liberty influenced the results of the Kyoto process?

media pluralism and a free public sphere guarantee *publicity* of the issue under debate

Were you satisfied with the way the media in Canada reported on the Kyoto process? (Were there waves of particularly high levels of attention; in comparison to other public debates, etc.?)

Possible sub-questions:

Did a press secretariat which was dedicated to the policy process exist and did this adequately inform media and support public debate on the issue through press conferences, publications, etc.?

Was media awareness of the policy process high enough to ensure public control over it?

For me, publicity means that media pluralism and a free public sphere exist. Would you say that the way publicity was applied influenced the results of the policy process?

//25min

5 The generation of interpretive knowledge

We have talked about many specific aspects of the policy process. I would now like to go back to a more abstract level.

- Based on the experiences you had, would you say that (a lack of) democratic quality influenced Canada's climate performance in the context of the Kyoto Protocol's formulation/implementation (climate policy targets, GHG emissions, etc.)?

- Imagine you are in the mid-1990s and in a position to design the whole process: how would you formulate the process design differently on the basis of your experiences?

//5min

A very last question

Can you think of anyone else who was deeply involved and whom I could contact regarding an interview? Do you have any documents you could send me?

//5min

Appendix C
Interview partners

Group	Name	Most relevant position in regard to Canada's Kyoto Protocol process	Interview date
executive (public service)	Confidential1	former ECan Public Service Official, responsible for international climate change negotiations	18 February 2014
executive (public service)	Confidential5	Public Service Official, ECan	11 February 2014
executive (public service)	Confidential6	former high ranking Public Service Official at ECan	12 February 2014
executive	David Anderson	Minister of the Environment, August 1999–December 2003	23 January 2014
executive (public service)	David Oulton	Chair of the National Climate Change Secretariat, 1998–2004	20 January 2014
executive	Edward Goldenberg	Senior Policy Advisor to PM Jean Chrétien, 1993–2003	4 February 2014
executive, business	F. Michael Cleland	Assistant Deputy Minister of the Energy Sector in NRCan, 1996–2000; President of the Canadian Electricity Association, 2002–2011	7 February 2014
executive (public service)	Paul Heinbecker	Chief Negotiator for Canada in Kyoto, 1997	29 January 2014
executive	Peter Kent	Minister of the Environment, January 2011–July 2013	27 January 2014
executive (public service)	Robert Slater	various positions in ECan from 1985 onwards, e.g. Senior Assistant Deputy Minister, 1997–2003	7 February 2014
executive	Stéphane Dion	Minister of the Environment, July 2004–February 2006	28 January 2014
policy evaluation and advisory	Confidential2	former member of the NRTEE	7 February 2014

Group	Name	Most relevant position in regard to Canada's Kyoto Protocol process	Interview date
policy evaluation and advisory	Confidential4	Public Service Official, CESD	6 February 2014
policy evaluation and advisory	David McLaughlin	President and CEO, NRTEE, 2007–2012	26 February 2014
policy evaluation and advisory	Scott Vaughan	CESD, 2008–2013	27 January 2014
parliamentary (executive)	John Godfrey	Member of the Standing Committee on the Environment and Sustainable Development, 2004 and 2006–2008; Minister of Infrastructure and Communities, July 2004–February 2006	22 January 2014
parliamentary	Karen Kraft Sloan	(Vice-)Chair of the Standing Committee on the Environment and Sustainable Development, 1994–2003; Parliamentary Secretary to the Environment Minister	22 January 2014
provinces (public service)	Confidential 3	high ranking Public Service Official in a ministry in Alberta	21 January 2014
society (ENGO)	Beatrice Olivastri	CEO of Friends of the Earth Canada	26 January 2014
society (ENGO)	Hugh Wilkins	Environmental Lawyer for Friends of the Earth in the Kyoto Protocol Implementation Act case in 2007	24 January 2014
society (ENGO)	John Bennett	Executive Director of the Sierra Club Canada, 2009–present (January 2015); active in Canada's green movement since the 1970s	20 January 2014
society (business)	John Dillon	various positions within the Canadian Council of Chief Executives, 1990–2015	17 January 2014
society (science)	John Stone	climate scientist with long-term involvement in climate policy-making	29 January 2014
society (ENGO)	Matthew Bramley	Senior Fellow, Pembina Institute	18 February 2014
media	Jeffrey Simpson	Journalist with *The Globe and Mail*	30 January 2014
media	Mike De Souza	Journalist with Postmedia News	28 January 2014
media	Shawn McCarthy	Journalist with *The Globe and Mail*	30 January 2014

Obviously, some interview requests were denied and there weren't available interview partners for all of the relevant and affected actors, e.g. the oil and gas branch or First Nations might be to a certain extent underrepresented, even though requests were made. However, standpoints, etc. are reconstructed as well as possible through other interview partners and documentation.

Index

Page numbers in bold refer to tables. Page numbers in italics refer to figures.